China and Southeast Asia

The **Institute of Southeast Asian Studies (ISEAS)** was established as an autonomous organization in 1968. It is a regional centre dedicated to the study of socio-political, security and economic trends and developments in Southeast Asia and its wider geostrategic and economic environment.

The Institute's research programmes are the Regional Economic Studies (RES, including ASEAN and APEC), Regional Strategic and Political Studies (RSPS), and Regional Social and Cultural Studies (RSCS).

ISEAS Publications, an established academic press, has issued more than 1,000 books and journals. It is the largest scholarly publisher of research about Southeast Asia from within the region. ISEAS Publications works with many other academic and trade publishers and distributors to disseminate important research and analyses from and about Southeast Asia to the rest of the world.

The **Center for Southeast Asian Studies (CSEAS)** at National Sun Yat-sen University, Kaohsiung, Taiwan, was established in October 1998. It has four major purposes: (1) to conduct research on Southeast Asia and regional integration, (2) to hold conferences and seminars on Southeast Asian studies, (3) to initiate academic exchanges with institutes and universities in Southeast Asia, and (4) to add to a collection of books, journals, government documents and newspapers on Southeast Asia. Since its inception, CSEAS has held two international conferences and a number of seminars. It has also signed exchange agreements with six universities and institutions in Southeast Asia.

China and Southeast Asia

Asia Global Changes and Regional Challenges

Edited by
**Ho Khai Leong and
Samuel C. Y. Ku**

ISEAS INSTITUTE OF SOUTHEAST ASIAN STUDIES
Singapore

CENTER FOR SOUTHEAST ASIAN STUDIES
National Sun Yat-sen University
Kaohsiung, Taiwan ROC

First published in Singapore in 2005 by
Institute of Southeast Asian Studies
30 Heng Mui Keng Terrace
Pasir Panjang
Singapore 119614
E-mail: publish@iseas.edu.sg
Website: http://bookshop.iseas.edu.sg

and

Center for Southeast Asian Studies
National Sun Yat-sen University
70 Lien-hai Road
Kaohsiung 804
Taiwan ROC

The responsibility for facts and opinions in this publication rests exclusively with the editors and the contributors and their interpretations do not necessarily reflect the views or the policy of the publisher or its supporters.

ISEAS Library Cataloguing-in-Publication Data

China and Southeast Asia : global changes and regional challenges / edited by Ho Khai Leong and Samuel C.Y. Ku.
1. China—Foreign relations—Asia, Southeastern.
2. Asia, Southeastern—Foreign relations—China.
3. China—Foreign economic relations—Asia, Southeastern.
4. Asia, Southeastern—Foreign economic relations—China.
5. Free trade—China.
6. Free trade—Asia, Southeastern.
7. Taiwan—Foreign relations—Asia, Southeastern.
8. Asia, Southeastern—Foreign relations—Taiwan.
I. Ho, Khai Leong, 1954–
II. Ku, Samuel C.Y., 1955–
DS740.5 A9C531   2004

ISBN 981-230-298-0 (soft cover)

Typeset by Superskill Graphics Pte Ltd
Printed in Singapore by Seng Lee Press Pte Ltd

CONTENTS

LIST OF TABLES

ABBREVIATIONS

ADB	Asian Development Bank
ACFTA	ASEAN-China Free Trade Agreement
AEC	ASEAN Economic Community
AFTA	ASEAN Free Trade Area
APEC	Asia Pacific Economic Co-operation
ARF	ASEAN Regional Forum
ASEAN	Association of Southeast Asian Nations
ASEM	Asia-Europe Meeting
CALD	Council of Asian Liberals and Democrats
CPP	Cambodian People's Party
CPM	Communist Party of Malaya
CEPA	Closer Economic Partnership Arrangement
CRTA	Committee on Regional Agreements
CU	Custom Union
DPP	Democratic Progressive Party
FDI	Foreign Direct Investment
EAEC	East Asian Economic Grouping
EHP	Early-Harvest Programme
EU	European Union
FTA	Free Trade Area
GATT	The General Agreement on Tariffs and Trade
GTAP	Global Trade Analysis Project
HS	Harmonized System
ICDF	International Co-operation and Development Fund
MFN	Most-Favoured Nation

MILF	Moro Islamic Liberation Front
NAFTA	North American Free Trade Agreement
NGO	Non-Governmental Organizations
NSC	New Security Concept
PGN	Policy of Good Neighbourliness
PLA	People's Liberation Army
PRC	People's Republic of China
PTA	Preferential Trade Agreement
RIA	Regional Integration Agreement
ROC	Republic of China
RTA	Regional Trade Agreement
SAM	Social Accounting Matrix
SCO	Shanghai Co-operation Organization
SCS	South China Sea
TACSA	Treaty of Amity and Co-operation in Southeast Asia
WHO	World Health Organization
WTO	World Trade Organization

CONTRIBUTORS

BA, Alice, D. (Ph.D., University of Virginia, 2000) is Assistant Professor in the Department of Political Science and International Relations, University of Delaware, Newark, DE. Her publications and research have focused on ASEAN-China relations, Asia's evolving regionalisms, and the relationship between regional and global governance. Her co-edited volume titled *Contending Perspectives on Global Governance* is forthcoming. E-mail: aliceba@UDel.Edu

CAI, Peng Hong is Director of Southeast Asia Study, Institute of Asia-Pacific Studies, Shanghai Academy of Social Sciences (SASS), China. Having graduated from International Politics of Fudan University in Shanghai (1982), he has since conducted research at SASS, during which he was Visiting Fellow of East-West Centre at Honolulu, Hawaii in 1992–93 and Visiting Scholar at IRPS, University of California, San Diego in 1995. His research and teaching interests include China's political and economic relations with East and Southeast Asia and international organizations. E-mail: paulcai@online.sh.cn

CHIRATHIVAT, Suthiphand (Ph.D., Université de Paris I-Pantheon-Sorbonne, 1982) is Associate Professor of Economics and former Dean of the Faculty of Economics at Chulalongkorn University. He is also chairman of Economics Research Centre and Centre for International Economics and editor of *Chulalongkorn Journal of Economics*. Concurrently, he holds various professional positions including: Advisor to the Minister for Foreign Affairs, Member of Thailand's Committee on International Economic Policy, and Corresponding Editor of *Journal of Asian Economics*. His more recent publications include *East Asia's Monetary Future: Integration in the Global Economy* (2004), and "ASEAN-China FTA: Background, Implications and Future Development", *Journal of Asian Economics* (2002). E-mail: csuthipa@chula.ac.th

CHEN, Jie (Ph.D., ANU, 1994) teaches at the Department of Political Science and International Relations, University of Western Australia. He works on foreign relations of Taiwan and China. He has published in various refereed journals including *Asian Survey, Pacific Review, Communist and Post-Communist Studies, Journal of Contemporary China, Journal of the South Seas Society* and *Issues & Studies*. His most recent publication is a book entitled *Foreign Policy of the New Taiwan: Pragmatic Diplomacy in Southeast Asia* (2002). E-mail: jiechen@cyllene.uwa.edu.au

CHU, Wai Lung (M.A., Warwick University Business School, 2001) is a Senior Research Assistant at the City University of Hong Kong. He has previously held several awards including a Li Po Chun (HK) scholarship and a Lady Margaret Hall (Oxford University) grant. His research experience includes questionnaire designing and data analysis specifically in the area of career decisions and cultural studies. He is also a consultant for a HK-government funded project serving small and medium-sized enterprises where he looks at particular managerial issues. E-mail: smchrisc@cityu.edu.hk

GOH, Evelyn (Ph.D., Oxford, 2001) is Assistant Professor at the Institute of Defence and Strategic Studies, Nanyang Technological University, Singapore. She writes on U.S. foreign policy, U.S.-China relations, and the security and international relations of the Asia-Pacific. She is the author of *Constructing the U.S. Rapprochement with China, 1961–1974: From Red Menace to Tacit Ally* (2004). E-mail: isclgoh@ntu.edu.sg

HAACKE, Jürgen (Ph.D., LSE, 2000) is Lecturer in the Department of International Relations, London School of Economics and Political Science. He is the author of *ASEAN's Diplomatic and Security Culture: Origins, Development and Prospects* (2002). His other publications include articles in *Pacific Review, International Relations of the Asia-Pacific, Asian Perspective, Millennium*, and *Review of International Studies* (forthcoming). In the context of the ESRC's New Security Challenges Programme, he is currently conducting research on how security cultures mediate responses by regional organizations to transnational challenges. E-mail: J.Haacke@lse.ac.uk

LIOW, Joseph Chinyong (Ph.D., LSE, 2003) is Assistant Professor at the Institute of Defence and Strategic Studies (IDSS), Nanyang Technological University, Singapore. His research interests include the international politics of Southeast Asia, political Islam, and the domestic politics and foreign policies of Malaysia. He has recently published in *Southeast Asian Research* (November 2003), *Third World Quarterly* (February 2004), and *Australian Journal of International Affairs* (June 2004), and has articles forthcoming in *Commonwealth and Comparative Politics* (July 2004), and *Studies in Conflict and Terrorism* (October 2004). His book titled *The Politics of Indonesia-Malaysia Relations: One Kin, Two Nations* is forthcoming. E-mail: iscyliow@ntu.edu.sg

MALLIKAMAS, Sothitorn (Ph.D., Wisconsin, 1990) is Associate Professor of Economics and Dean of the Faculty of Economics at Chulalongkorn University. He is former head of Chulalongkorn-Monash General Equilibrium Model Projects. He has conducted a number of research projects in the area of Thailand's trade liberalization for the Ministry of Commerce, including WTO, AFTA and FTAs. E-mail: msothito@chula.ac.th

MONDEJAR, Reuben (Ph.D., University de Navarra, IESE Business School, 1989; M.A., Harvard University 1987) is Associate Professor at the City University of Hong Kong where he is Director of the Master's in Global Business Management Programme. He was formerly Tutor in Southeast Asian Studies at Lowell House at Harvard University. He also served as Associate of the Centre for International Affairs at Harvard. His current research focuses on the various geopolitical and economic integration elements that are relevant to China and the ASEAN. He is a regular Asian affairs news commentator for international news providers CNBC, Star-TV, CNN, and BBC. He holds degrees in Economics, Finance, International Studies, and Organization Theory. He has held visiting appointments at Harvard, Cambridge (Wolfson & St Edmund's), and Oxford (Balliol) Universities. E-mail: mgreuben@cityu.edu.hk

WANG, Gungwu (Ph.D., London, 1957) is Director of the East Asian Institute; Faculty Professor in the Faculty of Arts and Social Sciences, National University of Singapore; and Emeritus Professor of the Australian National University (ANU). He taught at the University of Malaya (1957–68) and the ANU (1968–86), where he was Professor and Head of the Department of Far Eastern History and Director of the Research School of Pacific Studies. From

1986 to 1995, he was Vice-Chancellor of the University of Hong Kong. Among his recent books in English are *China and Southeast Asia: Myths, Threats, and Culture* (1999); *The Chinese Overseas: From Earthbound China to the Quest for Autonomy* (2000); *Don't Leave Home: Migration and the Chinese* (2001); *Bind Us in Time: Nation and Civilisation in Asia* (2002); *Anglo-Chinese Encounters since 1800: War, Trade, Science and Governance* (2003); and *Diasporic Chinese Ventures* (2004). E-mail: eaiwgw@nus.edu.sg

WANG, Jiangyu (SJD, University of Pennsylvania, 2003; M.Jur., University of Oxford, 2004; LL.M., University of Pennsylvania, 2000; Master of Laws, Peking University Law School, 1997; LL.B., China University of Political Science and Law, 1994) is Assistant Professor, Faculty of Law, National University of Singapore. He specializes in Chinese law, international economic law, and international commercial law. He practised law in the Legal Department of the Bank of China and Chinese and American law firms. He is a member of the Chinese Bar Association and the New York State Bar Association. E-mail: jywang@nus.edu.sg

WANG, Vincent Wei-cheng (Ph.D., Chicago, 1995) is Associate Professor of Political Science and International Studies, and Programme Co-ordinator of International Studies at the University of Richmond, in Virginia, USA. He has published extensively in the areas of East Asian politics and international relations, East Asian-Latin American comparative political economy, and science and technology issues in scholarly journals and books. He is currently working on public opinion issues pertaining to national security and justice. E-mail: vwang@richmond.edu

Editors

HO, Khai Leong (Ph.D., Ohio State, 1988) is Fellow at the Institute of Southeast Asian Studies, Singapore. His current research projects include China-ASEAN relations, corporate governance and administrative reforms in Southeast Asia. His works on China-ASEAN have been published in *Pacific Review*, *Journal of Contemporary China* and *Pacific Focus*. His other publications include *The Politics of Policy-making in Singapore* (2000) (The new edition was published as *Shared Responsibilities, Unshared Power. The Politics of Policy-making in Singapore* (2003) and *Performance and Crisis of Governance of Mahathir's Administration* (co-editor) (2001). His latest work *State,*

Market and Corporate Governance in Singapore is forthcoming. E-mail: hokl@iseas.edu.sg

KU, Samuel C.Y. (Ph.D., Ohio State, 1989) is Professor and Director at the Graduate Institute of Interdisciplinary Studies for Social Sciences and the Centre for Southeast Asian Studies, National Sun Yat-sen University, Taiwan. His major research interests include Southeast Asia's political development, Taiwan's relations with Southeast Asia, and Taiwan's foreign relations. He has published four and edited two Chinese books in Taiwan and more than thirty journal articles. His articles have appeared in such international journals such as *Issues and Studies, Contemporary Southeast Asia, Asian Profile, Asian Affairs — An American Review, Journal of Contemporary China, Journal of Asian and African Studies, World Affairs,* and *Asian Perspective.* E-mail: cyku@mail.nsysu.edu.tw

ACKNOWLEDGEMENTS

The editors would like to thank the following organizations and individuals: the Sun Yat-sen Institute of Interdisciplinary Studies and Centre for Southeast Asian Studies, for their generous administrative and financial support; Professors Michael Hsiao (Academia Sinica), Jyh-Lin Wu (National Sun Yat-sen University), Richard Yang (National Sun Yat-sen University) for their time and intellectual advice; Mr K. Kesavapany (Director, Institute of Southeast Asian Studies, Singapore) for enthusiastically initiating the idea of publishing this volume under the auspices of ISEAS; and Mrs Triena Ong (Managing Editor, Institute of Southeast Asian Studies) for professionally supervising the publication of the manuscript.

INTRODUCTION

China-ASEAN Relations: Confronting New Realities

Ho Khai Leong

The relations between the Association of Southeast Asian Nations (ASEAN) and China occupy a unique and important position in the foreign relations of the Asia-Pacific region. China and Southeast Asia's political, strategic and economic importance in the realm of international relations has been transformed by the region's unprecedented economic growth, unexpected financial crisis and turbulent political changes. In the economic front, there has been a five-fold increase in per capita income in the ASEAN region over the last four decades. The 1997 financial crisis, however, exposed the weaknesses of the corporate sector in ASEAN, which include questionable political inventions, poor investment structure, weak legal and accounting system. Simultaneously, the political development of the Southeast Asian states underwent a dramatic democratization process and leadership changes, making them barely recognizable.

China, on the other hand, also experienced economic changes that have allowed more people to become wealthy in a shorter period of time than in any other historical period. Its emergence as an economic, military and political power poses continuous challenge not only to the Southeast Asian states, but also to the great powers. Despite the fact that common economic interests and strategic concerns exist for both China and ASEAN, tensions and suspicions abound. China and its ten ASEAN neighbours of Brunei, Cambodia, Indonesia, Laos, Malaysia, Myanmar, the Philippines, Singapore, Thailand and Vietnam, are likely to share the same political and economic fate in an era of regionalism and globalization. While good neighbourliness and mutual trust are standard official rhetoric in the relationships, the complexities of China as a country and ASEAN as a regional organization intensify the enormous challenges ahead. The opportunities for co-operation and the challenges in dealing with problems arising from rapid economic and political transformation at both the global and regional levels will continue to confront their policymakers in years to come.

International and Global Changes

In the past decades, scholars have attempted to relocate the locus of conflict and competition from the military/security to the international/global economic realm. Globalization played a major role in the remarkable world economic expansion of the 1990s. Undoubtedly, it has contributed to rapid economic growth in parts of Asia, Europe, and Latin America. At the same time, the expansion of markets and opportunities promoted the expansion of democratic values and stability. A dramatic expansion of democratic governance can be evinced in Eastern Europe, Latin America and Southeast Asia. Economic forces are making the world more interdependent — states are, therefore, constrained in their ability to formulate selfish national interests. In general, countries have experienced the benefits of trade, open markets and more open systems of governance.

The expansion of world trade has had a powerful impact on both national and regional trade policy preferences. New opportunities have provided the impetus for previously protectionist regimes to turn towards a restructuring of their economies towards free trade and multilateralism. The new economic system has, therefore, transformed national economic structure and regional policy preferences. Current trade disputes are obstacles to effective globalization. Trade is the primary means of economic development for poor countries, and an important tool for growth and expansion for developed countries like the United States. Despite the benefits of trade, divisions among developing and developed countries are threatening the future of multilateral and bilateral free trade agreements.

It is against these backdrops that the relations between ASEAN and China have evolved in the last decades. ASEAN and China's policymakers look beyond their region for any emerging signs of economic developments that would have an impact on their regional and domestic policies. The failures of the world trade talks in Cancun and its impact on the WTO have shaken these economies.

Another global challenge is the counter-terrorism efforts by the United States-led alliances. The sensitivities of the Islamic countries in Southeast Asian cannot be dismissed. China's recent political and economic initiatives clearly need to be examined from this perspective against United State's military and economic presence in the Southeast Asian region. In the post-Cold War environment, the brave new world following the collapse of the Soviet Union's communist system heralded a dramatic reshuffling of global geopolitics, where the United States emerged as the world's sole superpower. Consequently, a novel paradigm of Sino-American relations has emerged. This paradigm has the tendency and potential to be predominantly rooted in adversarial competition rather than co-operation.

China, therefore, took advantage of the general anti-American sentiments prevalent in the Southeast Asian region after the invasion of Afghanistan and Iraq. Its gestures may be interpreted in terms of establishing partnership and genuine co-operation with ASEAN governments. Indeed, current Sino-ASEAN relations are marked by increased mutual tolerance and admiration. In response, the Southeast Asian nations have maintained a certain aloofness in its dealings with China so as to preserve equidistance.

Regional Challenges

One of the most important challenges can be seen in recent years within both the Ten+1 (ASEAN + China) and the Ten+3 (ASEAN + China, Japan and the Republic of Korea) frameworks. Despite the broadly based and steady improvement in China-ASEAN relations, significant issues have remained unresolved as a result of intra-ASEAN conflicts fighting for a competitive advantage and regime legitimacy. While progress has been significant, it is unclear, even in the short term, where it is heading. If China does not have its house in order, it is difficult to envision a progressive and stable Southeast Asian region in the long run. This is further exacerbated by the fact that much of the regional economic and political destiny is tight closely with China's developmental trajectories. Thus, while the recent signing of the Framework Agreement on China-ASEAN Comprehensive Economic Co-operation represented a new breakthrough, China-ASEAN relations are now confronting new realities in almost all areas. Financial co-operation, political linkages, economic integration, strategic and non-traditional security issues are but some of the more imminent items on the policy agenda.

The regional challenge for ASEAN and China are in the realms of political security, trade and development co-operation. While China is an enthusiastic participant in the ARF, it is still being socialized into the negotiating process, which requires parties to practise multilateral consultation. In the economic arena, the development of ASEAN-China co-operation has been dramatic; more so, given that both sides signed the Framework Agreement on Comprehensive Economic Co-operation in November 2002. The target to realize the Free Trade Area in 2010 for the ASEAN-6 and 2015 for Cambodia, Laos, Myanmar and Vietnam would be an extremely challenging task for both China and ASEAN. Development co-operation between ASEAN and China — which would include science and technology, tourism, public health, youth, and culture — is not foremost on the policy agenda. However, it would prove to be a key indicator of political commitment of both sides in the long run.

Globalism and Regionalism: Can the Twins Meet?

Scholars of international political economy typically consider the interactions of domestic and international factors, as they affect economic policy-making. In the case of China and Southeast relations, regional factors are the most important. Thus, theoretical exploration in international political economy can be promising. This academic frontier can only be achieved through solid research and progress *vis-à-vis* domestic and international interaction factors.

ASEAN-China interaction can be examined from the domestic as well as regional politics, and an examination of the principle economic interests at stake as well as the transit of these economic interests through organizations of regional political economics, determines the kind of distribution and aggregation. The impact of regional interests on intra-regional interaction, and *vice versa*, is at the core of regional and international connections. The task is made much more complicated when China is regarded as a region rather than a country. ASEAN as a region is also problematic as there are different levels of development within the organization. Endogenizing these two levels of analysis is, of course, an extremely complex exercise, and research in this area has met with some progress. But much more remains to be done. Can ASEAN act as an interest-aggregate institution representing collective interest? Can these interests be translated into positive outcomes in a strategic environment witnessing rapid economic and political transformation? The feedback to national regional policies through the regional organization *vis-à-vis* China's interest will depend on ASEAN's evolution in the next decade.

To answer some of the complexities of these problems, a conference on China and Southeast Asia was organized. A group of senior and upcoming scholars gathered at the scenic campus of National Sun Yat-sen University in Kaoshiung, in March 2004, with generous support from the Sun Yat-Sen Institute of Interdisciplinary Studies and Centre for Southeast Asian Studies. The intense discussions and the intellectual dialogue were both inspiring and stimulating. The product is this book.

Structure of the Book

Wang Gungwu's article, which, incidentally, was the opening address to the conference, addresses the changing perceptions of the rise of American power in the twentieth century from the Chinese and Southeast Asian perspective. He argues that the developments in the region are dependent on its perceptions of American power. In turn, this is a timely reminder that the "triangular relationships" between United States, China and Southeast Asia are symbiotic and should be pursued strategically in the future. He traces the development of American investment in Asia, and the responses of China and Southeast Asian. He points out that the United States has made even larger commitments to Asia, and China and Southeast Asia since early 2000. This commitment is marked by closer attention to Asia, and China and Southeast Asia as well as the creation of new alliances and networks of co-operation.

The completion of unfinished economic and financial sector reforms for the sake of regional economic integration is one of the top priorities of ASEAN member states. This would mean the realization of the ASEAN Free Trade Area (AFTA), which is considered the key to enhancing the region's competitiveness. The three chapters by Vincent Wei-Cheng Wang, Wang Jiang Yu, and Suthiphand Chirathivat and Sothitorn Mallikamas, discuss the China-ASEAN FTA from different perspectives. Vincent Wang argues that in light of regionalism in East Asia and China's new diplomacy, the China-ASEAN FTA is by and large driven by a political logic: firstly, to respond to challenges posed by competitive regionalism in the world economy; secondly, to secure material resources for China's economic modernization; and thirdly, to buttress China's growing influence and to counterbalance American and Japanese power in the Asia-Pacific region. China's "peaceful ascendancy" in international relations would bring about a future that is, at best, uncertain.

Wang Jiang Yu, however, offers a more optimistic analysis of this phenomenon. He argues that the emergence of China and the formation of China-ASEAN FTA would ensure more prosperity for the region. China's pursuit of great power status and regional and national security, though legitimate, must be hampered with the commitments to the multilateral trading system. Regional economic blocks should merely serve as the foundation for multilateral liberalization. Indeed, regionalism needs to serve multilateralism. The promotion of rule of law in China should be a paramount objective if it desires to build international confidence in the years to come.

The economists, Suthiphand Chirathivat and Sothitorn Mallikamas, offer an economic perspective of China-ASEAN FTA. As the trade relationship between ASEAN and China progresses, their continuous competition will intensify and pose great political and economic implications. However, they argue that the proper management of this development could bring about greater intra-regional trade and production networks with the potential to benefit both parties. As the ASEAN FTA is fast becoming a reality, its partnership and ultimate integration with China in the form of China-ASEAN FTA would certainly add a new dimension to the region's dynamism.

Reuben Mondejar and Chu Wai Lung are similarly optimistic. After a brief history survey of China and Southeast Asia, the authors argue that China is still at a transitional stage of development. Thus, China requires further engineering before it can contribute significantly to the Asia-Pacific development. China's problems — regional economic disparities, debt-ridden financial sector, inadequacies in legal regulations, industrial over-capacity etc. — could affect ASEAN indirectly; hence, ASEAN must consider these factors before committing itself. However, if China and ASEAN could work together to exploit each other positively, the prospects for a fruitful relationship, and ultimately integration, would be very bright.

One puzzling aspect of the dynamic relations between China and ASEAN is China's perception of ASEAN. In other words, how does Beijing view ASEAN? Jurgen Haacke provides a comprehensive account of the Beijing's historical and strategic position. China's relations with individual Southeast Asian countries are described in the author's attempt to cast a glance at the activities occurring "below" China-ASEAN relations at the regional level. In so doing, he offers a new perspective in the academic discourse.

While security issues occupy a central position in China-ASEAN relations, non-traditional security must also be examined. Cai Peng Hong provides a comprehensive account of the non-security issues confronting China-ASEAN relations — financial turmoil, environmental degradation, transnational crime, terrorism, issues related to separatism, SARS etc. — and concludes that the progress is only half complete. Much more has to be done if both China and ASEAN are committed to a secure and stable environment for economic development to take place.

Alice Ba notes that the emergence of "East Asia", made up of both Northeast Asian and Southeast Asian states, offers both challenges and opportunities for China as well as ASEAN. The paradox is embedded in the fact that East Asia offers ASEAN a chance for economic and political revitalization alongside arduous competition. For the regionalization process to move forward, there must be political trust and mutual confidence-building measures, which the author believes is conspicuously absent at the moment. The concept of "East Asia", or in a more general context, the East Asian Community, may be the ultimate challenge for all countries involved.

Ho Khai Leong argues that regime interests, defined in narrow national economic and political interests of countries concerned, may in the end prove to be the most significant impediments to the further advancement of Sino-ASEAN relations. As an economic region, ASEAN's connections with the rest of the world can be viewed at three levels: the global level, the regional level (Asia-Pacific) and the sub-regional level (ASEAN). Ho argues that ASEAN policymakers must first consolidate the AFTA before moving on to the proposal of the Asian economic community. However, the AFTA's inability to sustain long-term economic growth for the region has resulted in the intensification of its desire of economic co-operation and integration. In these developmental trajectories, China remains for many an enigma.

As much as we would like to recognize the validity of the "One-China policy", Taiwan's relations with ASEAN cannot be swept under the carpet. Taiwan's presence in Southeast Asia, both economic and cultural, need to be acknowledged as a reality; a reality that both China's and Southeast Asian policymakers will have to deal with. Chen Jie's and Samuel Ku's contributions remind us of the growing significance of Taiwan's diplomacy in Southeast Asia in the past two decades. Chen provides both macro and micro perspectives of Taiwan's pragmatic diplomacy in his comparison of the Lee Teng-hui and Chen Shui-bian administrations. The Go-South campaign initiated by Lee significantly raised Taiwan's politico-diplomatic position in Southeast Asian, while the DPP government under Chen Shui-bian has adopted a policy that sidelined the region. In turn, Taiwan-ASEAN relations have, unfortunately, continued to deteriorate, as elucidated by Samuel Ku. Chen also argues that the ASEAN states are not bystanders and as such, are also deeply concerned about cross-straits relations, for conflicts will bring dire consequences to China, Taiwan, and the Southeast Asian region.

Samuel Ku applies the interdependence theory — where the use of power in a situation of interdependence is shaped by sensitivity and vulnerability — to the relations between China, Taiwan and Southeast Asia. Although ASEAN does not recognize Taiwan as a sovereign state, the two entities are joined by multiple channels of communication. China appreciates the ASEAN countries' consistent adherence to the One-China policy and stresses that ASEAN cannot ignore Taiwan as an economic entity. After surveying the historical development of China and Taiwan with Southeast Asia, a triangular relationship that can be extremely complicated, Ku argues that China has emerged as a political hegemony in the wake of the 1997 financial crisis. He adds that its intention to continue this development is reflected in its proposal for regional integration.

The last two chapters deal with China's relations with individual Southeast Asian countries — Malaysia and Singapore respectively. Joseph Liow examines the transformation of Malaysia's China policy under the Mahathir administration from 1981 to 2003 and argues that there was indeed a gradual shift, albeit subtle, in Malaysia's posture towards China. In identifying the "bangwagoning-like" behaviour of Malaysia's China policy, he concludes that Malaysia's orientation towards China is part of a policy of hedge diplomacy towards Washington and Beijing. Evelyn Goh characterizes Singapore's response to an economically and politically powerful China as "deep engagement and strategic adjustment" and observes that Singapore's policymakers at the same time are "realist" enough to sustain close ties with the United States so as to maintain power equilibrium in the region.

Can ASEAN work as a collective? The continuous expansion of the organization with new members who do not necessarily partake in the experience of economic expansion cast doubts on this question. ASEAN requires much more effort to integrate the newer members to deal effectively to an emerging China. The Asia-Pacific region today is caught up in a dizzying swirl of economic, cultural, political, technological and social change. Enormous opportunities and challenges await policymakers and citizens alike who can harness these powerful currents to transform their societies; the task, however, is made more difficult by the fact that global forces and regional interests are often in conflict. China and Southeast Asia are confronting new realities which they must address together in order to compete and progress as individual nations as well as a regional entity.

References

Bert, Wayne. *The United States, China and Southeast Asian Security: A Changing of the Guard?* New York: Palgrave Macmillan, 2003.

Cai, Kevin G. "The ASEAN-China Free Trade Agreement and East Asian Regional Grouping". *Contemporary Southeast Asia* 25, no. 3 (2003): 387–402.

Haacke, Jurgen. "Seeking Influence: China's Diplomacy Toward ASEAN after the Asian Crisis". *Asian Perspective* 26, no. 4 (2002): 13–52.

Ho, Khai Leong. "New Directions in Taiwan-Southeast Asia Relations: Economics, Politics, and Security". *Pacific Focus* 10, no. 1 (1995): 81–100.

————. "Rituals, Risks and Rivalries: China and ASEAN in the Coming Decades". *Journal of Contemporary China* 10, no. 29 (2001): 683–94.

Hu, Weixing, "China's Security Agenda after the Cold War". *Pacific Review* 8, no. 1 (1995): 117–35.

Ku, Samuel C.Y. "Southeast Asia and Cross-Strait Relations". *Journal of Contemporary China* 7, no. 19 (1998): 421–42.

Suryadinata, Leo. *China and the ASEAN States: The Ethnic Chinese Dimension.* Singapore: Singapore University Press, 1985.

Vogel, Ezra F. *Living with China, US-China Relations in the Twenty-first Century.* New York: W.W. Norton & Company, 1997.

Wang, Qingxin. "In Search of Stability and Multipolarity: China's Changing Foreign Policy towards Southeast Asia after the Cold War". *Asian Journal of Political Science* 6, no. 2 (Dec 1998).

Wang, Gungwu. *China and Southeast Asia: Myths, Threats, and Culture.* Singapore: Singapore University Press, 1999.

Part I

GLOBAL CHANGES
&
REGIONAL PERCEPTIONS

1

CHINA AND SOUTHEAST ASIA
Changes in Strategic Perceptions

Wang Gungwu

Many books have been written since the start of the new century to discuss the relations between China and Southeast Asia. Most have concentrated on more immediate challenges like China's impact on Southeast Asian economic development and new ways of looking at the question of East Asian economic integration. Some have examined the problems for a larger Asia-Pacific region concerning long-term issues of defence and security. Yet others have dealt with Japanese and American reactions to China's initiatives in Southeast Asia, the interests of the European Community and the implications for global politics. This book seeks to combine the global changes with regional challenges. In that context, this essay shall focus on one of the key aspects of the subject, how regional developments depend on Asia's perceptions of the rise of American power in the twentieth century.*

Southeast Asia as a region found recognition by acting together as the Association of Southeast Asian Nations (ASEAN) in its relations with larger powers. The dramatic story of its growth in the course of about thirty years is yet to be fully told, but the process is inspiring, if not also a little surprising. Through the ASEAN Regional Forum and the larger Asia Pacific Economic

*An earlier version was presented as a lecture in Canberra at the Australian Defence College in August 2003.

Co-operation (APEC) meetings, the region was supported by the United States and key countries in Western Europe, Japan and Australia and, more recently, Korea and a reforming China. As a result, several of its original members moved quickly away from Third World status to be beacons to underdeveloped countries elsewhere. In this context, the region expanded to its present ten members and gained enough confidence to speed up its efforts to create a Free Trade Area. By 2002, six of its members had begun to reduce most of the remaining tariffs among themselves. They were thus ready to respond positively when China offered to negotiate a Free Trade Agreement with the whole region within ten years.

China, on the other hand, cannot be a region by itself nor does it need to be part of any region. It is a large historical polity bordered on all four sides by peoples it has had to befriend, control, or defend against. China was a magnet for traders when it was at peace, a rich target for envious and hostile neighbours when it was weak, and a dangerous enemy when it felt threatened and was aroused to defend its place as a civilization. Nor did others before modern times see China as any kind of region. It was only during the nineteenth century that, from the point of view of the British Empire, and ultimately also from that of various nations in Western Europe, China was grouped together with Japan, Thailand and various colonies east of British India in a fuzzy region that was called the Far East. When that centre of power shifted from Europe after the Second World War, during the era of the two superpowers, the United States and the Soviet Union, it was thought more appropriate to say that China was part of East Asia. More recently, with the growing recognition of a region called Southeast Asia, there have been efforts to see China as a part of the region to its north, that of Northeast Asia. For the understandable reason that this region includes an economic powerhouse like Japan and a potential power in a reunited Korea, that identification has not been a successful one. No regional grouping has emerged. On the contrary, recent moves reflecting the rivalry of the major powers seem to be leading to yet other kinds of groupings, including the idea of an Eastern Asia that encompassed both Northeast and Southeast Asia through the integration of ASEAN+3 (that is, China, Japan and Korea) and, more recently, even one that might include some of the members of the region further west, that of South Asia.

But even this move does not seem to meet the needs of contemporary geopolitics. There is the larger global picture in which China cannot look to any one region. Its land borders tie the country to Russia in what might be called "Northern Asia", to the new Muslim states in Central and West Asia and, across the Himalayas, to at least three of the countries in South Asia,

India, Pakistan and Nepal. One can see why Chinese rulers over the centuries saw their country as the centre of what is now called the continent of Asia. For the last century, new generations of leaders have seen that their interests are increasingly bound to the world beyond Asia to Europe and Africa and across the Pacific. China is no longer anybody's Far East. Could it be prosperous and feel secure just being part of Eastern Asia?

There are major points of concern that both China and Southeast Asia share. They are locked into a world trading system and no country or region is free to determine what kind of economy it wants. When their respective leaders talk of bringing China with Southeast Asia into a Free Trade Area, they do so knowing that they must contend with a global system that neither can control. Also, they are aware that rapid advances in technology have brought tensions to their respective value systems. These modernizing forces have generated powerful challenges to social stability. China and Southeast Asia need to have similar progressive goals. Otherwise, political divisions would make co-operation increasingly difficult. For one thing, China's economic and political power could encourage the Chinese people to develop a national pride that could generate fear among its neighbours, something that their leaders have sought to avoid for the past couple of decades.

No less important is the fact that China and Southeast Asia have both been fascinated by the growth of U.S. power. The United States has now made even larger commitments to Asia, and China and Southeast Asia are subject to closer attention than they have ever had. This U.S. commitment seems to be based as much on ideological and moral issues as on those of trade and power. Also, the U.S. war on terrorism since September 2001 has created new alliances and networks of co-operation that affect China and Southeast Asia. In particular, two new trends need to be better understood. On the one hand, the United States has shifted its position on China and, on the other, it seems that, in its future relations with Asian states, it would be prepared to be more interventionist than in the past. It is uncertain how China and Southeast Asia will ultimately fit into the new power structure that the United States projects across the Pacific to the Indian Ocean. Both China and Southeast Asia have to deal with developments linking religion to terror, and try to redefine their relationships with the United States. How the conflicts are resolved will also alter relations between Southeast Asia and China.

It is therefore important to understand what U.S. strategy towards Asia is, and how Asians see that strategy. That strategy is far from simple and clear-cut. How it was perceived at different stages during the past century is relevant to our subject and I shall try to trace that here. The Chinese had a glimpse of keen U.S. interest in the region when the United States followed the British in getting its share of the spoils of the Opium War by signing the Treaty of Wanghsia in 1844, but the United States kept a low profile, and the Chinese paid little attention during the nineteenth century to what lay behind U.S. actions. The Japanese had a foretaste of America's "manifest destiny" when the Black Ships arrived in Tokyo Bay in 1853, but this was the period of much more significant Anglo-French aggression elsewhere in Asia. It is understandable why what the Americans were demanding was seen merely as a minor variant of an extension of European power and largely associated with getting better trading conditions. The United States was still far from the Pacific power it was to become half a century later. Not until it had consolidated its control over the territories linking the Atlantic with the West Coast and across to Hawaii and Alaska did it begin to play a major part in Asian affairs.

The newfound American power impinged directly on the lives of an Asian people when the Spanish-American War led to the colonization of the Philippines. This was seen at the time as an act of replacing a failed colonial power, the Spanish, with one that was more modern and progressive. In any case, this new colony was clearly peripheral to the global ambitions of the great European powers. But the colony marked a new beginning for the United States in Asia. America began to flex its naval muscle more seriously. It identified with other imperial powers by joining in the intervention to free the legations in Beijing in 1900. It followed that with an Open Door policy seeking to prevent any power from making gains in China by excluding other powers. This represented a major commitment to Asian affairs and the Chinese saw this as a positive contribution to China's development compared with what the British and the French had demanded and what the Germans and the Japanese were asking for at the time. In particular, American willingness to return part of the Boxer indemnity funds to support the education of Chinese students in American colleges and universities was much appreciated. It led many Chinese to believe that China was an object of U.S. sympathy and generosity. Whatever strategy the United States had in Asia seemed to have been directed against China's enemies rather than China itself.

The first to feel the sharp point of growing American interest in Asia were the Japanese. The Open Door had limited Japan's gains after its defeat of the Russians in 1905, but this did not stop the Japanese from colonizing Korea and pushing into China's Manchurian provinces. Japan's emergence as the great naval power in the Far East during the First World War led to the Washington Conference of 1922, a strong move to limit Japanese expansion. Thereafter, the United States was divided between those who wanted to befriend a powerful Japan and those who feared its long-term threat to U.S.

economic interests in Asia. Japanese leaders in their turn gained many admirers among Asian elites, and this led Japanese strategists to gamble on their ability to win over other Asians against the West in a new Co-Prosperity arrangement that Japan would lead. This was at the root of the war in the Pacific of 1941–45, after which it was inevitable that the United States would intensify its strategic planning in Asia to defend U.S. global interests.

Thus, after the end of the Second World War, Southeast Asia came to be identified as an area that had strategic significance for the United States as a Pacific power, especially after the other European powers lost their respective colonies. And for the next half century, U.S. power was drawn deeper into the whole of the Western Pacific and into the Indian Ocean. We can discern three phases in this development for Southeast Asia. The first saw U.S. sympathy for anti-colonialism give way to a strong dedication to the defeat of international communism. The second followed the dissolution of the Soviet Union when the world had to learn to live with a single superpower that was strong enough to be interventionist in any part of the world. Since September 11, a third phase has begun as the U.S. response against terrorism directly involved parts of Southeast Asia. This region is now seen to be linked through its Muslim populations to the South Asian sub-continent as well as the Middle East.

Let me now point to some key features of U.S. power in Asia. For most of Southeast Asia before 1945, American activities mostly went unnoticed, and a relatively benign image of the United States was projected in the region until the 1950s. Awareness of U.S. wealth and power was growing, especially among the Japanese and the Chinese. The United States had made heroic efforts and sacrifices in the Pacific War of 1941–45 to defeat the Japanese and presented itself as a force in support of self-determination for all colonies. The independence of the Philippines in 1946 confirmed America's intentions, and the support for the Indonesian struggle against the return of the Dutch underlined the picture of an anti-imperial America. Also, there was the image of a magnanimous America reshaping Japan without a regime change, and making great efforts to turn that country into an ally, and this was accompanied by the efforts to save the nationalists in China from the Soviet ideology that had penetrated the Chinese Communist Party.

American strategy across the Pacific was centred on Japan and China, and Southeast Asian leaders recognized that their countries were but minor parts of a broad intercontinental sweep. What changed that perspective was when the United States "lost" China in 1949 and saw forces hostile to U.S. interests moving south into French Indochina. This led to a reversal of its anti-Empire stance and the Americans actually encouraged the French to stay on in

Vietnam. It was a decision that led to a division among the elites of the region largely into two groups, those for whom the U.S. commitment against the new threat of international communism was in their interest, and those who argued that the U.S. was showing an appetite for neo-colonialism and seeking to dominate the new nation-states. The division was a decisive factor in the creation in 1967 of ASEAN, with its five members (Indonesia, Thailand, Philippines, Malaysia and Singapore) that stood with the United States against the four mainland states (the Indochina states of Vietnam, Cambodia and Laos, plus Myanmar) that leant towards the People's Republic of China (PRC) and the Soviet Union.

This first phase had a dramatic mid-point when America lost the war in Indochina. A further shift in American strategy led to the making of a Sino-American "alliance" against the Soviet Union. The ASEAN half of Southeast Asia was quick to appreciate the change, and three members of the group, Thailand, Malaysia and the Philippines, established diplomatic relations with the PRC. In the 1980s, ASEAN played an active role together with Australia, the United States and the PRC, in sorting out the conflicts between Vietnam and Cambodia. That success enhanced ASEAN confidence and led to the decisive steps to invite the remaining four states in the region to join the organization.

For ASEAN, the active presence of the United States was always the key to the region's security. With that assured, it was possible for intra-ASEAN mechanisms to deal with all inter-state problems peacefully. This was a great advantage for the region's development. Most of that development could then ride on the economic growth in the United States and its other allies in East Asia, notably Japan, South Korea and Taiwan, not to say the British colony of Hong Kong. The optimism that this generated among a new generation of ASEAN leaders was unprecedented and the direct experience of U.S. "soft power" persuaded many sectors of the local elites to absorb American ideals and hopes and have a deeper appreciation of America's place as a superpower.

The second phase was a surprise to most because no one predicted the rapid disintegration of the Soviet Union. This was clearly a victory for United States' grand strategy. For the ASEAN states, the United States was now truly powerful in an unthreatening way. There have been assessments within the region of how U.S. strategy might change now that it was the sole superpower. Debates within the United States were followed with interest while Southeast Asian nations pursued their own diplomatic initiatives, mainly through the ASEAN Regional Forum (ARF) and their active support for APEC. There were adjustments to be made to the new global condition. For example, when angry voices were raised in the West in response to the Tiananmen debacle in

Beijing in 1989, Asian elites were asked to promote democracy, give more freedom to their people and check their human rights record. ASEAN leaders were reminded that they needed to do more in these areas if they wanted to retain American respect. Several of the leaders, notably in Malaysia and Singapore, responded robustly against these calls. They felt that they were doing well and were confident that their selective use of American and other Western values and methods to deal with their own needs had been effective.

One thing was obvious. The victory of liberal capitalism in a globalized market economy made clear that U.S. strategy in Asia is changing. What was unmistakable was the increasing attention given to the relations with the PRC now that America no longer needed China to balance the ambitions of the Soviet Union. As a result, even as ASEAN expanded rapidly to incorporate all ten nations in the region, some of the ambivalent attitudes towards the PRC among its old and new members became obvious.

The prominence of the PRC in U.S. strategy as well as in the calculations of the Southeast Asian leaders was heightened by the low growth in the Japanese economy, and even more so by the "miracles" of development on the Chinese mainland. No one could fail to notice that the reforms introduced by Deng Xiaoping from 1979 onwards had led to breathtaking changes. The fact that he looked favourably towards Southeast Asia, and especially towards the economic contributions of those nationals of Chinese descent in each of the Southeast Asian countries, was duly noted. It was inevitable that China's successes during the 1990s would lead to concerns among some of the region's leaders. ASEAN's American, Australian and Japanese allies were equally attentive towards the implications of China's wealth and power. But most observers were confident that economic growth within ASEAN itself would keep the region's problems to a minimum, and that the United States will continue to support that growth.

The region's optimism, as it turned out, was premature. In mid-1997, Thailand devalued its currency and this led to the spiral of banking defaults and business failures that the United States and its allies could do little to help. The dramatic events in Southeast Asia during the next four years, including the fall of the Suharto regime in Indonesia, the paralysis of leadership in Thailand, and the weakening of the newly enlarged ASEAN, have led to a new perception of China. Among some local leaders, this would include seeing China as an economic threat. The Chinese themselves have doubled their efforts to make friends and assuage the anxieties that this perception has caused. At the same time, the region has also noted the fact that China's success itself was directly linked to the American market and the broad implications this has had beyond questions of defence and national security.

Nothing prepared the nation-states of the world for the morning of 11 September 2001. The way that event galvanized the American people to action was impressive. Most Southeast Asian elites empathized with those who lost family and friends, but the U.S. Government's response provoked a range of different reactions. States that faced terrorism threats of their own were quick to support U.S. actions. But, when these threats were used to justify the war in Iraq, they touched the sensitivities of countries with large Muslim populations. At least five countries in the region have large Muslim populations, although Muslims are in the majority in only three of them. However, unlike those of the Middle East, most Muslims in Southeast Asia have preserved their local cultures in a Malay world framework. They are not Arabs or Taliban. Their "Malayness" allows them to adapt to the secular standards of modern society in their own way. There is now increasing pressure on the national elites of each country to crackdown on groups that support the enemies of the United States. For the ASEAN members who have benefited from American aid for decades, this would normally have been quite acceptable. But for them to single out their own Muslim nationals whose cross-border linkages might foster rebellion, subversion or terrorist attacks, they have to respond with great care.

Then there is the factor of China. For Southeast Asian states, the PRC is close to home. It is the northern neighbour of three of the states on the Southeast Asian mainland, that is, Vietnam, Laos and Myanmar, and is close to two others, Thailand and Cambodia. Historically, China's relations with these states have been distinct from those with the maritime polities in the region. For example, it had been relatively easy for China to exert pressure across the land borders from the provinces of Guangxi and Yunnan in times of disorder, whether they were rebellions or local rivalries. Although the preference had always been for trade and peace, traditional relations had been personal and feudal, and always bilateral. The PRC in recent years has tried to change that image and allay the fears of Southeast Asian nations about its growing power. But Southeast Asian leaders would like to be reassured that multilateral linkages prevail, not only between ASEAN and China in East Asia, but also that such linkages could be extended, wherever possible or necessary, to the larger Asia-Pacific and other major economic groupings.

The biggest challenge now is to ensure that the coming together of all ten nations into ASEAN will, in the long run, be fully justified. The sudden end of the Cold War has reduced the need for concerted ASEAN action on political and security grounds and stressed the need to pay more attention to economic challenges. The fact that China has been relatively unaffected by the downturn of the past four years has been seen as a contribution to the region's economic recovery. But, in the eyes of some leaders, that fact may turn out to be a potential obstacle to future developments. There is growing concern that more Foreign Development Investment (FDI) funds will be diverted to China, funds that would normally have come to Southeast Asia. For the first time in two centuries, China's economic performance has become a subject of intense debate among all Southeast Asian governments. Under the terms of the current debate, how can Southeast Asian countries ensure long-term co-operation with China?

A counter-argument would insist that economic growth is not a zero-sum game. If China's economy keeps on growing, and if Southeast Asian governments and entrepreneurs set out to attract more Chinese trade and investment into the region, there could also be benefits. The countries of Southeast Asia have had different experiences of China in the twentieth century. It may not be easy for them to agree what each might do and what the ASEAN group as a whole might do. Much will depend on how each country eyes China and how their leaders can iron out their differences of attitudes. Given the trend towards a weaker sense of national sovereignty and the drive towards borderless economic relations, these are serious challenges to existing mindsets.

How China sees the region as it becomes more powerful is another concern. For centuries, China saw the maritime ports and kingdoms and the tribal valley states of the Irrawady, the Salween and the Mekong as useful trading partners but no threat to China. Since the nineteenth century, Southeast Asia has been perceived as an area that could be used by powerful enemies for attacks against China. China's efforts ever since to seek security in the south have been aimed at the foreign powers operating in the region, but these then have often been seen as threats to Southeast Asian nations themselves. Indeed, during the height of the Cold War, the Beijing government used hostile rhetoric against the new national leaders who were thought to support the Western alliance, and this tended to incur the fear and anger of their peoples as well.

Since the Nixon-Kissinger initiative in 1971, Chinese views towards Southeast Asia have been gradually revised. The key lay in China's new relationship with the United States, but the fact that the region's national leaders could through ASEAN speak with one voice persuaded the Chinese leaders that ASEAN could actually help them make friends in the region and elsewhere. For most Southeast Asians, however, the idea that there are now millions of Chinese in China mastering the skills of modern business and building an irresistible economic superpower is an alarming one. A China inside the WTO that is capable of wielding the weapons of a globalized world to expand its own interests would need to be restrained. Recent memories of China's political instability, social unrest, revolutionary violence and occasional anti-foreign outbursts remain. Above all, China is difficult to read, even for a country like the United States with its vast intelligence networks. There is a wide spectrum of views and so many contradictory predictions about China's future that it is hard to believe that people are talking about the same country. At one extreme, China has been portrayed as the inevitable enemy of the United States that has to be contained now before it is too late. This is often based on predictions that China's economy will go on growing at more or less the dramatic rates of the past twenty years. That growth will enable China to build up its military capacities to the point when it will dominate its weaker neighbours and ultimately drive the Americans out of the Asia-Pacific.

China as a threat does not depend on its economic successes. A scenario that predicted economic failure could lead to a similar conclusion. It would portray a China that, when in deep economic trouble, would seek salvation through war. From this viewpoint, whether China prospers or not, it is seen to be potentially aggressive. There are many books that point to the negative factors that will ensure that China's economy, especially after it becomes open to WTO rules, has nowhere to go but down. These stress the deep inefficiencies in China's financial system and underline the irrationality of protecting loss-making state-owned enterprises. They point to the pervasive corruption in high places and emphasise the large number of unemployed disrupting the cities or roaming the countryside. The growing gap between rich and poor approaches the danger levels associated with the fall of earlier regimes in China. These authors also despair of the capacity of the Communist Party to remedy the situation from within. They describe the party as having lost credibility now that its ideology is bankrupt. And, not least, they also refer to the dangers of persistent unrest among China's minorities in border provinces like Xinjiang and Tibet.

Given the complexities of China and the propensity for the unexpected to occur, one cannot be dogmatic about what will happen there. We need to remember that the conditions for China's growth in 1978 were so poor that no one predicted the rapid transformations of the 1980s. Also, the aftermath of the Tiananmen tragedy in 1989 was so grim that no one foresaw the remarkable performances of the 1990s. Any realistic assessment must measure the country's immense problems against the exceptional things that its 1.3 billion people have been able to do. History provides no clear answers. When China was the great power in Asia, it did not need Southeast Asia for anything important and was content to encourage commerce in a highly regulated way.

For there to be genuine co-operation between China and Southeast Asia, at least two pre-conditions must exist. The first calls on Chinese strategists to recognize that Southeast Asia, among all the major regions that it borders, offers the greatest security for China. But this could only be so if the region is prosperous and stable. Therefore, China must assist the region to return to the growth trajectory that it had before 1997. Secondly, Southeast Asian leaders would have to consider if its recent heritage of fear and suspicion of China is still justified. If so, the dependence on a U.S. containment strategy in the region would remain and this has the potential to rekindle China's concern that the United States would work against its longer term quest for "wealth and power". But if China could dampen if not totally remove these Southeast Asian fears, then the chances for truly fresh beginnings in regional integration would greatly improve.

References

Amitav Acharya. *Seeking Security in the Dragon's Shadow: China and Southeast Asia in the Emerging Asian Order*. Singapore: Institute of Defence and Strategic Studies, 2003.

Bert, Wayne. *The United States, China and Southeast Asian Security: A Changing of the Guard?* New York: Palgrave Macmillan, 2003.

Broinowski, Alison, ed. *ASEAN into the 1990s*. New York: St. Martin's Press, 1990.

Cai, Kevin G. "The ASEAN-China Free Trade Agreement and East Asian Regional Grouping". *Contemporary Southeast Asia* 25, no. 3 (2003): 387–402.

Cheng, Joseph Y.S. "China's ASEAN Policy in the 1990s: Pushing for Regional Multipolarity". *Contemporary Southeast Asia* 21, no. 2 (1999): 183–200.

Curley, Melissa G. and Hong Liu, eds. *China and Southeast Asia: Changing Socio-cultural Interactions*. Hong Kong: Centre of Asian Studies, University of Hong Kong, 2002.

Fineman, Daniel. *Special Relationship: The United States and Military Government in Thailand, 1947–1958*. Honolulu: University of Hawaii Press, 1997.

Gong, Gerrit W., ed. *Southeast Asia's Changing Landscape: Implications for U.S.-Japan Relations on the Eve of the Twenty-first Century*. Washington D.C.: Centre for Strategic and International Studies, 1999.

Hood, Stephen J. *Dragons Entangled: Indochina and the China-Vietnam War*. Armonk, N.Y.: M.E. Sharpe, 1992.

Leifer, Michael. *ASEAN and the Security of South-East Asia*. London, New York: Routledge, 1989.

Liu Yongzhuo. *Zongguo dongnanya yanjiu de huigu yu qianzhan*. [*Southeast Asian*

Studies in China: Retrospect and Prospect] Guangzhou: Guangdong Remin Chubanshe, 1994.

Muni, S.D. *China's Strategic Engagement with the New ASEAN: An Exploratory Study of China's Post-Cold War Political, Strategic and Economic Relations with Myanmar, Laos, Cambodia and Vietnam.* Singapore: Institute of Defence and Strategic Studies, 2002.

Narine, Shaun. *Explaining ASEAN: Regionalism in Southeast Asia.* Boulder, CO: Lynne Rienner Publishers, 2002.

Paribatra, Sukhumbhand. *From Enmity to Alignment: Thailand's Evolving Relations with China.* Bangkok: Institute of Security and International Studies, Chulalongkorn University, 1987.

Steinberg, David, I. "Myanmar: Regional Relationships and Internal Concerns". *Southeast Asian Affairs 1998.* Singapore: Institute of Southeast Asian Affairs, 1998, pp. 179–88.

Sokolsky, Richard, Angel Rabasa and C.R. Neu. *The Role of Southeast Asia in U.S. Strategy toward China.* Santa Monica, CA: Rand, 2000.

Sukma, Rizal. *Indonesia and China: The Politics of a Troubled Relationship.* New York: Routledge, 1999.

Suryadinata, Leo. *Indonesia's Foreign Policy under Suharto: Aspiring to International Leadership.* Singapore: Times Academic Press, 1996.

Tin Maung Maung Than. "Myanmar and China: A Special Relationship?" *Southeast Asian Affairs 2003.* Singapore: Institute of Southeast Asian Studies, 2003, pp. 189–210.

Vatikiotis, Michael R.J. "Catching the Dragon's Tail: China and Southeast Asia in the 21st Century". *Contemporary Southeast Asia* 25, no. 1 (2003).

Womack, Brantly. "Asymmetry and Systemic Misperception: China, Vietnam and Cambodia during the 1970s". *Journal of Strategic Studies* 26, no. 2 (2003): 92–119.

Part II

CHINA-ASEAN FTA
Economic Statecraft
and
Policy Interests

2

THE LOGIC OF CHINA-ASEAN FTA

Economic Statecraft of "Peaceful Ascendancy"

Vincent Wei-cheng Wang

INTRODUCTION: RISING CHINA AND SOUTHEAST ASIA

The regional political and economic order in East Asia[1] has undergone a significant transformation since the end of the Cold War. One of the most important changes is China's growing clout and influence in this region. Several important factors contribute to this development: China's rapid and sustained economic growth (on average 9 per cent per year over the past two decades), Japan's relative decline as a result of its decade-long recession, the 1997–98 Asian Financial Crisis that decimated several high-flying Asian economies, and the stretching-thin of the United States' military resources and political capital due to the war on terror, the daunting task of rebuilding Iraq, and the challenge posed by a nuclear North Korea.

Whereas China's rise in the mid-1990s caused much concern among its neighbours and the United States,[2] China's further ascent in the early 2000s has instead generated more equanimity. This shift presents not only an intellectual puzzle but also an important policy question. China's expanding economy is now regarded more as an opportunity than a threat, and its more polished foreign policy exudes confidence and poise.[3]

One of the most dramatic events of the past decade was the announcement by ASEAN and China in November 2001 that they intended to create an FTA (Free Trade Area) between them within a decade. One year later, at the Eighth ASEAN-China Summit in Phnom Penh, Cambodia, in November 2002, ASEAN leaders and Chinese Premier Zhu Rongji signed a Framework Agreement on Comprehensive Economic Co-operation, which provided the groundwork for the eventual establishment of an ASEAN-China FTA by 2010 for the older ASEAN members (Brunei, Indonesia, Malaysia, the Philippines, Singapore, and Thailand) and 2015 for the newer members (Cambodia, Laos, Myanmar, and Vietnam). The agreement went into force on 1 July 2003.[4]

Comparing today with ASEAN's founding epoch, the contrasts cannot be more vivid: In 1967, China was mired in its angry self-imposed isolation called the Cultural Revolution, whereas ASEAN was established partly to form a collective counterweight against the regime that had exported revolutions and inspired guerrilla wars in Southeast Asia. Nowadays China is deeply engaged with the world and even assumes the hitherto unprecedented role as a trade promoter in East Asia.

What explain these changes? What are the political and economic impetuses for the ASEAN-China FTA? What is the relationship between China's current trade offensive and its "new" foreign policy thinking? Does it signify a long-term and fundamental shift in China's economic statecraft or represent a short-term tactical expedient aimed at buying the crucial time needed for China to develop into an unparalleled power in the region capable of safeguarding its core interests?

This chapter examines the ASEAN-China FTA in light of regionalism in East Asia and China's new diplomacy. It argues that China's FTA with the ASEAN is driven by a political logic to respond to challenges posed by competitive regionalisms in the world economy, to cement growing economic ties with Southeast Asian nations, to secure raw materials crucial to its economic development, and to ensure a peaceful and stable environment close to home so as to buttress China's growing influence and counterbalance American and Japanese power. It is thus a concrete example of economic statecraft employed to facilitate China's new foreign policy strategy — "peaceful ascendancy". ASEAN nations are attracted by the opportunities brought about by China's economic expansion and trade liberalization; they also seek to leverage their FTA with China to additional FTAs with important trading partners within (for example, Japan) or outside (for example, the United States) the region. However, because of the disparate levels of development and policy priorities of its members, ASEAN's FTA with China is likely to cause various challenges to individual members and the organization as a whole.

This chapter is divided into five parts. The first part is an introduction setting up the issue. The second part offers some background on regional trading arrangements, emphasizing the proliferation of such arrangements in the 1990s. The third part reviews the profiles of China's economic interactions with ASEAN. The fourth part examines the main political calculus in China's decision to pursue FTA with ASEAN, paying special attention to the larger strategic factors associated with China's desire to attain "peaceful ascendancy". The last part looks at some of the issues raised by ASEAN-China FTA and speculates its eventual success.

RISE OF REGIONALISM IN THE WORLD ECONOMY

Regional economic integration — the deepening of intra-regional economic interdependence in a given region, through intra-regional trade, foreign direct investment (FDI) and harmonization of commercial regulations, standards, and practices — probably predated the Westphalian international system. Regionalism is the political movement towards the creation or expansion of regional trade organizations or associations.[5]

The proliferation of regional trading blocs — often known as regional integration agreements (RIAs) — and the deepening of relationships among existing members of certain trading blocs are among the major developments in international relations in recent decades. Most industrial and developing countries in the world are members of a regional integration agreement, and many belong to more than one: over one-half of world trade takes place within such agreements.[6]

The past decade witnessed an especially sharp increase in regional trade agreements (RTAs).[7] According to World Trade Organization (WTO) figures, as the end of 2002, a total of 259 RTAs had been notified to the WTO and its predecessor, General Agreement on Tariffs and Trade (GATT); among them 176 RTAs are currently in force. An additional 70 RTAs are believed to be operational but not yet notified, and about 70 are under negotiation. Among WTO's 146 members, only Mongolia is not already in a RTA or engaged in negotiations on preferential agreements.[8]

One important reason for the increasing popularity of preferential trade agreements (PTAs) is the seemingly difficult process and bleak prospects for progress on the multilateral agenda — the latest example being the collapse of the WTO meeting in September 2003, after which U.S. trade representative Robert Zoellick warned that the United States might press ahead with bilateral and regional trade deals.[9]

Table 2.1 shows that 43 per cent of world merchandise trade now occurs under the umbrella of preferential trade agreements. If all RTAs currently under negotiation are successfully concluded before 2005, then over 50 per cent of world merchandise trade will occur among countries linked by preferential agreements.

Table 2.1 also shows that as of now, Western Europe leads in preferential trade (hence it evokes the image of "Fortress Europe"), whereas Asia is the least prone to trade on preferential terms. Indeed, the current proliferation of PTAs in Asia to a considerable extent represents a "catch-up" phenomenon.

PTAs are the obverse of the principle of non-discrimination trade policies. The Anglo-American Allies that planned the world economic system after World War II — which became known as the Bretton Woods system — believed that the discriminatory trade policies in the 1930s had contributed to the collapse of world trade and in turn to the Great Depression. They enshrined the non-discrimination policy into Article I of the GATT, requiring (unconditional) most-favoured nation (MFN) for all GATT members.[10]

However, since its outset, the GATT allowed a major deviation from the MFN principle. Article XXIV states that a group of countries may form a free

TABLE 2.1
Preferential Trade Share of intra-RTAs Trade in
Merchandise Imports of Major Regions, 2000 and 2005
(as of January 2003)

	2000	2005
Western Europe	64.7	67.0
Transitional economies	61.6	61.6
North America (incl. Mexico)	41.4	51.6
Africa	37.2	43.6
Middle East	19.2	38.1
Latin America (excl. Mexico)	18.3	63.6
Asia	5.6	16.2
World	43.2	51.2

Source: World Trade Organization, *World Trade Report 2003*, Geneva: WTO, 2003, p. 48.

trade area or custom union, dropping barriers among themselves, subject to a few requirements.[11]

Levels of Integration

Several formal regional trading agreements that denote differing levels integration need to be distinguished.[12]

(1) **Preferential Trade Arrangements:** The loosest type of arrangement is the granting of partial preferences to a set of trading partners. If the concessions are one-way, we term this a *preferential trade arrangement* — as seen in the unilateral concessions made by an industrialized country to less developed countries (LDCs), a practice that the GATT always permitted. If the concessions are reciprocal, we may call it *preferential trade area* (PTA) to describe the club of nations covered.

(2) **Free Trade Area (FTA):** If the members of a PTA eliminate *all* tariffs and quantitative import restrictions among themselves — that is, 100 per cent preferences — then they form a *free trade area* (FTA). They typically retain varying levels of tariffs and other barriers against the products of non-members.[13]

(3) **Custom Union (CU):** The next level of integration occurs when the members of an FTA go beyond removing trade barriers among themselves and set a common level of trade barriers *vis-à-vis* outsiders. This at a minimum entails a common external tariff, which is no higher than the average of the previously existing tariffs of the member countries. A full CU will set all trade policy for its members as a whole.

(4) **Common Market:** PTA, FTA, and CU are different models of "shallow integration", whereas common market and economic union constitute "deep integration". Beyond the free exchange of goods and services among members, a *common market* entails the free movement of factors of production: labour and capital.

(5) **Economic Union:** Economic union involves harmonizing national economic policies, including typically taxes and a common currency.

The European Union (EU) is the best example of a long process of increased level of integration and the most notable economic union. In contrast, neither the members of the North American Free Trade Agreement (NAFTA) nor the members of ASEAN FTA expect to literally eliminate all interior barriers to trade, as the name "free trade area" would imply. It should also be pointed out that not all trade among preferential trading partners takes place at preferential rates. Most agreements exclude certain sensitive sectors (for example, agriculture).

Motivations for Integration

Why do nations pursue regional integration? Largely speaking they do it for two sets of reasons: (1) politics and policymaking, and (2) economics.

As a World Bank publication asserts, "Regional integration is good politics: It meets political needs, such as security or enhanced bargaining power, and it satisfies influential lobbies."[14] Indeed, the main motivation for regional integration is often political, rather than economic. The first motivation is to use integration to consolidate peace and increase regional security. It is often assumed that creating linkages between economies can make conflicts more costly. Both Immanuel Kant's third definitive article of "perpetual peace" — cosmopolitan law[15] — and Thomas Friedman's "Golden Arches Theory of Conflict Prevention[16] affirm this insight. In the post-9/11 environment, U.S. Trade Representative Robert Zoellick justified his aggressive pursuit of FTAs with such nations as Jordan, Israel, Chile, Singapore, Australia, Morocco, southern Africa, and Western Hemisphere on national security ground. He argued, "While terrorism isn't caused by poverty…failed states, broken societies, extreme poverty, create the fertile ground in which the seeds of terrorism can grow, and therefore we have a very strong interest in having a pro-growth and opportunity economic policy that complements our security agenda."[17] Clearly the United States expected important strategic and political benefits from these FTAs, since the economic benefits were modest.

Second, by joining together the weak can become strong. Governments often seek to acquire greater bargaining power in multilateral negotiations by first tying in partner countries through regional commitments. At a regional level, a subset of countries could first strike their own agreement in order to increase bargaining power and press for a better outcome.

Third, regional agreements have been used to lock in institutional changes and reforms. For trade liberalization, regional agreements are a well-designed piece of commitment mechanism because they are built upon reciprocal preferences.

Fourth, vested interests, such as powerful national bureaucracies set up to negotiate trade agreements, or certain sectors of the society that stand to gain or lose, often lobby the governments to seek regional agreements.

Fifth, countries can benefit greatly from co-operation when they share resources — such as rivers, fishing grounds, hydroelectric power, or rail connection — or when they jointly to overcome problems — such as pollution and transportation bottlenecks. By virtue of enhanced trust, regional agreements can help in this regard.

Several economic rationales have also been marshaled for regional agreements, which can be summarized as the allure of reaping benefits from free trade without enduring the cost for adjustment. First, the theory of "second-best" holds that although multilateral agreements that aim at eliminating barriers across the board are almost always preferable, they are also more elusive. Hence, liberalization via a regional agreement might be more beneficial to the world than the *status quo*.

A second economic reason for governments to seek discriminatory liberalization is that they may be able to reap gains from trade in product areas where they cannot compete internationally. RTAs thus could serve the purpose of shutting out third-party competition from more efficient suppliers.

Third, small countries especially regard participation in regional agreements as a defensive necessity. They fear exclusion from markets and see participation as an insurance policy against being placed at a competitive disadvantage through discriminatory policies. Richard Baldwin calls this "domino theory" of regionalism — idiosyncratic incidents of regionalism triggered a multiplier effect that knocked down bilateral import barriers like a row of dominoes.[18]

As will be shown later, many of these characteristic political and economic considerations were clearly at work in the case of ASEAN-China FTA.

ASEAN AND CHINA: GROWING MORE INTERDEPENDENT, BUT NOT THE WHOLE STORY

ASEAN was established on 8 August 1967 in Bangkok by the five original member states — Indonesia, Malaysia, Philippines, Singapore, and Thailand. Brunei Darussalam joined on 8 January 1984, Vietnam on 28 July 1995, Laos and Myanmar on 23 July 1997, and Cambodia on 30 April 1999, expanding its membership to ten. The last four entrants are also called newer members, or ASEAN-4.

The ASEAN Declaration states that the aims and purposes of the Association are: (1) to accelerate the economic growth, social progress and cultural development in the region through joint endeavours in the spirit of equality and partnership in order to strengthen the foundation for a prosperous and peaceful community of Southeast Asian nations, and (2) to promote regional peace and stability through abiding respect for justice and the rule of law in the relationship among countries in the region and adherence to the principles of the United Nations Charter.[19]

Despite these common aspirations, ASEAN members vary considerably — from the tiny oil-rich sultanate of Brunei (population: 300,000) to the world's fourth most populous nation (and the largest Muslim country), Indonesia; from the miniscule economy of Laos to the potential giant, Indonesia; from the impoverished ASEAN-4 to the wealthy Singapore and Brunei. Table 2.2 presents several basic economic indicators.

The extreme disparity of ASEAN nations as shown in Table 2.2 raises several important questions. Experiences from other parts of the world, particularly Western Europe, demonstrate that (1) small states are often more active than large states in promoting integration (for example, the Benelux countries were often considered "core" members for each stage in the history of European integration); this is in contrast to the "hegemonic stability" theory, which holds that the existence of a hegemon, both willing and capable of shouldering the cost of maintaining an open system is the prerequisite to liberal economic regimes and institutions;[20] (2) homogeneity — comparable levels of development, ideological affinity, and compatible political systems — facilitates successful "deep" integration; (3) deeper integration among the existing members is often considered helpful for, if not essential to, "shallow integration" with newer members who are characterized by greater heterogeneity (for example, EU's "growing pain" or "hiccups" in integrating with the former communist countries of Eastern Europe).

ASEAN nations pride themselves for following certain "fundamental principles" in their relations with one another, as adopted in the Treaty of Amity and Co-operation (TAC) in Southeast Asia, signed at the First ASEAN Summit on 24 February 1976:

- Mutual respect for the independence, sovereignty, equality, territorial integrity, and national identity of all nations;
- The right of every state to lead its national existence free from external interference, subversion or coercion;
- Non-interference in the internal affairs of one another;
- Settlement of differences or disputes by peaceful manner;
- Renunciation of the threat or use of force; and
- Effective co-operation among themselves.[21]

In January 1992, the ASEAN Free Trade Area (AFTA) was established to eliminate tariff barriers among the Southeast Asian countries with an aim of integrating the ASEAN economies into a single production base and creating a regional market of 500 million people. Under AFTA, tariff rates levied on a wide range of products traded within the region be reduced to no more than five per cent. Quantitative and other non-tariff barriers are to be eliminated. The newer members were expected to realize AFTA by 2006–10.[22]

TABLE 2.2
China and ASEAN: Select Economic Indicators

	Brunei	Cambodia	Indonesia	Laos	Malaysia	Myanmar	Philippines	Singapore	Thailand	Vietnam	China
Population (millions, 2001)	0.3	12.2	209.0	5.4	23.8	48.3	78.3	4.1	61.1	79.5	1,271.8
GDP (US$ billions, 2001)	N/A	3.4	145.3	1.8	88.0	14.2*	71.4	84.9	115.3	32.9	1,159.0
GNI per capita (US$, 2001)	N/A	280	680	300	3,400	300*	1,030	21,100	1,960	410	890
PPP GDP (US$ bn, 2002 est.)	6.5	20.4	714.2	10.4	198.4	73.7	379.7	112.4	445.8	183.3	5,989.0
PPP GDP per capita (US$, 2002 estimates)	18,600	1,660	3,100	1,800	8,800	1,700*	4,600	25,200	7,000	2,700	4,700
Exports (US$ billions, 2001)	3.0	1.4	52.3	0.3	95.2	2.7	35.1	127.0	67.7	16.5	325.6
Imports (US$ billions, 2001)	1.4	1.7	32.1	0.6	76.8	2.5	33.5	113.0	58.1	16.8	295.3
FDI inflows (US$ millions, 2000)	N/A	125.7	-4,550.0	33.9	3,787.6	254.8	1,241.0	6,390.3	3,366.0	1,298.0	38,399.3

Notes: * Estimates
Sources: Author's compilation from *World Bank Indicators* Data Query <http://www.worldbank.org/data/dataquery.html>, The National Bureau of Asian Research, *Strategic Asia* Database <http://strategicasia.nbr.org/Data/CView/>, and the Central Intelligence Agency, *The World Factbook 2003* <http://www.odci.gov/cia/publications/factbook/index.html>.

Size is important, and China towers over each individual ASEAN member and all of them combined. AFTA intends to create a regional market of over 500 million people. But the combined ASEAN magnitude would only constitute 29 per cent of the population, 32 per cent of the GDP, and 46 per cent of the trade volume, of the combined ASEAN-China FTA, which, with 1.79 billion people, US$1.7 trillion in GDP, and US$1.36 trillion in trade volume, would become the world's largest FTA (calculated from Table 2.2). This is why there is a widely accepted view, expressed by former Singaporean Trade and Industry Minister George Yeo, that an integrated ASEAN is the only viable response to an economically-rising China.[23]

Table 2.3 shows the major export and import partners of individual ASEAN members and China. This table shows several interesting patterns. Although China is among the top five trade partners for each ASEAN member, it is not the most important (Myanmar's import is the only exception); its importance to these nations is comparable to that of Taiwan's or South Korea's. In fact, the United States is the top export partner of five out of the ten ASEAN members (and the United States is also China's top export market); and Japan is the top import partner of four ASEAN nations (and Japan is also China's top import source). So, economic arguments are insufficient to explain ASEAN-China FTA. If economy of scale is the main concern, then ASEAN nations (and for that matter China itself) should pursue FTAs with their largest trade partners — the United States and Japan. The fact that the smaller economies band together — a kind of economic "balancing" — shows that the main impetus for the China-ASEAN FTA is a political logic. The next section will examine some of the non-economic rationales for the ASEAN-FTA.

Although China's trade with ASEAN may not be as large or important as ASEAN's trade with the United States or ASEAN-Japan trade, it nevertheless has increased rapidly in recent years. Citing ASEAN official figures, Table 2.4 shows that from 1993 to 2001, total ASEAN export to China increased seven-fold, from US$4.5 billion to US$31.6 billion. During the same period, ASEAN import from China increased 5.5 times, from US$4.3 billion to US$23.8 billion. Two-way trade in 2001 stood at US$55.4 billion.

Table 2.5, using official statistics from China's Ministry of Commerce, highlights the importance of ASEAN-China trade but also helps place it in perspective. It should be noted that Table 5 groups together trade data of all fifteen member states of the European Union as one entity and the ten members of ASEAN as one entity. This accounting method serves to give the allure of elevated importance for EU and ASEAN — hence, it is politically easier to sell the FTA to ASEAN as a whole and to show that China's trade flows to various markets are "balanced". According to this

TABLE 2.3

Major Trading Partners of ASEAN Nations and China

(Percentage shares of the country's exports / imports)

	Brunei	Cambodia	Indonesia	Laos	Malaysia	Myanmar	Philippines	Singapore	Thailand	Vietnam	China
Export partners	Japan (40.3)	U.S. (60.2)	Japan (21)	Vietnam (26)	U.S. (21)	Thailand (31.4)	U.S. (26.2)	Malaysia (17.4)	U.S. (19.6)	U.S. (15.2)	U.S. (21.5)
	S. Korea (12.3)	Germany (9.1)	U.S. (13.2)	Thailand (19)	Singapore (17.4)	U.S. (13)	Japan (14.9)	U.S. (15.3)	Japan (14.9)	Japan (14.9)	Hong Kong (18)
	Thailand (12.1)	U.K. (7.1)	Singapore (9.4)	France (7.5)	Japan (10.9)	India (7.4)	China (7.4)	Hong Kong (9.7)	Singapore (8)	Australia (7.1)	Japan (14.9)
	Australia (9.2)	Singapore (4.4)	S. Korea (7.2)	Germany (5.3)	China (6.5)	China (4.7)	Taiwan (5.8)	Japan (7.1)	Hong Kong (5.4)	China (6.6)	S. Korea (4.8)
	U.S. (8.1)		China (5.1)		Hong Kong (5)		Singapore (5.7)	China (5.5)	China (5.2)	Germany (6.5)	
	China (6.4)		Taiwan (4.2)					Taiwan (4.9)	Malaysia (4)	Singapore (5.5)	
Import partners	Singapore (30.6)	Thailand (24.8)	Japan (14)	Thailand (59)	Japan (16.9)	China (27)	Japan (21.6)	Malaysia (18.2)	Japan (23)	S. Korea (12.7)	Japan (18.1)
	Japan (21.5)	Singapore (16.9)	Singapore (13.1)	Vietnam (12.3)	Singapore (15.9)	Singapore (19.5)	U.S. (18.6)	U.S. (14.3)	U.S. (9.6)	China (12.2)	Taiwan (10.5)
	Malaysia (17.4)	China (12.1)	U.S. (8.5)	China (7.9)	U.S. (15.5)	Thailand (12)	Singapore (7.8)	Japan (12.5)	China (7.6)	Japan (12.1)	S. Korea (9.7)
	U.K. (6.1)	Hong Kong (10.9)	China (7.8)		China (7.8)	Malaysia (9.1)	S. Korea (7.5)	China (7.6)	Malaysia (5.6)	Singapore (11.8)	U.S. (9.2)
	Hong Kong (14)	S. Korea (5.5)	S. Korea (5.3)		S. Korea (5)	Taiwan (6.3)	China (5.7)	Taiwan (4.6)	Singapore (4.5)	Taiwan (10.6)	Germany (5.6)
			Taiwan (5.1)		Taiwan (4.7)	S. Korea (5.3)	Hong Kong (4.5)	Thailand (4.6)	Taiwan (4.4)	Thailand (5.4)	
							Taiwan (4.1)				

Sources: Author's compilation from CIA, *The World Factbook 2003* <http://www.odci.gov/cia/publications/factbook/index.html>.

TABLE 2.4
ASEAN Trade with China by Country (1993–2001)

ASEAN Export to China
(Value in US$ Thousands)

COUNTRY	Export								
	1993	1994	1995	1996	1997	1998	1999	2000	2001
Brunei Darussalam	–	37.1	152.2	115.4	0.0	0.0	244.2	22,270.0	127,741.3
Cambodia	–	–	–	–	–	–	–	285,985.0	224,984.2
Indonesia	1,249,494.1	1,280,043.2	1,741,717.8	1,867,758.2	2,123,041.2	1,832,034.4	3,338,942.2	4,321,848.9	3,490,998.1
Malaysia	1,202,628.5	1,859,707.4	1,806,866.6	1,519,935.5	1,313,812.7	1,545,082.2	4,595,865.8	6,433,437.9	6,229,130.5
Myanmar	–	–	–	–	–	–	65,076.9	86,525.3	103,700.5
Philippines	173,874.0	163,967.0	212,938.6	327,921.7	244,411.6	343,682.6	2,521,925.8	2,570,611.5	2,372,582.0
Singapore	1,902,697.9	2,000,065.8	2,439,216.6	3,214,704.8	4,195,491.8	4,059,714.3	12,718,557.3	16,236,398.3	16,140,398.9
Thailand	–	–	–	543,696.6	1,291,132.0	1,422,072.6	3,231,764.2	5,077,586.6	2,862,555.1
TOTAL	4,528,694.5	5,303,820.5	6,200,891.8	7,474,132.2	9,167,889.3	9,202,586.1	26,472,376.4	35,034,663.5	31,552,090.6

Note: China including Hong Kong in 1999–2001

ASEAN Import from China
(Value in Thousand US$ Thousands)

COUNTRY	Import								
	1993	1994	1995	1996	1997	1998	1999	2000	2001
Brunei Darussalam	–	34,931.4	63,336.5	72,500.2	55,090.6	20,620.9	72,415.9	84,958.9	97,356.1
Cambodia	–	–	–	–	–	–	–	364,110.9	203,774.4
Indonesia	935,983.3	1,477,386.7	1,495,223.3	1,235,458.7	1,518,013.9	904,459.4	1,469,664.0	2,364,323.0	2,099,989.6
Malaysia	816,772.8	1,200,709.0	1,516,774.7	1,719,986.8	1,916,805.4	1,685,513.6	3,358,966.0	6,572,884.9	5,129,407.3
Myanmar	–	–	–	–	–	–	223,665.3	261,734.9	394,914.4
Philippines	180,662.9	294,046.6	475,876.6	676,506.8	871,565.5	1,198,911.2	2,265,960.7	1,984,916.9	2,212,320.0
Singapore	2,402,944.9	2,751,912.8	3,578,512.1	4,205,358.5	5,808,553.0	4,853,367.7	8,878,527.6	10,637,225.3	9,982,659.7
Thailand	–	–	–	1,307,809.3	3,312,855.6	2,548,662.2	3,138,797.8	4,210,755.3	3,712,652.5
TOTAL	4,336,363.9	5,758,986.5	7,129,723.2	9,217,620.3	13,482,884.0	11,211,535.0	19,407,997.3	26,480,910.1	23,833,074.0

Note: China including Hong Kong in 1999–2001
Sources: ASEAN Trade Statistics data query <http://202.154.12.3/trade/publicview.asp>.

TABLE 2.5
China's Top Ten Trading Partners
Unit: US$ billions; percentages

	Overall trade			Exports			Imports		
	Partner	Amount	Share	Partner	Amount	Share	Partner	Amount	Share
1	Japan	133.6	15.7	U.S.	92.5	21.1	Japan	74.2	18.0
2	U.S.	126.3	14.8	Hong Kong	76.3	17.4	E.U.	53.1	12.9
3	E.U.	125.2	14.7	E.U.	72.2	16.5	Taiwan	49.4	12.0
4	Hong Kong	87.4	10.3	Japan	59.4	13.6	ASEAN	47.3	11.5
5	ASEAN	78.3	9.2	ASEAN	30.9	7.1	S. Korea	43.1	10.4
6	S. Korea	63.2	7.4	S. Korea	20.1	4.6	U.S.	33.9	8.2
7	Taiwan	58.4	6.9	Taiwan	9.0	2.1	Hong Kong	11.1	2.7
8	Russia	15.8	1.9	Australia	6.3	1.4	Russia	9.7	2.4
9	Australia	13.6	1.6	Russia	6.0	1.4	Australia	7.3	1.8
10	Canada	10.0	1.2	Canada	5.6	1.3	Brazil	5.8	1.4

Sources: Ministry of Commerce of the People's Republic of China, "Top Ten Export Markets", "Top Ten Import Sources", and "Top Ten Trade Partners" (all dated 18 February 2004), online at <http://english.mofcom.gov.cn/article/200402/20040200183706_1.xml>, <http://english.mofcom.gov.cn/article/200402/20040200183744_1.xml>, and <http://english.mofcom.gov.cn/article/200402/20040200182458_1.xml>.

table, ASEAN is China's fifth largest overall trade partner, constituting 9.2 per cent of China's total trade; ASEAN is China's fifth largest export market and fourth most important import source. These more recent data, dated 18 February 2004, show that China's total trade with ASEAN amounts to US$78.3 billion.

To be sure, the United States remains the region's biggest trading partner, but trade between China and the rest of Asia is booming. Last October Chinese Premier Wen Jiabao urged Southeast Asian nations to achieve US$100 billion worth of trade with China before 2005 — almost double the 2001 figure of US$55.4 billion. By comparison, U.S. trade with the ten members of ASEAN was US$120 billion in 2001.[24] The race is on.

In sum, although increasing trade and investment ties have increased the economic interdependence between China and ASEAN, these relationships are still trailing the region's economic relationships with the United States, although the gap is narrowing. Although these economic facts justify an FTA, more important non-economic reasons explain why China "attaches great importance" to ASEAN-China FTA.[25]

POLITICAL LOGIC OF FTA: ECONOMIC STATECRAFT OF THE "PEACEFUL ASCENDANCY" POLICY

Commentators have offered various explanations for the initiatives taken by China to sign an FTA with ASEAN countries. Most of these accounts invoke standard economic arguments or fall under the category of conventional wisdom. For example, Kevin Cai identifies the three most crucial rationales for the ASEAN-China FTA: (1) such an FTA helps craft a response to intensified regionalism elsewhere (Europe and North America), (2) FTA helps cement the growing economic ties between China and ASEAN, and (3) FTA helps co-ordinate government policies — a need made painfully clear by the Asian Financial Crisis.[26]

Employing a computable general equilibrium (CGE) model based on international parity conditions, James Laurenceson finds that China's integration with the ASEAN-5 is already relatively advanced with respect to goods and services markets and he argues that future benefits from liberalization will be mainly felt in financial markets.[27]

Focusing on the ASEAN's four newer countries, Thitapha Wattanapruttipaisan believes that the ASEAN-China FTA will provide greater market access in resource- and agro-based products and some manufactured goods for the ASEAN-4, but will also see greater competition from China in both ASEAN-4's home and third-country markets.[28]

This chapter differs from all these theories by presenting a political logic of China's economic statecraft with respect to Southeast Asia. It argues that China's FTA with ASEAN countries is driven primarily by strategic considerations and that although the main instruments that it uses — FTAs — are economic, China's foremost goals are to ensure survival and to expand power — perennial core realist premises — in a changing (that is, more challenging) security environment. In short, China's FTA with ASEAN exemplifies the economic statecraft of China's "peaceful ascendancy".

The concept of "economic statecraft" involves the utilization of a state's economic tools (resources and capital) in its foreign policy conduct and is part of a state's statecraft — defined as the art of conducting state affairs. By employing either positive (rewards) or negative (sanctions) means, economic statecraft seeks to advance a state's interests through ways that are less coercive than military means.[29] Although many scholars equate economic statecraft with economic sanctions and consequently question the validity of economic statecraft since "sanctions never work",[30] positive incentives such as trade benefits or aid are no less of instruments for achieving a state's objectives and have not received the same amount of attention.

China's FTA with ASEAN is a good example of this positive approach, and this kind of approach has arguably better achieved the very same goals than what China's previous approach could achieve.

One of the most interesting developments to the scholarly and policy communities in the last two years is China's "new" foreign policy, which marks a significant departure from past practices in several key areas. Variously called "new diplomacy",[31] "peaceful ascendancy"[32] or "peaceful rise"[33] (*heping jueqi*), "independent foreign policy of peace", or "pragmatic, balanced strategy in foreign policy",[34] this new diplomacy contains several important elements.[35] First, it is stimulated by globalization and is based on the conviction that China's growth imperatives are tied with globalization. It relies both on China's domestic economy and the international marketplace to sustain and fuel growth. China's Fourth-Generation leaders[36] have concluded that the international environment that China faces has changed and the country must respond "correctly to a world which is becoming multipolar, to economic globalization, and to the trend of development in scientific and technological advancement".[37] Now is especially a "period of important strategic opportunity" for achieving China's paramount goal — in the words of one analyst, "it is all part of a single-minded focus on economic development oriented to making China an economic superpower in every respect...in the next two decades".[38]

Second, to achieve that goal, China must secure a peaceful international environment that is crucial to sustaining China's economic development and augmenting China's power. Peace in the Asia-Pacific region — China's backyard — is thus essential. Hence, China's "peaceful ascendancy" is designed to counter deep Asian apprehension about China as a competitor for trade, investment, and jobs. At a practical level, this means that when dealing with its most formidable challenger (the United States), China must "bide its time and hide its capacities" (*taoguang yanghui*) — avoiding a premature showdown or confrontation with the United States, especially in light of the Bush administration's imperial strategy; and when dealing with its nervous neighbours, China must replace its brusque "Great Power Diplomacy", which Third-Generation leaders like Jiang Zemin upheld, with a good-neighbour diplomacy.

The timing is ideal. As the United States is distracted by the war on terror, Iraq, and North Korea, and Southeast Asia is still grappling with the aftermath of the 1997–98 Asian financial crisis, China's peaceful rise presents an alternative policy agenda and opportunities to Southeast Asian nations. In light of America's single-minded pursuit of its own narrow agenda and Japan's diminished stature, China's "charm offensive" toward Southeast Asia — increasing investment and trade, and proposing myriad of FTAs throughout Asia — has won much good will in the region.[39]

Third, this new diplomacy is characterized by several important changes in style, if not substance: (1) Instead of acting like an aggrieved victim, China now aspires to be a responsible great power and is acting increasingly like one. (2) Whereas China used to distrust "multilateralism" for fear that multilateral institutions could be used to constrain or punish it, nowadays Chinese leaders recognize that deeply engaging these organizations help promote the country's trade and security interests and limit American power. For China, the word "multipolarity" sounds like a coded opposition to a world order characterized as "unipolar" (dominated by the United States) and to America's foreign policy style characterized as "unilateralism". (3) On many contentious and intractable issues, China has also adopted more pragmatic stances. On the South China Sea issue, China acceded to ASEAN's Treaty of Amity and Co-operation (TAC) and promoted peaceful dialogue over territorial disputes. On Taiwan, China has replaced its military bluster with economic enticement. (4) China is more aware that its rise has consequences for the Asia-Pacific region and beyond. So it is keen on easing the concerns of various countries. (5) China has become much more actively engaged in, and seeks to shape, regional affairs. Its hosting of the Six-Party Talk over North Korea's nuclear issue is a good example.

Fourth, the major instrument used in advancing China's fundamental objectives is its economic power, which is buoyed by its phenomenal economic growth, rapidly expanding domestic market, and voracious appetite for raw materials for its economic development. FTA with ASEAN helps cultivate goodwill among China's important neighbours, maintain peace and security in the region, defuse American influence, and secure key markets and raw materials needed for China's economic security. It is thus a *sine qua non* of "peaceful ascendancy" — the fundamental strategy of China's new diplomacy for survival and development.

To sum up, China's "peaceful ascendancy" is a comprehensive long-term strategy employing globalization as catalyst to accelerate China's economic development and elevate China's power and stature. The language is peace and stability, the style is constructive diplomacy, and the substance is economics — at least for now.[40] The key is ascendancy. The theory leaves open the question what happens *after* China has ascended: Will it have been fundamentally altered to become a *status quo* power as a result of the process of peaceful rise and embrace of globalization? Or will China now have the power to throw its weight around? In other words, is peace an end in China's theory of "peaceful rise" or simply a means for achieving ascendancy? No definitive answer can be ascertained at this moment, since the actual outcome is most likely some combination of these two views, and in any case is beyond the scope of this chapter.

China's FTA exemplifies the economic statecraft of this overall strategy. Geopolitics, rather than purely economic reasons, drives China to proactively conduct trade talks. The hallmarks of China's arrival as a major player in world and regional affairs include: (1) using multilateralism to counter what China considers U.S. unilateralism, (2) talking of the need for a new international political and economic order (multipolarity), and (3) promoting an East Asia pact to match European and North American free trade agreements.

ASEAN'S CALCULUS AND FTA'S IMPLICATIONS

What is the calculus for ASEAN nations regarding their FTA with China? How will this FTA impact ASEAN members? How will it affect regional and international balance of power? On the first question, this chapter suggests three fundamental reasons why ASEAN embrace the FTA with China.

First, each individual ASEAN member is too weak *vis-à-vis* China. To augment their bargaining power, ASEAN members must pool their resources together so as to overcome the very plausible collective action problem.

Facing an economically rising China, these nations conclude that if they are to have any hope of luring foreign investments, they need to trumpet their growing ties with Asia's next giant.[41]

Second, individual ASEAN members clearly see FTA with China as a logical step toward partaking in China's growing domestic market, made increasingly prosperous because of China's entry into the WTO (in December 2001) and the benefits arising from the phasing-in of China's pledged liberalization. China's offer of "early harvest" — a unilateral goodwill measure that would aid the less developed ASEAN nations (called ASEAN-4) in trade facilitation and would enable mutually beneficial adjustments ahead of the general schedule for the rest of ASEAN — is especially appealing to them.

Third, ASEAN nations see the FTA with China as a catalyst to accelerating their own integration (AFTA)[42] and a ploy with which to engage larger trading partners, such as Japan, the United States, and the EU. Already, ASEAN-China FTA is causing some concerns for Japan, and prompts Tokyo to redouble its endeavour in engaging an area that it has traditionally dominated. For example, in its summit meeting with ASEAN in December 2003, Japanese Prime Minister Junichiro Koizumi pledged US$3 billion in new aid to Southeast Asia (the region is already receiving 60 per cent of its overseas aid from Japan), and promised to work with the region to maintain security ties, liberate trade, and create a broad "economic partnership".[43] Interestingly, some analysts view Japan's new emphasis on fostering closer relations with ASEAN as being driven by one major consideration — not to be outdone by China.[44]

Even this cursory survey of ASEAN's motivation for FTA with China, limited by space, raises three important questions about the impact of the FTA on ASEAN.

First, China could turn out to be a fierce competitor. Rodolfo Severino, ASEAN's secretary-general, is aware that such industries as textiles, toy, and motorcycle manufactures will be negatively affected in the short term, but he believes long-term benefits will follow.[45] Because of its almost inexhaustible unskilled labour and huge amounts of FDI, China may pose a particularly great challenge to the ASEAN-4 in their home or third-country markets. Currently China is receiving the lion's share of FDI inflows to the entire developing world. As Table 1 shows, in 2000, China received more than three times the combined total of FDI inflows to the ten ASEAN nations. The FDI that is currently going into China (arguably motivated by the intrinsic value of China as an investment site) is unlikely to be distracted by an FTA with ASEAN, whereas some of the FDI going into ASEAN now may end up going into China (because of the region's new ties with the larger market). A *caveat* is in order. Chinese companies are keen on investing in Southeast Asia, especially in the resources sectors. This may mitigate China's competition for FDI with ASEAN somewhat.

Second, there are real concerns that ASEAN-China FTA may undermine AFTA. Some worry that China may distract a core trading group from pursuing its better interests by offering an FTA. These skeptics question whether China's real motivation is actually domination, as opposed to integration, and this could cause the ASEAN to fail to complete its own full integration, and instead try to cash in on the alluring Chinese economy.[46] This is especially true in that compared to China, which has a very clear strategic goal, as discussed earlier, ASEAN does not have a clear picture about its place in the new strategic environment of an emergent China. One Australian analyst thinks that under these circumstances the best that ASEAN can do is to lock itself in as a fringe player on the spokes of China's regional trade architecture, while further enhancing the attractiveness of China as the hub for regional investment and production.[47]

A historical metaphor is illustrative here. Historians John King Fairbank and Merle Goldman argue that traditional China, seeing itself as the superior Middle Kingdom, carried out its foreign policy based on a tribute system, which was a "reciprocal foreign relationship between superior and inferior" in that tribute offerings were normally reciprocated by lavish gifts from the emperor; hence, "accepting China's supremacy was materially worthwhile". In addition, the tribute system early became the institutional setting and indeed "cover for foreign trade".[48] Another scholar points out that China and its tributaries had far more interaction with each other than it commonly acknowledged. "Trade, both private and tributary, made up a significant portion of both government revenues and GNP. Under this system, these countries were a thriving, complex, and vibrant regional order" and the tributary system was "a form of disguised staple trade".[49]

This historical metaphor on the China-centric tribute system is at the heart of a current debate in International Relations — whether a hierarchical regional order in East Asia dominated by a rising China promotes more stability or instability. David Kang argues that East Asian regional relations have historically been hierarchic, more peaceful, and more stable than those in the West, and that when China has been strong and stable, order has been preserved.[50] He argues that:

> East Asian international relations emphasized formal hierarchy among nations while allowing considerable informal equality. With China as the dominant state and surrounding countries as peripheral or secondary states, as long as hierarchy was observed there was little need for interstate war.[51]

Theorizing on why China has successfully managed its relationship with Southeast Asia and Southeast Asian nations have increasingly accepted a normal China, Brantly Womack argues that China's successful diplomatic dealing with Southeast Asia during the reform era is mainly a result of China's successful exercise of leadership in its relationship with Southeast Asia — a relationship characterized by asymmetry.[52]

To argue that China's FTA with ASEAN evokes the ancient tributary system and threatens to institutionalize China's dominant position and ASEAN's subordinate status in the form of trade obviously risks the charge of being a false historical analogy. However, the analogy is not entirely inappropriate, either, as Kang's and Womack's lines seem to suggest. The Chinese are a history-minded people. After all, until recently their foreign policy was driven by the legacy of "century of humiliation". The main difference is that in the past, the Chinese believed in their cultural supremacy and cared more about the other peoples' acknowledgement of China's cultural eminence than actual conquest (again, Kang's description "formal hierarchy vs. informal equality") — in other words, the learning is only one-way. Today, China exists in a globalized world, and to survive in an increasingly challenging environment, China has proved that occasionally it can be a fast learner. It is learning the new rules and playing the new games. Learning is now two-way. Liking the FTA to the modern-day tribute system may be an exaggeration, but calling it the economic statecraft of China's "peaceful ascendancy" in light of China's fundamental goal of rising to preeminent power is a historically apt perspective.

As constructionists would like to point out, the structure of elites' beliefs and interests determine whether anarchy is conflictual or co-operative,[53] it is therefore inadequate to simply infer China's real intention from its behaviour. As China is seeking peaceful ascendancy, other countries hope that this portends a positive development and can thus interpret its more accommodating new diplomacy as a fundamental shift. However, the available evidence is not sufficient to warrant this optimism. After all, the Chinese seem to offer only a tactical reason for their restraint — "biding one's time and hiding one's capabilities". What will they do after they achieve their goal of becoming an economic superpower? Will economic success breed an aggressive nationalism? Will it convince Chinese leaders that China can finally take on the United States and turn the twenty-first century world order to *Pax Sinica*?

No one knows. Clearly with history in mind, U.S. Trade Representative Robert Zoellick recently said that China's increasing economic power and global influence must be integrated into the international community.[54] This is not just good economics; it is also good politics.

Notes

1. For the purpose of this chapter, the term "East Asia" encompasses both Northeast Asia and Southeast Asia.

2. For a useful compilation of commentaries on the implications of a rising China, see Michael Brown et al., eds., *The Rise of China* (Cambridge, MA: MIT Press, 2000). The two books that helped set the "great debate" over China were Richard Bernstein and Ross H. Munro, *The Coming Conflict with China* (New York: Knopf, 1997) and Andrew J. Nathan and Robert S. Ross, *The Great Wall and the Empty Fortress* (New York: Norton, 1997).

3. For an account on China's more confident diplomacy, see Evan S. Medeiros and M. Taylor Fravel, "China's New Diplomacy", *Foreign Affairs* 82, no. 6 (November–December 2003): 22–35.

4. ASEAN Secretariat, News Release, 4 November 2002, "ASEAN and China Sign Economic Pact", available at <http://www.aseansec.org/13169.htm>, and "ASEAN-China Dialogue", available at <http://www.aseansec.org/7585.htm>.

5. May T. Yeung, Nicholas Perdikis, and William A. Kerr, *Regional Trading Blocs in the Global Economy* (Cheltenham, UK: Edward Elgar, 1999), p. 17.

6. The World Bank, *Trading Blocs* (New York: Oxford University Press, for the World Bank, 2000), p. 1.

7. For example, of the 151 notified RTAs in goods since 1958, 29 entered into force in 1990–94, 64 in 1995–99, and 30 in 2000–02 — that is, 81 per cent of such RTAs went into effect after 1990. World Trade Organization, *World Trade Report 2003* (Geneva: WTO, 2003), p. 47.

8. *World Trade Report 2003*, p. 46.

9. "Road from Cancún Leads to Brussels: The Hypocrisy of Rich Countries Blocks Trade Liberalization", *The Financial Times*, 16 September 2003, p. 22.

10. Jeffrey A. Frankel, *Regional Trading Blocs in the World Economic System* (Washington: Institute for International Economics, 1997), pp. 2–3; and Jagdish Bhagwati, Pravin Krishna, and Arvind Panagariya, eds., *Trading Blocs: Alternative Approaches to Analyzing Preferential Trade Agreements* (Cambridge, MA: MIT press, 1999), p. 6.

11. These requirements are: (1) "Substantially all" barriers among the members be removed; (2) trade barriers against nonmembers not be made more restrictive than before; and (3) subsequent progress toward economic integration is supposed to be expeditious — normally not to exceed ten years. Frankel, *Regional Trading Blocs*, p. 3.

12. This part is based on Yeung, Perdikis, and Kerr, *Regional Trading Blocs in the Global Economy*, pp. 18–19; and Frankel, *Regional Trading Blocs*, pp. 12–17.

13. Some scholars caution that the term "free trade area" often mistakenly conjures a similar positive connotation as "free trade", but in fact it is a preferential trade area.

14. *Trading Blocs*, p. 11.

15. Immanuel Kant, "Perpetual Peace", in Lewis White Beck, ed., *Immanuel Kant: On History* (Indianapolis, IN: Bobbs-Merrill, 1963), originally published in 1795.

16. Thomas Friedman, *Lexus and the Olive Tree* (New York: Farrar, Straus and Giroux, 1999), pp. 195–217.

17. Peter Hatcher, "US Links Free Trade to Global Security", *Australian Financial Review*, 15 November 2002, p. 28.

18. Richard E. Baldwin, "The Cause of Regionalism", *World Economy* 20, no. 7 (November 1997): 865–88.

19. See ASEAN, "Overview: ASSOCIATION OF SOUTHEAST ASIAN NATIONS," available online at <http://www.aseansec.org/64.htm>.

20. See Immanuel Wallerstein, "The Three Instances of Hegemony in the History of the Capitalist World-Economy", *International Journal of Comparative Sociology* 24, no. 1–2 (1983).

21. "Overview: ASEAN".

22. ASEAN, *Southeast Asia: A Free Trade Area*, available in pdf form at <http://www.aseansec.org/12025.htm>.

23. "How ASEAN Can Hold Its Own Against China", *The Straits Times*, 12 November 2002. From *LexixNexis*.

24. Jane Perlez, "Asian Leaders Find China a More Cordial Neighbor", *The New York Times*, 18 October 2003, p. A1.

25. "China Attaches Great Importance to China-ASEAN Free-Trade Area", *Xinhua News Agency*, 23 October 2002.

26. Kevin G. Cai, "The ASEAN-China Free Trade Agreement and East Asian Regional Grouping", *Contemporary Southeast Asia* 25, no. 3 (2003): 387–404.

27. James Laurenceson, "Economic Integration Between China and the ASEAN-5", *ASEAN Economic Bulletin* 20, no. 2 (August 2003): 103–11.

28. Thitapha Wattanapruttipaisan, "ASEAN-China Free Trade Area: Advantages, Challenges, and Implications for the Newer ASEAN Member Countries", *ASEAN Economic Bulletin* 20, no. 1 (April 2003): 31–48.

29. David A. Baldwin, *Economic Statecraft* (Princeton, NJ: Princeton University Press, 1985) is a classic in the field of economic statecraft.

30. E.g., Gary Clyde Hufbauer and Jeffrey J. Schott, *Economic Sanctions Reconsidered: History and Current Policy* (Washington, D.C.: Institute for International Economics, 1985). In a recent revisit, Daniel W. Drezner et al., eds., *The Sanctions Paradox : Economic Statecraft and International Relations* (Cambridge: Cambridge University Press, 1999) seeks to solve the puzzle that despite the conventional wisdom that economic sanctions do not work in international affairs, why do countries wield them so often? Daniel Drezner argues that, paradoxically, countries will be most eager to use sanctions under conditions where they will produce the feeblest results. States anticipate frequent conflicts with adversaries, and are therefore more willing to use sanctions. However, precisely because they anticipate more conflicts, sanctioned states will not concede,

despite the cost. Economic sanctions are thus far less likely to be effective between adversaries than between allies.

31. Medeiros and Fravel, "China's New Diplomacy".

32. Yoichi Funabashi, "China is Preparing a 'Peaceful Ascendancy' ", *International Herald Tribune* (30 December 2003); "Author Sees China's Role in Pushing India, Pakistan Toward Détente", *Calcutta The Telegraph* (Internet version-WWW) in English 25 December 2003 (article by Jairam Ramesh, "China is Changing"), FBIS Transcribed Text, FBIS-NES-2003-1225, obtained via *World News Connection*.

33. Robert W. Radtke, "China's 'Peaceful Rise' Overshadowing U.S. Influence in Asia?" *The Christian Science Monitor,* 8 December 2003, p. 9.

34. "WWP: Beijing Adopts Pragmatic, 'Balanced' Foreign Policy", *Hong Kong Wen Wei Po (Internet version-WWW)* in Chinese 27 January 2004 [Dispatch from Beijing News Centre by reporter Liao Ya-meng, "China Adopts 'Balanced' Strategy in Foreign Policy"], PTS Translated Text for FBIS, FBIS-CHI-2004-0127, obtained via *World News Connection.*

35. The concept of "peaceful ascendancy" first appeared at last year's Boao Forum for Asia, and Zheng Bijian, vice president of the Central Party School took lead in studying the theory. The concept was formally introduced to Asia by Chinese President Hu Jintao on his tour of Southeast Asia last October. "WWP: Beijing Adopts" and Radtke, "China's 'Peaceful Rise' ".

36. "Fourth Generation" leadership refers to such leaders as Hu Jintao, Wen Jiabao, and Zeng Qinghong, that were elevated to top positions after the Chinese Communist Party's 16th National Congress in November 2002. See Susan Shirk, H. Lyman Miller, Gang Lin, Lowell Dittmer, Cheng Li, David Shambaugh, Richard Baum, *The 16th CCP Congress and Leadership Transition in China*, Wilson Centre Asia Programme Special Report No. 105 (Washington, D.C.: The Wilson Centre, 2002), pp. 1–48.

37. "Hu Jintao Summarizes China's World View in Political Bureau Study Session", *Beijing Xinhua Domestic Service* in Chinese 1155 GMT 24 February 2004 ["Hu Jintao at CPC Central Committee Political Bureau's Tenth Collective Study Session Stresses, Continue to Take a Broad View of the World While Analyzing the Situation, Improve the Ability to Work Well with Reform and Opening Up"], FBIS Translated Text, FBIS-CHI-2002-0224, obtained via *World News Connection.*

38. "Author Sees China's Role".

39. Jane Perlez, "China is Romping with the Neighbors (U.S. is Distracted), *The New York Times*, 3 December 2003, p. A1; "Asian Leaders Find China a More Cordial Neighbor", *NYT*, 18 October 2003, p. A1; "The Charm from Beijing", *NYT*, 9 October 2003; Radtke, "China's 'Peaceful Rise' "; Michael Vatikiotis and Murray Hiebert, "How China is Building an Empire", *Far Eastern Economic Review*, 20 November 2003.

40. One Indian writer quips, "It is all part of the new PRC syndrome — not the old

People's Republic of China, but a new Peaceful Rise of China". "Author Sees China's Role".

41. "Everybody's Doing It", *The Economist,* 28 February 2004, p. 62.
42. "How ASEAN Can Meet the Chinese Challenge", *The Business Times Singapore,* 1 August 2003, obtained via *Lexis-Nexis;* Michael Shari, "A New Front in the Free-Trade Wars; The ASEAN Nations Are Slashing Tariffs to Compete with China", *Business Week,* 3 June 2002, p. 23.
43. Audrey McAvoy, "Japan Pledges $3 Billion in Aid for Asia", *Associated Press,* 12 December 2003; Anthony Rowley, "Koizumi to Convince ASEAN on Integration", *The Business Times Singapore,* 1 December 2003. However, some analysts believe that because of Japan's heavy protection of its agricultural sector, an FTA with ASEAN similar to the ASEAN-China FTA appears unlikely.
44. Leslie Fong, "China's Not in Competition with Japan", *The Strait Times,* 19 December 2003; "ASEAN Must Deepen Ties with Japan", *The Business Times Singapore,* 31 July 2003; Kwan Weng Kim, "Japan 'to Remain Top ASEAN Partners for Next 20 Years'; but It Will Have to Jostle with China for the Position in 50 Years, says PM Goh", *The Strait Times,* 3 December 2003.
45. Barry Wain, "Some in ASEAN Have Issues with China FTA", *Australian Business Intelligence,* 8 October 2002, p100828119293 (*The Asian Wall Street Journal —* ABIX via COMTEX).
46. Garry Bowditch, "Trade Pact Carries Risk for ASEAN", *Australian Business Intelligence,* 12 November 2002, p1008316i2190 (*The Australian Financial Review —* ABIX via COMTEX).
47. Garry Bowditch, "Trade Pact with China Carries Risk for ASEAN", *Australian Financial Review,* 13 November 2002, p. 63.
48. John King Fairbank and Merle Goldman, *China: A New History,* enlarged edn. (Cambridge, MA: Harvard University Press, 1998), pp. 112–13.
49. David Kang, "Hierarchy and Stability in Asian International Relations", in G. John Ikenberry and Michael Mastanduno, eds., *International Relations Theory and the Asia-Pacific* (New York: Columbia University Press, 2003), pp. 172–73.
50. David C. Kang, "Getting Asia Wrong: The Need for New Analytical Frameworks", *International Security* 27, no. 4 (2002–03): 57–85.
51. Ibid., p. 67. For a critique of Kang's arguments, see Amitav Acharya, "Will Asia's Past be Its Future?" *International Security* 28, no. 3 (2003–04): 149–64.
52. Brantly Womack, "China and Southeast Asia: Asymmetry, Leadership, and Normalcy", *Pacific Affairs* 76, no. 4 (Winter 2003/2004): 529–48.
53. Alexander Wendt, "Anarchy is What States Make of It", *International Organization* 46, no. 2 (Spring 1992): 391–425. For a fuller account of Wendt's constructionist theory, see Alexander Wendt, *Social Theory of International Politics* (Cambridge and New York: Cambridge University Press, 1999).
54. "USTR Says China's Power Must Be Integrated Into World Community" (USTR Zoellick's 25 February remarks to Asia Society), e-mail update from "USINFO East Asia" <iipgeap@STATE.GOV>.

3

THE LEGAL AND POLICY CONSIDERATIONS OF CHINA-ASEAN FTA

The Impact on the Multilateral Trading System

Wang Jiang Yu

1. INTRODUCTION: CHINA'S RECENT REGIONAL TRADE AREA (RTA) INITIATIVES

One of the most striking features of international trade relations in the past decade is the fast growth of regionalism.[1] Insofar as it involves the question of trade and discrimination, regionalism is considered to be one of the oldest "trade and …" problems (Mathis 2001, p. 1). Furthermore, regionalism is part of international trade activities and it therefore bears the full nature of trade which is a multi-faceted issue encompassing economics, domestic politics, and national security and geopolitical concerns. For this reason, an individual effort towards regional preferential trade arrangements (hereinafter RTAs and RTA when appropriate) or free trade agreements (hereinafter FTAs or FTA when appropriate)[2] should be carefully examined in its special context and take into consideration the various non-economic factors underlying it.

While regionalism has been in existence for over half a century,[3] China jumped onto the bandwagon only very recently, embodied by the formation of the China-Hong Kong Closer Economic Partnership Arrangement (CEPA) and the China-Macao CEPA. China has also signed frameworks agreement for establishing free trade zones with the Association of Southeast Asian Nations (ASEAN), and is negotiating similar arrangements with Australia, New Zealand, and the Mercosure countries. The CEPAs, which are already in operation, are RTA-like arrangements between China and the two "special administrative regions" under the Chinese political sovereign, with the signatories acting as members of the World Trade Organization (WTO). The proposed China-ASEAN Free Trade Area, with a nice acronym "CAFTA", will create one of the world's largest FTA, standing besides with the North America Free Trade Area (NAFTA) and the European Union (EU), and the largest FTA made up of developing countries (ASEAN 2001).

Two fundamental questions need to be explored with regard to China's recent RTA approaches including CAFTA. First, what are the motivations behind the moves? Exploration for the motives are essentially important because they will decide the content, scope and all future acts of China as regards its pursuits for RTAs. Eventually, the RTAs participated by China, assumingly conforming to its strategic goals, will have profound implications on the fate of the multilateral trading system currently under the auspice of the WTO. As the WTO has noted, "political considerations will inevitably feature in decisions to establish regional trading arrangements". (WTO 2003c, p. 156) Political factors, especially realpolitik, play a key role in RTAs which is by no means less significant than economic considerations. This is especially true with regard to the CAFTA, affecting the trade and geopolitical positions of major countries in the region including ASEAN members, Japan, South Korea, Hong Kong and Taiwan.[4]

The second fundamental question concerns the complex impact of China's RTAs on the WTO-led multilateral trade system. This involves a two-level analysis. First, are the RTAs concluded by China consistent with the existing WTO rules, especially the most-favoured-nation (MFN) clause and GATT article XXIV? On its accession to the WTO China commits to implement the WTO agreement as well as the annexed Multilateral Trade Agreements. A violation of WTO obligations through RTAs will certainly cause serious concerns among other WTO members and further undermine China's credibility in international trade. Second, the impact of China's RTA approach on the future of the multilateral trade talks — currently the WTO's Doha Round negotiation — shall be examined. As there exists a potential conflict between the proliferation of regional trading blocks, which attempt to realize regional or bilateral trade liberalization, and the WTO regime, which thrives to liberalize trade multilaterally without preferential discrimination, exponents on both sides are now engaged in an enormously heated debate as to the orientation of the international trade system.[5] China's sheer size of population and territory, its top-ranking economy and trade volume, as well as its leadership position in the developing world, determines that the Chinese position on regionalism *versus* multilateralism can amend the direction of this ongoing debate.

This chapter is an attempt to outline and analyze the content of the CAFTA proposal, its negotiating process, as well as its impact on the multilateral trading system. Part 2 outlines briefly the scope, content, and negotiations of CAFTA. Part 3 discusses the economic and geopolitical motivations behind China's movement for CAFTA. Part 4 examines the relevant WTO rules on RTAs and evaluates the WTO consistency of CAFTA. Part 5 analyzes the impact of China's RTA approach on the multilateral trading system. In conclusion, this chapter argues that, China's pursuit of regional and national security and great power status through CAFTA is both legitimate, given that there are no meaningful WTO rules prohibiting this, and beneficial to the region, considering East Asia's troublesome geopolitical layout. However, China should be mindful of the importance of the multilateral trading system for achieving its goal. As a top trading power, China also has the responsibility to push for multilateral trade liberalization rather than being obsessed with regionalism. On the other hand, it shall be emphasized that the quest for regional trade arrangements demonstrates the many weaknesses of the WTO-led multilateral trading system. Regional movements for free trade, as China currently is after, shall be allowed and even encouraged to the extent that they do not create trade diversion and divergent rules from the multilateral trade system.

2. THE CHINA-ASEAN FREE TRADE AGREEMENT (CAFTA): SCOPE, CONTENT AND NEGOTIATING PROCESS

The Negotiating Process of CAFTA

At the ASEAN-China Summit in November 2000, Chinese Premier Zhu Rongji put forward a basket of proposals on strengthening co-operation in East Asia, which "seen in the long run", included China and ASEAN exploring the possibility on the formation of an FTA.[6] At his suggestion, a China-ASEAN Experts Group on Economic Co-operation ("Experts Group") was established to look into the possibility of establishing a free trade area between the two sides. In its final report issued in October 2001, the group suggested the establishment of a "WTO-consistent ASEAN-China FTA within ten years". It noted the profound implication of CAFTA as follows:

> [T]he establishment of a FTA between ASEAN and China will create an economic region with 1.7 billion consumers, a regional GDP of about US$2 trillion and total trade estimated at US$1.23 trillion... [T]he removal of trade barriers between ASEAN and China will lower costs, increase intra-regional trade and increase economic efficiency. The establishment of an ASEAN-China FTA will create a sense of community among ASEAN members and China. It will provide another important mechanism for supporting economic stability in East Asia and allow both ASEAN and China to have a larger voice in international trade affairs on issues of common interest. (ASEAN 2001, p. 2)

The report also recommended that China and ASEAN adopt a comprehensive and forward-looking framework of economic co-operation to forge closer economic relations in the twenty-first century. In November 2001, the Seventh China-ASEAN Summit endorsed the ideas envisaged by the Experts Group and initiated the negotiation progress. At the Eighth China-ASEAN Summit in Phnom Penh, Cambodia in November 2002, ASEAN and Chinese leaders signed the "Framework Agreement on the Comprehensive Economic Co-operation between ASEAN and China" (hereinafter the FA) which, coming into force on 1 July 2003, provides the groundwork for the eventual formation of the CAFTA by 2010 for six older ASEAN members and 2015 for the newly admitted members which are Cambodia, Lao PDR, Myanmar and Vietnam. The FA has been amended by a Protocol signed on 6 October 2003 by China and ASEAN at their 2003 annual summit in Bali, Thailand. The FA actually represents the first FTA initiative of both ASEAN (as a group) and China (outside the Greater China Area[7]) to develop free trade arrangements with foreign countries.

Scope and Measures for Economic Co-operation under the FA

With a view to establishing the CAFTA before 2010, the parties to the FA agree to strengthen co-operation through "progressively liberalize and promote trade in goods and services as well as create a transparent, liberal and facilitative investment regime".[8] This implies that the proposed CAFTA will cover trade in goods and services as well as trade and investment facilitation. In addition, the FA opens door for the parties to "explore new areas and develop appropriate measures for closer economic co-operation".[9] Specific measures towards the realization of CAFTA, which will be implemented progressively in the coming years, include the following:[10]

(a) elimination of tariffs and non-tariff barriers in substantially all trade in goods;
(b) liberalization of trade in services with substantial sectoral coverage;
(c) establishment of an open and competitive investment regime that facilitates and promotes investment within CAFTA;
(d) special and differential treatment and flexibility to the newer ASEAN member states, including Cambodia, Laos, Myanmar and Vietnam;
(e) flexible measure to allow the parties in CAFTA negotiations to address their sensitive areas in the goods, services and investment sectors with such flexibility to be negotiated and mutually agreed based on the principle of reciprocity and mutual benefits;
(f) trade and investment facilitation measures, such as simplification of customs procedures and development of mutual recognition arrangements;
(g) open attitude toward further liberalization in new areas/sectors; and
(h) establishment of appropriate mechanisms for the effective implementation of the FA.

Early-Harvest Programme (EHP) for Trade in Goods under the FA

In addition to the obligations to enter into negotiations for the ultimate free trade pact, the FA also establishes an Early Harvest Programme (EHP) which is implemented as of 1 January 2004 and aimed to materialize the results of immediate concessions offered by the parties, mainly by China. EHP allows the reduction of tariffs on certain products before the onset of CAFTA. Initially, it aims to implement tariff reduction on these products over three years: to 10 per cent before 2004, to 5 per cent before 2005, and to zero tariffs no later than 1 January 2006.[11] A distinctive feature of EHP is that China has given unilateral concessions to ASEAN members who felt they had not benefited as much from EHP, covering over 130 agricultural and manufacturing products.[12] In essence, it "allows ASEAN products to be exported to China at a very concessionary rate so that ASEAN countries can actually get benefits of a free trade agreement even before the agreement is finalized".[13] As a minor reciprocity, the ASEAN countries agree to give tariff concessions to China under the Harmonized System (HS) on tariff for agricultural products including meat, fish, fruit, vegetables and milk. In total, EHP has targetted for a host of some 600 products listed in Chapter 1–8 of the HS, mostly agricultural products which are to be unilaterally liberalized by China.[14] In addition, China agrees to grant WTO benefits (mainly MFN treatment) to those ASEAN members which are not yet the WTO's official members.[15]

Initially the FA followed a multilateral approach in terms of tariff reduction, namely, the tariff concessions under the HS based approach shall be multilateralized to all parties (that is, all ASEAN members and China) provided that the same products are included in their EHP. Because Philippine eventually had not finalized its EHP scheme with China, other countries in the region were not willing to give the Philippines a "free rider" status. In addition, the fear that some ASEAN countries like Thailand have more efficient farm sectors that could suppress the growth of the agricultural sector in others has also deterred ASEAN members to implement a multilateral approach under EHP. Malaysia, among the first, negotiated a clause in 2003 allowing it to offer lower agriculture tariff only to China as a reciprocity to the latter's concession under EHP.[16] This practice has been consolidated in the 2003 Protocol, which replaces the original Article 6(3)(b)(i) of the FA with a new clause. The new provision recognizes that, while a party may accelerate its tariff reduction and/or elimination under the EHP in relation to the rest of the parties, this will only be done on a unilateral basis. Meanwhile, one or more ASEAN members are still allowed to conduct negotiations and enter into acceleration arrangement with China to accelerate their tariff reduction or elimination, which shall be done, however, only on a bilateral or pluri-lateral basis.[17]

A good example of tariff acceleration arrangement is the China-Thailand "Agreement on Accelerated Tariff Elimination under the Early Harvest Programme",[18] which prescribes that China and Thailand shall eliminate tariffs on all vegetable and fruit products, which are mainly exported from Thailand, no later than 1 October 2003 which is ahead of EHP effective date, 1 January 2004, as well as the targetted zero tariff date, 1 January 2006.

Negotiation Agenda to Complete CAFTA

Goods not covered by EHP are subject to further negotiation within a timeframe. The FA categorizes these goods into two tracks. The first one, called the Normal Track, contains products tariff rates of which shall be gradually reduced or eliminated in accordance specified schedules (to be mutually agreed by the parties) over a period from 1 January 2005 to 2010 by the ASEAN-6 and China, and from 1 January 2005 to 2015 for the newer ASEAN members.[19] The Sensitive Track, including the second category of products which can be specified by an individual party on its own accord, does not impose a timeframe on further liberalization. It merely requires the parties to reduce (or eliminate when applicable) tariffs on those products "in accordance with the mutually agreed end rates and end dates".[20] In addition to tariff, the negotiations shall also include, among others, rules of origin, out-quota-rates, renegotiation of concession schedules, non-tariff measures, trade remedy laws, trade facilitations, as well as trade-related intellectual property protection.[21] In terms of the timeframe, the FA prescribes that the goods negotiations shall commence in early 2003 and be concluded by 30 June 2004.[22]

The FA, however, does not have a mandatory timeframe for the negotiations on services and investment, except that negotiations shall commence in 2003 and be concluded "as expeditiously as possible for implementation in accordance with the timeframes to be mutually agreed."[23] Substantive negotiations in these two areas have already started for the conclusion of the framework texts, and the first packages of commitments are set for the second half of 2004. The negotiations on services seek to progressively eliminate substantially all discrimination and prohibition of new discriminatory measures with respect to trade in services between the parties.[24] The FA also seeks the expansion in the depth and scope of liberalization of trade in services beyond those undertaken by China and ASEAN members under the GATS,[25] which could result in an acceleration of China's WTO commitments on services for ASEAN, like what China has done for Hong Kong and Macao. As for investment, the FA aims, through negotiations, "to obtain commitments on liberalizing the investment regime, increasing market access as well as commitments on protection of investment in the China market".[26]

Besides trade and investment, China and ASEAN have also identified five priority sectors for strengthened co-operation, including agriculture, information and communications technology, human resources development, investment, and Mekong River basin development, and eleven other activities, including standard mutual recognition and harmonization, electronic commerce, technology transfer, and specific projects such as the acceleration of railway project linking Singapore and China's southern city Kunming.[27] All these efforts indicate that the FA is indeed a herald for an all-embracing pact of economic co-operation.

Other RTA Initiatives involving China

The two completed RTAs are the aforesaid CEPAs with Hong Kong and Macao, respectively. The Mainland-Hong Kong CEPA was signed on 29 June

2003, which was the first RTA of both sides. Three months later, on 17 October 2003, China's central government concluded a similar agreement with the Macao Government, which is virtually modelled after the Hong Kong CEPA.

The major feature of the CEPAs is Mainland China's unilateral concessions to Hong Kong and Macao. Using the Hong Kong CEPA as an example, in goods trade, China has agreed to eliminate tariffs on imported goods of Hong Kong origin by stages. As from 1 January 2004, China undertook to eliminate tariffs on 273 categories of Hong Kong products, representing over 4,000 items. According to Hong Kong authority, this, together with China's commitments upon accession to the WTO, will cover 90 per cent of Hong Kong's domestic exports to China.[28] For other products, China will apply zero tariff rates latest by 1 January 2006 upon applications by Hong Kong manufacturers. But the most significant component of the CEPA is the service arrangement, covering service types including, among others, management consulting, conventions and exhibitions, advertising, accounting, banking, securities, insurance, logistics, movies, construction, shipping and value-added telecommunications services.

Compared with China's commitments to other WTO members states in its accession protocol (WTO 2001), CEPA gives Hong Kong businesses a "first move" advantage. In the prescribed eighteen industries, Hong Kong service providers can enjoy preferential treatment ahead of China's WTO timetable. For example, in management consulting, according to China's WTO commitments, wholly foreign-owned enterprises (WFOE) will not be permitted before 11 December 2007. CEPA, however, allows Hong Kong services providers to establish WFOE as from 1 January 2004. Certain preferential treatments extended to Hong Kong business even go beyond China's WTO obligations. Examples include that, in banking service, China's WTO commitments set up the minimum asset requirement as US$20 billion for an overseas financial institution to establish a branch and US$10 billion for a subsidiary in China. For a Hong Kong entity, the minimum asset requirement is US$6 billion.[29] In legal services, although China gives little concession to other WTO members, Hong Kong law firms are allowed to establish representative offices in China to operate in association with Mainland law firms, although the association may not take the form of a partnership. Chinese law firms can employ Hong Kong legal barristers or solicitors, while Hong Kong permanent residents with Chinese citizenship are permitted to sit the bar examination in the Mainland and acquire Chinese legal professional qualification. This is far beyond China's commitments in its WTO service schedule.

After the bold proposal for CAFTA, China has also reached out to a number of countries for free trade arrangements. China has engaged in a series of bilateral talks with the Mercosure (the South American Common Market) countries. The two sides have agreed in September 2003 to start with bilateral agreements in specific areas and mechanisms to increase integration and facilitate trade.[30] Another major move is being pushed in China's western front, under the auspice of the Shanghai Co-operation Organization (SCO) comprising China Kazakhstan, Kyrgyzstan, Russia, Tajikstan and Uzbekistan. The SCO was originally a pure political group formulated in 1996 to improve regional stability and counter the influence of Islamic fundamentalism in central Asia. Pushed by China, premiers of the five member states of the SCO signed a multilateral economic co-operation Framework Agreement to "deepen" the economic connections between member states and "improve the investment environment" on 23 September 2003 in Beijing. One of the plans prescribed in the agreement is to establish a free trade area within the SCO.[31]

China has also extended invitations to Australia and New Zealand which are regarded as part of the Western world and long-term U.S. allies.[32] On 25 October 2003, in a state visit by Chinese President Hu Jintao to Australia, China and Australia signed a Trade and Economic Framework which is regarded as "the first steps towards a free trade agreement worth billions of dollars" by *The Australian*.[33] A few days later the Chinese leader reached consensus with his New Zealand counterpart to start negotiations for reaching a free trade deal between the two countries.

3. THE POLICY AND GEOPOLITICAL MOTIVATIONS BEHIND CHINA'S CAFTA INITIATIVE

The Primary Motivations: Economics or Geopolitics?

Co-operation through free trade arrangements, by definition, is economic in nature. It is difficult, however, to conclude that China's recent RTA moves were economically driven. They are, at least, not for immediate and short-term economic benefits, though immediate unilateral concessions from China to other parties involved in the RTAs were immense. Using the CEPAs as example: Although Hong Kong and Macao will be the first choice to supply products and services with high value-added to the Mainland China market and thus reap immediate as well as long-term trade and employment creation, the immediate economic gain to the Mainland is not so obvious. That is probably why Hong Kong leaders said "[t]his agreement has given us an opportunity that our neighbouring countries can only dream of."[34] The *Wall*

Street Journal further noted that "the [CEPA] pact contains almost no concessions to China, because Hong Kong is already one of the freest economies in the world and doesn't impose import tariffs except on a handful of goods and services".[35] China's RTA framework agreement with ASEAN, especially the EHP, demonstrates similar feature of unilateral concessions to open up first to embrace other countries' exports to China, although the long-term benefit of CAFTA could be enormous to the parties of both sides, according to experts.

China's RTA approach, including the CAFTA initiative, is a strategic movement and shall be studied in a broader context which embraces both economics and geopolitics. In brief, it is part of China's regional and global strategy consistent with its national interest. As its economy and global influence grows fast, China has now acquired the confidence to proactively employ a variety of tactics and moves to achieve its interests. As the following sections show, although China's ultimate goal is not yet clearly manifested, its rhetoric and actions so far, fortunately, show that it is a pragmatic, constructive partner rather than a destructive player who only push its interest unilaterally.

Economic Security

It has been constantly argued that a country's RTA approach is often exercised as a defensive strategy against the proliferation of RTAs affecting (probably negatively) its interest, largely due to the fear of being "left-out". (Mansfield 1998, p. 527) suggests the formation of one RTA may prompt fears by outside countries that "it will degrade their competitiveness, thereby leading them to form a rival bloc". Likewise, "a state joining a [RTA] may generate concern by its economic rivals (outside the bloc) that this state's preferential access to an expanded market will furnish it with a competitive advantage, thus inducing its rivals to join this or that [RTAs] to obtain similar benefits". Arguably, the European integration (through initially the EEC and eventually the EU) spurred the formation of the NAFTA, and NAFTA and EEC jointly contributed to the surge of RTA initiatives in the Asia-Pacific region.

In essence, RTAs are related to the participating countries' economic security, which is defined as "the maintenance of given levels of welfare and state power through access to resources, finance and markets". (Thakur 1997, p. 52). Mansfield (1998) observed that, as a result of eroding hegemony, global recessions, and strategic interdependence provide strong incentives for countries to establish or enter into RTAs in order to help guarantee that their access to key foreign markets will not be curtailed and their competitiveness abroad will not be undermined.

While China did not express its fear of being "left-out" loudly, this fear was real considering that all its major trading partners and most of its neighbours were involved in RTAs. As a start, forming alliance with ASEAN is obviously the most rational choice, given firstly that the two other important players in the region, Japan and Korea, are not willing to be engaged in a FTA for various political and economic reasons (for example, see Wall 2003). In addition, China is in need of Southeast Asian countries' stable supply of raw materials and commodity components. Using China's appetite for energy as an example: China is now the world's second largest energy consumer after the United States and has been increasing dramatically its import of oil and natural gas (USCC 2003*a*). To meet its energy demands, China has the incentive to engage energy-rich countries including ASEAN members. The fast growing Chinese economy also increased China's reliance on ASEAN nations for commodity components to support its export economy or status as "world factory",[36] not to mention the fact that ASEAN also represents an increasingly important export market for China.

Wooing ASEAN for Regional Security and Influence

As noted by a commentator, "the ASEAN-China agreement is essentially politically motivated".[37] The essence is that, following the fact that China's economic growth has outperformed probably any country in the world for over a decade and it is inescapably heading towards becoming an economic superpower, China has assiduously pursued a strategy to transform its economic clout into political influence by practising "mature", "constructive", and "responsible" great power diplomacy.[38] China's main goal, at this time, is to build political trust with its neighbours and other important players in the region to strengthen regional security in favour of China. The CAFTA proposal, especially the EHP which gives early unilateral concessions to ASEAN states, is also directed to allay the fear of the "China threat" among China's weaker Asian neighbours, who have been suffering the loss of FDI to and struggling to compete with China for a decade.[39]

Competing with Japan (and even the United States) for regional leadership and influence is another concern of China as a rising regional and global power. Thus the CAFTA proposal is widely regarded as a way of pre-empting other powers' dominance of Asia.[40] Japan has been engaging with ASEAN since its founding in 1973 shortly after the organization's founding, yet largely because of Japan's deep-rooted "Looking West" orientation, it had never seriously initiated any comprehensive co-operation programme with ASEAN other than direct investment in the region. The Japanese economy's languishing growth in the past years has also encouraged Asia countries to look elsewhere for the engine of growth. As for the United States, it has been almost entirely occupied with the anti-terrorism campaign since September 11 of 2001. In China's perception, it is now probably the best time for it to rise up to take over the leadership position by stressing economic co-operation — which nations in the region, even including long-term U.S. allies Australia and New Zealand are in dire need of — in its diplomacy.[41]

The Ultimate Goal: Quest for "Peacefully Ascendancy" to Great Power?

In international relations, "how a country rises often has more drastic consequences for the world than the rise itself".[42] History and international relations scholars, such as Donald Kagan and Joseph Nye, have observed that since the era of the Greek city states, rising powers have tended to destabilize the established international system as they seek to make the system serve their interest.[43] Conceivably, the incumbent superpower will employ all the means it could possibly possess, including resorting to military, to contain, deter, or stop the development of the rising power. Arguably, there is only one instance in history an emerging great power had come to greatness without such a conflict; it was when the United States supplanted Britain as the dominating global power without a fight in the early twentieth century.[44] Certainly, China appears to be playing the role of the rising power in the early twentieth century. Clearly enough, given all the advantages possessed by the United States in the various areas of technology, human and natural resources, population, and, especially, the efficient and effective legal and political institutional structure, it will not possibly be "replaced" by any other nation, at least in the foreseeable future. But a rising power like China could grow as strong and great as the United States — this will literally cause the loss of the "single superpower" status of the United States. Furthermore, if a rising power exercises its strength in an aggressive, unilateral, and expansionist way, it will certainly damage the interests of other countries voluntarily or reluctantly involved in the plays with it.

Aware of its growing strength as a potential superpower and that this may cause concerns and even fear among other countries, Beijing's leadership has been seeking to sooth the worries of the international community. The wish is to give history a chance to witness a second time the peaceful emergence of a great power.[45] In a speech at Harvard during his U.S. visit in December 2003, Chinese Premier Wen Jiabao affirmed to the Americans that his country subscribed to the idea of "*heping jueqi*" — meaning "peaceful ascendancy" — after describing to them China's ambitious plan for economic and social development. To achieve this, he said, China needs a "peaceful international development and a stable domestic development".[46] Obviously, China's worldwide RTA movements, engaging primarily its Asian neighbours at this stage, is thus aimed at expanding its political influence through, peacefully, economic exchange and co-operation.

4. THE LEGAL ASPECT: WTO CONSISTENCY OF CHINA'S RTAS AND THE INADEQUACY OF WTO LAW

The Need for WTO Compliance

In theory, any WTO member's regulations and state activities relating to trade have to comply with WTO rules. As mentioned earlier in this chapter, by accession to the WTO, China has committed itself to abide by all the rules of the multilateral trade system, violation of which will be considerably detrimental to both its own credibility as well as that of the WTO. Thus, China's RTA approach, to the extent that international obligations are involved, will conform to WTO rules, provided there are relevant and meaningful WTO provisions in place.

The framers of CEPAs and the China-ASEAN FA, rhetorically, are very prudent on WTO compliance. One of the "General Principles" of the two CEPAs is "to be consistent with the rules of the World Trade Organization".[47] In the "Preamble" of the FA, the eleven countries bring their negotiations under the WTO framework by "reaffirming the rights, obligations and undertakings of the respective parties under the [WTO]". In the main text of the FA, substantive WTO obligations are mentioned in eight places, covering a variety of areas including tariff reduction, trade remedy laws and services.

The presumption is, of course, that there must be something in the GATT/WTO that can be "complied with". The GATT/WTO regime is founded on a core principle: non-discrimination which encompasses a "most-favoured-nation" (MFN) rule and a "national treatment" rule.[48] More relevant to RTAs is the MFN rule which, according to the WTO Secretariat, "is so important that it is the first article of the [GATT]" as well as "a priority in the General Agreement on Trade in Services (GATS) and the Agreement on Trade-Related Aspects of Intellectual Property Rights (TRIPS)."[49] Basically, the MFN clause requires a member of the WTO to extend unconditionally "any advantage, favour, privilege or immunity" affecting customs duties, charges, rules and procedures they give to products originating from, in or destined for any other country.[50]

By definition, regionalism is at odd with the MFN clause and the draftsmen of the GATT and WTO were aware of this; they created several exceptions for RTAs. Under the current WTO regime, RTAs are subject to three sets of rules. The first is Article XXIV of GATT 1947 which, as clarified in the *Understanding on the Interpretation of Article XXIV* of the GATT 1994, provides for the formation and operation of customs unions and FTAs on trade in goods. The so-called "Enabling Clause", formally called the Decision on Differential and More Favourable Treatment, Reciprocity and Fuller Participation of Developing Countries passed by the GATT Council in 1979,[51] permits preferential trade arrangements in trade in goods between developing country members. Finally, Article V of GATS, titled "Economic Integration", governs the formation of RTAs in the area of trade in services.[52]

Are the above rules effective in terms of judging the WTO-consistency of any RTA? One commentator notes that "RTAs are generally WTO-consistent", although "this is because the requirements of Article XXIV and the Enabling Clause and GATS are very weak and have never been enforced". (Lloyd 2002) This statement reveals the poverty of the WTO law in containing regionalism, which the WTO nevertheless views as an enemy of the multilateral trading system. The following sections examine the problems associated with the relevant WTO rules concerning regional trade integration, with particular attention paid to the CAFTA proposal.

The Substantive WTO Requirements: The Rules and the Problems

It is necessary to firstly identity the legal status of China's accomplished RTAs (the two CEPAs) and the half materialized CAFTA (the FA) under the WTO law, with which China and its trading partners vow to comply. GATT addresses two types of RTAs by drawing a distinction between custom union (CU) and FTA. Additionally it also governs the interim agreement leading to the formation of a CU or FTA. A CU, according to GATT Art. XXIV:8, is essentially an arrangement in which all participating countries adopt a common external trade tariffs and eliminate substantially trade barriers among themselves. China's RTAs, however, belong to the second type, namely they are FTAs, features of which are described as the following:

> A Free Trade Agreement/Area (FTA) is a reciprocal arrangement whereby trade barriers between participating nations are abolished. However, each member determines its own external trade barrier against non-FTA members independently. Most commonly, barriers to trade are reduced over time and in most cases, not all trade is completely free of national barriers.[53]

The two CEPAs are apparently FTAs and the CAFTA FA is an interim agreement leading to the formation of a FTA. In China's notification to the WTO Council for Trade in Goods and Council for Trade in Services regarding the CEPAs, they are described as "[to establish] a free-trade area within the meaning of Article XXIV of the GATT 1994 and [provide] for the liberalization of trade in services within the meaning of Article V of the GATS".[54] The FA makes it unequivocally clear that its purpose is to establish a "China-ASEAN FTA within 10 years".[55]

With regard to trade in goods, GATT has one general principle and two substantive rules governing RTAs. Paragraph 5 of GATT Article XXIV sets a principle for closer economic integration between WTO Members, stating that "the purpose of a [CU] or of a [FTA] should be to facilitate trade between the constituent territories and not to raise barriers to the trade of other contracting parties with such territories".[56] The two substantive rules are the "substantially-all-trade" (SAT) requirement and the "not-on-the-whole-higher" (NWH) requirement, embodied in GATT Article XXIV:8 and XXIV:5, respectively. In addition, pragmatically recognizing that a CU/FTA cannot came into being overnight, GATT also permits the formation of an interim agreement but states that it "shall include a plan and schedule for the formation of such [CU] or of such [FTA] within a reasonable period of time".[57]

Simply put, GATT Article XXIV:8 requires that parties to CUs or FTAs eliminate "*duties and other restrictive regulations of commerce*" with respect to "*substantially all the trade*" between their constituent customs territories.[58] Short and simple as it is, this requirement has nonetheless caused major difficulties in interpreting the conditions of Article XXIV, and even prevented the WTO itself from enforcing this provision. According to the Committee on Regional Trade Agreements (CRTA), the WTO's specialized agency for monitoring RTAs, two issues relating to this requirement have blocked the assessment of RTA's fulfilment of the relevant WTO law: the meaning of SAT, and the scope of list of "other restrictive regulations of commerce" (ORRC).[59]

As early as 1995, the WTO Secretariat has noted that "differences of opinion among participants in working parties regarding the interpretation of the [SAT] requirement have been a major reason why working parties have not reached a consensus on the GATT consistency of individual agreements" (WTO 1995, p. 13). Since the inception of GATT, there have been two approaches towards the interpretation of the SAT requirement. The first one is characterized as a "quantitative approach", which favours defining SAT as a statistical benchmark, such as a certain proportion of trade between the parties, to indicate that the coverage of a given RTA fulfil this rule. This problem with this approach is that "a single numerical definition or threshold" cannot suit the various different contexts in which SAT is used. Worse, it can be easily taken advantage of by countries to exclude a set amount of trade, including such sensitive sectors such as agriculture and textile. The other interpretation, called the "qualitative approach", would dictate that no sector (or at least no major sector) was to be excluded from intra-RTA trade liberalization. Ironically, this approach might not automatically result in free trade even if it includes all sectors. As noted by the CRTA, a number of suggestions have been proposed by members of the WTO in an attempt to bridge or complement the two approaches. However, no agreement has been reached (CRTA 2000).

The SAT requirement is further complicated by the mentioning of the ORRC in Article XXIV:8. This paragraph also states that, apart from SAT, WTO members may still "where necessary" exercise their rights to maintain duties or restrictions under GATT Article XI (quantitative restrictions), XII (balance-of-payment exception), XIII (non-discriminative administration of quantitative restrictions), XIV (exceptions to the principle of non-discrimination), XV (exchange arrangements) and XX (general exceptions).[60] The troublesome ambiguity still lies in the interpretation of this rule: were it to be constructed as an exhaustive list, members to RTAs then may not be able to agree on other trade restrictive measures, such as anti-dumping, safeguard, or countervailing duties which are not mentioned in the list; on the contrary, were it to be understood as non-exhaustive, then what other measures could be incorporated into the list is a highly contentious problem.[61]

The second substantive rule, the NWH requirement embodied in GATT Article XXIV:5, stipulates that in a FTA or interim agreement leading to it "the duties and other regulations of commerce" of the parties to FTA in respect of trade with third parties "shall not be higher or more restrictive than the corresponding duties and other regulations of commerce existing in the [parties] prior to the formation of the [FTA], or interim agreement as the case may be".[62] It has been generally recognized that Article XXIV:5 governs the external relations while Article XXIV:8 deals with mainly the internal trade liberalization of CUs or FTAs. Again, the language used here is short, but ambiguous enough to prevent the enforcement of the rule. Apart from the highly disputable, undefined terms such as "higher or restrictive", or "other regulations of commerce" (ORCs), one major problem is that, in order to determine if the NWH requirement is met, whether it is necessary that a country-by-country and product-by-product examination of the effect of increases in tariffs be undertaken. Heated debates have been generated since the GATT's examination of the legitimacy of the Treaty of Rome which established the EEC and to date, no agreement as to how Article XXIV:5's evaluation should be made has been reached among GATT/WTO officials and member-countries (WTO 1995; CRTA 2000). In one WTO case, *Turkey — Restrictions on Imports of Textile and Clothing Products*, a WTO panel indicated that Article XXIV:5(a) requires that the effects of the resulting trade measures and policies of the new regional agreement shall not be more trade restrictive, overall, than were the constituent territories' previous trade policies.[63] In essence, the panel concluded that the terms of this provision "do not address the GATT/WTO compatibility of specific measures that may be adopted on the occasion of the formation" of a new RTA.[64] This conclusion, although shared by the Appellate Body, is not yet the end of the debate, at least in the sense that the WTO's cases do not constitute legally binding *stare decisis*. Another very controversial and unsolved major issue relating to the NWH standard has been RTAs' rules of origin (ROOs). Since the formation of the EEC, it has been debated in the GATT/WTO that ROOs of RTAs have been designed and administered in a way to create new trade barriers to their trade with third countries. An additional concern is that the absence of GATT guidelines on ROOs for RTAs left RTA participants free to adopt whatever rules they may deem appropriate.

GATS Article V, the equivalent of GATT Article XXIV for services, is modelled closely on the latter. In the GATS, the "substantially-all-trade" ambiguity is only slightly abated, but by no means clarified. Most significantly, a RTA is required to have "substantial sector coverage",[65] with the term "substantial" understood "in terms of number of sectors, volume of trade affected and modes of supply".[66] Based on this, the requirement not to raise barriers to third countries is modified towards a tighter standard: it is applied sector by sector rather than "on the whole". For a covered sector "substantially all discrimination" is to be removed.[67] As observed by the CRTA, Article V has also caused many controversies and ambiguities but few of them were clarified.

The Notification and WTO Examination Process: Ill-Enforced Requirements

All RTAs concluded by WTO members require notification. The confusion and ambiguity caused by the relevant WTO notification rules is by no means less severe than that by the aforesaid substantive rules. GATT Article XXIV:7 indicates that any member deciding to enter into a CU or FTA shall promptly notify the WTO members "as will enable them to make such reports and recommendations to contracting parties".[68] GATS Article V:7(a) contains similar requirement. The major issue is that "the time at which notification of RTAs should be made is neither precisely formulated nor homogeneously expressed in the rules" (CRTA, 2000). Most RTAs, in practice, are already in force long before the WTO is in receipt of notification, despite the requirement in GATT XXIV:7(a) that members "shall promptly notify". WTO members have taken contrasting views with regard to the time of notification: one is that notification and submission of information should take place before entry into force — that will render most RTAs automatically illegal under the WTO law, and the other is that the lack of precision in the text implies a "regulatory forbearance" which reflects the "pragmatism" necessary to address complex negotiations for the formation of an RTA, especially in the context of the political difficulty of notifying agreements before ratification (CRTA 2000).

Most notified RTAs have been interim agreements. GATT XXIV:5(c) requires that these agreements include "a plan and schedule for the formation of a customs union or of a free trade area within a reasonable time." However, no definitions to the key terms ("interim agreement", "plan and schedule" and "reasonable time") are provided. Such lack of consensus has led to controversy as to whether any particular interim agreement qualified as such. Furthermore, with regard to interim agreement, Article XXIV provides for the contracting parties (now the WTO members) to make recommendations to the parties to the RTA, if they, after having studied plan and schedule included in the interim agreement, "find that such agreement is not likely to result in the formation of a [CU] or [FTA]" within a period that is reasonable. Accordingly, the parties shall not maintain or put into force such RTA if they are not prepared to modify it in accordance with these recommendations. As noted by John H. Jackson (2000, p. 104):

> The interesting thing about this procedural language is that it does not require advance or later approval of the Contracting Parties of GATT. Instead, it places the initiative with the Contracting Parties to put forward recommendations for changes in the preferential agreement. This means technically, once the agreement has been notified to the GATT, unless the Contracting Parties can somehow arrive at an agreed set of recommendations, the language of GATT permits the preference parties to go ahead. The presumption is thus in favor of the preferential arrangement.

Jackson (2000, p. 104) further notes that, to his knowledge, "the Contracting Parties of GATT have never made an agreed set of recommendations to notifiers of preferential agreements". As a result, "many such arrangements have been entered into and operated which arguably do not fully comply with the policy goals and the intent and spirit of Article XXIV of GATT".

Naturally, this kind of situation leads people to question the work of the WTO's Committee on Regional Trade Agreement (CRTA), which was established in February 1999 and charged with the principal duties, in particular (a) to oversee, under a single framework, all RTAs, and (b) to consider the systemic implications of the agreements for the multilateral trading system and the relationship between them.[69] There is evidence to suggest that CRTA has fulfilled the second mission, since it has released a number of valuable reports on this issue and instilled public awareness about the problems surrounding the difficulties imposed on the multilateral trading system by regionalism. However, CRTA's performance with regard to the first mission is an openly recognized failure. According to the committee's 2003 Report to the General Council of WTO, by the end of 2003, the Committee has currently under examination a total of 147 agreements; "no progress was, however, made on the completion of the examination reports".[70] In fact, no examination report has been finalized since the WTO's establishment in 1995. The WTO Director-General, in a number of WTO annual reports, concluded that the CRTA has failed "so far in assessing the consistency of the ... RTAs notified to the WTO, due to various political and legal difficulties, most of which inherited from the GATT years"[71] and that "since the establishment of the WTO, members have been unable to reach consensus on the format, let along the substance, of the reports on any of the examinations entrusted to the CRTA".[72] As a result, so far the CRTA has never approved any RTA as WTO-consistent; likewise, it has also not officially declared a single RTA as violating GATT/WTO rules.

So, is there any need to comply with WTO rules? Theoretically the answer is yes because, after all, if a country is a member of the WTO, the obligation to comply with the rules of the multilateral trading system is mandatory. However, a more useful answer is probably "no" because of the reasons implied in the above analysis. To summarize, first, the WTO rules on the introduction of RTAs are troublesomely ambiguous and could not be followed operationally. It is the inadequate WTO rules that should be blamed first before any criticism may be directed towards members' non-compliance (if any). Secondly, the nature of the WTO as a consensus-based institution prevents it from strengthening the enforcement of the existing rules, roughly starting with the examination of the EEC which was given up in early GATT days due to the clash of political interests, and never picked up again.

Although the reason behind the failure of enforcement is because of members' divergent interpretation of WTO rules, the real implication seems to be that almost no RTA could ever be declared unlawful under the current WTO regime and the process of CRTA examination can be ignored.

Experience shows that, to literally comply with GATT/WTO rules governing RTAs, members involved in RTAs need only to notify the WTO of the agreements either before or after their taking effect. Until the WTO substantially revises its rules governing regional economic integration, there is no imminent need for RTA members to worry about the compliance with the substantive WTO requirements. In this sense, since China has already notified the RTAs to the WTO, it can be assumed that those RTAs are to be deemed compatible by the WTO unless the WTO can render opposing reports and recommendations.[73]

5. A REALIST VIEW ON CHINA'S RTA APPROACH IN THE CONTEXT OF REGIONALISM V. MULTILATERALISM

This part intends to present a realist view on the emergence of China's RTA approach and its regional and global impact, in particular looking at its relationship with the multilateral trading system. Section A argues that pursuit of regional and national security is of paramount national interest for China and other East Asia countries, and regional economic integration through FTA is an effective instrument to achieve it. Section B points out that regional integration towards multilateralism-based broad liberalization is, however, in the long-term interest for peace and prosperity, concluding that China, as a top trading power, bears the responsibility to defend multilateralism while developing regional integration. In addition, it proposes recommendations for how China should act to strike the aforesaid balance.

National and Regional Security as A Legitimate Goal in International Trade Relations

In the absence of multilateral control through WTO rules, nations are free to pursue many goals in conducting regional integration through RTAs. The primary purpose of regional economic integration, according to a World Bank report, "is often political, and the economic consequences, good or bad, are side effects of the political payoff" (World Bank 2000, p. 11). Political benefits such as peace and security, quite rightly, are of the paramount concern in the minds of the framers of many RTAs, based on the rationale that regions that are economically highly integrated may tend to have less internal conflict. For example, the preamble to the 1951 treaty establishing the European Coal and Steel Community stated its aims as "to create, by establishing an economic community, the basis for broader and deeper community among peoples long divided by bloody conflicts". The founding fathers of the European Community (EC) even considered that economic integration would make war "materially impossible" (World Bank 2000, pp. 12–13).

Trade fosters global peace is a long-established liberal conviction. Theorists like Montesquieu and Kant and practitioners like Woodrow Wilson asserted the economic relations between states pacify political interaction. Literature of modern economics and international relations discloses that states fight for two reasons, and both are related to cost contests. Cost contests involve two elements. The first is that there is zero-sum competition for an excludable good. Secondly, states choose a settlement method, but the choice of method is non-zero-sum. The two reasons in connection to war are based on the understanding of the above two elements of the cost contests. First, states fighting each other must have incentives to compete, which is often the competition over an excludable good. States differ over issues that each cannot possess simultaneously. Secondly, there is uncertainty as to the private information about strategic variables (capabilities, resolve, and so on) possessed by each state. If states could credibly share private information, efficient *ex ante* bargains could be identified. Uncertainty firstly provides weak or unresolved states an opportunity to conceal weakness even as competition creates incentive to bluff. Only by imposing costly contests — by military fighting or similar acts — can states distinguish resolute opponents from those seeking to bluff. Furthermore, uncertainty also causes states to be not able to realize or overlook the likely consequences of contests (Gartzke, Li and Boehmer 2001, pp. 397–99).

Interdependence functions to promote peace in the sense that it helps to remove incentives for states to engage in conflict as well as to reduce the uncertainty states face when bargaining in the shadow of costly contests. The argument put forward by a group of international relations scholars is that "interdependence makes it easier to substitute non-violent contest for militarized disputes in signaling resolve", because "states that possess a range of methods of conflict resolution have less need to resort to the most destructive (and costly) techniques", while "states without linkages must choose between a very limited set of options, including — more often — war". (Gartzke, Li and Boehmer 2001, p. 400) Specifically, based on empirical studies and quantitative analysis, the argument concludes:

> Trade and direct investment increase cross-border economic contact and
> raise a state's stake in maintaining linkages. Monetary coordination and
> interdependence demand that states strike deals. Though such interactions,
> states create a broad set of mutually beneficial economic linkages. While
> these linkages may deter very modest clashes, their main impact is as a
> substitute method for resolving conflict. Political shocks that threaten to
> damage or destroy economic linkages generate information, reducing
> uncertainty when leaders bargain. Threats from interdependent states
> carry more weight than threats from autarchic states precisely because
> markets inform observers as to the veracity of political "cheap talk."
> Multiple channels of economic interactions help states to credibly
> communicate, increasing the "vocabulary" available to states in attempting
> to assess relative resolve. (Gartzke, Li and Boehmer 2001, p. 418)

Despite many other concerns such as supporting Hong Kong and pursuing the "Greater China Economic Circle" which is China's domestic matter, the major consideration behind China's RTA approach is engaging Asian neighbours for the sake of creating a peaceful and friendly regional environment for its economic development. China's goal, however, not only coincides with that of its neighbours but serves the supreme interest in the region, which is peaceful existence and enhance security.

Given East Asia's warring colonized history, diverse culture, extremely fragmented ideology groupings, long existed borders disputes, and deeply rooted mistrusts in regional politics, it is an area within which conflicts can be easily generated. Countries in East Asia, especially China and Korea, traditionally have lingering mistrust of Japan because of its history of aggression. Recently, China's rise as a regional and global power brings fear to its neighbours both economically and strategically. The conventional "China threat" theory has been in place for decades. Indeed, ASEAN was originally formed for the purpose of containing China when it was practising communism. The perception of threat from the "dragon" (China), however, has persisted into today's intra-Asia regional politics. One major dispute between China and its southern neighbours is that they all have laid claims to the Spratly islands and the Paracel islands (called *nansha* and *xiasha* islands, respectively, by the Chinese) in South China Sea, which are of strategic and potentially of economic importance. Since the 1970s, China had been involved in battles with Vietnam and exchanged fires with the Philippines and Malaysia over the islands (Shen 2002, pp. 100–01) Given the PRC's growing military might and uncompromising history in safeguarding its claimed territory, there is reason for China's small and weak neighbours to fear that the giant dragon might seek to resolve the disputes by force. This fear, in turn, can lead to political distrust, arms races, and eventually regional instability. Worse, China and its Asian neighbours would also not be able to share the benefits of each other's fast growing economies.

RTAs, if managed well, are certainly promoters of peace and common security. A World Bank publication describes the role of RTAs in this regard as follows:

> [T]trade relations, including [RTAs] and, especially, deeper arrangement, might assist political relations between member countries by developing means for avoidance and management of intramural conflict. The negotiations between leaders of neighboring countries that are required to form and operate an [RTA] tend to generate trust between them. This helps them identify with each other, understand each other's problems, and interpret each other's actions. Trade talks allow political and economic elites to form coalitions from subsequent collaboration and consensual action. (Schiff and Winters 2003, p. 192)

China's recent RTA movement is based on this rationale that RTAs can be used as an instrument to strengthen friendship with neighbours and enhance regional security which serves it long-term central task — economic growth and development of *zonghe guoli* [national strength]. Observers widely hold the view that "there's more than trade at stake" (Vatikiotis and Hiebert 2003). The geopolitical dimensions of China's economic diplomacy imply that "for Beijing, cementing closer economic ties with neighbouring East Asia states is also about establishing regional influence and leadership at the expense of the United States and other major economic powers", and that "China ... hopes to form at some point a counter power comparable to the United States and Europe by unifying Asian countries" (Vatikiotis and Hiebert 2003). However, there is no reason to presume that China is starring as "grandmother wolf" who took advantage of the innocence of Little Red Riding Hood. Perhaps more significant is that those economic diplomacy measures put forward by China will also "lock in" China's role as a promoter of regional stability. In the East Asia context, China's RTA approach is closely accompanied by a host of other efforts on increased support for and participation in regional security mechanisms. In November 2002, China co-signed the Declaration on the Conduct of Parties in the South China Sea with ASEAN, which reaffirms China's respect for and commitment to the freedom of navigation in and overflight above the South China Sea "provided for by the universally recognized principles of international law", and reiterates the principle for the parties to "resolve their territorial and jurisdictional

disputes by peaceful means, without resorting to the threat or use of force ....
In accordance with universally recognized principles of international law".
Furthermore, on 8 October 2003, in response to ASEAN's decade-long plea,
China, actually as the first country outside ASEAN, acceded to the Treaty of
Amity and Co-operation in Southeast Asia, a dispute settlement procedure
established by ASEAN in 1976. The treaty, in the form of recognized
international law, commits China to use peaceful means to resolve territorial
disputes. In addition, China is obligated not to "participate in any activity
which shall constitute a threat to the political and economical stability,
sovereignty, or territorial integrity" of other signatory states. These series of
strategic movements, according to an American observer, are underlined by
the intent to "ease ASEAN fears that China has territorial designs on the
South China Sea claims of littoral ASEAN members". But more significantly,
they contribute to the creation of an environment of peaceful co-existence
between China and Southeast Asia, given the fact that China is well positioned
to destroy unilaterally the stability in this area. Evidently, China's past behaviour,
very different from the current approach and based on restrained unilateral
acts and insistence on bilateral (rather than multilateral) talks, caused grave
concern among ASEAN members. China's new movement was certainly
embraced by its small neighbours with optimism. Very tellingly, after China's
accession to the Treaty of Amity, ASEAN's spokesman interpreted the ASEAN
understanding of China's motivation as follows:

> China needs a favorable environment in the region to continue its
> economic development, which is not inconsistent with ASEAN's strategic
> needs...China wants to be seen as a responsible member of the
> international community, a country that is prepared to follow the rules
> accepted by the international community...[On the part of ASEAN,]
> there is no other way to deal with China but to engage it in regional
> process. China is important as a neighbor politically, in terms of security
> and is also important as an emerging economic power (de Castro 2003).

Regional Integration and Multilateral Liberalization: the Moral Obligation to Ensure RTAs Serve as Building Blocks

Regional integration through free trade agreements has been shadowed by
heated debates featuring regionalism v. multilateralism. At the core of the
debates are the costs and benefits of regionalism. The classic model for
analyzing the economic effects of regional trade arrangements is still Jacob
Viner's scholarship on the concepts of trade diversion and trade creation
(Viner 1950). Viner explained how RTAs (including FTAs and CUs) have

opposite effects on welfare, or income. Trade creation takes place when, as a result of removal of tariffs on intra-area trade, domestic production of a good is displaced by imports from another member of the RTA, whose comparative advantage enables it to produce the goods at a lower cost. On the other hand, the preferential tariff rate established by a RTA may cause trade division, defined as a shift of production away from a lower-cost producer outside the RTA to a higher-cost source of supply within it. Viner concluded that the formation of a RTA will lead to improvement in economic efficiency and welfare if trade creation exceeds trade diversion. An opposite effect, harmful to economic efficiency and welfare, will be generated if trade diversion exceeds trade creation (Grimwade 1996).

Viner's main contribution was in showing that the formation of a RTA was not necessarily welfare-improving, or, using the more enthusiastic words of the eminent economist Jadish Bhagwati (1991, p. 59), "to destroy the common fallacy that a preferential move toward (total) free trade was necessarily welfare improving and thus to demonstrate that all preferential paths to (total) free trade were not monotonic in welfare". Following Viner, enormous literature on the benefits and costs of RTAs was generated. The modern version of the debates focuses on the role of RTA as a "stumbling block" or "building block" to multilateral trade liberalization. Bhagwati (1999) asserts that RTAs are by definition discriminatory and thereby trade diverting. While maintaining that trade diversion is likely to occur when a RTA is formed, he also argues that a RTA is inherently unhealthy even for its members because they are led by the RTA rules to engage in wasteful, discriminatory trade practices rather than trade induced by healthy market preferences. Both Bhagwati and Anne O. Krueger, another prominent opponent to RTAs, cite the rules of origin (ROOs) as a negative product of RTAs. They claim, for example, that the ROOs in one RTA more than likely do not coincide with the ROOs in many of other RTAs. Eventually, the incongruity of these different regulations governing the same subject matter could create a customs administration nightmare and call for the so-called "spaghetti-bowl" phenomenon (Bhagwati 1999, p. 36).

The many exponents of RTAs question the assumption of Bhagwati and his fellows in the debate. Economist Robert Z. Lawrence argues that the theory traditionally applied to RTAs (by Bhagwati, Krueger, and others) is too narrow to be applied to recent RTAs such as NAFTA, which involve much more economic integration than the elimination of tariffs and thereby has led to the reduction in barriers on services trade, investment, and other area (CRS Report 2002, p. 12). He concluded that these dynamic welfare enhancing characteristics of RTAs are likely to outweigh any trade diversion effect. But even for RTAs in general — meaning they include both traditional tariff-reduction RTAs and modern more comprehensive RTAs, Lawrence Summers (1991, p. 562) suggests that they are generally favourable tools for trade liberalization because of the following propositions: (1) under the existing structure of trade, plausible regional RTAs are likely to have trade creating effects that exceed their trade diverting effects; (2) even trade diverting RTAs are likely to increase welfare; (3) RTAs have other beneficial effects in addition to their impact on trade; (4) reasonable RTAs are as likely to promote global liberalization as to slow it down.

Obviously, the literature on the costs and benefits of RTAs does not offer conclusive answer on whether in general trade creation will exceed trade diversion or *vice versa*. It is, however, important to note that there is no major dispute as to the final goal: multilateral trade liberalization. The controversy is all about whether RTAs set up forces that encourage or discourage the evolution toward globally freer trade. In his highly regarded writing in 1996, economist C. Fred Bergsten (1996) praises the multilateral approach as follows:

> The global approach is fundamental superior because it maximizes the number of foreign markets involved and avoids the economic distortions (and political risks) of discrimination among trading partners. Indeed, the succession of GATT "rounds" throughout the postwar period has made a major contribution to the freeing of global trade.

Bergsten (1996) nevertheless argues that RTAs, in lieu of multilateral trade negotiations, are the next best thing and promote global free trade, due to the many deficiencies of the multilateral approach. Among other things, the regional approach is less time-consuming and less complicated to reach meaningful results, and RTAs often serve the priority national security concerns of countries involved. Hence a less controversial, or perhaps even common, point agreeable to both sides of the battle is that "the economic impact of regional arrangements depends on their particular architecture, including how far they go in reducing trade barriers and how many sectors they cover" (WTO 2003c, p. 62). Bhagwati (1991, p. 59) recognizes that Viner's model can lead to the conclusion that "preferential moves can indeed be welfare improving: It just depends on the parameters". A World Bank special report on trade regionalism concludes: "Whether or not trade diversion dominates trade creation depends on the specific circumstances" (World Bank 2001, p. 61).

The supreme principle is that a RTA should be designed, with appropriate policy choices, to supplement multilateral trade liberalization. This principle

is not inconsistent with the aforesaid position that national and regional
security is a legitimate goal to pursue in regional economic integration. There
is no inherent conflict between pursuing security in a RTA and setting up the
RTA to be friendly to trade liberalization on a global scale which we value.[74]
While we admit that regionalism is the "second-best" approach, it is important
to keep in mind that its general structure should not be inconsistent with a
policy that eventually meets the needs for the "first-best". There is, however,
a balance to make, namely, on the one hand, the international trade regime
should make itself ready to embrace the seemingly unstoppable trend of
regionalism, and, on the other hand, an international trade policy should be
formulated to encourage RTAs to achieve trade creation and avoid trade
diversion, both for the sake of members and to minimize harm to third-
countries. The bottom line, of course, is that RTAs should not be used for
protectionist purposes.

Leading trade powers, such as the United States, EU, and China, have
the responsibility to ensure that regionalism, which is actively pursued by
all of them, serves as "building blocks" for multilateral trade liberalization.
The arguments of both the proponents and opponents of RTAs should all
be credited to the extent that they have pointed out the positive and
negative aspects of RTAs in the world trading system. The technique is easy
to express but probably difficult to implement; using a Chinese idiom, it is
to *yangchang biduan*, meaning maximize favourable factors and minimize
unfavourable ones.

The United States has been a leader for free trade since World War II.
Until 2001, the United States had only two FTAs (the U.S.-Israel FTA and
NAFTA) while both were not initiated by itself. In the following years,
however, the United States had been proactively involved in bilateral trade
talks, having signed FTAs with Jordan, Singapore, Chile, Australia, and a
number of Central and South America countries. However, as one commentary
notes, "most of these [FTA] deals ... are unlikely to have a major impact of
the gigantic U.S. economy, given the amount of additional trade at stake:
Singapore, for example, is a city-state of more than 4 million whose dynamic
economy is already largely open" (Blustein 2002). Obviously, the United
States is implementing a strategy which can be characterized as "competitive
liberalization", a term that was allegedly first coined by Bergsten in his 1996
article which argues, in essence, that RTAs will trigger a wave of liberalization
towards global free trade as nations compete to open their market to one
another by joining RTAs due to the fear of being left-out" (Blustein 2002;
Bergsten 1996). Washington's regionalism aims to induce other major players
in world trade, including the EU, Japan and the coalition of a large number

of developing countries, to compete in the broader, multilateral agenda of the WTO, currently the Doha Round. The United States is pushing on two fronts: at the same time, it does not stop pressing other trading powers to act on multilateral talks. At the beginning of January 2004, U.S. Trade Representative (USTR) Robert Zoellick wrote to the trade ministers of other 146 WTO members, in which he indicated that "the U.S. does not want 2004 to be a lost year for the Doha Development Agenda" and suggested his approach to advancing negotiation in 2004 (USTR 2004*a*). With his "common sense" proposal, one month later Zoellick travelled all over the world and embarked on a global push to make strong progress in 2004 on multilateral trade negotiations. The trip, earning the support of many countries including China on a variety of sensitive issues which collapsed at the WTO Cancun Ministerial Conference in 2003, is hopeful in bringing about the restart of the Doha Round negotiations (USTR 2004*b*).

The above example is not necessarily suggesting that the United States is sincerely devoted to multilateralism. In fact, for many years the United States has been criticized for its overuse of aggressive unilateralism. The implication for China, however, is that trading powers, while pursuing regionalism to cure the deficiencies of multilateralism, should not lose sight on the multilateral approach towards global free trade. China became the world's fourth largest trading nation in 2002, and will be likely take the position of the third largest trader in 2003. Like the United States, EU and other leading trading powers, China also plays an important role in shaping international trade policy. In addition, China's traditional role as a leader of the Third World means that its behaviour will likely have an impact on the trade policy orientation of other developing countries. As a rising power which appears willing to shoulder a larger global responsibility, China should take a pragmatic RTA approach which helps balance its national objective and the multilateral trade liberalization. The proposed China-ASEAN Free Trade Agreement (CAFTA) should be designed in a fashion that helps this balance. Such a balance is very likely to be achieved if the RTA framework is constructed with the following considerations in mind.

1. *A Sound International Trade Policy has Two Faces.* First, it should be pragmatic enough to accommodate the security needs of trading nations, as long as those needs do not go against positive international law. In the East Asian context, in particular with respect to China and its neighbours, economic interdependence through integration has become essential for individual country's security needs as well as regional stability. There is no inherent conflict between these two goals. As noted by a World Bank report, even though RTAs can arise for essentially political reasons, there are strong returns

to ensure that they are set up with economic efficiency in mind. Only efficient, economically sustainable RTAs can help solve political problems, while a wasteful or divisive RTA could only produce opposite effects in the long run (Schiff and Winters 2003). In the case of China's RTAs with its neighbours, various authoritative studies show that the economic returns are strong and obvious. The ASEAN-China Expert Group's report on the feasibility of CAFTA suggests that "an ASEAN-China FTA will increase ASEAN's export to China by 48 per cent and China's exports to ASEAN by 55.1 per cent. The FTA increases ASEAN's GDP by 0.9 per cent or by US$5.4 billion while China's real GDP expands by 0.3 per cent or by US$2.2 billion in absolute terms" (ASEAN 2001). The larger welfare-improving effect of China's RTAs was also confirmed by a policy study of the United Nations Conference on Trade and Development, which uses the gravity model and the computable general equilibrium (CGE) model, two basic models in economics, to assess the empirical effects of RTAs. According to the study, for example, the simulation results of both models suggest the proposed Japan-Korea FTAs has negative coefficiencies in all experiments except agriculture, but expanding this arrangement to include China results in a positive estimated coefficient on trade integration between these economies, strongly significant in both manufacturing and overall merchandise, suggesting that "a bloc centred on China might be beneficial". Further expanding the arrangement to include ASEAN, results in highly significant positive efficiencies (UNCTAC 2001, p. 18). These results provide economic legitimacy for China and its neighbours' RTA initiatives in the region, although those initiatives themselves are essentially politics-driven.

2. *The Moral, but not Legal, Obligation to Pursue Multilateral Liberalization in Regional Initiatives.* As discussed above, multilateral liberalization is in the long-term interest of trading nations. However, because the process of pursuing multilateralism is too long and arduous, and the associated benefits might even be remote, and if in certain areas the collective action mechanism for global liberalization could not be established (to avoid the free-rider problem), countries should be allowed to pursue the "second best" approach which improves the economic welfare of the parties involved. After all, the world trading system does not require trading nations to be deontological; they are merely obligated to comply with the positive legal rules in the system. Apart from this long-term yet probably remote interest, countries can pursue the benefits of liberalized trade on a smaller scale as long as the detrimental effects are limited and non-obvious. This can be characterized as trading nations' "mid-term" interest.[75] In case trade diversion outweighs trade creation, the economies can still go ahead with a RTA as long as it enhances the mid-term

economic welfare of their countries. Theory and practice suggest that RTAs combining only small economies are likely to be trade diverting (Schiff and Winters 2003). However, especially for developing countries which desperately need to achieve development, RTAs should be assessed on the basis of national objectives and criteria, not according to whether they satisfy the relevant WTO articles or the purpose of the multilateral trading system. In the rare cases where there is a conflict, meeting the purpose (not necessarily positive laws) of long-term multilateral liberalization is probably only an abstract, moral obligation while meeting the objectives of economic development is a more urgent need.

3. *Promoting Rules Convergence as a Way of Promoting Multilateral Liberalization.* The well-known imprecision and ambiguity of GATT Article XXIV in particular and GATS Article V, as well as the inability of WTO members to reach consensus on the interpretation of these articles, has rendered the deadlock situation where there is no universally accepted understanding of all the important provisions in the articles. The effect is that members are in practice left free within quite a large range to unilaterally adopt their own interpretations of the disputed provisions. While this situation is clearly undesirable, the decisive movement toward its reform is not likely to be achieved in the near-term given the complexity of extorting sufficient political will from WTO members. For an individual WTO member who is willing to ensure the RTAs it is involved in are consistent with the spirit of the multilateral trading system, one of the best things it can do is to promote rules convergence and minimize the "spaghetti bowl" problems through the harmonization and adoption of common rules, especially in the highly divergent but crucial areas such as rules of origin, customs valuation, trade facilitation, and investment. Where there are relevant WTO provisions in place, the RTAs should follow those rules as closely as possible. In other areas where WTO rules are absent, international standards or "best practice" should be developed and adopted. China and its RTA partners are now in the best position to contribute to the convergence approach because most of the RTAs involving them are still in the negotiating stage.

6. CONCLUDING REMARKS

China's recent RTA initiatives, contributing significantly to the proliferation of regional trade arrangements, should be viewed in a broad context encompassing the country's and its neighbours' and economic, political and security concerns. Like other RTAs, this could run at odds with the goal of the multilateral trading system, although it is equally likely to supplement the process of multilateral trade liberalization. The ideal way is to use multilateral trading rules, embodied in the WTO regime, to control the direction of regionalism and minimize the adverse effects of multilateralism. The existing WTO rules, including mainly GATT Article XXIV and GATS Article V, are evidently weak, ambiguous and almost completely not enforced. Legally it could be argued that WTO members should be free to pursue a particular goal through trading behaviour in the absence of positive WTO rules which prohibit it. Taking a realist view, the idea of this chapter is that China's RTA approach is just another example that the international trade system should be pragmatic enough to accommodate the vital security needs of trading nations if prohibitive WTO rules are not in place. This is especially crucial in the East Asian context given its history and geopolitical layout; for example, China's complex political and military role in the region. An alternative route for East Asia without even politically-driven regional integration could be much less effective or even adverse for promoting regional prosperity and stability. Trading nations, especially leading trade powers like China, have, however, moral obligations to ensure that their RTAs serve as "building blocks" for multilateral trade liberalization by promoting rules convergence, although it is not suggested that they put this moral obligation above their national objective as there is no international legal obligation compelling them to do so.

Notes

1. Regionalism in the context of international trade was defined as "the promotion by governments of international economic linkages with countries that are geographically proximate" (Grimwade 1996). However, in recent decades regional trade agreements have been signed by countries located in different regions and even different continents, such as the U.S.-Israel Free Trade Agreement and the U.S.-Singapore Free Trade Agreement. To modify the traditional definition, regionalism can now be broadly characterized as the tendency towards the creation of preferential trade arrangements between a number of countries which discriminate against third countries.

2. The coverage of regional preferential trade arrangements is broadly defined here. Generally, RTA(s) and FTA(s) are used interchangeably in this article.

3. Jagdish Bhagwati has observed that there have been two phrases of regionalism in the post WWII period. The first phrase occurred in the late 1950s and early 1960s, represented by the European Community (EC), the European Free Trade Area (EFTA), the Latin America Free Trade Association (LAFTA), the Central African Customs and Economic Union (CACEU) and a few others. The second wave of regionalism, an ongoing phenomenon, first occurred in 1980s. The EU

and NAFTA are typical examples of FTAs concluded in this period. See Grimwade (1996).

4. The use of the terms "country" or "countries" follows the Explanatory Notes to Article XVI of the Uruguay Round Agreement Establishing the World Trade Organization, which provides "The terms 'country' or 'countries' as used in this Agreement and the Multilateral Trade Agreements are to be understood to include any separate customs territory Member of the WTO."

5. See for example, Bhagwati (1991). A very good recent account of this debate is a book edited by Richard Pomfret. Entitled *Economic Analysis of Regional Trading Arrangements* (Northampton, MA: Edward Elgar Pub., 2003), it features the masterful works of Jacob Viner, Harry Johnson, Robert A. Mundell, Paul R. Krugman, Lawrence H. Summers and many others prominent economists.

6. *Xinhua*, 2000.

7. The Greater China Area includes Mainland China, Hong Kong, Macao, and Taiwan.

8. FA, Art. 1(b).

9. FA, Art. 1(c).

10. FA, Art. 2.

11. Annex 3 of the FA, Part B. A slightly different schedule is used for the newer ASEAN members.

12. Annex 2 of the FA.

13. *Manila Times*, 2003*b*.

14. China, however, has excluded from EHP some agricultural products such as rice and palm oil, which are said to be major exports from ASEAN countries. These products are to be negotiated in the coming years.

15. FA, Art. 9. Currently Cambodia, Vietnam and the Lao PDR are not WTO members.

16. *Manila Times*, 2003*a*.

17. Only Brunei and Singapore are permitted to be parties to any arrangements that have been agreed on or will be agreed to between China and any other ASEAN states under the EHP. *See id*, Annex 2.

18. Text of the agreement is available on China's Ministry of Commerce website at <http://www.mofcom.gov.cn>.

19. The FA, Art. 3(4)(a)(i).

20. FA, Art. 3(4)(b).

21. FA, Art. 3(8).

22. FA, Art. 1(1).

23. FA, Art. 8(3).

24. The FA, Art. 4(a).

25. FA, Art. 4(b).

26. MTI of Singapore, 2004.

27. The FA, Annex 4.

28. HKTDC, 2003.

29. Ibid.
30. Bridges Weekly Trade News Digest, 2003.
31. CNA, 2003.
32. In November 2003 at the annual ASEAN+3 (China, Japan and Korea) Summit, then Chinese Premier Zhu Rongji also proposed to form a FTA with Japan and South Korea. The responses he received from the two East Asian countries were hardly positive. So far, there has been no substantial negotiation for a China-Japan-Korea FTA. The three countries, however, have agreed to start the feasibility study. As David Wall of the Royal Institute of International Affairs in London notes, "There is not much chance of a trilateral FTA in Northeast Asia for now then. Which is why Roh and Hu could only agree to leave it to academics to chew over, endlessly" (Wall 2003).
33. Lewis (2003).
34. Hong Kong and China Sign Free Trade Deal, *Financial Times*, 29 June 2003, Asian Edition 1.
35. Pottingger (2003).
36. Currently China mainly imports resource- or agriculture-based products (minerals, pulp, wood, vegetable oil and sugar) for ASEAN countries. Growing now is the share of machinery and electrical components for assembly into final goods in China (ASEAN 2001). China in recently has also been proactively buying national gas and oil fields in Indonesia.
37. Soesastro (2003).
38. USCC 2003b, statement of Bates Gill.
39. In 1980–2000, China's accumulated net FDI totalled US$209 billion while ASEAN's accumulated net FDI totalled on US$172 billion for the same period. See Phar (2003). CAFTA can slow this trend by providing multinationals with more incentives to invest or stay in ASEAN while meanwhile continuing to enjoy the benefits of China's huge domestic market.
40. Chua (2002). See also, Phar (2003).
41. The effect of China's "economic incentive" diplomacy, as I so call it, can be seen in Chinese President Hu Jintao's visit to Australia and New Zealand in October 2003. Local media hailed Hu's friendly gesture and policy declaration focusing on economic co-operation and political dialogue, and contrasted that with U.S. President Bush's almost sole concentration on security and anti-terrorism.
42. Funabashi (2003).
43. Paal (2000).
44. Paal (2000).
45. A Japanese newspaper noted that a researcher at a state-sponsored think-tank in Beijing commented that "China aims to grow and advance without upsetting existing orders" and the Chinese "are trying to rise in a way that benefits our neighbours" (Funabashi 2003).
46. Wen (2003).
47. See for example, China-HK CEPA, Main Text, Art. 2 (2).

48. General Agreement on Tariffs and Trade, 30 October 1947, Art. I and III [hereinafter GATT].
49. WTO, 2003*b*.
50. GATT, Art. I(1).
51. The Decision on Differential and More Favorable Treatment, Reciprocity and Fuller Participation of Developing Countries, Decision of 28 November 1979, L/4903 [hereinafter the Enabling Clause].
52. General Agreement on Trade on Trade in Services, 15 April 1994, Marrakesh Agreement Establishing the World Trade Organization [hereinafter WTO Agreement], Annex 1B, Art. V.
53. APEC, 2001.
54. "Closer Economic Partnership Arrangement between China and Hong Kong, China", *Notification from the Parties*, 12 January 2004, WT/REG162/N/1, S/C/N/264, and "Closer Economic Partnership Arrangement between China and Macao, China", *Notification from the Parties*, 12 January 2004, WT/REG163/N1, S/C/N/265.
55. FA, Art. 2.
56. GATT, Art. XXIV:5.
57. GATT, Art. XXIV:5(c).
58. Ibid., Art. XXIV:8 (emphasis added).
59. CRTA, 2000.
60. GATT Art. XXIV: 8(b).
61. In fact, this problem has generated a good number of disputes before the WTO's Dispute Resolution Body (DSB). See for example, Turkey — Restrictions on Imports of Textile and Clothing Products, 22 October 1999, WT/DS34/AB/; United States — Definitive Safeguard Measures on Imports of Circular Welded Carbon Quality Line Pipe from Korea, 15 February 2002, WT/DS202/AB/R; and Canada — Certain Measures Affecting the Automotive Industry, 31 May 2000, WT/DS139/AB/R, WT/DS142/AB/R.
62. GATT, Article XXIV: 5(c).
63. *Turkey — Restrictions on Imports of Textile and Clothing Products,* WTO panel report, 31 May 1999, WT/DS34/R, paras. 9.120–21 [hereinafter the panel report of *Turkey — Textile*].
64. Ibid., para. 9.122.
65. GATS Art. V:1(a).
66. GATS Art. V:1(a), footnote 1.
67. GATS Art. V:1(b).
68. GATT, Art. XXIV:7(a).
69. For the terms of reference of the CRTA see WTO document WT/L/127, 7 February 1996.
70. CRTA, *Annual Report 2003*.
71. WTO, *Annual Report 2002*, p. 114.
72. WTO, *Annual Report 2003*, p. 111.

73. There is a counter-argument saying that the legal status of RTAs in the WTO can be considered as remaining unclear, and thus WTO members are preserved with the rights under dispute settlement procedures with regard to RTAs in any event. *See* WTO Secretariat, 2002b: para. 24. This argument, however, does not go against the *prima facie* compatibility of an RTA. Furthermore, even though a RTA is challenged before the DSB for non-compliance with the WTO framework, the DSB, based on above analysis, does not possess the legal tools to examine the legal standing of RTAs *vis-à-vis* WTO rules. In *Turkey–Textile,* the panel observed that "it is arguable" that panels do not have jurisdiction to assess the overall compatibility of a customs union with the requirements of Art. XXIV of GATT. In the end, the panel assumed *arguendo* that the arrangement between Turkey and the EC is compatible with the requirements of GATT Article XXIV:8(a) and 5(a). The Appellate did not address this issue.
74. Bergsten (1996) argues that "regional and global liberalization initiatives have mutually reinforcing throughout the past three decades or more" and that "the fears of some observers that regionalism would derail globalism have been demonstrably overcome".
75. In the analytical framework of this article, the long-term interest, referring to the eventual goal of global trade liberalization, is certainly the goal without major dispute. The mid-term interest is worth pursuing because the benefits are obvious and damage to other members of the international trade community are non-obvious, limited, and not a result of international legal obligations. The short-term interest refers to those benefits which can be achieved at the expense of massive environmental damage, human rights violations, or direct violations of the positive rules of international trade law.

References

APEC (Asia Pacific Economic Co-operation). *A Complete Guide to the Regional Trade Agreements of the Asia-Pacific.* Written by T. Martyn for the APEC, March 2001.

ASEAN. *Forging Closer ASEAN-China Economic Relations in the Twenty-First Century.* A report submitted by the ASEAN-China Expert Group on Economic Co-operation, October 2001. Available at <http://www.aseansec.org.>.

———. *Annual Report 2000–2001.* ASEAN Secretariat.

———. *Annual Report 2002–2003.* ASEAN Secretariat.

Bergsten, C.F. Competitive Liberalization and Global Free Trade: A Vision for the Early 21st Century. Working paper 96–15. Washington D.C.: Institute for International Economics, 1996.

Bezlova, A. " 'One Country, Two Systems' Under Fire". *Asia Times Online.* 17 July 2003. Available at <http://www.atimes.com.>.

Bhagwati, J. *The World Trading System at Risk.* Hertfordshire: Harvester Wheatsheaf, 1991.

————. "Multilateralism and Regionalism in the Post-Uruguay Round Era: What Role for the US?" In *Multilateralism and Regionalism in the Post-Uruguay Round Era: What Role for the EU?*, edited by O. Memedovic, et al. Boston: Kluwer Academic, 1999, pp. 31–38.

Blustein, P. "U.S., Singapore Near Pact on Trade: Talks are First of Many Bush Administration Plans to Pursue for Bilateral Deals". *The Washington Post,* 20 November 2002.

Bridges Weekly Trade News Digest. "From the Regions: China Intensifies Regional Trade Talks", 7, no. 32 (1 October 2003).

CNA (China News Agency). 上海合作组织成员国总理会晤：温家宝提三倡议 [SCO Premiers' Summit: Wen Jiabao Puts Forward Three Proposals]. 23 September 2003. Available at <http://www.chinanews.com.cn.>.

Chua, L.H. "China-ASEAN Trade Pact — A Landmark Agreement?" *The Strait Times*, 4 November 2002.

CRS Report. "Free Trade Agreements: Impact on U.S. Trade and Implications for U.S. Trade Policy", Congressional Research Service, the U.S. Library of Congress. Prepared by W.H. Cooper, 9 April 2002.

CRTA (Committee on Regional Trade Agreements of the World Trade Organization). *Synopsis of "Systemic" Issues Related to Regional Trade Agreements.* 2 March 2000. WT/REG/W/37.

————. *Annual Report 2003.*

De Castro, I. "China Snuggles up to Southeast Asia", *Asia Times Online,* 7 October 2003. Available at <http://www.atimes.com>.

Dunoff, J. L. "Rethinking International Trade", *University of Pennsylvania Journal of International Economic Law* 19 (1998): 347–89.

Funabashi, Y. "China's Long-Term Strategy: Peaceful Ascendancy". *International Herald Tribune/The Asahi Shimbun,* 2 December 2003.

Gartzke, E., Q. Li and C. Boehmer. "Investing in the Peace: Economic Interdependence and International Conflict". 55, no. 2 (2001): 391–438.

Grimwade, N. *International Trade Policy.* London: Routledge, 1996.

HKTDC (Hong Kong Trade Development Council). "CEPA and Opportunities for Hong Kong". News release, 20 October 2003. Available at <http://www.tdctrade.com/econforum/tdc/tdc031002.htm.>.

Jackson, J.H. *The Jurisprudence of GATT and the WTO: Insights on Treaty Law and Economic Relations.* Cambridge: Cambridge University Press, 2000.

Lewis, L., J. Kerin and N. Wilson. "China: New Economic Era Begins". *The Australian*, 25 October 2003.

Lloyd, P. "Implications for the Multilateral Trading System of the New Preferential Trading Arrangements in the Asia Pacific Region". PECC Trade Forum paper, Vancouver, 11–12 November 2002. Available at <http://www.pecc.org.>.

Mackay, A. "A Trade Bridge to the Mainland". *Financial Times*, 31 December 2003.

Manila Times, The. "Malaysia Early Harvest Clause a Way Out for RB". 7 April 2003*a*.

————. "ASEAN, China Launch First Stage of Free-Trade Plan". 7 October 2003*b*.

Mansfield, E.D. "The Proliferation of Preferential Trading Arrangements". *Journal of Conflict Resolution* 42, no. 5 (1998): 523–43.

Mathis, J. *Regional Trade Agreements in the WTO*. Hague: T.M.C. Asser Press, 2001.

MTI (Ministry of Trade and Industry) of Singapore. *ASEAN-China FTA Facts Sheet*, 2004. Available at <http://www.mti.gov.sg>.

O'Sullivan, F. "Chinese Minister Says Free Trade Deal Likely". *The New Zealand Herald*, 13 January 2004.

Paal, D.H. "The Regional Security Implications of China's Economic Expansion, Military Modernization, and the Rise of Nationalism". In *The Security Environment in the Asia-Pacific*, edited by H. Tien and T. Cheng. Taiwan: The Institute of National Policy Research, 2000, pp. 79–91.

Pottinger, M. "A Back Door to China Opens Wider — Hong Kong Fleshes Out its Chinese Trade Accord, Giving Multinational Hope". *The Wall Street Journal*, 30 September 2003.

Phar, K.B. "ASEAN and China's Regional Concerns". *Asia Times Online*, 21 January 2003. Available at <http://www.atimes.com.>.

Phoenix TV News. 大陆邀台签 CEPA; 台陆委会反对 [The Mainland Extends CEPA Offer to Taiwan, but Taiwan's Mainland Affairs Council is Opposed to It], 13 November 2003. Available at <http://www.phoenixtv.com>.

Schiff, M. and A.L. Winters. *Regional Integration and Development*. Washington D.C.: World Bank and Oxford: Oxford University Press, 2003.

Shen, J. "China's Sovereign over the South China Sea Islands: A Historical Perspective". *Chinese Journal of International Law* 1 (2002): 94–157.

Soesastro, H. "Dynamic of Competitive Liberalization in RTA Negotiations: East Asia Perspectives". PECC Trade Forum Paper, 22–23 April 2003. Available at <http://www.pecc.org.>.

Summers, L. "Regionalism and the World Trading System". In *Trading Blocs: Alternative Approaches to Analyzing Preferential Trade Agreements*, edited by J. Bhagwati, P. Krishna and A. Panagariya. Cambridge: The MIT Press, 1991, pp. 561–66.

Thakur, R. "From National to Human Security". In *Asia-Pacific Security: The Economics-Politics Nexus*, edited by S. Harris and A. Mack, St. Leonards. NSW: Allen & Unwin Australia Pty Ltd, 1997.

UNCTAD (U.N. Conference on Trade and Development). *Assessing Regional Trade Arrangements in the Asia-Pacific*. Policy Issues in International Trade and Commodities: Study Series no. 15, U.N. Doc. UNCTAD/TAB/16, 2001.

USCC (U.S.-China Economic and Security Review Commission). *China's Energy Needs and Strategies*. Public Hearing. 108th Congress, United States. Washington D.C., 30 October 2003*a*.

————. *China's Growth as a Regional Economic Power: Impacts and Implications*. Public Hearing. 108th Congress, United States. Washington D.C., 4 December 2003*b*.

USTR (Office of the United States Trade Representative). Zoellick Embarks on Global Push to Make Strong Progress in 2004 on the Doha Trade Negotiations. USTR press release, 8 February 2004. Available at <http://www.ustr.gov>.

———. Transcript of Ambassador Robert B. Zoellick, Press Conference, Beijing, China. 12 February 2004. Available at <http://www.ustr.gov>.

Vatikiotis, M. and Hiebert, M. "Free Trade Agreement: China's Tight Embrace". *Fast East Economic Review,* 17 July 2003.

Viner, J. *The Customs Union Issue.* Carnegie Endowment for International Peace, 1950.

Wall, D. "East Asia FTA? Dream On". *Japan Times,* 2 July 2003.

Walsh, B. "Will CEPA Make Any Difference". *Time (Asia),* 14 July 2004/vol. 162, no. 1. Available at <http://www.time.com/timie/asia.>.

Wen, J. "Turning Your Eyes to China". Speech of Chinese Premier Wen Jiabao at Harvard University, 10 December 2003.

World Bank. *Trade Blocs.* A World Bank Policy Report. Washington D.C. Oxford: Oxford University Press, 2000.

WTO (World Trade Organization). *Regionalism and the World Trading System.* Geneva: WTO Secretariat, 1995.

———. *Protocol on the Accession of the People's Republic of China.* Decision of 10 November 2001 of the WTO. WT/L432. Geneva, 2001.

———. *Annual Report 2002.* Geneva: WTO Secretariat, 2002.

———. *Compendium of Issues Related to Regional Trade Agreements.* TN/RL/W.8/ Rev. 1, 1 August 2002*b*.

———. *Annual Report 2003.* Geneva: WTO Secretariat, 2003.

———. *Understanding the WTO.* Geneva: WTO Secretariat, 2003*b*.

———. *World Trade Report 2003.* Geneva: WTO Secretariat, 2003*c*.

———. "Membership". Geneva: WTO. <www.wto.org>, 2004.

Xinhua (Xinhua News Agency). 朱镕基出席第四次中国东盟领导人会晤 [Zhu Rongji Attends the Fourth China-ASEAN Summit]. 25 November 2000.

———. 温家宝希望"安排"能为香港带来更多商机 [Wen Jiaobao Wishes CEPA will Bring More Business Opportunities to Hong Kong], 19 July 2003.

4

THE POTENTIAL OUTCOMES OF CHINA-ASEAN FTA

Politico-Economic Implications for Participating Countries

Suthiphand Chirathivat and Sothitorn Mallikamas

1. INTRODUCTION

The last few years of the twentieth century that marked East Asia in both politics and economics, especially for many countries in the ASEAN region, was the Asian crisis, and the emergence of China. Now, the first few years of the new century have been hit by the event of the September 11 attacks that choked the growth engines of the world, in particular the United States and to a certain extent, the EU and Japan. The threat of a war against terrorism and a worsening world economy combined to make East Asia look vulnerable.

Most countries in the region are readjusting to the new reality of the world economy. ASEAN countries, for instance, cannot afford to have another crisis and thus need to boost their own economic resilience. China, on the other hand, has not been deterred from its commitment to remain open and globally integrated, as a new member of the WTO and a strong new growth engine of the world. Relatively speaking, ASEAN economies have been weakened by the crisis, while China poses a formidable challenge, thus ASEAN needs to reconsider its own position *vis-à-vis* the rise of China.

The proposed establishment of an ASEAN-China Free Trade Area (or ASEAN-China FTA) comes at a time of an uncertain global environment.[1] China called on ASEAN countries to set within ten years an economic partnership between the two.[2] It gave special and differential treatment and flexibility to the least developed members of ASEAN. It was agreed that the ASEAN-China FTA would be established by 2010 between China and the original members of ASEAN plus Brunei, and by 2015 for the newer ASEAN member states.[3] Response from the ASEAN countries differed but overall they agreed to work toward these new challenges posed by China.

There will be many preparations needed for both sides in an FTA. Like it or not, this new challenge will be there with the emergence of China and the rethinking of ASEAN's own economic integration. As the agreement started in 2003, the negotiations are actually taking place quite intensively. The details of the FTA need to take into consideration possible implications for participating countries which remain to be interpreted.

2. CONTEXT

Until recently, the ASEAN Free Trade Area (or AFTA) had been the only regional trading arrangement in East Asia. Japan and Singapore then signed an FTA in January 2002 and ASEAN-China FTA set a framework agreement in November 2002. Since these initiatives, there have been more negotiations targetted to set framework agreements for FTAs in East Asia and several of these agreements have started to be formally enacted. Thus, it looks like an ASEAN-China FTA is a natural response to the growing popularity of FTAs regionwide.

Several factors explain the recent rapid expansion of bilateral FTAs in East Asia. (Lloyd 2002; Urata 2003). Rapid expansion of bilateral FTAs in other parts of the world has caused East Asian countries to form its own FTAs. An FTA is also attractive because it provides preferential access to both sides, promotes economic growth, and may draw the attention of outsiders to become more involved with the grouping. For some countries, an FTA provides external pressures to pursue useful and effective domestic policy adjustments which would be otherwise difficult to attain. It also encourages the use of regional trading frameworks to promote economic and other types of co-operation.[4]

Looking closer at the formation of an ASEAN-China FTA, one would find that ASEAN, as a region, is losing its economic attractiveness due to the crisis while China is viewed as an appealing global economic partner. The reality is that China appears to be diverting direct foreign investment from the Southeast Asian region as it also competes with ASEAN for exports to third markets (Chirathivat 2001, 2002), (Panichpakdi and Chifford 2002). Linking the two sides together in an FTA would reinforce each one's own position within the regional and global context.

Trade liberalization has been gradual in ASEAN and China. For ASEAN, progress varies among countries with Singapore being the most advanced, the ASEAN-5 well on their way to liberalization, and CMLV[5] (Cambodia, Myanmar, Laos and Vietnam) not even in the WTO yet, but with all now involved in the AFTA. China, on the other hand, has committed to a comprehensive package of market liberalization in its negotiations to enter the WTO. China's accession to the WTO will require a lot of changes, and this will not be quickly or easily understood throughout China.

The result of the liberalization process has been a large increase in foreign trade for both ASEAN and China. The reduction in tariff and non-tariff barriers has been motivated on different fronts. Multilateral institutions like the WTO encourage member countries to liberalize multilaterally and unilaterally. Since the 1990s, the regional approach to liberalization has also gained momentum (Bhagwati, Krishna and Panagariya 1999). Different countries in various regions including the AFTA, have taken initiatives to liberalize among themselves. In fact, except for CMLV, the rest of the ASEAN countries are close to completing their free trade area. China's trade liberalization is very much watched by outsiders on the extent and progress of its commitments to the WTO.

Both ASEAN and China should be considered as natural trading partners due to their geographical proximity, strong economic growth, rise of income per capita and range of new product diversity and its availability. ASEAN has mostly recovered from the Asian crisis while China is still moving at a high rate of growth. Both ASEAN and China are expected to see continuing growth in the medium term. Within this context, ASEAN-China economic relations have grown rapidly in recent years as detailed in a report by the ASEAN Secretariat:

> ASEAN-China trade totaled US$39.5 billion in the year 2000. ASEAN's share in China's foreign merchandise trade has been continuously on the rise, increasing from 5.8 per cent in 1991 to 8.3 per cent in 2000. ASEAN is now China's fifth biggest trading partner. Meanwhile, the share of China in ASEAN's trade has grown from 2.1 per cent in 1994 to 3.9 per cent in 2000. China is now the sixth largest trade partner of ASEAN.[6]

Even in 2003, China's trade with ASEAN hit a record high of US$78.3 billion, surging by 42.8 per cent year-on-year, according to the Chinese customs statistics.[7] ASEAN has started to benefit from its trade surplus with China. Indeed, China's imports jumped to 57.7 per cent to reach a level of US$47.3 billion while China's exports to ASEAN grew at a pace of 31.1 per cent to US$30.9 billion, leaving a trade deficit of US$16.4 billion in 2003. China mainly bought machinery products and parts, animal fat and plant oil, and mineral and agriculture products from ASEAN countries such as Malaysia, Indonesia and Thailand; and sold machinery and electronic products, chemicals, fabrics and garments.

China's increasing imports seem to be concentrated on China's needs of raw materials and parts and components.[8] With China's growing economy and recovery of ASEAN countries, bilateral trade will continue to grow with China becoming a new drive for the East Asian region. Thus, there is strong potential for further linking trade and investment between ASEAN and China despite both claiming their major export markets in the developed countries and both being major destinations among LDCs for foreign direct investment. Meanwhile, both ASEAN and China have identified existing measures that hamper their trade and investment.[9]

Mutual benefits through economic co-operation between ASEAN and China are seen as essential to develop further economic linkages between them, with an ASEAN-China Free Trade Area as a desirable option. An ASEAN-China FTA was seen by the parties as:

> "An important move forward in terms of economic integration in East Asia" as well as "a foundation for the more ambitious vision of an East Asian Free Trade Area, encompassing ASEAN, China, Japan, and Korea".[10]

In November 2002, at the annual ASEAN-China summit meeting, a "Framework Agreement on ASEAN-China Economic Co-operation" was signed. With this framework, both sides set a free trade area within ten years, with special and differential treatment given to ASEAN's new members.[11] As part of these liberalization bilateral arrangements,[12] individual ASEAN countries are open to negotiate with China for their specific market sectors.

3. IMPLICATIONS

With the ASEAN-China FTA set to become an integral part of the future course of ASEAN-China economic relations, one could ask what would be the economic benefits of such an initiative. Certainly, there are strategic interests for both sides to be considered. How would ASEAN deal with China's dominance in an economic area with a population of 1.7 billion, GDP of about US$2 trillion and total trade estimated at US$1.23 trillion?[13] It will be the largest FTA in the world in terms of population and one made up of developing countries at different levels of development.

For the ASEAN-6 (Indonesia, Malaysia, the Philippines, Singapore, Thailand and Vietnam), average tariff rates on Chinese products are already low compared to Chinese tariff rates on ASEAN products which are still quite high even with China's accession to the WTO (see Table 4.1). Non-tariff barriers imposed by China against ASEAN are also in general much higher than the reciprocal non-tariff barriers (see Table 4.2).

TABLE 4.1
Import-Weighted Average Tariff Rates

Unit: %

ASEAN applied to China		China applied to ASEAN	
Fruits & vegetables	5.0	Fruits & vegetables	27.4
Coal	9.4	Oil seeds	21.4
Food products	5.0	Petroleum products	8.4
Electrical goods	4.8	Rice	112.8
Drinks/tobacco	6.2	Chemical, rubber & plastic products	19.2
Machinery	3.4	Electrical Goods	16.6
Average	2.3	Average	9.4

Source : Chulalongkorn and Monash General Equilibrium Model (CAMGEM), Chulalongkorn University.

TABLE 4.2
Import-Weighted Average Incidence Rates of Non-tariff Barriers

Unit: %

ASEAN applied to China		China applied to ASEAN	
Other commodities	13.6	Other commodities	76.6
Milk products	17.0	Rice	100.0
Drinks/tobacco	51.2	Metal products	83.7
Textiles	7.3	Leather products	76.8
Mineral products	9.6	Forestry products	96.8
Average	9.2	Average	69.1

Source: Same as Table 4.1, UNCTAD databases.

In a FTA, abolishment of trade barriers will allow trade expansion between ASEAN and China which could be realized through trade creation or through trade diversion. The removal of trade barriers will lower costs, expand intra-regional trade and increase economic efficiency. This will help to boost real income in both regions as resources flow to sectors where they can be more efficiently and productively utilized.

In addition to the increased trade within the FTA, non-members might come to engage in greater trade and investment with the FTA members as their economies become more outward oriented. By enlarging the market, establishment of the ASEAN-China FTA will intensify competition, increase investment and bring about economies of scale which will have spillover effects in research and development and technological improvement in the long-run. It remains to be seen what would be the "dynamic" time-path (Bhagwati 1993) of such a creation.

There are, however, also potential concerns associated with an ASEAN-China FTA. Even after the FTA is fully implemented, varying degrees of discrimination across products and countries will remain due to differences in the rules of origin. The rules of origin create significant costs for administrative surveillance and implementation. This could cause complications if different countries in ASEAN and perhaps China get involved in an increasing number of separate but overlapping FTAs.[14] That is why in preference to an FTA, some economists[15] advocate a customs union which is characterized by a common external tariff (CET) equivalent to the lowest tariff prevailing in any of the member countries.[16]

Apart from the issue of rules of origin, a large number of members in an FTA might confuse investors as to which rules, obligations and incentives correspond to which partner. Also, the time and effort that will be required to negotiate and implement the FTA are still unknown, and the process may distract attention from the bigger WTO agenda. At this point, ASEAN and China have yet to start the long process of negotiations for trade liberalization under the FTA.

4. SIMULATION RESULTS

The effects of an ASEAN-China FTA have been simulated for this chapter using the model of the Global Trade Analysis Project (GTAP)[17] as adapted in the Chulalongkorn and Monash General Equilibrium Model (CAMGEM) of Chulalongkorn University, Thailand. The model contains forty-five countries and fifty production sectors. The structure of the model is outlined in Appendix 4.1.

In the modeling exercise, it is assumed that rates of trade protection are reduced to zero with all tariff barriers eliminated.

WHAT COULD HAPPEN TO CHINA?

Macroeconomic Impact

The results from GTAP simulation show that ASEAN-China FTA will lead to a decline in price level due to the reduction of China's import tariff rates. In addition, FTA will result in higher demands for China exports due to the reduction of ASEAN's tariff rates and greater competitiveness of China products in the world market. Higher export demands lead to greater demands for primary inputs such as labour and land. As a result, average wage rate will increase by 0.61 per cent while land rent will increase by 0.23 per cent. In addition, the import tariff cut will result in a decline the GDP deflator by 0.17 per cent (see Table 4.3).

Tariff elimination between ASEAN and China will boost the total China's exports by 2.37 per cent. The trade creation effect will lead to a sharp rise in China's exports to ASEAN by 23 per cent, Vietnam by 91.6 per cent, Thailand by 55 per cent and Phillipines 46.6 per cent. In addition, the exports to other countries will slightly expand due to cost reduction from import tariff cut which strengthens the competitiveness of Chinese products in the world market. (see Table 4.4.)

The ASEAN-China trade agreement will also create trade diversion. China will increase its import value from ASEAN by 53.3 per cent while decrease its import value from USA by 2.39 per cent Japan by 1.31 per cent, and the EU by 1.5 per cent (see Table 4.4).

The FTA has impact not only on external demand but also internal demand. Higher export income and lower commodity prices will increase private consumption in China by 0.4 per cent. Aggregate savings will rise by 0.17 per cent. Private investment is expected to increase by 0.74 per cent, caused mainly by greater export opportunities. Overall, the welfare of China will improve by US$1,787 million (see Table 4.3).

Sectoral Impact

The GTAP results show both positive and negative FTA impact on each sector in Table 4.5. On the positive side, some sectors such as textiles, apparel, motor vehicles and parts, and electronic equipment are expected to gain from improving market access to ASEAN's market due to lower barriers. While

TABLE 4.3
Macroeconomic Impact of ASEAN-China FTA

Country / Variable	ASEAN			China			Korea	Japan	USA	EU	ROW
	Overall	Internal	External	Overall	Internal	External					
Rental price of capital (%)	0.19	-0.11	0.30	0.00	-0.25	0.24	-0.02	-0.01	0.01	0.01	0.01
Rental price of land (%)	3.64	0.07	3.55	0.23	-0.60	0.83	-0.19	0.07	0.11	0.14	0.18
Labour wage rate (%)	0.97	0.09	0.88	0.61	0.15	0.45	-0.16	-0.06	-0.03	-0.03	-0.05
Average price of primary factor (%)	0.76	-0.02	0.78	0.28	-0.11	0.39	-0.10	-0.04	-0.02	-0.02	-0.01
Price of GDP (market price) (%)	0.55	-0.17	0.72	-0.17	-0.52	0.35	-0.09	-0.04	-0.02	-0.02	-0.01
Import price (%)	0.03	-0.01	0.04	0.04	0.05	-0.01	0.02	0.04	0.00	-0.01	0.01
Export price (%)	0.34	-0.11	0.44	-0.11	-0.37	0.26	-0.05	-0.03	-0.01	-0.01	0.00
Terms of trade (%)	0.31	-0.09	0.40	-0.14	-0.42	0.27	-0.07	-0.07	-0.02	-0.01	-0.01
Aggregate capital stock (%)	0.83	0.26	0.56	0.74	0.54	0.20	-0.16	-0.06	-0.05	-0.04	-0.07
Real GDP (factor cost) (%)	0.38	0.09	0.29	0.30	0.18	0.12	-0.07	-0.02	-0.01	-0.01	-0.03
Real GDP (market prices) (%)	0.38	0.12	0.27	0.36	0.24	0.12	-0.08	-0.02	-0.02	-0.01	-0.03
Real private consumption (%)	0.46	0.04	0.41	0.40	0.24	0.15	-0.09	-0.03	-0.02	-0.01	-0.04
Real government consumption (%)	0.52	-0.05	0.57	0.09	-0.09	0.18	-0.05	-0.02	-0.01	-0.01	-0.02
Real investment (%)	0.83	0.26	0.56	0.74	0.54	0.20	-0.16	-0.06	-0.05	0.00	-0.07
Real saving (%)	0.78	0.05	0.73	0.17	-0.06	0.23	-0.10	-0.02	-0.01	-0.01	-0.02
Export volumes (%)	0.95	0.45	0.48	2.37	1.98	0.37	-0.05	0.01	-0.01	-0.01	-0.05
Import volumes (%)	1.27	0.43	0.82	3.44	2.74	0.66	-0.16	-0.11	-0.05	-0.03	-0.08
Trade balance (millions $)	-177.68	-319.63	147.87	-979.93	-1238.35	267.45	74.37	190.61	233.46	149.70	262.68
Welfare (million $)	2986.22	190.09	2785.73	1787.05	587.59	1191.72	-101.86	-332.42	-118.56	-180.48	-167.15

Source: Same as Table 4.1.

TABLE 4.3
Macroeconomic Impact of ASEAN-China FTA

Country / Variable	Thailand			Malaysia			
	Overall	Internal	External	Overall	Internal	External	Overall
Rental price of capital (%)	−0.06	−0.30	0.21	0.26	−0.10	0.36	0.22
Rental price of land (%)	9.96	0.38	9.71	3.85	0.20	3.70	0.62
Labour wage rate (%)	0.93	0.12	0.87	1.05	0.12	0.99	0.55
Average price of primary factor (%)	0.77	−0.15	0.92	0.87	0.00	0.90	0.40
Price of GDP (market price) (%)	0.40	−0.40	0.77	0.58	−0.17	0.75	0.33
Import price (%)	0.02	0.00	0.02	0.05	−0.01	0.06	0.05
Export price (%)	0.59	−0.22	0.81	0.36	−0.10	0.46	0.25
Terms of trade (%)	0.57	−0.21	0.79	0.31	−0.08	0.40	0.20
Aggregate capital stock (%)	0.75	0.62	0.23	0.60	0.27	0.41	0.40
Real GDP (factor cost) (%)	0.33	0.29	0.06	0.46	0.13	0.36	0.18
Real GDP (market prices) (%)	0.32	0.34	0.01	0.44	0.15	0.32	0.19
Real private consumption (%)	0.48	0.21	0.28	0.67	−0.05	0.74	0.18
Real government consumption (%)	0.23	−0.05	0.26	0.67	0.27	0.41	0.30
Real investment (%)	0.75	0.62	0.23	0.60	0.38	0.51	0.40
Real saving (%)	0.82	0.19	0.65	0.80	0.40	0.78	0.32
Export volumes (%)	1.05	1.04	0.17	0.79	−55.07	184.97	0.62
Import volumes (%)	1.45	0.96	0.67	1.05	0.07	0.78	0.92
Trade balance (millions $)	−59.98	−212.86	117.15	135.30	54.33	596.16	−12.13
Welfare (million $)	422.33	254.20	555.05	282.13	0.09	0.63	113.91

Source: Same as Table 4.1.

TABLE 4.3 – cont'd

Indonesia		Phillipines			Singapore			Vietnam		
Internal	External	Overall	Internal	External	Overall	Internal	External	Overall	Internal	External
–0.09	0.32	–0.12	–0.26	0.11	0.15	–0.04	0.19	–0.24	–1.02	0.26
0.04	0.57	0.75	–0.55	1.14	2.00	0.16	1.86	2.34	1.82	2.00
0.06	0.54	0.18	–0.10	0.24	1.02	–0.19	1.28	1.95	0.92	0.43
–0.01	0.44	0.08	–0.22	0.26	0.56	–0.11	0.70	1.35	0.44	0.56
–0.08	0.43	–0.27	–0.55	0.23	0.53	–0.10	0.66	–0.21	–1.80	0.48
0.00	0.04	0.05	0.00	0.03	0.04	–0.03	0.07	0.11	0.02	0.09
–0.08	0.35	–0.18	–0.34	0.12	0.21	–0.05	0.28	0.02	–0.79	0.37
–0.08	0.31	–0.23	–0.34	0.09	0.17	–0.03	0.21	–0.08	–0.80	0.28
0.18	0.26	0.21	0.12	0.08	1.08	–0.23	1.39	1.53	1.37	–0.12
0.07	0.13	0.08	–0.03	0.07	0.58	–0.12	0.74	0.68	–0.02	0.01
0.08	0.13	0.11	0.02	0.05	0.60	–0.13	0.76	0.78	0.23	–0.03
0.02	0.30	–0.02	–0.39	0.13	0.90	–0.15	0.96	0.67	–1.54	0.19
0.18	0.26	–0.20	0.12	0.08	0.76	–0.23	1.39	–0.10	1.37	–0.12
0.41	0.26	0.21	1.84	0.12	1.08	–0.12	1.15	1.53	5.55	–0.12
0.45	0.56	–0.04	1.05	0.19	0.98	–0.16	1.38	0.73	5.08	0.02
–46.66	31.89	1.68	19.18	–17.94	0.94	11.04	–41.30	2.86	–66.37	9.87
0.08	0.27	1.07	–0.31	0.21	1.13	–0.17	1.23	2.87	–0.81	0.24
82.70	361.03	–2.76	–115.72	60.17	–31.10	–97.18	638.58	–34.51	–61.19	19.28
0.04	0.16	–72.62	–0.17	0.10	229.26	–0.18	1.14	–8.09	–0.18	0.11

TABLE 4.4
Impact of ASEAN-China FTA on Trade Flows (%)

	CHINA	ASEAN	THAI	MALAY	INDO	PHI	SING	VIET	JAPAN	USA	EU	ROW	Total
CHINA	-100.00	23.07	55.01	28.36	23.67	46.58	1.52	91.59	0.04	0.13	0.12	0.07	1.91
ASEAN	53.27	-0.79	64.74	–	–	–	–	–	-1.41	-0.83	-1.04	-1.21	0.76
THAI	63.33	5.45	0.00	-1.42	-4.62	-5.28	0.79	-6.05	-1.82	-1.11	-1.45	-2.38	0.74
MALAY	52.98	–	-2.40	0.00	-1.61	-3.35	0.37	-6.01	-1.51	-0.98	-1.24	-1.58	0.63
INDO	26.85	–	-2.70	-0.71	0.00	-2.94	0.76	-10.06	-0.75	-0.63	-0.72	-0.78	0.46
PHI	31.34	–	-1.17	0.95	0.78	0.00	1.73	-4.80	0.55	2.18	0.91	0.72	1.55
SING	68.58	–	-1.67	-0.55	-0.79	-3.27	0.00	-8.72	-0.83	-0.76	-0.83	-0.85	0.83
VIET	10.06	–	-1.18	9.08	-0.77	3.92	1.20	0.00	1.93	-0.52	4.96	0.51	2.80
JAPAN	-1.31	0.23	-0.81	0.33	-0.27	-0.88	1.24	-5.73	0.00	0.05	0.05	0.03	-0.07
USA	-2.39	0.54	-0.34	0.81	0.00	-0.76	1.19	-3.58	0.02	0.00	-0.02	-0.02	-0.04
EU	-1.50	0.38	-0.25	0.50	0.03	-1.69	1.23	-3.81	-0.02	-0.02	-0.02	-0.03	-0.04
ROW	-2.08	0.63	-0.55	0.62	-0.24	-1.14	1.52	-3.90	0.15	-0.03	-0.02	0.02	-0.09
Total	1.61	1.03	0.95	0.97	0.67	0.43	1.17	1.43	-0.07	-0.05	-0.03	-0.07	0.07

Source: Same as Table 4.1.

Impact of ASEAN-China FTA on China's Production Sectors

Sector	MFN		Output			Price	Exports	Imports	Change in Trade balance
	ASEAN	China	T	I	E				US$ mil.
	%	%	%	%	%	%	%	%	
Agriculture									
1 Paddy	0.00	0.00	-0.83	0.15	-0.95	0.16	-0.18	-2.40	0.01
2 Wheat	0.00	0.00	-0.52	-0.04	-0.48	0.20	-0.81	-0.20	3.59
3 Cereal grain	0.76	1.76	-0.52	0.02	-0.53	0.20	0.37	-0.07	1.42
4 Veg, fruit, nuts	5.04	27.43	0.31	0.29	0.06	0.37	2.68	35.32	4.94
5 Oil seeds	1.45	21.25	-4.23	0.03	-4.35	-0.51	6.84	-6.01	42.93
6 Sugar cane, sugar beet	2.00	0.00	-2.87	-0.56	-2.31	-0.36	2.39	-7.51	53.78
7 Plant-based fibres	0.29	8.14	1.02	0.26	0.73	0.44	-1.03	1.90	-26.91
8 Other crops	2.96	15.88	-1.17	0.28	-1.40	0.01	4.30	26.38	-180.48
9 Livestocks	2.22	7.83	0.43	0.18	0.26	0.08	-0.46	0.57	-0.13
10 Other animal products	3.36	20.60	0.35	-0.03	0.37	0.25	-0.69	1.74	-13.53
11 Raw milk	0.00	0.00	0.64	0.04	0.59	-0.26	0.34	0.34	0.00
12 Wool, silkworm cocoons	2.06	7.17	1.96	-0.60	2.53	-0.93	4.13	-0.55	15.00
Natural Resources									
13 Forestry	2.42	2.19	0.37	0.11	0.26	0.42	-1.81	3.41	-15.32
14 Fishing	10.40	17.62	-0.17	0.06	-0.22	0.18	-0.21	2.27	-2.18
15 Coal	9.36	3.37	0.48	0.09	0.38	0.30	-0.73	1.47	-9.00
16 Oil	0.43	7.90	0.19	-0.12	0.29	0.17	0.23	2.63	-63.17
17 Gas	13.90	0.00	0.48	-0.02	0.50	0.26	2.40	0.68	-3.48
18 Other minerals	3.42	0.44	0.59	-0.03	0.59	0.15	0.93	1.08	-7.02
Agro-industry									
19 Meat products	1.55	23.92	0.67	-0.31	0.95	-0.22	1.94	0.31	2.65
20 Poultry, seafood	4.86	25.71	-0.47	-0.41	-0.10	0.16	-0.05	45.37	-61.40
21 Veg, oils and fats	1.98	35.13	-7.49	-0.15	-7.40	-0.59	3.37	25.30	-548.45
22 Dairy products	7.32	12.59	0.65	0.36	0.32	-1.33	12.77	-0.93	3.21
23 Processed rice	0.00	112.79	-3.28	0.09	-3.39	-0.25	4.54	251.27	-515.79
24 Sugar	0.54	26.06	-6.28	0.18	-6.41	-0.11	2.51	22.62	-275.03
25 Other food products	4.97	27.69	0.24	0.26	0.00	-0.20	4.16	10.47	-18.81

continued on next page

TABLE 4.5 – cont'd

Sector	MFN		Output			Price	Exports	Imports	Change in Trade balance
	ASEAN	China	T	I	E				US$ mil.
	%	%	%	%	%	%	%	%	
Manufacturing — labor intensive									
26 Beverages, tobacco products	6.22	49.72	0.97	2.06	-0.55	-0.27	39.74	68.11	91.08
27 Textiles	11.35	22.05	1.22	0.53	0.67	-0.03	5.45	2.18	107.29
28 Apparels	4.51	31.50	1.02	-0.92	1.86	-0.09	1.37	3.58	307.92
29 Leather products	6.91	10.18	0.70	-1.54	2.11	-0.04	0.83	1.28	122.29
30 Wood products	14.68	6.88	-0.76	-0.38	-0.40	-0.25	2.01	10.15	-189.18
Capital intensive									
31 Paper prods., publishing	5.08	11.14	0.33	0.18	0.16	0.00	2.42	1.72	-40.87
32 Petroleum, coal products	0.32	8.36	0.51	0.21	0.32	0.05	6.66	1.51	18.89
33 Chem, rubber, plastic prods.	6.35	19.16	0.50	0.26	0.24	-0.08	3.08	1.64	-81.25
34 Other mineral products	8.37	19.20	0.77	0.42	0.38	0.08	4.29	5.83	45.51
35 Ferrous metals	3.68	11.20	0.89	0.25	0.60	0.09	4.06	1.43	98.26
36 Other metals	2.33	6.90	0.52	-0.01	0.48	0.03	2.34	2.34	-47.86
37 Metal products	7.05	13.51	0.78	0.36	0.41	0.05	3.46	2.59	75.58
Technology									
38 Motor vehicles and parts	10.71	20.11	1.40	0.85	0.68	0.01	58.74	1.38	213.89
39 Other transport equipment	0.14	5.19	1.04	-0.10	1.03	0.01	3.47	1.76	17.90
40 Electronic equipment	4.81	16.63	2.09	0.82	1.44	-0.29	4.07	2.74	255.91
41 Other machinery, equipment	3.35	10.20	0.59	-0.04	0.60	0.02	1.65	1.49	-263.55
42 Other manufactures	3.14	14.47	0.59	-0.32	0.88	-0.01	1.21	2.01	138.62
Services									
43 Electricity	0.00	0.00	0.49	0.17	0.33	0.12	-0.66	0.84	-3.37
44 Gas manufacture, distribution	3.00	7.72	0.44	0.22	0.25	0.18	0.42	0.42	0.00
45 Water	0.00	0.00	0.42	0.16	0.27	0.11	0.44	0.44	0.00
46 Construction	0.00	0.00	0.74	0.25	0.51	0.10	-0.39	0.40	-1.58
47 Trade, transport	0.00	0.00	0.49	0.06	0.43	0.01	0.04	0.37	-31.76
48 Finance, business, recreation	0.00	0.00	0.41	0.02	0.39	0.08	-0.30	0.51	-37.66
49 PubAd., defence, edu., health	0.00	0.00	0.12	0.20	-0.06	0.21	-0.79	0.67	-14.14
50 Dwellings	0.00	0.00	0.42	0.11	0.32	0.07	0.45	0.45	0.00

Note:
T: Total Effects, I: Internal Effects, E: External Effects
Source: Same as Table 4.1

sectors such as textiles, other food products, motor vehicles, and other mineral products gain from lower input costs due to lower China's tariffs. On the negative side, some sectors may experience lower output resulting from import substitutions.

Positive Impact from Market Access into ASEAN Market

Apparel benefits from ASEAN's tariff reduction of 4.5 per cent. Exports to ASEAN will increase by 31.5 per cent. Moreover, the lower cost of apparel due to China's tariff cut, together with a better market access into ASEAN, lead to an increase in the total sectoral exports by 1.4 per cent and a rise in the trade balance for the products by US$307.9 million.

Electronic equipment will benefit from ASEAN's tariff reduction of 4.8 per cent. As a result, the exports to ASEAN will increase by 16.6 per cent while the total sectoral exports will increase by 4.1 per cent. The output of electronic equipments will expand at the rate of 2.1 per cent. The trade balance for the products will rise by US$255.9 million.

Positive Impact from Lower Costs

Other food products will benefit mainly from the lower costs of production due to China's tariff rate cuts. When tariff rates of agricultural products are reduced, the intermediate input costs of other food products will decline, resulting in the decrease of costs by 0.2 per cent. This greater competitiveness will rise the export demand by 4.2 per cent. Lower price, improvement of Chinese income and higher export demand will raise the output of other food products by 0.24 per cent.[18]

Textiles will benefit, not only from ASEAN market access but also from lower cost of production due to China's tariff rate cuts. When tariff rates of its intermediate input are reduced, the intermediate input cost of textiles will decline, resulting in the decrease of cost and price by 0.03 per cent. This greater competitiveness will rise the export demand by 5.5 per cent. An increase in wearing apparel outputs, improvement of Chinese income and higher export demand will raise the output of textiles by 1.2 per cent.

Electronic equipment will not only benefit from a better market access into ASEAN but also from lower costs of production. The cost and price of Chinese products will reduce by 0.3 per cent and this will result in a higher export demand.

Negative Impact from Import Substitution

Rice will experience a decline in outputs due to import substitution. China's tariff reduction of 112.8 per cent will increase imports from ASEAN by 234 per cent while the sectoral total imports will rise by 251 per cent. As a result, the output of rice will drop by 3.3 per cent and the sectoral trade balance will decline by US$515.8 million.

Sugar is expected to face a decline in outputs due to import substitution. China's tariff reduction of 26 per cent will increase imports from ASEAN by 103 per cent while the sectoral total imports will rise by 22.6 per cent. As a result, the output of sugar will drop by 6.3 per cent and the sectoral trade balance will decline by US$275 million.

Vegetable oils is likely to have a slightly lower output caused by import substitution, particularly from Malaysia. A 35.1 per cent cut in China's tariff will lead to a 146 per cent increase in import from ASEAN. Total import in the sector will increase by 25.3 per cent while the trade balance will decline by US$548.5 million.

Poultry and seafood will face a higher competition from ASEAN. A 25.7 per cent tariff cut in imports of poultry and seafood will increase imports from ASEAN by 89 per cent. The output in this sector will decrease by 0.47 per cent and the trade balance will worsen by US$61.4 million.

WHAT COULD HAPPEN TO ASEAN?

Macroeconomic Impact

ASEAN-China FTA will mainly benefit ASEAN through an increasing market access in China's huge market. A rise in ASEAN's exports, such as rice, sugar, vegetable oils, textiles and leather products increases the demand for primary factors of products. Wage and rental price of land will rise by 1.0 per cent and 3.6 per cent, respectively. This leads to an increase of 0.6 per cent in the GDP deflator. The higher demand for Thailand's exports will rise in the export price index by 0.34 per cent (see Table 4.3).

The FTA results in a significant trade creation. Namely, there will be a 53.3 per cent surge in ASEAN's exports to China while ASEAN's imports from China will rise by 23 per cent. This leads to an increase in the total exports of 0.95 per cent. Due to cheaper products from China and expansion of the overall economy, ASEAN's total imports from China and the rest of the world will increase by 1.27 per cent. As a result, trade balance may decline by US$177.7 million (see Table 4.4).

The FTA will create some trade diversion effects. The intra-trade within ASEAN members will significantly decline. For example, exports of Thailand to Vietnam and the Philippines will be declined by 6 per cent and 5.3 per cent respectively, while the exports of ASEAN to the United States and Japan will drop by 0.83 per cent and 1.41 respectively.

The FTA expands not only ASEAN's external sector but also internal sector. Gross domestic investment in ASEAN will rise by 0.83 per cent. While the private consumption and savings will increase by 0.46%and 0.78 per cent respectively. As a result, the real GDP will increase by 0.38 per cent. This leads to a 545.2 per cent increase in welfare of the ASEAN (see Table 4.3).

Sectoral Impact

According to the GTAP results of sectoral impact shown in Table 4.6. Like China's case, the FTA creates both positive and negative impacts on productive sectors. On the positive side, some sectors such as rice, sugar, vegetable oils, and textile, chemical, rubber and plastic products, and vehicles and parts may benefit from more exports to China. On the negative side, due to lower ASEAN's lower trade barriers, imports from China will cause a decline in ASEAN's output of vegetables and fruits. In addition, better cost competitiveness of other Chinese food products, apparel and leather products due to the FTA is likely to cause ASEAN output to suffer.

Positive Impact from Market Access into China's Market

Rice, particularly from Thailand and Vietnam, will benefit from a 112.8 per cent reduction in China's import tariff. As a result, the exports to China will increase 234.4 per cent, causing total exports and production of rice to increase by 24.7 per cent and 3.5 per cent respectively. The trade balance will rise by US$468.7 million. The domestic price of rice will increase by 2 per cent.

Sugar, particularly from Thailand and Vietnam, will benefit from a 26 per cent reduction in China's import tariff. As a result, the exports to China will increase by 103.1 per cent, causing total exports and production of sugar to increase by 23 per cent and 5.9 per cent respectively. The trade balance will rise by US$328.7 million. The domestic price of sugar will increase by 1.3 per cent.

Vegetable oils, particularly from Malaysia, will benefit from a 35.1 per cent tariff reduction. The exports to China will grow by 146 per cent while

TABLE 4.6
Impact of ASEAN-China FTA on ASEAN's Production Sectors

Sector	MFN		Output			Price	Exports	Imports	Change in Trade balance
	ASEAN	China	T	I	E				US$ mil.
	%	%	%	%	%	%	%	%	%
Agriculture									
1 Paddy	0.00	0.00	3.04	0.03	3.00	2.86	-9.01	3.90	-4.44
2 Wheat	0.00	0.00	-0.26	0.10	-0.36	0.44	-0.54	1.36	-19.55
3 Cereal grain	0.76	1.76	-0.27	0.01	-0.28	1.72	-3.84	3.95	-26.03
4 Veg, fruit, nuts	5.04	27.43	-0.41	-0.12	-0.28	1.67	-1.98	5.14	-72.94
5 Oil seeds	1.45	21.25	2.56	0.00	2.56	2.69	-5.90	6.56	-50.68
6 Sugar cane, sugar beet	2.00	0.00	1.63	0.03	1.59	2.20	-9.09	4.21	-79.64
7 Plant-based fibres	0.29	8.14	0.26	0.01	0.24	1.89	-4.00	3.62	-67.16
8 Other crops	2.96	15.88	-1.00	-0.05	-0.94	1.30	-1.56	1.94	-83.56
9 Livestocks	2.22	7.83	-0.29	0.06	-0.35	1.66	-5.36	3.61	-8.74
10 Other animal products	3.36	20.60	-0.03	0.02	-0.04	1.39	-1.29	3.18	-24.16
11 Raw milk	0.00	0.00	-0.31	0.06	-0.38	1.52	0.19	0.19	0.00
12 Wool, silkworm cocoons	2.06	7.17	0.80	0.26	0.53	0.42	0.98	2.43	-3.43
Natural Resources									
13 Forestry	2.42	2.19	0.25	0.13	0.12	0.57	-1.13	1.54	-17.24
14 Fishing	10.40	17.62	-0.08	0.04	-0.12	1.10	-3.29	2.32	-30.36
15 Coal	9.36	3.37	-1.90	-0.33	-1.55	0.73	-3.36	2.23	-39.01
16 Oil	0.43	7.90	-0.65	0.14	-0.78	1.03	-0.57	1.07	-140.26
17 Gas	13.90	0.00	-1.33	0.07	-1.39	0.84	-2.48	1.59	-111.67
18 Other minerals	3.42	0.44	-0.69	0.14	-0.82	0.54	-2.35	1.21	-134.52
Agro-industry									
19 Meat products	1.55	23.92	-0.29	0.12	-0.40	1.07	2.14	2.00	-7.70
20 Poultry, seafood	4.86	25.71	0.37	0.01	0.36	0.87	1.20	2.44	28.53
21 Veg, oils and fats	1.98	35.13	6.67	0.14	6.48	0.85	13.12	1.46	834.87
22 Dairy products	7.32	12.59	-0.40	0.07	-0.47	0.53	-0.32	0.59	-9.99
23 Processed rice	0.00	112.79	3.53	0.02	3.48	2.07	24.74	3.20	468.70
24 Sugar	0.54	26.06	5.89	0.03	5.82	1.34	23.06	2.03	328.71
25 Other food products	4.97	27.69	-0.11	0.04	-0.15	0.68	0.01	1.66	-16.72

26 Beverages, tobacco products	6.22	49.72	1.60	-0.67	2.27	0.41	25.77	7.44	148.11
27 Textiles	11.35	22.05	3.34	0.14	3.16	0.02	9.64	3.67	388.90
28 Apparels	4.51	31.50	0.38	1.73	-1.32	-0.07	0.90	5.93	22.24
29 Leather products	6.91	10.18	-0.16	1.89	-2.01	0.05	0.33	3.50	-52.17
30 Wood products	14.68	6.88	0.33	0.13	0.20	0.42	0.40	2.53	51.17
31 Paper prods., publishing	5.08	11.14	0.79	0.06	0.72	0.30	2.16	1.12	21.81
32 Petroleum, coal products	0.32	8.36	0.16	0.13	0.03	0.42	-0.46	0.62	-66.45
33 Chem, rubber, plastic prods.	6.35	19.16	1.74	0.05	1.68	0.38	3.77	1.55	285.45
34 Other mineral products	8.37	19.20	0.54	-0.35	0.88	0.31	3.62	3.00	-46.99
35 Ferrous metals	3.68	11.20	0.56	-0.04	0.59	0.20	3.21	1.17	-118.81
36 Other metals	2.33	6.90	1.79	0.21	1.56	0.29	2.73	1.02	31.49
37 Metal products	7.05	13.51	0.78	-0.25	1.02	0.14	3.07	2.23	-32.26
38 Motor vehicles and parts	10.71	20.11	0.80	0.27	0.51	0.12	8.11	1.41	-78.38
39 Other transport equipment	0.14	5.19	0.48	0.54	-0.07	0.21	0.93	0.85	-41.92
40 Electronic equipment	4.81	16.63	0.51	0.37	0.14	0.10	0.60	0.93	161.05
41 Other machinery, equipment	3.35	10.20	0.86	0.46	0.38	0.08	0.95	0.76	-241.74
42 Other manufactures	3.14	14.47	-0.07	0.34	-0.41	0.17	-0.07	0.99	-99.44
43 Electricity	0.00	0.00	0.59	0.12	0.46	0.38	-2.10	1.23	-0.06
44 Gas manufacture, distribution	3.00	7.72	0.56	0.09	0.47	0.50	0.64	0.64	0.00
45 Water	0.00	0.00	0.50	0.12	0.37	0.35	0.46	0.46	0.00
46 Construction	0.00	0.00	0.79	0.25	0.53	0.29	-0.99	0.98	-49.57
47 Trade, transport	0.00	0.00	0.02	0.14	-0.12	0.42	-1.14	1.16	-694.37
48 Finance, business, recreation	0.00	0.00	0.07	0.14	-0.06	0.37	-1.38	0.98	-339.90
49 PubAd., defence, edu., health	0.00	0.00	0.22	-0.03	0.25	0.56	-2.06	1.40	-138.85
50 Dwellings	0.00	0.00	0.45	0.06	0.39	0.28	0.63	0.63	0.00

Row group labels (left margin): Manufacturing — labor intensive (26–30), Capital intensive (31–37), Technology (38–42); Services (43–50).

Note:
T: Total Effects, I: Internal Effects, E: External Effects
Source: Same as Table 4.1.

total exports will increase by 13.1 per cent. As a result, output in this sector will expand by 6.7 per cent while trade balance will rise by US$834.8 million.

Textiles will benefit from a 22 per cent reduction in China's tariff rate and an expansion in China's apparel sector. ASEAN's export of textiles to China is likely to grow by 133 per cent, leading to a 9.6 per cent surge in total textile exports. As a result, the production will expand by 3.3 per cent while the trade balance will gain US$388.9 million.

Chemicals, rubber and plastic products are likely to gain from a 19.2 per cent cut in tariff barriers. ASEAN's exports to China will surge by 77.6 per cent while the total exports will grow by 3.8 per cent. This leads to an output expansion of 1.7 per cent and the trade balance will increase by US$285.4 million.

Vehicles and parts will benefit from a 20.1 per cent tariff cut. The exports of automobile industry to China will grow by 473.5 per cent while its total exports will increase by 8.1 per cent. As a result, production will expand 0.8 per cent.

Negative Impact from Lower Cost of Imports

Vegetables and fruits will experience a decline in output due to import substitution. ASEAN's tariff reduction of 5 per cent will increase imports from China by 19.8 per cent while the sectoral total imports will rise by 5.1 per cent. As a result, the output will drop by 0.4 per cent and the sectoral trade balance will decline by US$72.9 million.

Apparels, like food, will face a higher competition from Chinese lower cost of production and ASEAN's 4.51 per cent tariff cut in imports. These will increase imports from China by 107.5 per cent. Total imports of apparels are likely to increase by 5.9 per cent. As a result, the output in this sector will decrease by 0.38 per cent.

The overall result of the simulation is that there are trade gains for both ASEAN and China from forming an FTA. Trade creation will more than offset trade diversion for ASEAN while for China there is no obvious trade diversion. It remains to be seen how ASEAN and China will use these opportunities to strengthen their economic relationships. The simulation shows that China would look increasingly at ASEAN as an alternative source of inputs for natural resource-based or intermediate products. China still needs sources of imported inputs to satisfy the needs of its manufacturing industries which domestic suppliers may not be able to meet. With continuing strong growth in China, ASEAN could come to play a crucial role in supplying China's demand for such products.

5. FRAMEWORK AGREEMENT

The idea to form an ASEAN-China FTA was in response to the suggestion by the former Chinese Premier Zhu at the Sixth ASEAN Summit in November 2000. Then, a joint study by the ASEAN-China Expert Group was called for. A year later, at the following Seventh ASEAN Summit in November 2001, the report by the expert group was adopted.[19] This includes the proposal for a framework on economic co-operation and the establishment of an ASEAN-China FTA in ten years with special and differential treatment and flexibility to the newer ASEAN members. The leaders also agreed that the framework should provide for an "early harvest" in which the list of products and services will be determined by mutual consultation.[20]

ASEAN and China are working to adopt a framework of economic co-operation containing six major elements, some of which could be implemented sooner than others. These elements are as follows:[21]

- Trade and investment facilitation measures which cover a wide range of issues like the removal of non-tariff barriers, mutual acceptance of standards and conformity assessment procedures to promote trade in services.
- Provision of technical assistance and capacity building particularly to new members of ASEAN to expand their trade with China.
- Trade promotion measures, consistent with the WTO rules, to be given to the non-WTO members of ASEAN.
- Expansion of co-operation in various areas such as finance, tourism, agriculture, human resource development industrial cooperation, intellectual property rights, environment, energy, etc.
- Establishment of an ASEAN-China FTA within ten years, with special and differential treatment given to ASEAN's new members.
- Establishment of appropriate institutions between ASEAN and China to carry out the framework of cooperation.

The former ASEAN Secretary General, Rudolfo Severino, noted in 2001 that:

> when viewed and carried out in this light, as well as the competition, between ASEAN and China bears enormous promise for the peoples of ASEAN and China and for the enterprises operating them. The dynamics between ASEAN and China as competitors and partners will then prove of tremendous benefit to all.[22]

The proposed FTA would thus allow each side to respond to the challenges and seize the opportunities. ASEAN member governments are adopting important policy measures, perhaps the most important since the creation of AFTA. It is then up to the business community to seize the opportunities and respond to these challenges. The governments of both sides have agreed to work out details of the proposed agreement. Indeed, the framework agreement on an ASEAN-China FTA came into effect after the signing at the Eighth ASEAN Summit in Phnom Penh in November 2002, with enough progress of the ASEAN-China negotiations to allow both sides to conclude essential points outlined in the framework agreement.[23]

Essentially, this framework agreement recalled the decision made at the Seventh ASEAN Submit in Brunei on November 2001 regarding a framework on economic co-operation, and to establish an ASEAN-China FTA within ten years with special and differential treatment and flexibility for the newer ASEAN member states and with the provision for an "early harvest" for products and services to be determined by mutual consultation. In order to move ahead with the agreed framework, both ASEAN and China agreed to enter into negotiations in which duties and other restrictive trade regulations shall be eliminated on substantially all trade in goods between both parties:

- The first set of products involves the implementation of an "early harvest" programme, at the latest, 1 January 2004. This would concern the product coverage, tariff reduction and elimination, implementation timeframes, rules of origin, trade remedies and emergency measures applicable to the programme.[24]
- The second set of products includes those "normal track" items, not covered by the early harvest programme for which parties could phase out all tariff rates at the end of the framework agreement, from 1 January 2005 to 2010 for ASEAN 5 and China and from 1 January 2005 to 2015 for newer ASEAN members and the Philippines.
- The last set of products, which is to be kept to a minimum, covers "sensitive track" items, such as industries that need time to adjust, and for these, inclusion in the FTA would be step by step, and respective applied rates reduced and eliminated with timeframes to be mutually agreed between the parties.

According to these principles, the two parties should gradually lower tariff rates on globally competitive products at a faster pace than on sensitive products. Also, for the newer ASEAN members and the Philippines, China would offer the right to implement tariff reductions a few years later.

In fact, FTA provisions would go beyond reduction of tariffs to cover also reduction and elimination of non-tariff barriers, liberalization in services trade and liberalization in investment. However, it will take time to negotiate all these issues in the process of establishing the FTA. It remains to be seen how both sides would identify and continue to work on the issues.

6. PARTNERS IN A NEW OPERATING ENVIRONMENT?

ASEAN linking up with China in an FTA is expected to boost the region's attractiveness for investment. Such integration among the two sides seems to be necessary given the increasing competition in the global economy following the Asian crisis and China's entry into the WTO. China's WTO entry together with the strong flow of foreign direct investment into the country serves as a wake-up call to all Asian countries to improve their competitiveness. For its part, China looks to ASEAN to improve ties and strengthen economic relationships in support of its growth. The ASEAN-China FTA agreement could also attract outsiders like Japan, the United States, the EU and others to take a closer look at their partnerships in the region.[25]

On the other hand, some ASEAN members are still reluctant to open their markets to China, fearing a flood of Chinese goods. The increased competition in ASEAN's domestic markets as a result of liberalizing trade with China could negate any potential benefits from having better access to the Chinese market and to the FDI now flowing into China. ASEAN still needs to be careful in such an FTA not to sacrifice its own interests, but bringing China to see the co-prosperity that might take shape in connecting to the ASEAN region.

The CMLV countries would benefit by waiting till a later stage to liberalize tariffs while Indonesia, Malaysia and Thailand are more prepared to open up their markets. Thus, most ASEAN countries, at the moment, are busy working to re-evaluate individually their own positions with China. There are costs and benefits with any liberalization exercise. Proper sequencing is still essential because domestic industries might need time to adjust. Overall, countries must seek to get benefits that outweigh the costs.

Sceptics argue that ASEAN needs to exercise caution and work to ensure a win-win result. The devil is in the details. Much of the FDI flowing into China may not have been diverted from ASEAN as these capital flows are directed toward different objectives and are not competing with similar flows to the ASEAN region. Moving into an ASEAN-China FTA may not address ASEAN's needs to strengthen its own grouping. The optimists argue that ASEAN could gain a better access to China in an increasingly production-based network in East Asia where the role of China will be more and more pertinent.[26] The next five to ten years will see the result of ASEAN's repositioning *vis-à-vis* China and the rest of Asia.

For China, the country has become active in regional economic processes. For ASEAN, they already did so in the AFTA process. Whatever the arguments given, the proposal to establish an ASEAN-China FTA has given breath to the debate about forming an FTA for all Asia. This would mean that Japan and Korea, for example, could join the FTA agreement as well. This also contributes to a new round of debate about the timing for East Asia to form a trade group in the wake of the much stronger economic blocs in Europe and the Americas.

It is in this sense, that an ASEAN-China deal could be useful politically to keep the momentum going and pressure other countries to get on with the free trade programme for fear of losing benefits. Furthermore, with bilateral free-trade pacts proliferating within the region, the firming up of an East Asian FTA is moving closer. Singapore is negotiating simultaneously with Japan, the United States, Australia, New Zealand and South Korea. Thailand is doing a similar exercise with China, Australia and New Zealand. A Japan-Korea free-trade agreement is being considered by both sides. This trend creates strong impetus for an Asia-wide FTA. While new deals may boost trade, however, there must be avoidance of a confusing "spaghetti bowl" of conflicting and overlapping rules (Bhagwati 1997).

The ASEAN-China FTA has contributed to new thinking about East Asia, not just as a geographic concept, but as an institutional arrangement. This regional approach may take time to realize, but it still ought to be seen as the most desirable option. It is still the case that ASEAN and China are considered developing countries with strong dependency on outside markets rather than a self-contained group. However, by creating an ASEAN-China FTA, and developing appropriate institutions to carry out co-operation, both regions could gain in the long run.

7. CONCLUSION

As trade and other economic linkages between ASEAN and China grow rapidly, they have also become competitors for both markets of their products and services, and also for investments. This trend is obvious since the crisis, which caused many ASEAN countries to slow down economically while China poses formidable challenges since its accession into the WTO. The prospect of heightened competition causes ASEAN to reposition and redefine their competitiveness. Looking ahead, the next few years would be key to the ASEAN region to hasten the integration of the regional market and make further adjustment to respond to the rise of China.

Indeed, the opening-up of the Chinese economy to the world could also serve as a tremendous opportunity for ASEAN, with differences varying from country to country. As the Chinese economy will continue to grow, it is clear that China would become even more an ASEAN's major trading partner and *vice versa*. There are strong prospects for intra-regional trade and production networks brought about by rising income, product differentiation and economies of scale. Linking ASEAN and China together with a focus on regional, sub-regional or even very localized potential spots for high growth and investment could help further growth in a regional context and also in the global economy.

Several challenges have to be overcomed in forming an ASEAN-China FTA. Politically, China proposed such a scheme to ASEAN. While individual ASEAN members might have responded differently, they agreed, however, to such a formation. The agreed timeframe has been fixed for China and the original members of ASEAN plus Brunei, to set a free trade zone by 2010, while the remaining four new ASEAN member countries have to follow suite by 2015. The negotiations are taking place and quite intensively. Hopefully, it will not turn out to be China negotiating with individual ASEAN countries given the differing interests of each ASEAN country, while ASEAN deals in an FTA with China.

Looking from a long-term perspective, there would be trade gains for both sides. Trade creation would offset trade diversion overall with some ASEAN exports diverting from current trade partners to China. With China's strong growth, imports from ASEAN could be absorbed by exports without causing significant trade diversion. China could look at ASEAN as an additional source of input for natural resource-based and intermediate products.

An ASEAN FTA is, substantially, now a reality. Indeed, the six original signatories to the AFTA agreement has achieved its target of zero-to-five per cent tariffs from intra-regional trade. Forging economic links with China in an FTA will add dynamics and a new dimension to the whole region. In fact, the ASEAN market is integrating to an important level now with the actual integration of the additional Chinese market. Thus, the activities of the multinational companies, especially firms from Japan, the United States, and the EU, for example, can focus their relocation in a more widely extended area to allow for efficient resource allocation at the regional level. The formation of an ASEAN-China FTA could also favour the concept of an "ASEAN Economic Community" (Dutta 2002). In other words, East Asia is being transformed from a mere geographic concept into a regional institutional arrangement and this may be only the beginning of such a process.

APPENDIX 4.1

Summary of the Global Trade Analysis Project (GTAP) model applied in this study:

This chapter makes use of the GTAP model known among economists in the area. The Chulalongkorn CAMGEM Project is based on this model and has been applied to a number of important global trade analyses. The GTAP model in its latest version contains forty-five countries and fifty production sectors.

The model (ASEAN Secretariat 2001) is structured on the following elements: (a) a regional household whose Cobb-Douglas preferences are defined over composite private expenditures, composite public sector expenditures and savings; (b) demand arising from private expenditures governed by a constant difference of elasticity (CDE) function; (c) production described by a multi-level Leonlief-type production function defined over value-added and intermediate inputs generated from the Social Accounting Matrix (SAM) constructed for each region, with value-added produced through a constant elasticity of substitution (CES) function; (d) macro closure of a CGE model with balances in each region composed of government deficit or surplus, aggregate saving and investment, and balance of trade.

Finally, the equilibrium of the model is defined as a set of prices and quantities for goods and factors in all regions such that (a) demand equals supply for all goods and factors; (b) each industry earns zero profit; and (c) gross investment equals aggregate savings in each region. The model is neo-classical in nature as prices in each region's product and factor markets are assumed to be flexible and arable land for agriculture in each region is assumed to be fixed.

Notes

1. From Prime Minister Zhu Rongji at the ASEAN China Summit in Singapore in November 2000.
2. Export Group's Report was considered at the ASEAN-China Summit in Brunei in November 2001.
3. See "Framework Agreement on Comprehensive Economic Co-operation between the Association of Southeast Asian Nations and the People's Republic of China", in <http://www.aseansec.org/1B197.htm>.
4. ASEAN-China and Japan-Singapore are clear examples of comprehensive economic framework that include wide coverage of mutual economic co-operation.
5. The new members of ASEAN included Vietnam (in 1997) and Cambodia (in 1999).
6. ASEAN Secretariat (2001). "Forging Closer ASEAN-China Economic Relations in the Twenty-first Century", a report submitted by the ASEAN-China Expert Group on Economic Cooperation, October 2000, p. 1.
7. *Bangkok Post*, 9 February 2004.
8. Quoted as major reason for this growing deficit.
9. See ASEAN Secretariat (2001), op. cit, pp. 26–27.
10 See ASEAN Secretariat (2001), op. cit.
11. The Philippines, also due its uncertain economic environment, asked to join the group of ASEAN's new members to liberalize with China at a later date.
12. Within a multilateral policy framework.
13. In comparison to the EU and NAFTA, each possesses a GDP size of over US$9 trillion. ASEAN Secretariat (2001), op. cit., p. 30.
14. Singapore-Japan FTA has been formalized while Singapore continues to negotiate with the United States, Australia and New Zealand. Thailand has also entered into dealing a FTA with Australia, New Zealand and perhaps Japan and even China as well.
15. Like A. Krueger, "Problems with Overlapping Free Trade Areas" in *Regionalism and Multilateral Trade Arrangements*, edited by T. Ito and A. Krueger (Chicago: The University of Chicago Press, 1997).
16. However, a major disadvantage of a customs union is that it requires greater degree of policy co-ordination and collective decision-making and budgetary mechanisms to distribute the tariff revenue between members. Rajan, R. and R. Sen, "Singapore's New Commercial Trade Strategy: The Pros and Cons of Bilteralism", Centre for International Economic Studies, Adelaide University, Discussion Paper NC 0202, 2002, p. 11.
17. In a 45-regions and 50-sectors GTAP model.
18. It should be noted that according to the GTAP model, a sharp rise in food product output and primary input constraint may limit output growth in apparel and leather products.

19. A report submitted by October 2001. See <http:// www.aseansec.org/newdata/ asean_china_bc.htgm>.
20. See Press Statement by the Chairman of the Seventh ASEAN Summit and the three ASEAN+1 Summits, ASEAN Secretariat (2001), (unpublished).
21. Ibid.
22. See further details in ASEAN Secretariat (2001), ibid., p. 29.
23. See note 3.
24. Details as appeared in Annex 3 of the Framework Agreement.
25. Japan's manufacturers are also under threat from China's cheap labour and cheap goods. Unemployment has been rising across the country and it is vital to adopt new technology and find new ways to compete. Japan's industries are now struggling with the shifting of industries to the region as a way to survive. *Far Eastern Economic Review*, 25 April 2002.
26. Indeed, a new geoeconomic configuration that is taking place in which China is playing an active role will change the way we view East Asia as well as the world's political economy. In Rolf, Jim, "Welcome in Asia: China's Multilateral Presence", in *Asia's China Debate*, Asia-Pacific Centre for Security Studies, 2003, pp. 2–5, (unpublished).

References

Bhagwati, J. Regionalism and multilateralism: An overview. In *New Dimensions in Regional Integration*, edited by M. Jaime de & A. Panagariya. Cambridge: Cambridge University Press, 1993.

Bhagwati, J., P. Krisna and A. Panagariya. *Trading Blocs: Alternative Approaches to Analyzing Preferential Trade Agreements*. Cambridge: MIT Press, 1999.

Chirathivat, S. "Interdependence between China and Southeast Asian Economies on the Eve of the Accession of China into the WTO". In *China Enters WTO: Pursuing the Symbiosis with the Global Economy*, edited by Yamazawa, I. and K. Imai. Tokyo: The Institute of Developing Economies, 2001.

Chirathivat, S. "ASEAN-China Economic Partnership in an Integrating World Economy". *Chulalongkorn Review* 14 (2002a): 98–114.

Chirathivat, S. "ASEAN-China FTA: Background, Implications and Future Development". *Journal of Asian Economics* 13 (2002b): 671–86.

Dutta, M. *Asia Economic Community: Intra-community Macro-and Micro-economic Parameters*. A paper presented at the annual meeting of AEA in Atlanta, GA, 1 June 2002 (mimeograph).

Gomory, R.E. and W.J. Baumol. *Global Trade and Conflicting National Interests*. Cambridge, Massachusetts: The MIT Press, 2002.

Krueger, A. "Problems in Overlapping Free Trade Areas". In T. Ito and A. Krueger, *Regionalism and Multilateral Trade Arrangements*. Chicago: The University of Chicago Press, 1997.

Lloyd, P.J. "New Bilateralism in the Asia Pacific". *The World Economy*, 2002.

Lloyd, P.J. and D. Maclaren. "Openness and Growth in East Asia after the Asian Crisis". *Journal of Asian Economics* 11 (2000): 89–105.

Mallikamas, S. *A Study of Thailand's Readiness to Establish Free Trade Areas*. CAMGEM Development Project, Faculty of Economics, Chulalongkorn University, 2002.

Neary, P. "Of Hype and Heperbolas: Introducing the New Economic Geography". *Journal of Economic Literature* 39 (2001): 536–61.

Panagariya, A. "Preferential Trade Liberalization: The Traditional Theory and New Developments". *Journal of Economic Literature* 38 (2001): 287–331.

Panitchpakdi, S. and M. Clifford. *China and the WTO*. Singapore: John Wiley & Sons (Asia) Pte Ltd., 2002.

Rajan, R. and R. Sen. *Singapore's New Commercial Trade Strategy: The Pros and Cons of Bilateralism*. Centre for International Economic Studies, Adelaide University, 2002 (mimeograph).

Sunthonkhan, D. *China's Accession to the WTO and its Impacts on Thailand: The GTAP Model Approach*. Master thesis (in Thai). Faculty of Economics, Chulalongkorn University, 2002 (mimeograph).

The World Bank. *Globalization, Growth, and Poverty: Building an Inclusive World Economy*. A World Bank policy research report. Washington D.C.: A co-publication of the World Bank and Oxford University Press, 2002.

The World Bank. *China Engaged: Integration with the Global Economy*. Washington D.C., 1997.

UNCTAD. *World Investment Report*. Geneva, 2001.

Urata, S. "A Shift from Market-led to Institution-led Regional Economic Integration in East Asia". Paper prepared for JSPS-NRCT Workshop on "Perspectives of Flows, Middle Class, State and Market for Asia", Bangkok, 14–15 January 2003.

Wang, Z. "The Impact of China's WTO Entry on the World Labour-intensive Export Market: A Recursive Dynamic ECG Analysis". *The World Economy* 22, no. 3 (1999): 379–405.

Yang, Y. and C. Zhong. China's Textile and Clothing Exports in a Changing World Economy. *The Developing Economies* 36, no. 1 (1998): 3–23.

Zhao, H. "Foreign Trade in the People's Republic of China: Past Performance and Future Challenges". *Asia*, 1997.

Part III

CHINA-ASEAN RELATIONS
Domestic, Regional and International Politics

5

THE SIGNIFICANCE OF BEIJING'S BILATERAL RELATIONS

Looking 'Below' the Regional Level in China-ASEAN Ties

Jürgen Haacke

Much attention has been devoted to recent developments in China-ASEAN ties at what might be called the regional level.[1] In contrast, only few analyses have explored — above all from a comparative perspective — what role and significance individual ASEAN countries have played in China's strategic, political and economic considerations relative to Southeast Asia.[2] Equally, only few works have offered a comparative study of recent developments between Beijing and individual ASEAN states and the importance of these bilateral ties for advancing China's relations with ASEAN as a diplomatic grouping.[3] It may well be that the strong interest in East Asian regionalism can in part explain this neglect.[4] Nevertheless, the relative lack of interest in the relationship between China and individual ASEAN states is somewhat surprising taking into account the importance that bilateralism has traditionally assumed in Beijing's foreign policy. Indeed, it is imperative to remember that although China has dealt with ASEAN in both the Cold War and the post-Cold War periods, formal China-ASEAN relations date back only to 1991.[5] Moreover, one might argue that at the regional level China-ASEAN interaction received its greatest boost even only after the Asian financial crisis.[6]

The purpose of this chapter is two-fold: the main goal is to investigate how Southeast Asian states matter to Beijing and what the state of individual bilateral relationships is. The chapter will, second, briefly discuss how developments in bilateral ties have provided a platform for Beijing on which to advance relations with ASEAN as a grouping. The chapter is divided into four sections. The first section briefly outlines the general international and domestic context in which China's foreign policy towards Southeast Asian states has been formulated, particularly after 1989. Section Two starts by exploring how China's Southeast Asia policy has been embedded within broader policy initiatives, before turning to identify some of the key expectations that Beijing seems to have in relation to the continental and maritime states of the ASEAN region. The third section examines the importance that Chinese leaders and analysts have attributed to individual states in Southeast Asia, with particular reference to the post-Cold War period and provides an overview and summary assessment of China's bilateral relations with ASEAN states, again primarily from a Chinese perspective. The final section looks how evolving bilateral ties have allowed Beijing to build a platform on which to promote deeper co-operation at the regional level.

THE CONTEXT OF CHINA-SOUTHEAST ASIA RELATIONS

An analysis of China's ties with Southeast Asian states is best located in the wider context of China's political ambitions pursuant to its informal ideology, its evolving political, economic and security agenda and, as such, the challenges it has faced both at home and the wider East Asia region. China's Southeast Asia policy, therefore, has not been immune to perceived changes in the international environment and developments in China's general foreign policy outlook, not least in relations with the other major powers.[7] After the establishment of the People's Republic in 1949 until the early 1970s, for instance, Beijing's policy toward Southeast Asia was formulated in the context of China's struggle for security and equality that informed relations with Moscow and the United States. In other words, Southeast Asia policy was subsumed during this period under the struggle against imperialism and from about 1958 onwards the parallel struggle against revisionism and social imperialism.[8] Domestic factors have also mattered. While the 1950s still saw Beijing emphasise mutual coexistence on the basis of respect for basic principles of international society, as illustrated by its stance at the Bandung Conference in 1955, PRC foreign policy in the 1960s was characterized by a marked degree of interference, the apex of which was reached during the years of the Cultural Revolution. In the wake of China's decision to opt for strategic alignment with the United States in the late 1960s, and its successful attempt to take over the China seat at the United Nations, there also followed the normalization of some of China's bilateral ties with some Southeast Asian states: Malaysia, Thailand and the Philippines. In the 1980s, Beijing's Southeast Asia policy was shaped in large measure by the Cambodian Conflict and the PRC's objective to deny Hanoi, which was viewed as a client state of the Soviet Union, sub-regional hegemony in Indochina. This involved reversing Vietnam's installation of a puppet regime in Phnom Penh and securing the withdrawal of its troops. During the early 1990s, after the violent suppression of street protests in 1989 and related all-out efforts to ensure the long-term survival of the Communist Party, policy toward Southeast Asia received increasing attention, partly to offset the political fallout with Western countries and the need to restore the PRC's international image. With regime legitimacy dependent on rapid economic advance, the Chinese leadership under both presidents Jiang Zemin and Hu Jintao have continued Deng Xiaoping's promotion of domestic economic reform, with Southeast Asia playing a crucial part in China's overall strategy, both in terms of the perceived need for a stable periphery and deeper economic exchanges.[9] These considerations have been re-explored and taken forward in the context of changing Sino-American relations and China's promotion of multipolarity.[10] Efforts to outflank Japan's search for a leadership role and the undermining of Taiwan's pragmatic diplomacy have also increasingly constituted key objectives in China's Southeast Asia policy.[11] In other words, then, the importance of Southeast Asian countries in Chinese eyes has been a function of Beijing's political ambition, strategic preoccupations, security interests and developmental strategy.

The importance of particular Southeast Asian states to China has in addition depended, albeit not necessarily in this order, on a country's geographical proximity, its ideological and foreign policy orientation, the market size and potential, its relations with other great powers, and its position within Southeast Asia. Notably, attaching particular importance to select neighbours has for Chinese policymakers not always implied that the nature of this relationship was considered to be amicable or problem-free. Beijing's troubled ties with Vietnam for much of the Cold War period since the 1960s are a prime example. Chinese leaders went to substantial length to assist Vietnam in their resistance against the restoration of French colonial rule and the suppression of Vietnamese nationalism. However, bilateral relations suffered severely in the wake of China's strategic embrace of the United States in the early 1970s and reached their nadir when Vietnam defied Beijing and used force to displace the visceral Khmer Rouge. As the case of Vietnam moreover illustrates, the specific nature of relations between China and its immediate continental Southeast Asian neighbours has not merely been influenced by structural influences emanating from great power relations. The health of bilateral ties has also depended on Chinese assessments about the extent to which the foreign leaderships concerned have demonstrated sufficient regard for Chinese strategic and security interests and recognized the latter's core identity claims. To the extent that China's Southeast Asian neighbours felt unwilling or unable to recognize these interests or claims, PRC relations with individual Southeast Asian states have over time varied in warmth and depth.

POLICY INITIATIVES APPLIED TO SOUTHEAST ASIA

From around the mid-1980s onwards, China developed two major policy initiatives. Neither was exclusively designed for Southeast Asia, but was palpably applied to the region. The first came under the name of Policy of Good Neighbourliness, the second under the label of New Security Concept. The Policy of Good Neighbourliness (PGN) served primarily to enhance relations with countries on China's periphery in the context of a rapidly changing international environment and China's impressive economic rise; the New Security Concept (NSC) has in addition advocated a particular pathway to national and regional security.

China's leadership was well aware of the distrust within Southeast Asia that its unstinting support until the late 1980s for a separation of government-to-government and party-to-party relations had generated. The PGN, which was first developed before the end of the Cold War, hence served above all the purpose of confidence building and reassurance. It was accompanied by the refrain that China would neither practise hegemonism, nor approve of the suppression or bullying of small and weak countries. After June 1989, it was also designed to help Beijing overcome the loss of international status, to assist in sustaining if not accelerating China's economic growth on which political regime legitimacy has come to depend, and to parry the emerging "China threat" discourse. Muni has summarized the goals of the PGN as involving (1) unqualified support for political systems, particularly in what would later be the new ASEAN member states, and the befriending of the respective leaderships; (2) strategic engagement in the interests of sub-regional stability; (3) calls for closer economic co-operation; and (4) the intensification of cultural and political exchanges.[12] To some extent, therefore, the success of the PNG was to rest on China's rising soft power.

China's espousal of a New Security Concept since 1997 can be regarded as the second main policy initiative linked to making a contribution to the debate on a new order (which is not confined to Southeast Asia) and practical relations with the PRC's neighbours.[13] Essentially, China's new concept of security, which has been slightly developed since it was first systematically outlined,[14] argues that the use of force or threat to use force cannot fundamentally resolve disputes and challenges. It therefore stands in opposition to confrontation and military blocs as well as the idea of "absolute security" and emphasises four core elements: mutual trust, mutual benefit, equality, and co-operation/co-ordination.[15] These elements have also been conceptualized as the "four no's": no hegemonism, no power politics, no arms races and no military alliances.[16] Consequently, China's new concept of security stresses particular pathways to stability and peace (confidence building, common security, co-operation and peaceful resolution of disputes) and, above all, the application of certain instruments of regional order (diplomacy and economic interdependence).[17]

The Chinese Government is quite happy to stress that co-operation under the New Security Concept should be flexible and diversified in "form and model", no doubt so as to accommodate those features of the present regional order Beijing that does not find objectionable, be it a loose forum in which to have a security dialogue (ARF) or a "security mechanism", yet to be established. It is also noteworthy that the new security concept is allied to China's defence concept which has been summarized as "to love peace, to value defence, to seek unification, to promote unity and resist foreign aggression".[18]

Implicit Expectations

As is often the case, formally stated policy and attendant public discourse do not necessarily tell the full story about a country's intentions and ambitions. In China's case too, it is possible to identify certain expectations that even though they flow from China's identity and related moral claims, as well as from its security interests, these are not always expressly captured in China's diplomatic rhetoric. Primarily for reasons of geographical distance, these expectations have not been uniformly applied to continental and maritime Southeast Asia. This is not to say that some of the expectations held within China about neighbouring continental Southeast Asian states do not also pertain to the maritime states, but arguably they do not generally do so in quite the same way.

Chinese leaders seem to have at least four — often unspoken — expectations about what continental Southeast Asian countries should not do or be. First, Beijing has never been happy to see these countries allow other major powers to establish foreign bases on their territory. Beijing violently objected to the construction and use of such bases in Thailand during the Second Indochina War as well as to the Soviet Union's military presence and use of bases in Vietnam after 1978. The wide support within Southeast Asia for the more limited policy of "places, not bases" has consequently attracted far less wrath from Beijing. However, when, as in the case of Cam Ranh Bay, the issue of the long-term future of a former base has again come up, Beijing has not been shy to communicate its point.[19]

Second, irrespective of Beijing's discourse in relation to sovereign equality, it is a historical fact that Chinese leaders prefer continental Southeast Asian countries not to assume a strategic centrality within this sub-region that would not only impair China's security interests but also question China's regional status. Nayan Chanda has argued in this context that Beijing's support in the first half of the Cold War for independence and neutrality of the monarchies in Laos and Cambodia served this very end because it limited Vietnam's influence over these two countries.[20] Zhou Enlai's attempt to break the deadlock in the 1954 Geneva Conference by highlighting Vietnam's refusal to admit to the existence of forces in Laos and Cambodia perhaps illustrates the length to which Beijing was prepared to go in this regard, even at a time when relations with Hanoi were warm.[21] China's determination to prevent the establishment of an Indochina Federation after the Vietnam War followed the same instincts, even though considerable political and especially military support for the anti-Vietnamese Khmer Rouge was at best of mixed success in thwarting Hanoi's sub-regional ambitions. The point remains relevant, as China's ongoing efforts to promote the pursuit of an independent foreign policy in Cambodia and Laos make clear.

Third, Chinese leaders also expect their immediate Southeast Asian neighbours to be attentive if not sensitive to the Middle Kingdom's lesser security interests and identity claims, even as these evolve. There is moreover the expectation on China's part that regional neighbours consult on those developments that have tangible implications for Beijing. This is not to say that Chinese leaders have sought to curtail the independence of continental Southeast Asian states, particularly as regards the development of contacts with outside powers. Indeed, such a move is, certainly at this moment in time, regarded as something of a retrograde step that would likely only rekindle precisely those suspicions that China has for years been keen to overcome once and for all.

Fourth, and closely related to the last points, Chinese leaders would prefer not to see major instability on their southern periphery arising from either interstate or intrastate conflict. There are two chief reasons for this: First, the PRC wishes to avoid external involvement by major powers in conflicts along its periphery. Secondly, Beijing is concerned about such conflicts easily undermining confidence in the countries concerned, with possible adverse repercussions for economic development.

China's expectations in relation to ASEAN states' behaviour have obviously been disappointed at times. However, when expectations have not been met, or been in doubt whether they would be, Chinese leaders have been sufficiently adept at re-emphasizing their point. This was illustrated in February 2003 when Beijing's Vice-Foreign Minister, apparently "gravely concerned", felt obliged to provide friendly advice to the ambassadors of Thailand and Cambodia to avoid a deterioration of their relations over the burning of the Thai Embassy and other Thai interests in Phnom Penh. More recently, Beijing has communicated to Myanmar its displeasure about the recalcitrant stance adopted by the Chairman of the State Peace and Development Council over the issue of Daw Aung San Suu Kyi and the negative implications for national resilience and Yangon's foreign relations.

Maritime Southeast Asia

While the PRC government considers the continental Southeast Asian countries as making up China's soft underbelly and playing an important part in the country's development strategy, Southeast Asia's maritime states are also recognized in Beijing as having considerable strategic, political and economic importance. After all, the countries play considerable economic roles and they straddle major sea-lanes of communication that have grown in significance as China's global trade has expanded. Economically, the maritime states have mattered much more than the continental Southeast Asian states — safe perhaps for Thailand. With fairly or even highly developed economies, some maritime Southeast Asian countries have been regarded as both example and partner in the context of the domestic reform process.

China's expectations of the maritime Southeast Asian states are not as far-reaching as those held *vis-à-vis* the continental ASEAN countries. To the extent that countries have committed themselves to non-alignment, no foreign bases, or a nuclear weapons free zone, the Chinese Government expects that commitments of this nature will not be reversed. However, unlike in the case of the continental Southeast Asian states, Chinese officials appreciate that maritime ASEAN is not quite in their immediate backyard. A second expectation is that the maritime ASEAN countries remain crucially involved in promoting China's continued development as well as their own national and regional resilience. Third, where there is danger of territorial dismemberment, Beijing expects regional support for territorial integrity and unambiguous respect for basic principles of international society, unless special circumstances warrant a different approach. Beijing also expects those maritime countries in Southeast Asia that are host to sizeable ethnic Chinese communities which have been encouraged to participate in the PRC's economic transformation to do just that without fear of negative repercussions.

Having spelled out the basic policy contours within which China's policy toward Southeast Asia has been cast and noted several of the expectations that China seems to have *vis-à-vis* both the continental and the maritime states, the following main section of the chapter provides an overview of how Chinese decision-makers look at individual Southeast Asian states, particularly in the post-Cold War period. This is coupled with an overview and assessment of developments in Beijing's ties with the ten ASEAN member states.

CHINA'S RELATIONS WITH ASEAN MEMBER STATES

Recognizing the necessary limitations of providing within the available space a country-by-country overview of China's perceptions of and ties with members of the Association, this section will nevertheless offer a cursory account of key relevant points. In line with the focus adopted so far, the analysis focuses on the strategic-security, political and economic dimensions of China's relations with ASEAN members. The analysis will begin with the continental Southeast Asian states before moving on to the maritime countries.

Thailand

As one of three countries that established diplomatic relations with the PRC in the mid-1970s, Thailand was the first Southeast Asian country to move from enmity to co-operation, if not alignment, as a consequence of the mutual objective to drive Vietnam out of Cambodia.[22] From China's perspective, Thailand's significance has derived from three considerations: First, its geostrategic location in continental Southeast Asia. There are two points here. Thailand was, and still is, regarded as a political (and military) counterweight to Hanoi. China also has an interest in building a canal across the Kra Isthmus that would help reduce both transportation costs and dependency on existing trade routes through the Strait of Malacca.

Secondly, Thailand is regarded as a key player within the association. This was the case in the 1980s, when Thailand co-steered ASEAN's collective diplomacy as a frontline state. In the aftermath of the Asian crisis, China analysts have noted Bangkok's successful attempt, particularly under current Prime Minister Thaksin Shinawatra, to re-position Thailand at the core of the association. Third, Chinese analysts moreover see Thailand as able and willing to make a positive contribution to sub-regional stability in continental Southeast Asia and to initiate useful steps to address a range of non-traditional security challenges.[23]

Fourth, China also hopes to make Thailand, which enjoys a relatively high level of economic development compared with many parts of south-western China, a partner in the development of the PRC's south-west, particularly Yunnan and Sichuan. Chinese central policymakers and the regional business community in this context also see Thai support for the development of the Mekong River Basin as crucial to increase regional trade and investment flows with China.[24]

Finally, Thailand is important because though it has on the whole remained a resolute U.S. ally, Bangkok has on occasion signalled an apparent willingness to voluntarily defer to Beijing.[25] With multipolarity in mind, Beijing is keen to promote the bilateral relationship in all areas, so as to ensure that military ties between Bangkok and Washington are not harmful to Chinese interests.

Recent Developments

Sino-Thai relations have become increasingly stronger over the last few years. This is due in part to Beijing's response to the Asian crisis, which hit Thailand rather hard, but found Washington less than fully alert to Thailand's predicaments. In contrast, Beijing provided financial assistance to Bangkok, retained its currency peg to the dollar and stimulated bilateral trade through a range of measures. Bangkok reciprocated by becoming the first ASEAN country to sign a bilateral framework agreement on future co-operation with China in early 1999. Since then, the People's Republic has become increasingly important as a market for Thai goods, not least in the broader context of the only limited success of the Indochina-strategy of former Prime Minister Chatichai Choonhavan, and the realization that Thailand's economic health demands enhancing trade and investment flows with all major markets. Like other regional economies, Thailand has been affected by Japan's prolonged sluggish economic growth and inconsistency in demand from the United States and other markets.

The accession to power of the Thaksin government in February 2001 has reinforced the dynamism inherent in China-Thailand relations. In line with his policy of "forward engagement", Premier Thaksin Shinawatra has enthusiastically pushed Thailand's economic agenda *vis-à-vis* the PRC, and particularly the liberalization of trade. China did make concessions to Thailand in the context of its WTO accession, but these failed to satisfy the trading community. In contrast, the Thailand-China bilateral FTA on agricultural produce, which had a start date of October 2003, was the first of its kind in the context of the China-ASEAN "early harvest" tariff reductions and has been hailed by some Thai officials as the most important bilateral economic achievement in the post-Cold War period.[26] The provisional evidence suggests that Thai exports in fruits and vegetables have risen massively.

Bilateral political and security co-operation has also expanded. On the occasion of Thai Premier Thaksin Shinawatra's visit to Beijing in August 2001, the two sides issued a joint communiqué which reaffirmed their 1999 Joint Statement and stated that it had been "agreed to consolidate the existing traditional friendship and work for strategic co-operation".[27] In the event, China supported Thailand's initiative to kick-start the Asia Co-operation Dialogue as well as efforts to stabilize relations with Burma/Myanmar, and, more recently, to break the political deadlock in Myanmar through the "Bangkok process". Bangkok has in turn continued to pursue a One-China policy, albeit not always without ambivalence, and has pleased Beijing by stamping down on Falungong activities. Recently, the Thaksin government pledged that Thailand "would forever remain China's most sincere friend", while outgoing President Jiang Zemin stated that there were "no outstanding issues".[28] Emphasizing Bangkok's importance for PRC diplomacy, Thailand was the first foreign destination for President Hu Jintao in October 2003. Thailand was also the first country within Southeast Asia with whom Beijing decided to create a bilateral consultative mechanism for political affairs.

Bilateral security co-operation and military exchanges are unobtrusive but continuous. Security consultations focus on terrorism, narcotics and the situation in Myanmar. Both sides are interested in combating transnational security challenges affecting their border regions. It was former Defence Minister Chavalit Yongchaiyudt who proposed to institutionalize high-level defence meetings to annually review military co-operation in the light of the evolving strategic situation in East Asia. The first formal security meeting between defence officials took place in December 2001. Thailand's Supreme Commander also regularly visits China. Other elements of co-operation include port calls and weapons purchases. China has offered sizeable loans to allow Thailand to purchase weapons and spare parts. However, for "cross-border" contingencies, Bangkok continues to rely on the United States, which recently designated the country a major non-NATO ally.[29]

In sum, therefore, the bilateral relationship has been progressively broadened and raised to higher levels. While acknowledging Bangkok's eagerness to demonstrate deference on key issues, Chinese leaders recognize that Beijing would not succeed if an attempt were made to push Bangkok beyond equidistance in its relations with the major powers. As Chinese analysts acknowledge, at issue is Thailand's willingness to be mindful of the direction and strength of the wind blowing at the Kingdom.[30] In view of this, Beijing seems intent on working towards even better relations with Bangkok.

Burma/Myanmar

China's relations with Burma/Myanmar are officially described as "traditional, good neighbourly and friendly" and classified as a *pauk hpaw (siblings)* relationship.[31] Although bilateral ties have deepened since the accession to power of the State, Law and Order Restoration Council (since 1997: the State Peace and Development Council), Chinese influence over Myanmar is perhaps more limited than is often suggested. According to Poon Kim Shee, "Sino-Myanmar ties are uneven, asymmetrical but nevertheless reciprocal and mutually beneficial".[32]

Myanmar's significance for the People's Republic derives in part from its geographical location given it is here that South Asia, Southeast Asia and (North) East Asia intersect. Myanmar shares a 2,220 km-long border with China, as well as borders of 1,450 km and 2,100 km in length with India and Thailand respectively, and offers easy access to the Andaman Sea, the Malacca Strait and the Indian Ocean. Burma/Myanmar has for years served as a buffer between China and India and other parts of Southeast Asia.[33] Strategically, Myanmar is important for Beijing in the context of China's two-ocean strategy (Pacific and Indian). Since the mid-1980s, Burma/Myanmar has also increasingly been recognized as potentially playing a major role in China's development strategy.[34]

In the context of China's western development strategy, Burma/Myanmar has in particular been viewed as an important trading outlet for the Chinese provinces of Yunnan and Sichuan with other economies in South and Southeast Asia. Burma boasts railheads at both Myitkyina and Lashio (in north-eastern Myanmar) both of which can be easily accessed from China. Apparently Chinese authorities have also hoped to benefit from the establishment of a trade route that would involve barges transporting goods from a new container port at Bhamo, a town on the eastern bank of the Irrawaddy River, to

Mandalay and then on to Minhla from where they would be transported by road to the a deepwater port of Kyaukpyu in the Bay of Bengal.[35]

Beijing has no interest in seeing Myanmar pander to foreign powers with interests inimical to those of Beijing and any one power acquiring greater sway over Yangon than Beijing currently possesses. From a Chinese point of view, it is also important to prevent instability in Myanmar that could result in the central authorities losing control over the border areas, particularly if this resulted in a further exacerbation of the drug flow into China or foreign intervention.

Recent Developments

Myanmar was the last of the new ASEAN members to be visited by former President Jiang Zemin. However, Jiang's visit in December 2001 has given Sino-Burmese relations an important boost, in part because the military regime badly wanted it and partly because not all had previously been well in Yangon-Beijing ties. Above all, the visit appears to have prompted an acceleration of economic co-operation.

Since the early 1990s, official trade had jumped from a few million to several hundred million US dollars. Myanmar had also attracted several hundred thousand Chinese entrepreneurs and farmers that boosted cross-border trade, on which no reliable statistics exist, however. At the same time, various impediments to further improvements in bilateral economic ties characterized the 1990s. China was dissatisfied with the limited steps taken by the SPDC to reform Myanmar's economy. Myanmar's continued official exchange rate was equally viewed as an obstacle to trade. Official trade then suffered a major reversal after the Asian crisis. Casting doubt on an agreement reached in principle, the SPDC proved reluctant to implement a Chinese proposal to establish a container port at Bhamo, from where the navigable Irrawaddy River provides access to Mandalay and the Bay of Bengal, and to enhance existing port facilities at Kyaukpyu in the Arakan.[36] Other issues have related more directly to border trade, which suffered after the accession to power of the SPDC in 1997.[37]

Since 2001, technical and economic co-operation have gathered added momentum especially in trade, and Chinese assistance with industrial projects and infrastructure has been considerable. According to official sources, bilateral trade including border trade for the first time exceeded US$1 billion in 2003.[38] In March 2004, the two sides also agreed on a feasibility study in relation to the construction of a rail link in northern Myanmar to the Chinese border.

While Sino-Myanmar economic co-operation has been enhanced, political and security co-operation has continued. In rhetorical terms, both countries agreed in 1999 to work towards a "sustainable, stable, good-neighbourly and mutually-trusted friendly co-operation relationship". In an apparent reference to the improvements between China and Thailand, Yangon has pointedly declared that it is Myanmar that is China's "most sincere" and "most reliable". Beyond such declaratory positions, political ties have involved further high-level visits, mutual diplomatic support and the reaffirmation of basic principles of international society. High-level exchanges, for instance, included SPDC Chairman Senior General Than Shwe's visit to China in January 2003. As regards political support, Beijing has, for instance, defended Myanmar on the issue of forced labour against pressure from the International Labour Organization.[39] Chinese leaders also *de facto* supported the military regime against the oppositional National League for Democracy although Beijing has become concerned about the implications for political stability flowing from the bitter stand-off between Senior General Than Shwe and National League for Democracy leader Aung San Suu Kyi. Seeing the SPDC faced with significantly increased castigation after the events of 30 May 2003, Beijing has offered "friendly advice" to Yangon's generals in relation to the future political process and Myanmar's relations with foreign critics.[40]

Security and military co-operation clearly proceed apace but their full extent is arguably not always entirely clear. In the early to mid-1990s, Yangon purchased significant amounts of weaponry from the PRC that helped the SLORC/SPDC to secure ceasefire with most of the ethnic insurgents. China reportedly also upgraded Myanmar's radar facilities in the Coco Islands and assisted with the construction of a naval base in Sittwe.[41] While military co-operation including weapons purchases and intelligence exchange seem ongoing, the Burmese military appears uneasy about too dependent a relationship with China, not least against the background of its long tradition of strategic neutrality, which may have been relaxed but not abandoned after the SLORC won power. Consequently, the SPDC has turned to Russia for MIG 29 fighters. Myanmar's military regime has also responded positively to India's recent political and economic advances as well as proposals for some security co-operation.

Sino-Myanmar security co-operation meanwhile is strongly focused on confronting non-traditional security threats. Chinese officials estimate that in 2003 about 80 per cent of the drugs produced in the Golden Triangle region were shipped either to or through China.[42] For China, the drug influx has been accompanied by problems of border security, crime, corruption and attendant problems of declining legitimacy, social instability and a massive health threat in view of the close link between drug use and the spread of HIV/AIDS. China now appears to be undertaking interdiction measures and joint strikes with Myanmar against local centres of drug production, alongside anti-drug enforcement training and the long-term emphasis on crop-substitution and development.[43]

China-Vietnam

Sino-Vietnamese relations have seen considerable advances following normalization in 1991 but remain difficult.[44] Chinese analysts regard Vietnam as a country that enjoys an important geographical location within continental Southeast Asia, and with which China shared a professed ideology. At the same time, it is acknowledged that Vietnam's fierce nationalism has historically often put the two neighbours at odds with one another. Following the end of the Cambodian Conflict, Beijing clearly considered it crucial that Vietnam should not regain effective control over the Indochina region. Although positive about Vietnam's accession to ASEAN in 1995, Chinese leaders and analysts have evidently been keen to avert a scenario by which Vietnamese nationalists within the communist leadership would seek to transform an enlarged ASEAN into an anti-China club. Beijing has moreover directly pursued several further objectives *vis-à-vis* Vietnam: to build better bilateral trade relations, to assist the country's economic transformation, to build mutual confidence, and to resolve border conflicts amenable to compromise.

Recent Developments

Following the beginning of their reconciliation process in 1991 on what essentially were Chinese terms, Beijing and Hanoi have succeeded in developing the bilateral relationship, but several challenges remain. In the economic field, the two sides have undertaken steps to (1) enhance the efficiency of Vietnam's industry, (2) develop the country's industrial infrastructure, (3) expand trade, and (4) address the problem of illicit border trade. All these efforts have generally met with at least some success. Vietnam has made progress in learning from the PRC on how to achieve the transition from a socialist economic to a mixed economy with a strong market-based system without an attendant loss of power on the part of the ruling Communist Party. Chinese investments in Vietnam have grown, even if they still lag far behind those of other states. Official trade with Vietnam, however, has more than doubled since 1998 to reach US$3 billion per annum in 2001, with the next official target being set at US$5 billion. These are considerable figures when compared with other trade figures. In some sectors, however, especially in garments, Vietnamese and Chinese exports increasingly compete in foreign markets. In other areas, like agriculture, Vietnam has of late experienced a drop in exports to China, as the country was not accorded the same "early harvest" tariffs cuts that were extended to some of its other neighbours.[45]

In spite of normalization dating back to more than a decade ago, the Chinese and Vietnamese leaderships are still not fully at ease. To be sure, the substance of communiqués on bilateral ties and the agreements reached on the delimitation of the land border and the Gulf of Tonkin in 1999 and 2000 respectively attest to the general improvement of bilateral ties already achieved. Moreover, Beijing has also engaged Hanoi in a comprehensive process of mutual confidence building through systematic exchanges at government and party levels, and also by dint of military contacts.

Looking into the future, the two sides endeavour to "achieve long-term stability, good neighbourliness, friendship and all-round co-operation". What makes bilateral relations difficult, however, is its political-psychological dimension. Within much of Vietnam's political elite (and the wider public) there is a continued sense of resentment *vis-à-vis* China that feeds on the rejection of Chinese superiority and the feeling of historically having been given a raw deal by the northern neighbour. At the same time, Hanoi knows that it has to face up to Beijing's continued geopolitical interests in Indochina and China's growing international stature.

Not surprisingly, in such a context, Vietnam's moves to improve relations with China have proved controversial at home. Alleged concessions made to China during negotiations with Beijing over the land border and the delimitation of the Gulf of Tonkin were a factor in costing Le Kha Phieu his position as General Secretary of the ruling Communist Party in April 2001. To Beijing's chagrin, such reassessment of bilateral agreements with China have also impeded practical progress in relation to the demarcation of the land border. The remaining disputes over the Paracels and the Spratlys have meanwhile continued unabated,[46] with little sign of a possible compromise in the immediate future. Vietnam is happy to see further improvements in bilateral relations, but is reluctant to do so again at the expense of political acts that could be interpreted as entailing undue deference.

China-Cambodia

Sino-Cambodian ties also qualify as "traditional friendship of long standing" and as being "stable and sound". Indeed, within only ten years of the end of the Cambodia conflict, Chinese investors and traders have economically penetrated the Kingdom,[47] and the People's Republic has regained political influence in Phnom Penh.

Although China and Cambodia do not share a joint border, Beijing has for long viewed Cambodia as occupying an important geostrategic position given that the country is flanked by Thailand to the northwest, and Vietnam to the east/northeast. Given its geostrategic location, China has historically favoured Cambodia's existence as a neutral state and it has been a persistent policy objective to nip in the bud any efforts to establish in Beijing's backyard an Indochinese bloc with a distinct and hostile security identity. To prevent such a scenario, China also relies on Cambodian nationalism, which historically has been directed at Vietnam (and Thailand). Cambodia's geostrategic significance also derives in part from its access to the Gulf of Thailand. This is illustrated by Beijing's proposal for the establishment of an export-processing zone on Koh-Kong Island in the Gulf of Thailand.[48] Notably, history is in itself a major factor why Cambodia remains important to Chinese leaders, not least due to the questions surrounding Beijing's support for the Khmer Rouge in the 1970s, answers to which could conceivably impact on China's image and raise questions about how Beijing has itself dealt with history.

Recent Developments

Beijing has had very close personal and political ties with then Prince Norodom Sihanouk, who was reinstated as monarch in September 1993. However, it was China's subsequent comprehensive withdrawal of support from the Khmer Rouge and the disengagement from Vietnam by Hun Sen's Cambodian People's Party (CPP) that allowed the Chinese Government to slowly restore good ties with Cambodia in the mid-1990s. Final reconciliation between Hun Sen and the Chinese leadership occurred during a visit by the former to China in 1996. To further the development of bilateral ties, China has since repeatedly pledged and provided assistance for Cambodia's national reconciliation and its reconstruction. When Hun Sen ousted Prince Ranariddh as First Prime Minister in a bloody coup in July 1997, which also had the unexpected consequence of delaying Cambodia's admission to ASEAN for another two years, Beijing avoided joining the chorus of international condemnation. And after the Asian crisis precipitated foreign (particularly Thai) investors to rethink both their existing and planned projects, China implemented and strengthened agreed economic co-operation. Notwithstanding the remaining practical difficulties of investing in Cambodia, Chinese entrepreneurs are increasingly well represented, playing a role in all sectors of the Cambodian economy. While there is some concern in Phnom Penh about increasing Chinese influence in the economy, Cambodia greatly appreciated China's decision in November 2002 to write off all debts that had matured by then and, unlike Western donors, not to attach conditions to assistance provided. Also, Chinese investments and trade with China have been a boon for Cambodia's infrastructure and exports. While trade in textiles has largely centred on the United States, China-Cambodia trade amounted to US$320 in 2003, with an official target of US$500 set for 2005. While still relying heavily on Western donors, Premier Hun Sen counts on major Chinese assistance in the areas of infrastructure, telecommunications and agriculture, as he made clear in his most recent visit to China in April 2004.

Sino-Cambodian political ties have improved but may have some way to go. Cambodia scored brownie points with Beijing when Hun Sen ordered shut Taipei's cultural and economic office in Phnom Penh in 1997. Hun Sen equally prevented a purely international tribunal to pursue crimes committed by the Khmer Rouge. His resistance was apparently due in part to considerations of deference to Chinese requests to avoid the coming to light of embarrassing details of China's erstwhile support for Pol Pot's fratricidal regime. In this context, former Chinese President Jiang Zemin reportedly impressed upon Cambodia's leadership the importance of defending sovereignty against outside encroachments including an international tribunal of Khmer Rouge leaders. In the event, Cambodia's National Assembly adopted relevant legislation in 2001, and the UN and Phnom Penh signed an agreement on the genocide tribunal in June 2003. Although their importance should not be overstated, the above examples illustrate that China has acquired a measure of influence over Cambodia. However, from a Chinese perspective, bilateral relations could be better still. One of the four points in then Prime Minister Zhu Rongji's 2002 proposal for further promoting the relationship was further enhancing co-ordination in international and regional affairs.

China-Laos

Since their normalization of ties in the late 1980s, Beijing and Vientiane have established a cordial relationship. That said, Laos' significance for China pales somewhat in comparison to that of other continental Southeast Asian states. Indeed, Laos has never enjoyed the same level of importance as Cambodia as a cushion against Vietnam and Thailand, and the same remains true now.

With its difficult topography and its small and mostly rural population, Laos is also of only limited interest as a market for Chinese products. Nevertheless, the fuller exploitation of the Mekong to Luang Prabang is a key

Chinese objective. As in the case of Cambodia, an increasing number of Chinese traders and entrepreneurs have settled in parts of Laos. In addition, the fact that the Lao economy remains heavily dependent on external assistance has been exploited by Beijing to improve the country's infrastructure in the overall context of China's Mekong policy. When the Lao kip depreciated rapidly in 1999, the PRC provided generous export subsidies and interest-free loans to stabilize the currency.

The two sides have also engaged in various forms of limited security co-operation. The focus has in part been on non-traditional security concerns, not least along the 505-km long border. China is also considered to have provided Laos with training support, equipment, weapons and ammunition to allow Vientiane to deal with restive anti-regime Hmong that China had supported during the Third Indochina war.[49] Such support has not allowed China to undermine Laos' security relationship with Vietnam, however. Indeed, Chinese leaders acknowledge and respect the close personal relationships that many of the more accomplished revolutionaries within the ruling circle of the LPRP have had with Vietnam, and they are sensitive to the fact that the younger generation of leaders, widely reputed to be interested in deepening relations with Beijing, will still need more time to make a difference in this regard. For the moment, CCP leaders seem happy to see the Lao Government opt for a foreign policy that, for the time being, gives pride of place to the special relationship with Vietnam.

China-Philippines

Relations between Beijing and Manila are complex and difficult. From China's perspective, the Philippine leaders have generally operated outside the core of ASEAN, not least due to the country's status as a staunch ally of the United States.[50] However, during the post-Cold War period the Philippines has assumed much greater importance for CCP policymakers given the tensions characterizing bilateral relations over Taiwan and Manila's response to Chinese encroachments in the South China Sea. When difficulties first arose in the early 1990s, Beijing felt that it was necessary to ensure that movements toward reinterpreting Manila's practice of the One-China policy should be stopped, including the attempted passage of the Philippine-Taiwan Mutual Benefits Act (also known as the Philippine-Taiwan Relations Act).[51] This legislation was to serve the purpose of stimulating trade and attract badly required foreign direct investment, which the Mainland was unable to provide at the time. Manila's adherence to the One-China policy has remained a concern, in line with developments in Philippine domestic politics. Following the occupation of Mischief Reef (Panganiban Reef) in 1994–95, the Philippines consistently and vociferously protested this move as well as other perceived encroachments and at times has gone as far as engaging itself in seemingly provocative behaviour to reassert its claims in relation to the Spratly group and Scarborough Shoal.[52] Part of the underlying problem has been Manila's failure as yet to determine the precise extent of the Philippine territorial sea and its exclusive economic zone. More importantly from Beijing's perspective however, has been Manila's eagerness to draw the other ASEAN countries and particularly, the United States, into the territorial dispute with China. Consequently, for Beijing, the Philippines had throughout the 1990s the capacity to assume the role of a spoiler in as much as Manila was believed to have the potential to retard the development of Beijing's overall relations with ASEAN and to play party in a suspected attempt to build an arc of containment around the PRC. Indeed, by constantly warning in dramatic terms of what some scholars have called Beijing's "creeping assertiveness", Manila seemed intent to make its position the yardstick for progress in evolving multilateral talks on the elaboration of a code of conduct between China and ASEAN with respect to the South China Sea.

Recent Developments

Ironically, although Sino-Philippine post-Cold War relations have been overshadowed by Beijing's 1994–95 occupation and subsequent fortification of Mischief Reef, the issue became such a major thorn in bilateral ties that Beijing and Manila eventually agreed that the South China Sea conflict should not affect the normal development of relations. That has proved difficult given the high number of incidents ranging from the placing of territorial markers, the exploitation of fishery resources and the continued fortification of existing structures in contested waters and territory. The difficulties in leaving Mischief Reef to one side moreover stem in part from a sharp sense of vulnerability and resentment among the Philippine elite that has led Manila not only to internationalize the dispute but also to normalize military ties with Washington, its long-time ally. Such bonding, expressed in the 1998 Visiting Forces Agreement and the 2002 Mutual Logistics Support Agreement as well as a resumption of military exercises in the South China Sea, has in turn disturbed Beijing.

In contrast to its relations with most other ASEAN countries, the PRC encountered several structural problems when, in the second half of the 1990s, it attempted to put ties with the Philippines on a better footing in the economic realm. One concerned the Philippines' trade structure and its competitiveness. Indeed, in 1999 a comparatively low level of trade and investment characterized the bilateral economic relationship, with only 1.64 per cent of Philippine exports going to the PRC.[53] In 2000, China successfully proposed to the Philippines to use the occasion of the twenty-fifth anniversary of the establishment of diplomatic relations to draw up a Joint Statement on the framework of bilateral relations in the twenty-first century, with the promotion of economic exchanges a core aim. In 2002, the volume of trade already exceeded US$5 billion, with a healthy trade surplus on the Philippine side.[54]

To address the problem of high farm-to-port transportation costs that still undermine the competitiveness of Philippine agricultural products, China has offered Manila preferential loans to improve necessary infrastructure. Beijing has furthermore provided assistance to enhance agricultural yields. Although also offered a bilateral "early harvest" agreement with Beijing, Manila has felt obliged to opt out of the lowering of agricultural tariffs, apparently due to reasons linked to smuggling in northern Luzon and other structural deficiencies.

If the above steps were designed to promote confidence and reduce Philippine anxiety over possible Chinese economic domination, this objective has also starkly underpinned China's political and security initiatives of the past few years. One pillar on which to improve bilateral relations has focused on promoting high-level exchanges. In this regard, it is noteworthy that Philippine President Gloria Macapagal-Arroyo concluded that her state visit to China in 2001 had raised the bilateral relationship to a more "mature and enduring level". China and the Philippines have also promoted military-to-military exchanges, including a port call to Shanghai by the Philippine navy. Building on earlier Chinese suggestions, Beijing in September 2003 proposed to undertake joint oil exploration in contested waters in the South China Sea. It has also sought to forge counter-terrorism co-operation between Manila and the Shanghai Co-operation Organization in which Beijing is playing the lead role. In the event, these proposals have not yet altered the basic dynamics of Sino-Philippine relations. These find expression in Manila's policy toward the United States and what Philippine officials continue to describe as "irritants" in the South China Sea.

China-Malaysia

Although China-Malaysia relations were marred by suspicions at the beginning of Dr. Mahathir's first term as Prime Minister, his remaining tenure in office saw increasingly better bilateral ties. A major reason for significant progress in the bilateral relationship was Beijing's decision at the end of the Cold War to distance itself from the Communist Party of Malaya. The subsequent improvement is due in many ways to Kuala Lumpur's conscious policy decision to develop ties with China to promote the national interest.[55]

From the PRC's perspective, meanwhile, Malaysia's significance has stemmed in part from its international outlook and position within ASEAN. Indeed, politically, the People's Republic has regarded Malaysia as something of a soulmate in international politics and regional affairs since the end of the Cold War. Dr. Mahathir's advocacy in the early 1990s of a new form of regionalism that centred on East Asia rather than the Asia-Pacific signalled a measure of political discomfort with the United States that Beijing shared. Beijing was also impressed at the time at how Malaysia vigorously defended the principle of non-interference against arguments in favour of human rights and democracy, which Beijing perceived as a strategic discourse designed to achieve peaceful evolution. Economically, Malaysia has been considered important given its significant ethnic Chinese minority, and the attendant potential for mutually beneficial economic exchanges. In the event, significant progress in bilateral relations have depended on Malaysia's long-time Prime Minister Dr. Mahathir Mohamad (who left office in late October 2003) developing in the 1990s an increasingly pragmatic and friendly attitude toward the People's Republic, following intense suspicions toward China only a decade earlier.

Recent Developments

Economic interdependence has vastly increased since Dr. Mahathir led a massive delegation to Beijing in June 1993 to stimulate bilateral trade and investment flows. Kuala Lumpur's trade volume with Beijing now surpasses that of all other ASEAN countries and can be expected to reach higher levels. When then Vice-President Hu Jintao visited Malaysia in April 2002, it was agreed to form the Malaysian-China Business Council with a view to further enhancing trade and investment. China's development is expected to have a mixed impact on the Malaysian economy, but Kuala Lumpur anticipates that it will gain from the "early harvest" agreement as well as China's efforts to build capacity in the new ASEAN member states. Recent Malaysian steps toward promoting a green revolution in countryside are clearly in part aimed to further penetrate the Chinese market.

Following the political departure of Indonesian President Suharto, Malaysian Prime Minister Dr. Mahathir Mohamad became the longest-serving head of government within ASEAN. Although Chinese analysts have appreciated that ASEAN was always unlikely to want to be led by Dr. Mahathir, they could until the end of his tenure trust him to adopt a declaratory foreign policy position that explicitly or implicitly mirrored that of the PRC in relation to a number of issues. For instance, both often railed against power politics and unilateralism in much the same way. This is illustrated, for example, by the official discourse in both capitals in the context of NATO's war in Kosovo in 1999. At the same time, Malaysia has taken care not to damage relations with Washington.

Although the PRC and Malaysia contest territory and waters in the South China Sea, Malaysian leaders have for more than a decade publicly stressed that China is not viewed as a threat. This stance has not always been taken at face value given more ambivalent private comments from within the community of defence officials and analysts. Whatever the extent of residual distrust of China, Malaysia and China have not only agreed about the best possible way to deal with the South China Sea conflict, but also generated rumours of PRC-Malaysia collusion against other claimants. Meanwhile, available evidence suggests that Malaysian leaders remain preoccupied with security threats from their immediate neighbourhood.[56] Practical Sino-Malaysian security co-operation, which was written into the Joint Statement Concerning Future Co-operation of May 1999, seems to involve mostly the exchange of visits by military leaders and port calls.

Malaysia's current Prime Minister, Abdullah Ahmad Badawi, and the new Deputy Prime Minister, Najib Tun Razak, whose father Tun Razak established diplomatic ties with the PRC in 1974, have both committed themselves to promote greater interdependence with Beijing. The two leaderships have already agreed on a visit to China by the new Premier to celebrate the thirtieth anniversary of the establishment of diplomatic relations as well as the 600-year anniversary of the landing of General Zheng He [Cheng Ho] on Malaysian shores in 1405. There are also plans for the king to pay a state visit to the PRC.

China-Brunei Darussalam

Although the two countries pride themselves to be able to look back at more than 1000 years of friendship, Beijing's relations with the Sultanate have developed only rather slowly (but smoothly) following the establishment of diplomatic relations in 1991. On the basis of a state visit by President Jiang Zemin and the finalization of a long-term contract that has allowed China to purchase crude oil from Brunei to serve its diversification strategy in sourcing energy supplies a breakthrough in relations was achieved in 2000. The miniscule trade volume of the 1990s has since jumped to US$340 million in 2003 as China has secured 10 per cent of Brunei's daily oil-producing capacity. Brunei's investments in the PRC have similarly picked up after the two sides agreed on signing an investment protection treaty. The Chinese leadership is particularly interested in seeing such investments support its western development strategy. Political and security co-operation between China and ASEAN's smallest member have yet to evolve.

China-Singapore

The post-Cold War period has seen a deepening of the Sino-Singaporean economic partnership and the further institutionalization of political ties. At the same time, China-Singapore relations have at times exposed political sensitivities and disagreements, particularly in politico-security questions. As a predominantly ethnic Chinese city-state located in the heart of Southeast Asia, Singapore has enjoyed particular importance in the eyes of Chinese decision-makers. Particularly in terms of trade and investment, Beijing has hoped to benefit from strong ties with the city-state. For China, the Singapore experience has also been of interest because the city-state has combined an economic success story without parallel in the region with a formidable record as a beacon of political stability. In the early 1990s, following the establishment of diplomatic relations, Singapore remained important for Beijing because Chinese leaders could moreover trust their counterparts in the city-state to advocate *vis-à-vis* their American partners a policy of sustained engagement of the PRC. Singapore was also helpful because its government played an important role in elaborating a theory of Asian values that could serve as a justification for authoritarian government.[57] In the second half of the 1990s, Singapore's significance may on the whole have declined a little as developments moved on, but it assumed a new importance for China by promoting ASEAN regional economic integration.

Recent Developments

In the early 1990s Singapore had eagerly sought to continue mediating between China and the outside world, a role it had begun to fashion for itself during the Cold War. In 1993, for instance, Singapore had hosted Singapore the so-called Wang-Koo talks, which involved Wang Daohan, President of the Association for the Relations Across the Taiwan Strait and his Taiwan counterpart Koo Chen-fu, Chairman of the Taiwan-based Straits Exchange Foundation. Singapore had moreover tried successfully to bring China into newly established regional multilateral institutions, especially the ASEAN Regional Forum. A year later, Singapore and the PRC agreed on the establishment of the flagship Suzhou Industrial Park (SIP) project to advance the development of Shanghai's hinterland. This inter-governmental project was meant to involve a comprehensive software transfer that would allow the Chinese side to learn how to provide efficient economic management and public administration that were deemed crucial to attracting foreign investments. Notably, Singapore's role of mediator has experienced several setbacks in succeeding years and not all have been ironed out. Beset with difficulties at the local level, the SIP project has also required high-level intervention.[58] Continued mediation between Mainland China and Taiwan proved impossible as cross-strait relations became more confrontational. Moreover, Beijing increasingly voiced its displeasure at Singapore's defence relations with Taiwan and the perceived ambivalence characterizing the city-state's One-China policy. Efforts to forge a stable balance of power between Beijing and Washington have also proved difficult. Chinese leaders have not been terribly enthusiastic about Singapore's strenuous efforts to entrench the present regional order, including those pillars that build on U.S. reassurance and deterrence, notwithstanding their understanding that these efforts flow in part from the perceived need in Singapore to address the issue of increasing Chinese power and apprehensions about the city-state's future if Southeast Asia's regional order were to undergo a dramatic transformation.

While obviously still keen to exploit the opportunities for economic co-operation, Singapore has over the last few years become a little wary of the implications of China's rapidly improving relations with almost all ASEAN countries in the context of instability in relations between Washington and Beijing. As a result, Singaporean leaders have reiterated that the United States is a force for stability and prosperity and taken steps to reinforce its strategic partnership with Washington. Notably, when China approached one ASEAN member after another to win support for the idea of signing a statement on the future development of bilateral ties, Singapore appears to have been the only ASEAN country to pre-empt China's diplomats by itself putting forward an inconspicuous draft. This anticipatory move was successful and resulted in what is arguably the only bilateral statement agreed by the PRC between 1999 and 2000 that is relatively short on detail and more ambiguous in its wording than statements sanctioned by fellow ASEAN states.

Against this background, Beijing seems to have been interested to reinvigorate China-Singapore economic and political ties. Leading a delegation to the city-state in 2002, Hu Jintao discussed China's interest in co-operation in high-tech industrial sectors, the development of its western provinces,

Chinese companies' efforts to go global as well as training and exchange of talents. A year later, the two sides agreed to set up a China Centre in Singapore to allow the PRC to showcase goods and services. More importantly, a bilateral co-operation council directed by the two Prime Ministers and co-chaired by their deputies has been agreed. Singapore has characterized this move as another high point in the relationship and hopes to build on the agreement as a stepping-stone for its continued involvement in the rapid growth of Chinese economy. In the context of Singapore's drive in favour of bilateral FTAs with its key trading partners, the Republic has also favoured on such talks with Beijing. However, for the moment, Singapore is content to wait for the conclusion of China-ASEAN negotiations in relation to goods. Having already successfully negotiated the creation of bilateral free trade agreements with the United States and Japan, Singaporean officials argue that the island republic can afford to bide its time, not least so as not to reinforce claims that the city-state is moving too fast and too far ahead of fellow members of the association. That said, Chinese academics and policy advisers estimate that China's strong economic growth and particularly its ability to attract foreign direct investment in increasingly sophisticated areas of industrial production as well as (potentially) in the services industries presents Singapore with a formidable long-term challenge.

While their political relations are very sound, Beijing and Singapore continue to differ on what the future regional order should look like. While China continues to espouse its New Security Concept, Singapore has little time for it, not least because its leaders see China's policies and possible intentions in relation to military modernization, the South China Sea and Taiwan as potentially destabilizing. Singapore's government is keen on a continued forward presence of the U.S. military and the continuation of the San Francisco Treaty system to effectively balance China. Moreover, it helped to initiate the Shangri-La Dialogues and has given its support to many of the multinational responses to security challenges that the U.S. Pacific Command has proposed. At the same time, Singapore seeks to deepen U.S. engagement with Southeast Asia across the board in order to give U.S. policy greater legitimacy to counteract the rise in Chinese influence won, for instance, through the ASEAN+1 process. This strategy is to some extent at odds with China's political aspirations and preferred security order.

China-Indonesia

There can be little doubt that the Chinese leadership aspires to significantly enhanced relations with Indonesia. To Beijing's vexation, political and security ties lack behind developments in the economic sphere. Indonesia's significance for China in the post-Cold War period, at least until the onset of the Asian financial crisis, was in part a reflection of Jakarta's centrality within the association, and Beijing expects Jakarta to reclaim its former status. Mindful of its own growing international trade, the importance attributed to Indonesia is moreover a reflection of Indonesia's geographical position and the fact that it straddles important sea-lanes of communication. Beijing also has long-standing concerns over the treatment of the ethnic Chinese community in Indonesia. These factors continue to inform Chinese policy towards Jakarta. But there are additional reasons why Beijing is interested in enhanced ties with Jakarta. First, Chinese leaders are keen to persuade Jakarta to forego the persistent balance of power motive that characterized its foreign policy *vis-à-vis* Beijing under President Suharto and still has adherents in the bureaucracy and army. Second, after the political demise of Suharto in May 1998, when Indonesian politics became gripped by a tortuous and imperfect process of democratization and decentralization, which at times threatened its territorial integrity and for a while put an end to straightforward ethnic and religious co-existence, Indonesia's continued stability assumed considerable political importance for Beijing, not least in the light of its own fissiparous condition. At the same time, China for the first time since the 1960s saw the opportunity to make significant progress in bilateral relations, particularly in political-strategic terms and to develop Indonesia as an important economic partner, whose economy is viewed as increasingly complimentary to the Chinese economy.

Recent Developments

Sino-Indonesian relations were normalized in 1990, but they remained strained even during the final years of the Suharto presidency. These strains echoed above all the deep-seated suspicions of the People's Republic held by Indonesia's military, which in policy terms translated into Jakarta's support for the sustained engagement of the United States in the ARF and the unprecedented signing of a security treaty with Australia in 1995.[59] These events prompted a rethink and charm offensive on the part of Beijing. Although China's restrained reaction for many weeks in view of what seemed an anti-Chinese pogrom in Jakarta in May 1998 reinforced the point that Beijing valued highly any possibility of improving bilateral ties, these were upgraded through a symbolic act of diplomatic courtesy only at the beginning of the presidency of Abdurrahman Wahid. Following two years that saw Indonesia humbled by the experience of the Asian crisis, Wahid made to the PRC in 1999 in what was declared as his first official visit abroad in the context of his new Asia policy. On that occasion, the two sides signed an important communiqué that served as the foundation for their May 2000 statement on future political, economic and security co-operation.

Notably, of all ten joint statements on bilateral co-operation signed by the PRC with the ASEAN countries during 1999-2000, the Indonesia-China statement was arguably the most assertive in tone in that it called for a "just and more balanced new international political, economic *and security* order".[60] That assertiveness was more the expression of Indonesia's frustration with its post-crisis political-strategic downsizing than a reflection of a newly found mutuality with Beijing. Indeed, close observers within Indonesia maintain that China-Indonesia ties have remained "one-sided" in that Jakarta, although keen to promote economic exchanges, has not developed a clear political strategy to dealing with China,[61] in contrast to the Chinese Government, which has also been interested in expanding the relationship to include a strategic dialogue. As Chinese Premier Zhu Rongji put it when visiting Indonesia in November 2001, China hopes to "continue consultations and co-operation with Indonesia on regional and international political, economic, and security issues of common concern".[62]

For the moment, high-level exchanges, the political symbolism of Jakarta's explicit commitment to a One-China policy and Beijing's commitment to Indonesia's territorial integrity as well as efforts to stimulate economic interaction very much form the essence of bilateral ties. Both sides moreover argue for the "democratization" of international relations and express concern about U.S. unilateralism. More success has been achieved in boosting economic ties. Bilateral trade has multiplied quickly to reach about US$10 billion, including trade via Hong Kong;[63] Chinese investments in Indonesia by July 2003 have soared massively from a cumulative total of US$282 million in 1999. With soaring energy requirements that increasingly have to be met from abroad, it is no surprise that most high-ticket Chinese investments to date have come about in the context of Beijing's search to diversify its increasing energy supplies. This has included the purchase by China National Offshore Oil Corporation of the Widuri and Cinta fields in Indonesia for US$585 million.[64] China also awarded to Indonesia without tender a contract to supply Liquified Natural Gas (LNG) to Fujian for twenty years.

In contrast, co-operation in security and defence remains underdeveloped, ostensibly due to the residual distrust against China still harboured within the TNI. The clarification that Jakarta once sought in relation to China's claims in the South China Sea, not least to determine whether there is an overlap with Indonesia's EEZ claim to waters around the Natunas, has apparently not been forthcoming. However, the two sides have started a dialogue over weapons sales and future co-operation in related research. Part of the background to this is that Chinese weapons would come with no strings attached, in contrast to Western-sourced systems that cannot be used in Aceh. Also, unlike with Washington, purchases from Beijing would also not be hostage to congressional politics.

BILATERAL RELATIONS AS A PLATFORM FOR SINO-ASEAN TIES

The rapid development of bilateral relations has been a common feature in China's ties with Southeast Asia in the post-Cold War period, particularly after the Asian crisis. Consistent features of China's bilateral ties in recent years have been a high number of high-level visits and official exchanges, a significant upsurge in trade and mutual investments and the increasing institutionalization of bilateral relations. To be sure, interactions between the PRC and individual ASEAN countries have not all proceeded at the same pace. While some have developed beyond the expectations of most analysts, others remain stifled even when agreement to move the relationship forward regardless of conflict has been reached. Still others develop in a subdued manner in view of the prevailing ambivalence still pervading parts of Southeast Asia when it comes to relations with Beijing.

Having examined the bilateral relationships, it would also seem that China's expectations about how in particular the continental ASEAN states should relate to China have been largely fulfilled. Both China's core identity claims and security interests are sufficiently respected. No Southeast Asian country has sought sub-regional hegemony in the aftermath of the Cambodian conflict and no ASEAN state has pushed for the establishment of new military bases by external powers, although some have offered to provide the United States with improved access. On sensitive political issues, like Taiwan, ASEAN countries have widely supported Beijing, albeit not always without equivocation. Co-operation to improve stability in the border areas has been multi-faceted. As regards the maritime countries, China can claim to have made strident advances, irrespective of the remaining issues, problems and suspicions in some capitals. No maritime country is openly challenging China, even though some have turned to the United States to reinforce the existing order.

Overall, there can be no doubt that in comparison to the Cold War era China now possesses some influence in Southeast Asia. But qualifications are important. Beijing's ability to exercise influence is variable, even within continental Southeast Asia. In maritime Southeast Asia, the lure of mutually beneficial economic exchanges has generally not translated into major political influence. From Beijing's perspective, this is no cause for concern. Indeed, in China's view, the extent of improvement in bilateral ties with several Southeast Asian countries since the late 1990s must be reason for elation.

That Chinese leaders believe that strengthening bilateral ties with individual members has been critical for advancing overall China-ASEAN relations is without doubt. Certain ASEAN members are publicly credited with assuming a particular import in moving China-ASEAN ties forward. As noted, Thailand is regarded to have assumed such an important role. Malaysia has been similarly praised, as has Singapore, albeit the latter perhaps not as much recently as in the past. What applies to the past, seems also to be valid for the future as Beijing believes that it can rely, for example, on the "comprehensive development of Sino-Thai relations" to "promote the continuous development of the relations" with ASEAN.[65]

This expectation is not an expression of Chinese high-mindedness but reflects the reality of greater economic interdependence and opportunity for both itself and ASEAN-10. China's new diplomacy and the economic opportunities it is offering have provided a strong foundation for mutually beneficial economic relations and successful multilateral endeavours. The dispensation of economic handouts and the willingness to absorb significantly more exports from the ASEAN countries has rendered the People's Republic a serious economic partner with whom ASEAN governments can and should deal individually and collectively. Notably, as the example of the agreed ASEAN-China FTA demonstrates, Beijing has moreover sought to accommodate particular concerns of all ASEAN countries in reaching an agreement with the association. This has allowed member states to see encouraging coherence in China's bilateral and regional policies.

From China's perspective, improvements in bilateral ties have also provided a platform for overall China-ASEAN ties insofar as — unlike in the mid-1990s — Beijing's restraint and generosity has made it much more difficult for individual states in Southeast Asia to maintain that Beijing is not acting in good faith, which would allow them to hope to be able to torpedo regional level agreements considered unwanted or unfavourable. Indeed, in moving on the regional level relationship the Chinese leadership has not found it necessary to draw on any policy instruments that would have undermined its own efforts to come across as a benign power *vis-à-vis* individual ASEAN states. As was illustrated by the negotiations in the run-up to the Declaration on the Code of Conduct, Beijing has perhaps politically benefited from intramural differences. More generally, China evidently also benefits from the understandable inclination of all ASEAN states to pursue first and foremost, the respective national interest.

Although ASEAN countries on the whole acknowledge that China has behaved rather responsibly in the wider region and undertaken initiatives to improve both the atmosphere and substance of bilateral ties, suspicions about long-term intentions persist in some quarters. As such, bilateral relations have provided Beijing with a strong platform, albeit not one that is completely immune to shocks. Should bilateral ties with key ASEAN states not only unexpectedly languish but suffer major reversals, agreements already attained might prove more difficult to implement, and consolidation rather than new initiatives could for a while easily become the name of the game of Sino-ASEAN ties. The Chinese leadership knows that bilateral relations need further strengthening and it has been very open about its wishes for the longer term: closer co-ordination on international and regional issues, deeper economic ties and co-operation in dealing with transnational security challenges. Meanwhile, even if some bilateral ties were to further advance, it is not self-evident that this would translate into further stunning progress in the regional level China-ASEAN relationship.

Arguably, strong or improving bilateral relations with ASEAN member states also only provide a platform for the development of China-ASEAN ties in the overall context of Southeast Asian assumptions about the future of China and strategic stability in East Asia. In other words, the platform's static balance is, for the time being, secured by China's strong domestic economic performance and relatively stable Sino-U.S. relations. Neither can be taken for granted.

CONCLUSION

This chapter has attempted to cast a glance at what goes on "below" China-ASEAN relations at the regional level: China's bilateral relations with individual member states. Following a brief contextualization of China's Southeast Asia policy, it has spelled out in some detail the importance that China attaches to individual countries within the association and analyzed key developments in bilateral ties to highlight their increasing depth and breadth, particularly after the Asian crisis. The chapter has argued that the steadily improving state of bilateral relations between China and the countries of Southeast Asia has largely both rested on Chinese initiative and depended on Beijing's adroit use of foreign policy instruments. The argument has moreover been that enhanced bilateral relations have given Beijing a platform to put the relationship with

ASEAN on a new footing. However, while improving bilateral relations offer the PRC a platform for greater achievements at the regional level, the platform will itself need continued attention and reinforcement.

Acknowledgements

The author gratefully acknowledges funding from the British Academy (Sino-British Fellowship Trust) to conduct interviews on PRC foreign policy towards Southeast Asia. Many thanks also go to the numerous academics and officials in Beijing, Guangzhou, Xiammen and Kunming who kindly gave of their time for this project, particularly Professor Han Feng, Assistant Director of the Institute of Asia-Pacific at the Chinese Academy of Social Sciences.

Notes

1. See for example Alice Ba, "China and ASEAN: Renavigating Relations for a 21st Century Asia", *Asian Survey* 43, no. 4 (2003): 622–47. Also see "Overview of ASEAN-PRC Relations", online at <http://www.aseansec.org>.
2. For an exception see S.D. Muni, *China's Strategic Engagement with the New ASEAN: An Exloratory Study of China's Post-Cold War Political, Strategic and Economic Relations with Myanmar, Laos, Cambodia and Vietnam* (Singapore: IDSS Monograph no. 2, 2002).
3. For an exception see for instance Joseph Y.S. Cheng, "Sino-ASEAN Relations in the Early Twenty-first Century", *Contemporary Southeast Asia* 23, no. 3 (December 2001): 420–51.
4. On this, see for instance the contributions in Mark Beeson, ed., *Reconfiguring East Asia: Regional Institutions and Organisations after the Crisis* (London and New York: RoutledgeCurzon, 2002). Also see Douglas Webber, "Two Funerals and a Wedding? The Ups and Downs of Regionalism in East Asia and Asia-Pacific after the Asian Crisis", *The Pacific Review* 14, no. 3 (2001): 339–72.
5. Important developments in the formal inter-regional relationship include: (1) The ASEAN-China Senior Officials Meeting, agreed in 1994; (2) China's acceptance as one of ASEAN's dialogue partners in 1996; and (3) the establishment of the ASEAN-China Joint Co-operation Committee in 1997.
6. Among the important documents are: (1) Framework Agreement on Comprehensive Economic Cooperation (including ASEAN-China Free Trade Area) (2002), (2) Declaration on the Conduct of Parties in the South China Sea (2002), (3) China's accession to the Treaty of Amity and Co-operation (2003), and (4) the Joint Declaration on Strategic Partnership for Peace and Prosperity (2003).
7. On informal ideology, see Stephen Levine, "Perception and Ideology in Chinese Foreign Policy" in Thomas W. Robinson and David Shambaugh David, eds.,

Chinese Foreign Policy:Theory and Practice (Oxford: Clarendon Press, 1994), pp. 30–46. Also see Michael Hunt, *The Genesis of Chinese Communist Foreign Policy* (New York: Columbia University Press, 1996).

8. See Michael Yahuda, *China's Role in World Affairs* (London: Croom Helm, 1978). Also see John Gittings, *The World and China, 1922–1972* (London: Eyre Methuen, 1974).

9. For the theme of stability along China's periphery, see Michael D. Swaine and Ashley J. Tellis, *Interpreting China's Grand Strategy: Past, Present, and Future* (Santa Monica, CA: RAND, 2000).

10. On China's relations with the great powers see, for instance, Jennifer Anderson, *The Limits of Sino-Russian Strategic Partnership* (Oxford: Oxford University Press for IISS, 1997); Reinhard Drifte, *Japan's Security Relations with China: From Balancing to Bandwagoning* (London: RoutledgeCurzon, 2003); James Mann, *About Face: A History of America's Curious Relationship with China, From Nixon to Clinton* (New York: Vintage, 2000).

11. For these points, see Jürgen Haacke, "Seeking Influence: China's Diplomacy toward ASEAN after the Asian Crisis", *Asian Perspective* 26, no. 4 (2002): 13–52. Also see Chen Jie, *Foreign Policy of the New Taiwan: Pragmatic diplomacy in Southeast Asia* (Cheltenham: Edward Elgar, 2002).

12. Muni, *China's Strategic Engagement with the New ASEAN*, p. 20.

13. For a general overview of the development of China's concept of security, see Wu Baiyi, "The Chinese Security Concept and its Historical Evolution", *Journal of Contemporary China* 10, no. 27 (2001): 275–83.

14. Jiang Zemin, "Promote Disarmament Process and Safeguard World Security", address at UN Disarmament Conference, Geneva, 26 March 1999, <www.china-un.org/eng/zghlhg/cj/unga/t29298.htm>.

15. Zhan Maohai, "China's Security and Military Doctrine", paper presented at 1st IISS Asia Security Dialogue, Singapore, 31 May–2 June 2002.

16. Chu Sulong quoted in Denny Roy, "China's Reaction to American Predominance", *Survival* 45, no. 3 (2003): 70.

17. *China's Position on the New Security Concept*, 31 July 2002, available online at <www.fmprc.gov.cn>.

18. Zhan Maohai, "China's Security and Military Doctrine", p. 2.

19. See Ian James Storey and Carlyle A. Thayer, "Cam Ranh Bay: Past Imperfect, Future Conditional", *Contemporary Southeast Asia* 23, no. 3 (December 2001): 452–73.

20. Nayan Chanda, "China and Cambodia: In the Mirror of History", *Asia-Pacific Review* 9, no. 2 (2002): 2–3.

21. Chen Jian, *Mao's China and the Cold War* (Chapel Hill & London: University of North Carolina Press, 2001), chapter 5, esp. pp. 138–44.

22. See Sukhumbhand Paribatra, *From Enmity to Alignment: Thailand's Evolving Relations with China* (Bangkok: Institute of Security and International Studies, Chulalongkorn University, 1987); R.K. Jain, *China and Thailand, 1949–1983* (New Delhi: Radiant Publishers, 1984), pp. xxxvii–lxxxvi.

23. Interviews, Beijing, January 2004.
24. Michael Vatikiotis, "Outward Bound", *FEER*, 5 February 2004, pp. 24–27.
25. See Michael Vatikiotis, "Catching the Dragon's Tail: China and Southeast Asia in the 21st Century", *Contemporary Southeast Asia* 4, no. 1 (2003): 71.
26. Interview, 5 January 2004.
27. See *China-Thailand Joint Communiqué*, Beijing, 29 August 2001, online at <www.fmprc.gov.cn/eng/17357.html>.
28. Lyall Breckon, "Focus is Elsewhere, but Bonds Continue to Grow", *Comparative Connections*, January–March 2003, online at <www.csis.org/pacfor/cc/0301Qchina-asean.html>.
29. Interview with Thai official, 5 January 2004.
30. Interview, Beijing, 26 February 2003.
31. For an overview of the bilateral relationship, see Tin Maung Maung Than, "Myanmar and China: A Special Relationship", *Southeast Asian Affairs* 2003, pp. 189–210.
32. See Poon Kim Shee, "The Political Economy of China-Myanmar Relations: Strategic and Economic Dimensions", *Ritsumeikan Annual Review of International Studies* 1, no. 10 (2002): 34.
33. See Mohan Malik, "Sino-Indian Rivalry in Myanmar: Implications for Regional Security", *Contemporary Southeast Asia* 16, no. 2 (September 1994), pp. 137–56.
34. See Pan Qi, "Opening the Southwest: An Expert Opinion", *Beijing Review* 28, no. 35 (2 September 1985): 22–23.
35. See Bertil Lintner, "China's Ambitions in Myanmar: India Steps Up Countermoves", *Strategic Comments*, July 2000, reprinted at <http://www.asiapacificms.com/articles/myanmar_influence/>.
36. See David I Steinberg, *Burma: The State of Myanmar* (Washington: Georgetown University Press, 2001), pp. 224, 233.
37. Steinberg, *Burma: The State of Myanmar*, p. 159.
38. *People's Daily*, "Sino-Myanmar Bilateral Economic, Trade Ties Get New Momentum", 22 March 2004, <http://www.english/peopledaily.com.cn/200403/22/eng20040322_138147.shtml>.
39. Muni, *China's Strategic Engagement with the New ASEAN*, p. 45.
40. Interview, Beijing, January 2004.
41. It has been widely argued that Burma/Myanmar has also been of interest to Chinese military for purposes of intelligence gathering on Great Coco Island in the Bay of Bengal, which is located 30 nautical miles north of India's Andaman Group, but rumours that Beijing is interested in Hainggyi Island as a Chinese naval base may have insufficient foundation. Certainly within China these rumours have been widely denied, not least by officials from the Ministry of Defence. One interviewee said that while he doubted the rumours, he hoped they were true.
42. CSIS, *Transnational Threats Update* 2, no. 6 (March 2004): 6. For background information, see for example Bertil Lintner, *Burma in Revolt: Opium and Insurgency since 1948*, second edn. (Chiang Mai: Silkworm Books, 1999)

43. Also see Information Office of the State Council, *Narcotics Control in China*, June 2000.

44. On Sino-Vietnamese relations see Chang Pao-min, "Sino-Vietnamese Relations: Prospects for the Twenty-First Century", in *Vietnamese Foreign Policy in Transition*, edited by Carlyle A. Thayer and Ramses Amer (Singapore: ISEAS, 1999), pp. 130–47.

45. Lyall Breckon, "SARS and a New Security Initiative from China", *Comparative Connections*, <www.csis.org/pacfor/cc0302Qchina_asean.html>.

46. On the Spratlys, see Greg Austin, *China's Ocean Frontier: International Law, Military Force and National Development* (St. Leonards: Allen & Unwin, 1998); On the Paracels, see Stein Tønneson, "The Paracels: The 'Other' South China Sea Dispute", *Asian Perspective* 26, no. 4 (2002): 145–69.

47. See James K.Chin, "Dragon and Naga: Challenges and Pitfalls in Bilateral Economic Collaboration" in this volume.

48. Muni, *China's Strategic Engagement with the New ASEAN*, p. 86.

49. Ibid., p. 74.

50. Interview, Beijing, January 2004.

51. Aileen San Pablo-Baviera, "Philippine-Taiwan Relations", in *China-ASEAN Relations: Political, Economic & Ethic Dimensions*, edited by Theresa C. Carino (Manila: DeLa Salle University, 1991), p. 113.

52. Haydee B. Yorac, "The Philippine Claim to the Spratly Islands Group", in *China-ASEAN Relations: Regional Security and Cooperation*, edited by Theresa C. Carino (Quezon City: Philippine-China Development Resource Centre, 1998), pp. 67–87. You Ji has argued that China's occupation of Mischief Reef was provoked by the Philippines. See his *The Armed Forces of China* (New York: I.B. Tauris, 1999), p. 223.

53. Aileen San Pablo Baviera, "Philippines-China Relations: A Vision for Cooperation", *Currents* 11, no. 1 (January–June 2000): 1–2.

54. See Chinese Ministry of Foreign Affairs, China-Philippines bilateral relations <http://www.fmprc.gov.cn/eng/wjb/zzjg/yzs/gjlb/2762/default.htm>.

55. Malaysia's China-policy has been described as "bandwagoning". For this argument, see Joseph Liow's chapter in this volume.

56. Andrew Tan, "What's Behind Malaysia's Defence Build-up?", *IDSS Commentaries*, June 2003.

57. Alan Chong, "Singaporean foreign policy and the Asian Values Debate, 1992–2000: Reflections on an Experiment in Soft Power", *The Pacific Review* 17, no. 1 (2004): 103.

58. Following the expression of misgivings in public the SIP has apparently made better progress. According to official Chinese sources the project had by April 2002 attracted a cumulative total of US$13.15 billion in investments. See *People's Daily*, <http://english.peopledaily.com.cn/2002505/10/eng20020510_05429.shtml>.

59. See Michael Leifer, "Indonesia and the Dilemmas of Engagement", in *Engaging China: The Management of an Emerging Power*, edited by Alastair Iain Johnston and Robert S. Ross (London and New York: Routledge), pp. 87–108.

60. My emphasis. In the Communiqué the formulation had only made reference to the objective of a "more just and balanced world order".

61. Hadi Soesastro, "Indonesia-China Relations — But Where is the Beef?", <www.kompas.com/kompas_cetak/0204/01/English/indo.htm>.

62. Chinese Ministry of Foreign Affairs 2001, "Premier Zhu Held Talks with Indonesian President Megawati Sukarnoputri, 7/11/2001", online at <www.fmprc.gov.cn/eng/20460.html>.

63. For an analysis on the shift toward economics in the relationship, see Samuel C.Y. Ku, "Indonesia's Relations with China and Taiwan: From Politics to Economics", *Asian Perspective* 26, no. 4 (2002): 227–56.

64. See Dhume and Lawrence, "Buying Fast into Southeast Asia", p. 31. Also see Amy Myers Jaffe and Steven W. Lewis, "Beijing's Oil Diplomacy", *Survival* 44, no. 1 (Spring, 2002): 115–34.

65. See *People's Daily*, <www.english.peopledaily.com.cn/200309/03/eng20030903_123605.shtml>.

6

NON-TRADITIONAL SECURITY AND CHINA-ASEAN RELATIONS

Co-operation, Commitments and Challenges

Cai Peng Hong

INTRODUCTION

Like other parts of the world, East Asian nations including China and ASEAN have been genuinely concerned about non-traditional security issues, particularly since the 1997 financial crisis and 2003 SARs. With this background, this chapter will focus on the new developments in political and security relations between China and ASEAN, especially in their co-operation, roles and prospects in addressing "non-traditional security" issues. Non-traditional security is a term in debates within China as well as international academic circles, but the ASEAN-China joint declaration has adopted the concept, generally defining it under the state's sovereignty. I will therefore review the bilateral relations development along the lines of traditional security but will emphasize on the non-traditional security, particularly in view of China's signing of the Treaty of Amity and Co-operation in Southeast Asia (TACSA), which originally implies and serves as a foundation of traditional security.

I regard non-traditional security as a new phenomenon and doubt whether a realist approach will still be of help, but consider a liberal approach as being possibly useful, to facilitate co-operation. This is a policy analysis and thus, any statement or claim that nations like ASEAN members and China have made would be looked at as an important step towards co-operation in the fight against non-traditional security issues and further co-operation in the future security of East Asia.

CHINESE PERSPECTIVES OF "NON-TRADITIONAL SECURITY"

Since the end of the Cold War, Chinese policymakers and academics have reviewed and discussed the concept of security, coincident with the "lively debate over the meaning of security" worldwide (Tow and Trood 2000, p. 13). Such discussions and reviews have generated a clear contour of academic perception in China over non-traditional security from a state-centric view, to a blend of state-centric and neo-liberalist security concerns that include not only the protection of the foundations of the state against external threats but also other types of security values and other types of threats, although there is still some ambiguity within the policy-making circles.

Taking a realist approach, Chinese security studies have traditionally focused on external threats to state security and internal instability possibly affecting the legitimacy of a government or current authority. As a revolutionary regime emerged in 1949, China made every effort to consolidate state power in its initial years. For revolutionary leaders like Mao Zedong and others, what made sense in security were those military threats against the new state from external sources, mainly from the U.S.-led West at first, and then from the former Soviet Union (USSR) (Mao 1994). Domestic factors that seemed to threaten the viability of the new regime primarily include remnants of the KMT regime in Taiwan and perhaps revisionists inside the Chinese Communist Party (CCP) and government. From the realist theory, a nation's security means ensuring the survival of a nation state from an external aggressor trying to occupy land and overthrow the ruling regime, and from internal subversion, although that theory emphasizes less on internal threats. This state-centric paradigm dominated the agendas of security policy studies in academic and policy circles for more than thirty years.

Immediately after the end of the destructive Cultural Revolution (1966–76), Deng Xiaoping's rehabilitation in 1977 heralded a new age in China, which embarked on economic reform. Deng re-evaluated and then abandoned Mao's thoughts on global war. According to Deng's new thinking in the early 1980s, neither a new world war nor a mass military aggression directed against China would be possible in the foreseeable future. This indicated that traditional threats of security to the state would be stressed less and less but new issues would contribute to a new security situation with the shift in national strategy to economic construction. With the end of the Cold War, the bipolar world order disappeared. Instead, the whole world seemed to shift towards a new focus, that is, economic development. That this phenomenon has taken place without any major war among the big powers, further supported Deng's previous view and in China, Deng's argument that "economic development is irrefutable" has taken on an irreversible momentum. The discussion on security under the new situation was mainly conducted in academic circles. To understand Chinese research on the conceptual debates, the following analysis of the studies on non-traditional security has been divided into three stages.

The first stage starts from the end of the Cold War to the year 1997. Although some arguments of the Club of Rome group had been introduced into China in the early 1980s, some non-military issues expressed as "world problematique" like poverty, environmental degradation, uncontrolled urban spread, insecurity of employment, alienation of youth, rejection of traditional values, and inflation and other monetary and economic disruptions, did not draw Chinese attention until the early 1990s, when the USSR split up and the Cold War came to an end. With the end of the bipolar world order, President Jiang Zemin exposed non-traditional security concerns such as conflicts among ethnic groups and religions, economic competition and North-South gaps in his speech to the Chinese Communist Party Congress in 1992 (Jiang 1992*a*). Since then, non-traditional security issues have been stressed in the Chinese Government and academic circles. Policy analysts started reconsidering the security meaning and suggested some new ideas such as comprehensive security and a common security concept for the common interests of all nations and social progress. The contents of the concept extended from traditional security to economic, science and technology, environment, culture and many other areas, which are now called non-traditional security issues. The embodiment of this new thinking was the new security concept put forward as an initiative by China in 1996 and embedded into the document "Sino-Russian Joint Statement on the Multipolarization of the World and the Establishment of a New International Order" signed on 23 April 1997.

The second stage is from around 1997 to the terrorist attacks on 11 September 2001, during which non-traditional security issues had increasingly become a source of growing concern in China as well as the world. The financial crises like the 1997 financial crisis that hit Southeast Asia, the 1998 Russian financial storm and the 2001 case that almost dismantled Argentina's economy alerted the Chinese to the financial issues ahead. These issues bear on economic and financial security (Zhang and Zhou 2000). Meanwhile, the new security concept has been implemented through diplomatic activities. The establishment of Shanghai Co-operation Organization in 2001 and its further development should be regarded as a new institution dealing with non-traditional as well as traditional security issues.

The third stage commences with the September 11 attacks to the present. Non-traditional security has been gradually established almost at the same level of priority as that of traditional security on the agendas of China's national security strategy. China made it clear that non-traditional security issues are terrorism, illicit drugs, HIV/AIDS, piracy, illegal migration, environmental security, economic security, information security and others (PRC Government 2002*a*). China has defined the concept and features of non-traditional security in its official documents issued since 2002 such as "*China's Position Paper on Enhanced Co-operation in the Field of Non-Traditional Security Issues*" (29 May 2002), "*China's Position Paper on the New Security Concept*" (31 July 2002) and "*Declaration of China-ASEAN Co-operation on Non-traditional Security Issues*" (4 November 2002). The most significant is the viewpoint that "the elements of traditional and non-traditional threats to security are intertwined", in which the term "non-traditional threats" first appeared in a top official document, a report delivered by Jiang at the sixteenth National Congress of the Communist Party of China (CPC) on 8 November 2002 (Jiang 1992*b*). The SARs (Severe Acute Respiratory Syndrome) epidemic occurred in early 2003 and then the special China-ASEAN Summit on the SARs issue held in Thailand on 29 April 2003 spurred China to further emphasize non-traditional security issues.

Non-traditional security research in China has been a government-directed academic activity for a long time. With the Chinese society opening up increasingly, it is normal that academics have diverse ideas on academic issues including non-traditional security. Although the mainstream defines it as the elements of threat to the security of sovereign countries, including threats to human beings and social development except for military, political and diplomatic conflicts (Fu, Y. 2003), academic debates on non-traditional security have led to various points of view including human security with its extensive themes. This is mainly because of the influence of Western international relations theories introduced to China.

The theory of international political economy (IPE) has had a significant impact on Chinese academics, particularly with the emergence of *The Political Economy of International Relations* by American scholar Robert Gilpin (Gilpin

1987*a*), which had its Chinese translation published in 1988. The contribution that the IPE theory and approach made to Chinese academic circles is that it widened Chinese insights into international politics with an emphasis on its security research, though the IPE book did not refer to the term non-traditional security. Gilpin's explanations of international trade, international finance, activities of transnational companies, dependence and development and exploration of international economic order were classic statements of the new field, and theoretical foundation for the intellectual development of Chinese international politics. Meanwhile, the neo-realist approach started focusing on international co-operation outside threats of a military nature against the state from external sources. Although the argument on hegemonic stability (Charles, K. 1970 and Gilpin 1987*a*) and the co-operation theory after hegemony (Keohane, R.O. 1984) are still pursued, liberal views reflecting to some extent a new probe for a co-operative security gradually emerged. Besides, I would also like to touch on the North-South gap, an essential issue in current studies of non-traditional security which was stressed by Robert Gilpin, whose argument was that poverty and underdeveloped countries would deeply affect the future of the world and human beings (Gilpin 2002*b*, p. 295).

The neo-liberalist theory plays an even more important and influential role. The complex interdependence approach has shown that a hierarchy of issues has not been enough to explain the agendas of inter-country relations, and those issues that are considered as low politics, including oil, resources, environment, population, use of ocean and space, have been viewed as being as important as those of high politics. The argument by Keohane and Nye that military force plays a secondary role has been significantly amended to propose a new alternative core concept of security (Keohane and Nye 2002, p. 28). The fact that Keohane and Nye's book was first published in Chinese translation and distributed in China in 1988 and then again in 2002 shortly after its third version in 2001, strongly demonstrates that the neo-liberalist approach has gained the attention of Chinese academics, some of whom advocate neo-liberalism because these scholars' security concerns have shifted to new phenomena including economic and social issues, away from traditional thinking. Liberal views and their influence are gaining ground, particularly with the SARs incident in 2003, and the value of security concerns cover almost all those ideas the liberals espouse, including individual and community (public) health, sustainable economic development, environmental protection, human security and even individuals' spiritual growth and human rights.

The environmental degradation and resource decline have become increasingly central to the academic debates and governmental development agendas. China paid attention to international politics on the environment or ecological politics only less than a decade ago (Wang, Y. 1998, pp. 585–613). These days the Chinese Government has emphasized the "scientific development concept", indicating that environmental issues and resource scarcity have been linked to non-traditional security, as a serious issue that may have an adverse effect on the national strategy. Premier Wen Jiabao stressed the need to balance the development of man and nature, which shows that their harmonious development as an overall planning in the national strategy has become a key issue (Wen 2004). The environmental concerns have been labelled non-traditional security in academic circles but undoubtedly the politics of environmental studies is still in its infancy and no stringency of theoretical and academic framework has been established. To solve the issues of the relations between non-traditional security and the environment, the questions raised by Lorraine Elliott are still awaiting responses from Chinese academic and policy circles: who or what is made secure; what core values are threatened; what are the types of threats and the nature of the problem and how should insecurity be managed and how should security be attained (Elliott, L. 2001, p. 438).

Divergent views in the debate over the concept of human security have reached a new outcome recently. A few years ago, the debate was dominated by those who strongly rebuked the Western hostile elements for having ulterior motives in trying to bring human rights as a pressure to bear on China. The 2003 SARs incident renewed the debate and finally China's top leaders did not oppose human security publicly but President Hu Jintao signed the 2003 APEC Summit Declaration, in which human security has been stressed and required to be enhanced to secure trade in the Asia and Pacific region (APEC Secretariat 2003).

Increasingly, non-traditional security challenges such as economic crises and environmental degradation have been attracting academic attention but the study is still a new field in China. My argument is that the non-traditional security still lies within the fundamental framework of security studies, particularly with the current global pattern where there is no efficient governance under an ideal world government. Therefore the non-traditional security issues are a somewhat expanded range of traditional security meaning (connotation). The central government of the state is truly and increasingly paying more attention to non-traditional security issues, for instance, the viewpoint that "putting people first" (*yi ren wei ben*) as a new doctrine has been covering almost all policy papers. However, it would be absolutely impossible for China at the moment to accept it as its commitment to human security, that "the sovereignty of states must no longer be used as a shield for gross violations of human rights" (The UN Secretary-General in his Nobel lecture on 10 December 2001). China is also unable to share the same degree of concern over some issues such as Western values being a part of individual rights.

CHINA APPROACHES ASEAN FOR CO-OPERATION IN NON-TRADITIONAL SECURITY

China has had good relations with the nations of Southeast Asia for a long time. After the 1949 Revolution, there appeared to be almost no connection among China and most of the archipelago nations because of the Cold War. Beginning with the first half of the 1970s, China gradually normalized relations with those nations and the normalizations were established upon the basis of common political strategy against then Soviet expansionism. By 1991, China had restored its diplomatic relations with all individual ASEAN nations and then Chinese Foreign Minister Qian Qichen attended the opening session of the Twenty-fourth AMM in Kuala Lumpur, laying the foundation for further developing co-operation with ASEAN. The policy adjustment by China was contributive to the establishment of good-neighbourly relations, particularly with the Chinese withdrawing support to local communist activities and cutting its relations with the Khmer Rouge, which resulted in improving and resuming China's relations with Vietnam.

However, improvements in relations in the early 1990s may not have totally dissolved some nations' long-standing concerns about China's intention in the South China Sea and some unsettled land-bordering disputes, because sovereignty and territorial integrity have been regarded as core interests for both sides. Many ASEAN nations were newly established after WWII and cherished their sovereignty and other elements of high politics, which are closely connected with traditional security issues. Their perspectives and traditional security concerns, similar to China's, were therefore manifested in a set of ASEAN documents. The fundamental principle of the "Treaty of Amity and Co-operation in Southeast Asia" (1976) is to keep "independence, sovereignty, equality, territorial integrity" in the hands of the state and to reject "external interference, subversion or coercion".

Although some legacy from history or the Cold War could not fade away overnight, the new events as mentioned above like the end of the Cold War and the process of globalization have spurred China to reconsider the traditional security concept and its contents. Meanwhile, ASEAN nations have just made some amendments to their development strategy focusing on internal economic construction to make up what they had lost in the period of the Cold War. Moreover, some new phenomena like information technology, big container transportation, population immigration and others have been transnationalized. Economic development should be protected from those new phenomena but ASEAN began suffering from issues such as transboundary haze pollution, drug trafficking, women and children smuggling and others. It also seems from then on that China clearly made some concrete concessions to ASEAN to improve its relations with ASEAN. China assented to a proposal by ASEAN in 1992 to resolve the South China Sea issue through peaceful means "without resort to force". With a commitment to abide by the United Nations Convention on the Law of the Sea to solve the South China Sea issue, China did not publicly reject Indonesia's claim over the Natunas in 1995 when then Foreign Minister Ali Alatas paid an official visit to Beijing (*The Straits Times*, Singapore, 22 July 1995). The 1997 financial crisis was a chance for both China and ASEAN to go hand-in-hand to overcome the negative outcomes of globalization. When the International Monetary Fund aid plan with the support of the United States did not generate a welcome result, China made bilateral loans to Indonesia and Malaysia and kept the Chinese currency (RMB) rate unchanged during the crisis. These unprecedented acts by China were viewed as responsible and friendly, so China should not be looked upon as the China before the 1990s. It seems that the time is mature for both sides to start their co-operation in tackling non-traditional security issues.

NON-TRADITIONAL SECURITY ISSUES CHALLENGE ASEAN

As with China, with the end of the Cold War and globalization, non-traditional security issues have emerged from within and outside Southeast Asia. Globalization is an opportunity for China and ASEAN nations but China feels more favoured because it has brought to China unprecedented economic growth with extraordinary achievements. In Southeast Asia, some do not trust that globalization would bring opportunities but argue that it brought only the economic crisis in 1997 (Tan and Boutin 2001, p. 5). Clearly, the 1997 financial crisis was a significant turning point for both sides in getting together to strengthen their co-operation in the new field of non-traditional security. This would be a possible juncture to define the basic timeframe for the bilateral co-operation in non-traditional security out of the traditional security concept, and I will explain below after outlining the non-traditional security issues confronting ASEAN. In fact, there are several other non-traditional security issues if security is not defined narrowly within a state-centric concept but from a liberal perspective.

One is environmental degradation such as transboundary pollution problems. Like the haze pollution which erupted in 1996–97, the transboundary issue has obviously had some deleterious effects on sustainable development and human health not only in one nation but regionally. Environmental issues have now become central to the agenda of development in ASEAN and environmental security, which has been increasingly accepted as a part of the regional security agendas and we have a term "environmental insecurity" (Tan and Boutin 2001, pp. 438–39). ASEAN member nations agreed to designate the year 2003 as Environment Year, with the theme "Together Towards Sustainable Development", indicating that environmental problems have been dealt with at the regional level.

Next is transnational crime. According to the United Nations Convention Against Transnational Organized Crime, transnational organized crimes such as money-laundering, corruption, piracy and others should be prevented and combated. For instance, on piracy, almost 70 per cent of global pirate attacks took place in the sea areas of Southeast Asia and have increasingly become a serious challenge to regional and even global trade security because one third of world trade transportation shipping passes through the sea channels in Southeast Asia (*Christian Science Monitor*, 27 December 2000 edition). In addition, there are crimes and corruption widespread throughout the region including human and drug trafficking.

Resource-disputed issues exist regionwide. Fishery, water, forestry, energy and other natural resources are always in scarcity, but it seems it has been increasingly leading to serious issues in the region since the end of the Cold War. This is partly because of large-scale economic construction driven by market demand and partly because some maritime and land boundaries have not been well defined. The resource-disputed issues at the regional level include water issues between Malaysia and Singapore; fishery disputes between Myanmar and Thailand, also Vietnam and China; and the sovereignty conflict in South China Sea between the Philippines and China, which still remains very serious among China and some ASEAN nations concerned because oil and other mineral deposits have been the focus of the region's attention.

Terrorism is a serious issue that looms large. If a non-traditional security issue is defined as what has transcended national borders in terms of its effects and the solution requires regional as well as international co-operation, the terrorist issue is a significant challenge in ASEAN, seriously affecting the civil societies and economic development in the region. After the September 11 attacks, the terrorist activities and threats have escalated in Southeast Asia and the situation has deteriorated. Individuals suspected of links with al-Qaeda were rounded up in Singapore, Malaysia and the Philippines. There have been also some terrorist networks, including the extremist Jemaah Islamiyah, believed to have several branches located in the Philippines, Singapore, Malaysia and Indonesia, and their aim is to set up a nation for their cause. The terrorist group was responsible for both the Bali attack and the 5 August 2003 bombing at the J.W. Marriott Hotel in Jakarta. In addition, there are still some "loopholes" at the border areas for such elements to hide and with no tight and strict prevention and measures established, some members of the extremist groups sometimes managed to escape. It seems that the international terrorists including those of al-Qaeda are closely connected with the region's terrorist groups, which are weaving a network to form a second front.

Separatism can be viewed not only as a non-traditional security issue but a traditional one as well. If it becomes worsened to the extent that a separatist movement becomes an internal threat to a present authority, almost to the extent of possibly overthrowing a legal government, it is a traditional security issue. When it becomes a factor that it may cause a society to become unstable, this separatist movement could be regarded as a non-traditional security threat because it gives cause for worry that it may have some secret connections with international terrorist groups. Some ASEAN member nations are now confronting such threats. The Free Aceh Movement or Acehnese separatist group is an obvious issue for the Indonesian Government because it generates internal instability. The Philippines is facing a more serious separatist issue in Mindanao, a place where the Moro Islamic Liberation Front (MILF) has reportedly tried to turn the place into "the new Afghanistan" — a training ground for the Jemaah Islamiyah, Southeast Asia's regional terrorist network. In Thailand, renewed separatist efforts resulted in a recent clash in Pattani. Prime Minister Thaksin Shinawatra pointed out recently that "it is possible that there were some foreigners involved in the incident" (*The Nation*, 3 May 2004).

The above issues have had obvious spillover effects transcending national borders, with some other security issues existing in the area, for instance, some human security issues including bird flu and SARs, which were stressed in the 2003 APEC Bangkok Declaration. These transnational non-traditional security issues require China and ASEAN nations to co-operate to find solutions. The last four or five years saw the co-operation that both sides have experienced and some good results have been produced.

One is that both sides have jointly fought against the threats from the economic and financial fields. As a result of globalization and growing interdependence, the most negative consequence — the 1997 financial crisis, alerted China and ASEAN nations to take measures to address economic security issues. Following its loans to some ASEAN nations, China respected those measures taken by ASEAN nations such as Malaysia to overcome financial difficulties. China supported the Malaysian initiatives at the 1998 APEC meeting to strengthen economic and technological co-operation. China and other ASEAN nations took co-operative action to set up the Chiang Mai Initiative. At the fifth leaders' summit in Brunei in 2001, to erase any doubts and misgivings that some ASEAN nations had because of Chinese WTO access, former Premier Zhu Rongji agreed to establish a free trade area with ASEAN within a decade. It is expected that China would fully respect ASEAN's willingness, and their ideas and suggestions, in the process of building an ASEAN-China FTA. In 2002, the Framework Agreement on Comprehensive Economic Co-operation Between ASEAN and the People's Republic of China was signed, officially initiating the process for the establishment of a China-ASEAN free-trade area. It would seem that the co-operation for regional security in its initial stages rests more on economics. With this momentum, in 2003, trade between ASEAN and the PRC totalled $78.25 billion, a 42.8 per cent increase over the previous year, making China the sixth and ASEAN the fifth biggest trading partners for each other (data from China's Customs). Even as Southeast Asia is still recovering from the 1997 financial crisis, more bilateral trade has increased China and ASEAN members' economic interdependence. Recent figures show that trade and the FTA process make countries in Southeast Asia more profitable.

Sino-ASEAN co-operation to combat transnational organized crimes and the joint activities have been advanced. Transnational crimes have increasingly become pressing problems that China and many ASEAN countries are facing. China and Myanmar intensified cross-border co-operation to carry out joint raids on several heroin production plants. Starting from 2001, China with some ASEAN nations including Myanmar, Laos and Thailand, held a ministerial meeting on drug issues and the joint project has been kept on and even attracted India to participate in 2003. The significant Joint Declaration of ASEAN and China on Co-operation in the Field of Non-Traditional Security Issues (2002 ASEAN-China's Joint Declaration) signed by heads of China and the ASEAN nations at the Sixth ASEAN-China Summit in Phnom Penh on 4 November 2002, was a milestone in the advancement of the China-ASEAN co-operation relationship in the area. The leaders agreed that transnational crimes such as trafficking in illegal drugs, people-smuggling including trafficking in women and children, sea piracy, terrorism, arms-smuggling, money-laundering, international economic crime and cyber crime all belong to non-traditional security issues which have become important factors of uncertainty affecting regional and international security and are posing new challenges to regional and international peace and stability. Following up on these agreements, China joined the ASEAN-China Dialogue meeting held in Hanoi in June 2003 and the two sides agreed to strengthen bilateral and multilateral co-operation and exchange information and experiences in combating transnational organized crimes. Besides, China hosted a symposium in Beijing on 25 August 2003 on combating transnational organized crimes, with participants from police officers and academic representatives from ten ASEAN member nations and China. The official Chinese perspective on the co-operation is that combating transnational organized crimes will ensure that the economic co-operation and FTA between China and ASEAN will be smoothly conducted and securely set up. China also hopes the joint measures will bring bilateral relations to a higher level and a stable region ahead. To further enhance the co-operation in fighting transnational organized crimes, the Chinese police and the ASEAN nations' police are jointly making a mid- and long-term plan to meet the new situation in the new period.

China's participation in the SARs Summit made a significant contribution to the co-operation in dealing with non-traditional security issues. SARs and other infectious diseases are not only a matter of public health, but also threats to national and regional security. The 2002 ASEAN-China's Joint Declaration did not raise the issue but the Special China-ASEAN Summit on the SARS issue on 29 April 2003 did make up for what had apparently been neglected. About six years ago, China and ASEAN had joined hands for the first time to combat the 1997 financial crisis, and this was the second time both had come together to fight a new enemy, SARs, in terms of non-traditional security. Although China's belated response was severely criticized for initially playing down the seriousness of the problem partly because of its treating SARs as a medical problem and partly because of bureaucratic procedures, the fact that China's performance from silent denial to sincere acknowledgement and a quick movement to Bangkok by the newly appointed premier for comprehensive co-operation with ASEAN, has reflected China's determination and sincerity in the fight against SARs, a new and non-traditional security issue. The emergent conference and face-to-face meeting by leaders of ASEAN and China pushed forward the bilateral co-operation in the special field to a new level, with the meeting achieving successes and playing a significant role in controlling the spread of the epidemic in the region, reducing its negative effect on the regional economy and helping people regain their confidence. This was demonstrated in a joint statement issued by ASEAN and Chinese leaders after the meeting, expressing their deep concern over the mounting threat to the life and health of the people in Southeast Asia, China and other parts of the world. They stressed the need for collaborative efforts not only in the ASEAN region but also in the rest of the world to effectively tackle the challenges posed by the deadly virus.

Strictly speaking, terrorism may also be assigned to the category of transnational organized crimes under non-traditional security issues. China stressed that counter-terror is a top priority on the agenda for co-operation in combating transnational organized crimes. Terrorist activities in Southeast Asia have their own characteristics, different in nature from other transnational organized crimes. Transnational organized crimes may be committed through special methods including some, but not all, forms of international terrorism. Given the large Muslim population living and working in the region and economic gaps, the issue poses some dilemma as to how to define terrorism. On the one hand, one should combat terrorism because the terrorists have been launching attacks on civil societies; but on the other hand, one should not forget that poverty might be a hotbed of terrorism. The United States denies the connection between poverty and terrorism but in the ASEAN nations, some do believe that poverty is the origin of terrorism. My argument is that it is unnecessary to have a definite causality between terrorism and poverty, but some connection should not be excluded. We must not overlook but consider poverty as a factor of some bearing.

EVALUATING SINO-ASEAN RELATIONS IN COMBATING NON-TRADITIONAL SECURITY ISSUES

China should be half satisfied with the progress it has made in its relations with ASEAN. With its rapidly growing economy and timely supports provided to ASEAN, the image of China has been changing from a revolutionary country to a regional power that is accountable and friendly. Economically, China is viewed as a place with prospects of profit, an advantage for ASEAN businessmen and entrepreneurs to take. It seems that ASEAN nations are making more efforts to get access to the Chinese market. Politically and in terms of security, bilateral co-operation may have generated some positive results by now but it is probably not easy to advance, even in the area of non-traditional security. To evaluate the trends and prospects of the ASEAN-China relationship in the near future, it is necessary to consider the power and interests of state actors in some other policy-decision situations including those of a non-traditional security nature, which could be revealing about policy tendencies. One is China's policy on non-traditional security in terms of priority and its consequent impact. The next is ASEAN's views on outside players like the United States and Japan and their different instruments for achieving their goals in Southeast Asia. The final section looks at a possible future by introducing an analysis of the institutions based on the Treaty of Amity and Co-operation in Southeast Asia (TACSA) which China has signed.

NEW AGENDA OF CHINA'S POLICY

A people-based or "people first" policy requires new leaders to pay more attention to non-traditional security issues. For the Chinese leaders headed by Hu Jintao, the central task at present is to develop the economy and improve people's livelihood. They do not expect that a global war will occur in the foreseeable future or at least in the first twenty-year period of the new century. Neither will a mass-destructive aggression be committed against China. They believe China should grasp this period of opportunity to quicken the pace of economic development "for the goal of building a well-developed society in all areas". Thus the Chinese cardres and officials at various levels have been urged to dedicate themselves to the interests of the public, govern for the benefit of the people, set their minds to serving the people wholeheartedly in their work and "always keep the safety and livelihood of the people in mind" and do their best "to lift the needy out of poverty and difficulty"(Hu, J. 2003). Thus, the traditional military threats (mainly referring to the big powers) to the state have been considered reduced, and non-traditional security issues should be stressed for its close connection with the short- and middle-term goal of economic development. Therefore, it is natural for Chinese leaders to attach importance to non-traditional security issues and reorient its policy position to a higher level, sometimes as a top priority on the agenda. Logically, China would hope for a peaceful international environment to pursue the goal of economic development, and regional stability is particularly vital to that end. To address non-traditional security issues, China has adjusted its foreign policy with emphasis on neighbouring countries and its co-operation with ASEAN. However, China must have its own evaluation of those issues and arrange them in order of urgency because of the different goals of China and ASEAN and other factors including American troops returning to Southeast Asia. The central question in the non-traditional issue areas for China is how to make choices for its own core national interests without jeopardizing the good relations with its neighbouring ASEAN nations.

One of the top priority issues is the separatist campaign, along with religious extremism and terrorism. The "East Turkistan" in Xinjiang may be an important issue but the most pressing is the separatist issue in Taiwan. The Taiwan issue is a legacy of the internal war in the 1940s and is still alive, reminding Chinese of the divided society and unintegrated territory. Nationalism has increasingly become a powerful force, with the leaders aware of pressures from the common Chinese people with a strong sense of nationalism. The separatists, including those who want to declare Taiwan independence, the Zang (Tibetan), and East Turkistan separatists, have not been state actors but non-governmental actors. According to the Chinese constitution and law, all those territorial lands belong to China and the demands of the separatists desperate for independence are actually conducted by criminals. So, those Taiwanese claiming independence are legally regarded as separatists. One can see from the current situation that there exists a very uncompromising conflict between the strait. Particularly, on the part of the Mainland, a dominating view is that the separatists should be regarded as non-governmental actors, who cannot be recognized as governmental actors in the sense of international relations. Some even view the independence claimants as international terrorists, being non-governmental actors with weapons of mass destruction. If those weapons were used to attack, China's modernization efforts would have been greatly sabotaged and the "goal of building a well-developed society" would have been in vain. Therefore the cadres have also been urged to stay diligent, vigilant and prepared against potential danger and adversities in peace time (Jiang, Z. 2002*b*). The "potential danger and adversities" refer to all kinds of non-traditional security issues including the declaration of Taiwan independence. As the Taiwan independence claimants belong to non-state actors threatening the security of the state and China's territorial integrity, it is rational that China puts this issue as a top priority on its agenda. According to this logic, it is natural for us to expect China to have rearranged its policy priorities.

A MATTER OF PRIORITY

First, China will certainly stand firm on the claims over sovereignty and territorial integrity, most importantly, concerning Taiwan. A concrete declaration for independence by Taiwanese leaders must trigger a new war. It is unimaginable that the Chinese leaders will be indifferent to such a declaration without any action. The Chinese regard treasonous behaviour as the most disgraceful. The one who surrendered the sovereignty of Taiwan to Japan in 1895 under humiliating terms has earned opprobrium probably till the end of history. The "land for peace" method could be used while dealing with Myanmar in the 1950s and with other neighbouring nations but not where

Taiwan is concerned. It appears that a new thinking on Taiwan is inconceivable at present although the United States supports such an approach.

Second, China will stand along with ASEAN to promote economic co-operation and fight against any factors that would be harmful to the economic development of both sides. Economic and financial security issues have been raised to a high level in Chinese strategy and China is unlikely to prefer solutions that may sacrifice long-term aggregate benefits for short-term relative gains at the expense of its good relationship with ASEAN. One can expect that China will continue to try its best to make concessional supports in the process of building Ten+1 FTA with ASEAN.

Third, China is now aware of the challenging situation for its future economic development because of the uneven construction and is now appealing to the country for scientific and sustainable development. China will enhance co-operation with ASEAN in combating non-traditional security threats. Combating sea piracy benefits both ASEAN and China. Considering that China has become a big oil consumer and importer, jointly protecting the sea channels in the Southeast Asia could be arranged into the agendas. Success will depend mainly on multilateralism in the region.

Fourth, China will keep on implementing agreements and declarations signed with ASEAN to combat transnational crimes, epidemics and environmental degradation.

One can conclude from the above order of priority that the most pressing non-traditional security issue on the Chinese agenda is the factor of Taiwan independence. Then comes the emphasis to seek a quick economic development for the goal to be a well-developed society for the whole country and in the process, China must stand up to all non-traditional security issues possibly harmful to its development programme.

TRADITIONAL TO NON-TRADITIONAL ISSUES IN SINO-ASEAN RELATIONS

While China reiterated its determination to combat terrorists and address non-traditional security issues, this does not mean that China is detracting from the focus on traditional state-centric security. It seems that China will not soften its position and alter its policy of claiming the offshore territories. However, a flexible policy is not unimaginable. Given the fact that China has signed the Declaration on the Conduct of Parties in the South China Sea, it will not provoke any incidents. China has made several concessions to relevant countries since the end of the 1980s. An important one was that it accepted the concept that a sovereignty dispute exists over the Spratlys sea areas. It also made clear that China and Indonesia had no dispute over the Spratlys and the surrounding waters. (Sinaga 1995). The flexibility will not be available on the Taiwan issue. China may adopt a tolerant and restrained attitude to a recent Vietnamese action opening an island in the Spratlys as a resort to attract international tourists. But to Taiwan, China will not put up with independence, away from China. That would be definitely intolerable.

Undoubtedly, non-traditional security and traditional security issues are inextricably linked, especially when the nature of the state has remained completely unchanged for almost four centuries. Therefore, we have to admit that non-traditional security only belongs to traditional security, in a relationship of subordination. Traditional security deals strictly with the state-to-state affairs between sovereign nations, which has dominated current international politics. Non-traditional security is an extension of traditional security but not superior to traditional security. Non-traditional security copes not only with inter-country relations but with relations within a country (sovereign nation) as well. Relations within a country cover those of local and central governments as well as those of person-to-person and other social roles. Standing firmly on those basic principles expressed in the UN Charter and Treaty of Amity and Co-operation in Southeast Asia (TACSA), China and ASEAN have come together on common grounds for economic co-operation and to combat non-traditional security issues.

TACSA AND LEGAL RESPONSIBILITY

We may consider the establishment of the Ten+1 co-operative mechanism under TACSA as a cornerstone for Sino-ASEAN relations. This heralds a new image of China with its accountability for regional security because it laid a legal foundation for Sino-ASEAN co-operation in security. ASEAN leaders adopted the TACSA in 1976, which has initially been a guideline regulating the relations of ASEAN member nations. The treaty stipulates that membership requires any Southeast Asian nation that wants to be a member of the organization to accept and sign this important document before joining it. The TACSA's goal is "to promote perpetual peace, everlasting amity and co-operation". It stipulates that the relations of members should be guided by six principles:

1) Mutual respect for the independence, sovereignty, equality, territorial integrity and national identity of all nations;
2) The right of every state to lead its national existence free from external interference, subversion or coercion;

3) Non-interference in the internal affairs of one another;
4) Settlement of differences or disputes by peaceful means;
5) Renunciation of the threat or use of force;
6) Effective co-operation among themselves.

This important document stresses co-operation and regional peace, requiring members to bear the necessary responsibilities facilitating political and economic co-operation. Such co-operation should not limit its spheres of membership but expand to external regions and international organizations. Principles Four and Five deal with peaceful means to settle disputes between members, indicating ASEAN members commit themselves not to resort to force. Should serious disputes emerge among members, a High Council would be summoned to take necessary methods and measures with mediation, inquiry or conciliation "for the prevention of a deterioration of the dispute or the situation". These principles and co-operative spirit are consistent with the basic principles of the UN Charter. With the situations changing, the TACSA was amended separately in 1987 and 1998. The main amendment is that "States outside Southeast Asia may also accede to this Treaty" on the condition of the consent of all ASEAN members. The third amendment done at the Ninth ASEAN Summit held in Bali, Indonesia, in October 2003, made it clear again that the treaty is open to countries outside ASEAN. To respect the willingness of ASEAN, China assented to join in the treaty and China's signature strengthens and consolidates the legal foundation of bilateral relations. To the Chinese Government, the treaty's aim is to respect sovereignty of the state, independence, non-interference in each other's internal affairs and peaceful settlement of dispute, which are all consistent with Chinese foreign policy and the spirit of the UN Charter. Obviously, these principles are completely consistent with the traditional security research paradigm.

For China, this is an appropriate time to overcome the fallacy of the "China threat", which stemmed from the West but has spread worldwide. China's rise and sovereignty disputes over the South China Sea soon prompted some talk about the "China threat" in Southeast Asia. It seems that what worried some Southeast Asians were Chinese military as well as economic and ideological threats (Broomfield 2003). In addition to TACSA, Chinese Premier Wen Jiabao and heads of ASEAN signed a joint communiqué on a strategic partner relationship at the Bali Meeting in October 2003. This is the first time that China has ever made a strategic partnership with a regional organization. This creates the possibility of pushing Sino-ASEAN co-operation into a new field of security but more than that, is the fact that China has expressed its willingness to abide by a regional institution, an important step as it bears a legal responsibility.

The establishment of the Ten+1 co-operative mechanism under TACSA could be viewed as a common and important foundation for security co-operation. Chinese participation demonstrates China's esteem for ASEAN. Further, the TACSA may be regarded as some form of collective security ensuring regional stability and security. China conveys its will to abide by the treaty and that it is not a threat. With TACSA as a foundation of political relations, ASEAN and China accept the mainstream policy view that traditional state-to-state relationship dominates international politics. Presumably, China may have made a breakthrough in its policy adjustment from one of non-alignment to an ambiguity. This is a favourable ambiguity benefiting China to join quietly in a political and security treaty such as the TACSA. The policy adjustment may be a response to Jiang Zemin's report at the Sixteenth Party Congress, in which Jiang did not reiterate the non-alignment policy, a basic and important policy stated in previous Party Congress reports. It seems that China has been willingly bound to a regional group. Undoubtedly this is a triumph for ASEAN.

For China, it seems rational to stress non-traditional security while sticking to the traditional security concept. Since non-traditional is security subordinate to traditional security, no matter what non-traditional security issues have been raised to a high level, the issues are still dealt with under the traditional security paradigm. While non-traditional security issues cross national borders, any activities to cope with those issues must be within or under the governance of present governments concerned. It is noted that many non-traditional security issues are posed by NGOs in Southeast Asia but not in China. This does not indicate that state governments have no rights to govern actions and measures related to non-traditional security issues. Many non-traditional security issues in fact emerge within borders and some NGOs from other nations may request to be involved in the process of dealing with them. This may be allowed but only under the state's permission. Therefore, it is flexible for China to adopt a new policy to cope with non-traditional security issues and also an opportunity for China to implement the policy.

ASEAN AND OTHER OUTSIDE PLAYERS

By the end of the 1990s, ASEAN has reached its goal with all nations of Southeast Asia joining in. It tries to be a multilateral group with one voice on the regional and global stages, conducting a policy of balance towards major powers including the United States, and China. ASEAN deals carefully with China, Japan and the United States and tries to plan new regional strategies in order to address traditional and non-traditional threats. Counter-terrorism campaigns have been shaping the new political map of Southeast Asia with some ASEAN nations more active than others. As mentioned in the previous sections, on the counter-terrorism front, ASEAN seems somewhat inclined towards the United States, and big powers have been wooing ASEAN. How to use the opportunity to serve their countries depends on ASEAN statesmen's capabilities. Of more concern are the big powers like the United States and Japan with their motives and intentions toward Southeast Asia.

The United States has to confront the reality of terrorism domestically and worldwide including Southeast Asia. The U.S. invasions of Afghanistan and Iraq caused a negative and new wave of anti-U.S. sentiments among the Muslims. Reportedly Southeast Asia's regional terrorist network operates with the international terrorist network.

Clearly, a way should be found to wipe out terrorist elements in Southeast Asia. One way is to strengthen regional co-operation and ASEAN nations did. In 2001 at the APEC meeting in Shanghai, ASEAN leaders expressed their determination in counter-terrorism. They signed the Declaration on Joint Action to Counter Terrorism in 2001. Collective actions have proven to be effective. A good example is the co-operation between Malaysia and Singapore to jointly destroy the extremist groups. The other way for ASEAN is to use something like "outsourcing", that is, the U.S. troops.

It appears that China's participation in anti-terrorist activities in Southeast Asia is not going smoothly. The reality is that China-ASEAN's approach to combating extremist terrorism has been different from that adopted by the United States with ASEAN in the past years. The United States has a history in its relations with some ASEAN nations on security co-operation where it highly valued ASEAN and called Southeast Asia the "second front" after Afghanistan in the U.S. war on terror. In August 2002, ASEAN and the United States signed the Joint Declaration for Co-operation to Combat International Terrorism to jointly combat terrorism. The United States used traditional security methods to fight against Islamic extremist elements and other terrorists, dispatching a certain number of U.S. troops to the Philippines. U.S. forces returned to a location very close to China. It may be assumed that the goal of the American mission is to train Philippine troops to hunt Abu Sayyaf rebels, an Islamic extremist group labelled as a terrorist organization, but meanwhile, it is certain that the United States could also use the opportunity to monitor China. The Philippine President Gloria Macapagal-Arroyo admitted early April 2004 that U.S. troops had been used to monitor

China (Wang 2004) . The United States conferred the title "Non-NATO Ally" to some ASEAN members so that these nations' status would be different from previously. As traditional military means could only be used against traditional enemies, the United States does not regard terrorists as a non-traditional but traditional security issue. China has not been included in the same camp in the anti-terrorism campaign in the region. This may suggest that Sino-ASEAN co-operation in non-traditional security would be restrained by the American factor and not be easy to upgrade to a higher level.

The United States has taken advantage of the counter-terrorist campaign to quickly dispatch troops to Southeast Asia and this shows that the United States' influence has not waned but remains. It appears that the region has not become captive to "a single power", but is still under the influence of the United States. The Bush administration prefers unilateralism in combating virtual enemies like terrorists, and we doubt such a policy can play a balancing role in the region. Some Southeast Asians have grumbled about the fact that counter-terrorism has become an overriding task. The complaint reminds us of the serious reality that ASEAN member governments may need some measures to solve and eradicate the root causes of worsening social, economic, and political conditions, which may have been breeding existing and potential terrorists.

Undoubtedly, the ASEAN-Japan Summit held in Tokyo in December 2003 indicates Japan is further recovering its relations with Southeast Asia. For ASEAN nations, it is rational to strengthen their relations with Japan because increasingly they have been having a closer relation with China and India in recent years. They need a balance in the region's interest. For Japan, the momentum of the co-operation between China and ASEAN may produce some pressures. The Japanese Government may be aware that the competition between China and Japan is on the basis of opening up, co-operation and development and this virtuous competition must benefit regional co-operation. Japanese Premier Koizumi had remarked that China was not a threat but an opportunity to Japan. ASEAN is clearly seeking a comprehensive co-operation with Japan that is not only economic but political, military and in non-traditional security as well. It still remains to be seen whether ASEAN would truly accept Australia and New Zealand into the East Asian Community. Another obstacle is whether the Japanese market is open to ASEAN agricultural products.

External powers are increasingly interested in Southeast Asia and ASEAN nations may have various demands in terms of their different situations. China's policy is to let ASEAN play an important role in the process of regional economic integration. ASEAN will surely benefit more and more in the process but it could be dangerous if Chinese interests were played off against those of the United States and Japan or any other powers. At present, not only China, but also Japan and India are inclined to adopt multilateralism to push regional co-operation forward. TACSA is an institutional base for these Asian nations and ASEAN to get together to play their roles.

CONCLUSION

Since the end of the Cold War, non-traditional security issues have challenged China and ASEAN nations as well as the world. With the possibility of a world war reduced and the process of economic globalization speeded up, governments have designed economic plans for the goal of creating well-developed societies. These are the people-based strategies but they need a peaceful environment to fulfil the goals.

To have secure and stable environments for economic development, China and ASEAN have joined together to combat non-traditional security issues. This co-operation has been mainly conducted in the fields of illicit drug trafficking, HIV/AIDs, piracy, illegal migration, environmental security, economic security, information security and others. As counter-terrorism has been regarded as a special global war, the combat has become part of traditional high politics. As the political system of China is inconsistent with those of core ASEAN nations, China is unable to become a normal participant in the fight against terrorists in Southeast Asia. The United States will continue its war against terrorism in the short term and use Southeast Asia as a second front. The American troops returned to Southeast Asia have the effect of killing two birds with one stone. Terrorist activities have been defined not only as traditional but also non-traditional security issue-areas. The United States has not viewed terrorism as low politics but used traditional forces to combat terrorists. Counter-terror war has been dominated by the United States and some governments of Southeast Asia have followed the standards of the United States. China's co-operation with ASEAN to combat terrorism cannot compare with U.S. co-operation with ASEAN. China's relations with ASEAN in security still have some way to catch up.

References

APEC Secretariat. *Key APEC Documents 2003*, Singapore: APEC Secretariat, 2003.
Buzan, B., O. Waever, and J.D. Wilde. *Security: A New Framework For Analysis*, (Chinese translation), Hanzhou, China: Zhejiang People's Publishing House, 2002.

Elliott, L. "Regional Environmental Security: Pursuing A Non-Trading Approach". In *Non-traditional Security Issues In Southeast Asia*, edited by Tan, Andrew T.H. and Boutin, J.D.K. Singapore: Institute of Defence and Strategic Studies, Nanyang Technological University, 2001, pp. 438–67.

Emma, V.B. "Perceptions of Danger: The China Threat Theory". In *Journal of Contemporary China* 12, no. 35 (2003): 265–84.

Fu, Y. "The Period of Strategy and Non-traditional Security Issues". *Studies on Mao Zedong and Deng Xiaoping Theories*, Shanghai, no. 5 (2003): 82–88.

Gilpin, R. *The Political Economy of International Relations*. Princeton University Press, 1987*a*.

————. *The Political Economy of International Relations* (Chinese version). Shanghai: People's Publishing House, 2002*b*.

Ho, Khai Leong. "Rituals, Risks, and Rivalries: China and ASEAN in the Coming Decades". *Journal of Contemporary China* 10, no. 29 (2001): 683–94.

Hu, J. Addresses Symposium on 'Three Represents' Thought. *People's Daily*, 3 July 2003.

Ku, Samuel C.Y. "The Political Economy of Taiwan's Relations with Southeast Asia". *Contemporary Southeast Asia* 17, no. 3 (December 1995): 282–97.

Jiang, Z. "Speeding up Pace for Open[ing]-up and Modernisation Construction to Reach a Better Triumph On the Socialist Cause With Chinese Characteristics". A report delivered at the Thirteenth National Congress of the Communist Party of China (CPC), *People's Daily*, 14 October 1992*a*.

Jiang, Z. "Build a Well-off Society in an All-Round Way and Create a New Situation in Building Socialism with Chinese Characteristics". A report delivered at the Sixteenth National Congress of the Communist Party of China (CPC) on 8 November 2002. *People's Daily*, 17 November 2002*b*.

Keohane, R.O. *After Hegemony: Cooperation and Discord in the World Political Economy*. Princeton: Princeton University Press, 1984.

Keohane, R.O. and J.S. Nye. *Power and Interdependence* (Chinese version from English version copyright 2001). Beijing: Peking University Press, 2002.

Kindleberger, C. *Power and Money: the Economics of International Politics and the Politics of International Economics*. New York: Basic Book, 1970.

Mao, Z. *Selections On Diplomacy from Mao Zedong* (*Mao Zedong Waijiao Wenxian*). Beijing: Central Literature Press, World Knowledge Press, 1994.

PRC Government. "China's Position Paper on Enhanced Cooperation in the Field of Non-Traditional Security Issues" (29 May 2002). Beijing: Ministry of Foreign Affairs, the People's Republic of China, 2002*a*. <www.fmprc.gov.cn/eng/wjb/zzjg/gjs/gjzzyhy/2612/2614/t15318.htm>.

————. "China's Position Paper on the New Security Concept" (31 July 2002) Permanent Mission of the People's Republic of China to the United Nations office at Geneva and other International Organizations in Switzerland, 2002*b*. <http://www.china-un.ch>.

————. "Declaration of China-ASEAN Cooperation on Non-traditional Security

Issues" (4 November 2002). Beijing: Ministry of Foreign Affairs, the People's Republic of China. Beijing: *Xinhua News Agency*, 13 November 2002.

Sinaga, S. Alatas: China Makes No Claims on Oil-rich Islands. *The Straits Times* (Singapore), 22 July 1995.

Tan, Andrew T.H. and J.D.K. Boutin. *Non-traditional Security Issues In Southeast Asia*. Singapore: Institute of Defence and Strategic Studies, Nanyang Technological University, 2001.

Tow, W.T. and Russell Trood. "Linkages between Traditional Security and Human Security". In *Asia's Emerging Regional Order: Reconciling Traditional and Human Security*, edited by W.T. Tow, R. Thakur, and In-Taek Hyun. Tokyo-New York-Paris: The United Nations University Press, 2000, pp. 13–32.

Wang, C.J. "United Military Exercises of the Philippine-US Once Used to Target at China". In *Global Times*, Beijing 7, no. 2 (April 2004).

Wang, Y. *Western International Politics: History and Theories*. Shanghai: People's Publishing House, 1998.

Wen, Jiabao. *Report on the Work of the Government*. Delivered to the Tenth National People's Congress held in Beijing on 5 March 2004.

Zhang, Y. and J. Zhou. *Economic Security*, Shanghai: High Education Press, 2000.

7

THE POLITICS AND ECONOMICS OF "EAST ASIA" IN CHINA-ASEAN RELATIONS

Alice D. BA

Since the late 1980s, East and Southeast Asia have been adapting to changes associated with the ending of the Cold War, especially the reprioritization of U.S. economic and strategic interests in Asia. Those changes introduced new realities in Southeast Asia's relations with Northeast Asia, including new security concerns, the intensification of economic and trade linkages, and general blurring of lines between Southeast and Northeast Asia. China's growing economic and political presence is considered an especially significant development that is compelling a reorganization of the regional political economy. In particular, these changes, along with the challenges of a fast-paced and changing global economy, have generated growing momentum behind a reorganization along East Asian lines.

For the member states of the Association of Southeast Asian Nations (ASEAN), the emergence of "East Asia" made up of both Northeast Asian and Southeast Asian states[1] offers as much challenge as opportunity. On the one hand, "East Asia" promises the thirty-plus-year-old organization and its economies a chance at economic and political revitalization at a time when China's economy looms especially large and at a time when ASEAN itself is undergoing a period of reevaluation. On the other hand, "East Asia" also holds out the danger that ASEAN and its voice will eventually be subsumed within a larger grouping that also includes larger powers. Also, though relations between China and ASEAN have improved in significant ways, many in ASEAN remain wary and concerned about China's growing economic and political influence. This chapter examines the economics and politics of "East Asia" in the context of ASEAN-China relations.

The chapter begins with a brief discussion of China's particular economic challenge to the ASEAN economies and the ways that this challenge is re-centering a regional political economy that had been built upon Cold War relationships and priorities. The chapter then turns to a discussion of ASEAN's and China's respective and evolving views of "East Asia". Particular attention is paid to how the economics and politics of their relations, especially since 1997, are affecting the lines along which East Asia's reorganization is taking place and the prospects for an East Asian regionalism. While economic developments, especially the demands and dilemmas of competing in an ever more challenging global political economy, are compelling a rethinking of regional growth strategies and regional co-operation along East Asian lines, developments also point to important reservations about this East Asian trend. Politics remains the most important complicating factor in regionalization processes (economic and political); however, politics may also provide additional arguments for "East Asia".

CHINA'S ECONOMIC CHALLENGE

The 1990s were a time of much change for China and ASEAN. In particular, shifting U.S. priorities in East and Southeast Asia underscored long-standing questions about U.S. security guarantees and compelled ASEAN states to rethink their relations with China. Political-security preoccupations loomed especially large over relations. Competing claims and conflicts over the Spratly Islands, along with military modernization efforts on the parts of both China and ASEAN, were perhaps the two issues that most defined ASEAN-China relations in the 1990s. Despite predictions of conflict, however, relations have mostly stabilized and indeed improved in significant ways.

Post-Cold War uncertainties also created new incentives on the parts of both China and ASEAN to increase and expand their engagement of one another. In part, the ASEAN states, especially, saw bilateral and regional engagement processes as important fall-backs should there be further U.S. retrenchment. ASEAN states, for example, saw engagement processes as serving important reassurance functions that could ease relations with China in the event of weakened U.S. security guarantees. As for China, though at first suspicious of regional processes, it saw expanded engagement as a way to stabilize its periphery and to ensure a peaceful regional environment conducive to growth and development.

Economic and trade incentives also supported ASEAN's expanded engagement of China. The attention paid to the political-security aspects of relations sometimes obscures the fact that by the early 1990s, economic and trade considerations had already begun to loom large in relations, especially on ASEAN's side. At first, China drew attention because of the lure of a potentially huge consumer market for ASEAN goods. As in the political-security realm, this economic interest in China similarly reflected new calculations that had to do with Washington's shifting priorities in East and Southeast Asia — perhaps no surprise given Washington's efforts to link trade and security issues. In particular, a sluggish U.S. economy had sparked a backlash against Asian trading partners, which were doing relatively well at the time. Told by U.S. representatives that they could no longer rely on the United States to be their engine of growth (Savetsila 1988),[2] ASEAN economies began to see Japan and increasingly China as providing alternative — or at least supplementary — support in driving ASEAN growth. U.S. efforts to link trade to Asian human rights practices, along with the U.S.-led creation of the North American free trade arrangement, only underscored the need to diversify ASEAN's trading relationships and to mitigate ASEAN's particular dependence on the United States and especially the U.S. market to buy ASEAN goods. At the same time, ASEAN economies had also begun to recognize that as much as China represented a tremendous economic opportunity, it was also a tremendous economic challenge to ASEAN's smaller economies, which had to compete against China's cheaper labour and larger market. The creation of the ASEAN Free Trade Area, for example, was an attempt to create an economy of scale that could improve ASEAN's overall competitiveness. While a collective ASEAN market was far from rivalling the size of China's (it was only half the size), it nevertheless made the ASEAN region more attractive than it might otherwise have been. Thus, AFTA was as much a response to China's economic challenge, as to North American and European integration. Economics and trade have only become more, not less, important in relations between China and ASEAN.

In fact, ASEAN concerns about competition from China have grown increasingly more acute since the 1997–99 Asian financial crisis. In particular, the 1997–99 crisis adversely affected the ability of ASEAN economies to compete for both trade and investment *vis-à-vis* China (which had been much less affected). Since the crisis, economic concerns have mostly eclipsed the political-security concerns that so dominated and defined their relations in the early and mid-1990s. While China's actions during the crisis — especially its willingness to keep its promise not to devalue the renminbi[3] — helped soften its image in Southeast Asia, ASEAN economies remain deeply concerned about China's growing economic and political presence. In that the net result of the crisis was to shift the overriding focus of relations to economic issues, the 1997–99 Asian financial crisis can be seen to mark an important turning point in relations (Ba 2003).

Southeast Asia generally rebounded more quickly than many originally expected; however, the 1997–99 crisis nevertheless pointed to ASEAN's vulnerabilities to global, economic forces and the challenges of sustaining economic growth in a fast-changing global economy. Also, the fact that China was more insulated and thus less affected by the crisis underscored the sense of shifting fortunes and intensified insecurities felt by ASEAN's smaller economies, especially about their ability to compete against the size and dynamism of China's. China's entrance into the World Trade Organization in 2001 has only made China more attractive to international investors, and has thus done little to reassure an ASEAN that remains wary of China's influence.

ASEAN concerns about China focus on its ability to attract increasing amounts of trade and investment. In the area of trade, ASEAN concerns include Chinese competition in both domestic and third party markets. This is especially true of ASEAN's lesser developed economies that more directly compete against China; however, many expect that China's presence will soon be felt more intensely in higher technology areas as well, areas that ASEAN's more developed economies have been competitive. By some accounts, the financial crisis may have sped up the process. Concluded Voon and Ren, for example, "It is very obvious…that China has benefited overall at the expense of the ASEAN-4 economies [due to the crisis], as reflected for instance in the improvements in Chinese primary exports as well as in exports of machinery and transport equipment". (Voon and Ren 2003, p. 169)

An especial source of tension in relations is the widespread perception in Southeast Asia that investors have abandoned ASEAN for China. By most estimates, China is receiving about 30–50 per cent of all foreign direct investment headed for East Asia. While it is difficult to determine exactly how much of the foreign direct investment received by China since 1997 is new investment versus old investment diverted from ASEAN, the fact remains that China has been drawing the lion's share of Asia-bound FDI. According to Greg Felker, ASEAN saw its share of FDI headed for developing Asia fall from an average of 40 per cent during the 1989–94 period to a mere 10 per cent in 2000. By contrast, the trends for China are the opposite. In 1998 it received 50 per cent of the FDI headed for developing Asia. In 2000, it received two-thirds (Felker 2003, p. 258). Even if the decline in ASEAN-bound FDI in absolute terms is overstated, as some have argued,[4] the perception in Southeast Asia is nevertheless that FDI to China is having what Ho Khai Leong describes as a "hollowing out effect" (Ho 2001, p. 693; Leung 2003), and this perception has contributed to a growing sense of crisis across much of Southeast Asia.

A related but also more significant concern has been the number of high profile plant closings in Southeast Asia and relocations of production facilities to China on the parts of Japanese manufacturers and other multinationals, a trend that was detailed in a July 2002 article by the *Nihon Keizai Shimbun*.[5] UNCTAD's 2002 *World Investment Report* affirmed conclusions that China has emerged as "the leading destination by far" in terms of investment by Japanese manufacturing transnational corporations, and the top recipient of all inbound foreign investment to developing Asia and indeed the developing world.[6]

Some have expressed surprise at ASEAN's eroding economic position in the regional economy (Voon and Ren 2003). Some see this phenomenon in part reflective of ASEAN's particular position as East Asia's middle tier economies which now find themselves facing competitive pressures from both above and below. According to Felker, for example, "Sluggish FDI and export trends suggest that Southeast Asia's ailing tiger economies are caught in a "structural squeeze" between an ascendant China and more advanced NIEs like South Korea and Taiwan" (Felker 2003, p. 259). In some cases, there is also additional competition from less developed ASEAN economies.

Felker's nuanced observations also point to Southeast Asia's failure to "develop more sophisticated production profiles", and describes that failure as both structural and political — a function of "captive development" but also the failure of existing governance arrangements to adapt (Felker 2003). While Felker is more optimistic than some about Southeast Asia's economic prospects, the challenges are no less great. All ASEAN capitals acknowledge the enormity of the challenge, even if they have yet to fashion "fully formed strategic response to China's competitive pressure or to other changing global conditions" (Felker 2003, p. 273). Meanwhile, as a collective, ASEAN has also faced difficulties in co-ordinating a response due to new questions about the organization's directions and coherence, domestic preoccupations, as well as diminished confidence since the financial crisis.

In the face of what Felker describes as China's "potent combination of competitive advantages: the world's only fast-growing economy, the biggest potential domestic market in a range of products, and the promise of easier access with the country's accession to the World Trade Organization"(Felker 2003, p. 279), ASEAN economies have sometimes exhibited a combination of urgency and paralysis, and characterizations of the economic challenge posed by China often contain a hint of futility. Said Singapore's Prime Minister Goh Chok Tong, for example, "Our biggest challenge is...to secure a niche for ourselves as China swamps the world with her high-quality but cheaper products...How does Singapore compete against 10 post-war Japans, all industrializing and exporting at the same time?" (Felker 2003, p. 257)

In the face of such a challenge, there appears to be growing sentiment that closer economic co-operation with China is fast becoming less an opportunity but a necessity. The slowdown experienced by the U.S. economy the last two years has only bolstered this conclusion (Choong 2001). Such sentiments played an important part in overcoming China's reservations about entering into a comprehensive economic co-operation framework, including the creation of ACFTA, proposed by China. Even in cases like the Philippines where domestic interests initially were able to convince the Congress to reject the executive branch's decision to enter into ACFTA are now once again on board — mostly out of a fear of being left behind.

EAST ASIA'S ECONOMIC REORIENTATION

According to the World Bank's *East Asian Integrates* report, the 1997–99 crisis and China's accession to the World Trade Organization in November 2001 are two events of "historic proportions" for East Asia (Krumm and Kharas/ World Bank 2003). They are historic because they signal a shift in the economic balance of power in East Asia. This shift is about more than China's moving up the regional economic hierarchy or regional production chain; it is also about a more fundamental reorientation of a regional political economy that had been very much defined and driven by U.S. Cold War policies and economic dominance. U.S. wars in Korea and Vietnam, for example, helped power growth in the higher tier Asian economies like Japan, Taiwan, and Korea, which also benefited from U.S. Cold War trade policies aimed at ensuring a stable, non-communist East Asia. While U.S. military and economic aid, and U.S. expenditures during the Korean and Vietnam Wars most directly affected Japan, Taiwan, and South Korea, they also had an effect on Southeast Asian development and their trade relationships.[7] Supported by U.S. Cold War interests, Japan's post-World War II recovery especially helped develop a regional political economy in which East Asian economies came to rely disproportionately on the U.S. market and Japanese aid, investment, and capital (Siazon 1995, p. 25).[8] The net result of those Cold War policies, combined with colonial economic legacies, was that much of East and Southeast Asia found themselves producing disproportionately for the U.S. market (Stubbs 1989). The centrality of the U.S. economy to East and Southeast Asian growth strategies only underscored its regional dominance, even hegemony, in other areas.

In the 1990s, however, the ending of the Cold War, especially with Washington's unwillingness to support East and Southeast Asian growth and growth strategies, destabilized the foundations of that regional political economy. Meanwhile, China's embrace of market reforms began to direct growing economic attention and interest from its neighbours, which saw China as both a major investment opportunity and supplemental driver of Southeast Asian growth. Especially given its size and potential, China's reintroduction into the regional economy could not help but have an impact on trade and investment flows. Indeed, in East and Southeast Asia, trends suggest not only an intensification of economic activity between China and other regional actors, but also a long-term reorientation of the regional economy around China's growing economic presence. Put another way, there are signs that East Asia's economic center of gravity is shifting. While the U.S. and Japanese economies remain (and will remain) important in East Asia's political economy, regional economic activity increasingly revolves around China.

In the case of Korea, China has already become its most important trading partner. According to the *Korea Herald*, the bilateral trade volume between the two economies grew by an annual rate of 22 per cent between 1992 and 2000. By the end of 2002, bilateral trade was worth $41.2 billion dollars or 13.1 per cent of Korea's total trade volume. Meanwhile, Korean investment in China tripled between 1999 and 2003 (from $1.3 billion to $4.1 billion), surpassing both the United States and Taiwan to become China's third largest source of FDI (Kim 2004).

Even those most wary have been unable to resist China's gravitational pull. In the case of Taiwan and Japan, the amount of trade and investment with China continues to grow despite explicit government reservations and recommendations to diversify their investments to places like Southeast Asia, instead of China. Taiwan's "go south" initiative, whose primary objectives were to "to divert local companies' investment funds from China to Southeast Asia" and "to strengthen Taiwan's diplomacy relations with Vietnam and the ASEAN states" (Ho 2001, p. 692), for example, has done little to discourage Taiwanese investment in the PRC. In 2003, Taiwan's businesses invested 46 per cent of their global investment in mainland China (Leow 2003).[9] Taiwan, like Korea, also "recorded a 50 per cent increase in their exports to China in 2002, while exports to the United States remained flat" (Gordon 2003).

Similarly in Japan, growing concerns about its growing economic ties with, if not dependence on, China led the Ministry of Foreign Affairs (MOFA) to explicitly list a free trade area with China as a mid- to long-term priority, behind ASEAN, Korea, and even Mexico, which were identified as near term priorities. Debates in the ruling Liberal Democratic Party (LDP) have been especially explicit in its concerns that Japan's investment in, and official development assistance to, China is "helping to finance China's prosperity" at Japan's economic, political, and even strategic expense (Nebeshima 2002; "Japan Will Not Slash..." 2002). As in the case of Taiwan, however, such warnings have not done much to reverse economic trends. Despite Tokyo's scaling back its investment to China, investment in China by Japanese firms remain strong. Drawing on preliminary 2002 trade figures, Gordon also notes that "for the first time since 1961, Japan imported more from China than from the United States" (Gordon 2003). In 2004, China surpassed the United States to become Japan's largest trading partner (*Financial Times*, 25 March 2004).

The general reorientation around China is also evident in Southeast Asia. While interdependencies remain weaker compared to their other trade relationships, here, as well, long term trends suggest a shift of regional activity towards China. In the case of China's trade with the ASEAN-4 economies, for example, trade since 1986 grew faster than their combined trade with the United States.[10] Gordon's comparison of 1996 and 2002 trade figures shows a 138 per cent increase in ASEAN's exports to China, but a decrease in ASEAN exports to both the United States and Japan (21 per cent and 4 per cent respectively) (Gordon 2003; Krumm and Kharas/World Bank 2003; Cai 2003). Though neither China nor ASEAN currently command a huge share of each other's trade, ASEAN states' decision to sign onto ACFTA, despite important reservations, was an important acknowledgement from ASEAN states that they expect China's economic importance to grow, not diminish. For example, though collective ASEAN is only China's fifth largest trade partner, after the United States, Japan, the EU, and Hong Kong, its share of China trade has been increasing at an annual rate of about 20 per cent for the last ten years (Pangestu and Gooptu 2003). Recently, China's Ministry of Commerce reported that trade volume between China and ASEAN for the first half of 2003 increased 45.3 per cent compared to year previous.[11] While most agree that the China market for ASEAN goods is currently underdeveloped (Wong and Chan 2003), ACFTA suggests both the expectation that it will become more important and the desire of governments to further develop that aspect of the relationship.

As noted above, ASEAN economies have been concerned about their over-reliance and particular dependency on the U.S. market since the late 1980s. The recent U.S. economic downturn has only underscored those concerns. According to UNCTAD Singapore, Malaysia, and Thailand all saw their exports to the United States contract by 5 per cent as a result of the U.S. economic downturn in 2001 (UNCTAD 2002). For much of Southeast Asia, which sees economic growth as integral to political, as well as economic, stability, China can provide an alternative and supplementary motor of Southeast Asian growth. It is also important to point out that such concerns about the need for ASEAN to diversify economic partners and in particular about the need to dilute its over-dependence on the U.S. market is not new; rather, concerns have been growing since the late 1980s with shifting U.S. Asia policies. The last decade and a half also points to shifts in thinking about U.S. interests in relation to Southeast Asia, as well as the global economy in general. As the ASEAN-China Expert Group on Economic Co-operation concluded, closer co-operative ties between China and ASEAN are "a natural response to regional and global developments during the course of the past decade" (ASEAN-China 2001, pp. 4, 6, 7). The emphasis here is on long-term trends. The U.S. and Japanese economies will remain important to Southeast Asia; however, the potential and dynamism of China's economy, combined with unhappiness with U.S. and Japanese policies, has heightened ASEAN interest in China and development of a more integrated East Asian regional economy. Moreover, there remains "a lot of potential for trade expansion" between China and ASEAN, especially if governments are able to encourage the creation and development of trade niches, core competencies, and other complementarities (Wong and Chan 2003, p. 525). It is significant given the Cold War dominance of the U.S. market that East Asia has already emerged as "the largest single market for its own exports" (Ong 2003, p. 59).

THE POLITICS OF ASEAN-CHINA RELATIONS: BILATERALISM OR REGIONALISM?

As suggested above, despite the intensification of economic relations, it is mostly politics that complicates relations between China and ASEAN, and regionalization processes in general. While economic trends illustrate that politics has not posed a particularly large obstacle in economic regionalization processes the last decade, the process has become more politicized since the financial crisis as states realize that the economic and political are inextricably intertwined. The debates in Taiwan and Japan over their investments in China are good illustrations.

ASEAN members share many of the concerns expressed by Japan and Taiwan about economic trends. While ASEAN states tend not to view China as a military threat in the ways that Japan and Taiwan do, their concerns about China are intensified by the fact that they are smaller actors. Economic arguments in favour of closer economic integration may be persuasive, but they have not eliminated ASEAN's concerns about being dominated by larger powers, in fact, quite the contrary. The asymmetries are especially evident in bilateral relationships between China and individual member states, but also between China and ASEAN as a collective. Just as ASEAN states have desired to mitigate its economic dependence on the United States by developing relations with China, they have desired to make sure its relations with China are similarly balanced by other relationships. These concerns have also added to the arguments in favor of broadening bilateral China-ASEAN agreements to be more inclusive of other regional actors.

ASEAN's concerns and reservations have not gone unnoticed by China, which has responded with overtures and diplomatic visits, all aimed to reassure. China's concerted efforts to "court" and reassure ASEAN are an indication of both China's heightened sensitivity to ASEAN concerns, as well as the relationship's heightened importance in China's regional priorities. Since the 1997–99 financial crisis, Chinese officials and leaders, including China's new president Hu Jintao, have made a number of high profile visits to Southeast Asia, where they underscored interdependence themes, in addition to highlighting the ways that a China-ASEAN relationship could help them each navigate a tough and often fickle global economy. Chinese initiative in proposing the comprehensive economic framework and ACFTA, which was signed in 2002, is of particular note. Especially given this post-crisis context, in which ASEAN had lost much of its lustre in the eyes of other actors (read, Western economies, especially the United States), China's overtures have been notable and appreciated.

On China's part, these overtures serve China's interest in portraying itself as a valuable partner and responsible power. They also speak to China's cognizance that, in Womack's words, "The difference between the perception of China as a threat and China as an opportunity lies to a great extent in China's political credibility. Hence, politics has mattered, does matter, and will matter, regardless of the mushrooming of economic ties" (Womack 2003–04). For China, good and stable relations with ASEAN serve a variety of interests. Perhaps most of all, a friendly regional environment will mitigate U.S. influence or efforts to leverage ASEAN and allow China to focus on domestic growth and reforms. According to Sheng Lijun, China's pursuit of ACFTA and better relations with ASEAN is also motivated by a concern that "international forces" might use economics and China's economy to play up the "China threat" in Southeast Asia (Sheng 2003). Thus, it is important to underscore the point that China's interest in ASEAN is proactive but also defensive. China is less interested in creating an anti-U.S. coalition (and certainly, ASEAN is not) than it is in neutralizing anti-China policies on the part of Washington.

From ASEAN's vantage point, China's ACFTA proposal also had a welcome, though perhaps unintended, effect and that was to generate renewed interest in ASEAN on the parts of other actors. Soon after China's proposal, the United States, Japan, Korea, and even India each followed with FTA proposals of their own.[12] The U.S. "Enterprise for ASEAN Initiative" (EAI) was most welcome as an indication of continued U.S. interest in ASEAN; however, the initiative was also substantively weak. As a bundle of bilateral agreements, the EAI not only failed to engage ASEAN as a region, but the conditions attached to it meant that not all ASEAN economies were even eligible. Japan's proposal was also both welcome and disappointing, though compared to the United States, there has been a more concerted effort to impress upon ASEAN its commitment to relations. This is because while Japan may be ambivalent about assuming a more formal leadership role and relatedly reluctant to upset its relations with the United States, neither is it comfortable with China assuming a leadership role in the region. On ASEAN's side, members have welcomed Japan's renewed attention not only because of the importance of their economic relations with Japan but also because ASEAN would prefer that China's influence be offset by other relationships.

Nevertheless, one of the biggest obstacles to a more explicitly identified East Asian regionalism is the China-Japan relationship. And as Robert Sutter has discussed, there are those who anticipate "an intensified rivalry for leadership in Asia" between China and Japan (Sutter 2002). In Japan, especially, China's proposed ACFTA "was widely seen as an attempt by Beijing to try to usurp the leadership role in Southeast Asia which has traditionally been played by Tokyo" ("China's Hu Jintao..." 2002, p. 7). Thus, Japan's counterproposal — in the form of a "Comprehensive Economic Partnership (CER)", a ten-year process of building a "broad-based economic partnership covering not only liberalization of trade and investment, but also trade and investment promotion and facilitation" (Kaur 2002) — soon after China and ASEAN announced their intent to pursue a joint free trade area was no surprise and is perceived by many in ASEAN as a transparent effort to counter China's influence.[13] In prioritizing a Japan-China FTA behind other trade relationships, Japan's foreign ministry also appears to be actively excluding China from regional plans. According to the "MOFA strategy", Japan would pull ASEAN and Korea into an "umbrella" economic partnership before concluding an FTA with China and well ahead of ACFTA's target date (Nebeshima 2002; "Japan Will Not Slash..." 2002). Whether or not Japan can keep these arrangements distinct, however, remains to be seen, especially given its own relatively intense economic relations with China.

On ASEAN's side, there are also reasons to be wary of an explicitly East Asian arrangement. Most of all, ASEAN is concerned that its voice will be lost in the larger grouping. Recent debates about Malaysian Prime Minister Mahathir's offer of a million dollars as seed money to create a secretariat for the APT process in Kuala Lumpur highlight the tensions and reservations regarding East Asian regionalization processes and their potential effects on ASEAN and the ASEAN Secretariat ("ASEAN+3"). Mahathir also pressed to have the APT's name formally changed so that it would explicitly identify its "East Asian" composition ("ASEAN+3"). Though other members felt some pressure to support the proposal on account of Mahathir's impending retirement — a "gift" to a long-time ASEAN leader — most ASEAN members were not supportive of the proposal. Indeed, only the Philippines expressed any significant support. As for the others, Thailand, Indonesia, and Singapore, all saw the APT secretariat — which represented a formal and physical expression of the East Asia idea — as "steal[ing] the shine" from the ASEAN Secretariat,[14] if not a potential threat to ASEAN and/or ASEAN interests. At the very least, they argued, the creation of the secretariat should wait until ASEAN was in a stronger position. Thailand's preference, for example, was to "strengthen the ASEAN Secretariat" (Abdullah 2002) in Jakarta first so that ASEAN would be better able to manage the APT process. Then, as the director-general of the ASEAN Department of Thailand's foreign ministry put it, "at least we will continue to steer it".[15] Opponents to the proposal also expressed concern that unless the ASEAN Secretariat was strengthened first, ASEAN would, in the words of one ASEAN diplomat, not only "lose its luster as a regional entity" but would also "be 'neutralized' by the North Asian giants, especially China" (Parameswaran 2002). In this sense, ASEAN does not yet appear ready or confident enough to move beyond the existing APT framework. One long-time reporter for Bangkok's *The Nation* put it in the following way: "Deep down, opponents [of the APT Secretariat] fear the new secretariat will transform ASEAN+3 to 3+ASEAN..." (Chongkittavorn 2002). To call the APT process "East Asia" would be even worse, a sign that ASEAN had been completely eclipsed by the larger body; at least "ASEAN+3" provided an explicit reminder of ASEAN's existence.

On the other hand, ASEAN would also like its bilateral relationship with China offset by other arrangements and the presence of other powers economically, as well as politically. As suggested above and as illustrated by the two years it took for ASEAN to study China's ACFTA proposal, ASEAN economies did not enter into that agreement with China without reservations. To have other economies in the mix would therefore also have a reassuring effect. Again, this is one reason that the FTA proposals from Japan, Korea, and others have been most welcome. Similarly, East Asian processes like the APT process, which include both Japan and Korea, also can help mitigate Chinese influence.

Not everyone is convinced that East Asia's reorientation will take place along East Asian lines. Some, for example, see the proliferation of bilateral trading arrangements in East Asia as particularly contrary to broader regionalization (and liberalization) processes (Ravenhill 2003). And indeed, the proliferation of bilateral arrangements, with its "spaghetti bowl effect of different rules and regulations" (Krumm and Kharas 2003), does complicate East Asian regionalization processes (political or economic). In this sense, East Asia has experienced contrasting trends in bilateralism and regionalism — both of which have been influenced to some extent by ACFTA. On the other hand, this emerging web of multiple and overlapping free trade agreements may also provide additional arguments for giving more serious consideration to an East Asian free trade area. Southeast Asian economies, especially, are ill-equipped and without the human resources to negotiate and implement so many different agreements. Moreover, many of these economies are pursuing bilateral, as well as regional, agreements out of fear of being left out — in other words, what they seek is *inclusion*, not exclusion which may introduce different dynamics than if they were pursuing such agreements for other reasons.[16] They are reactionary to agreements being pursued in other regions, as much to various initiatives being pursued closer to home. Relatedly, ASEAN remains concerned about attracting investment and business to Southeast Asia. If these bilateral agreements are shown to have the opposite effect, however, they may in fact prompt a more serious discussion of a more truly regional approach to free trade. In fact, Singapore, whose very active bilateralism is responsible for much of the current debate within the region, sees its bilateralism as a reaction to the slow pace of ASEAN's own integration efforts and thus a way to pressure others to pick up the pace[17] or alternatively, to create a system of "interlocking web of FTAs in the region" (Lien 2003).

Others similarly have raised the possibility that these arrangements, especially those between ASEAN (as a group) and the three Northeast Asian powers, might "converge" to form an East Asian arrangement.[18] Even better for ASEAN is if ASEAN could serve as a kind of "hub" or focusing point for regionalization activities. For this to happen or to be effective, however, ASEAN states, individually and collectively, would have to more proactive and consistent in terms of the FTAs being negotiated.[19]

There is also another reason for supporting East Asian regional integration processes, especially if the APT name is retained. That reason has to do with some of the understood lessons of the financial crisis, as well as the effects of that crisis on ASEAN's reputation and coherence. According to Terada and others, one of the more important lessons learned from the financial crisis was that for better or worse, relations between and among East Asian economies had become tied together by a growing interdependence (Terada 2003; Choi 2003). Even China and Vietnam, whose economies were less open and thus more insulated in 1997–99, know that next time, they are unlikely to be so unaffected. As Yu Yongding, Director of the Institute of World Economics and Politics at the Chinese Academy of Social Sciences, put it, for example: "The contagion effect showed that East Asia is a region, and no economies in the region are completely immured from the negative impact if one economy in the region collapses" (Yu 2001, p. 5; Zhang 2002c; Sheng 2003, p. 7).

In the case of ASEAN especially, the crisis dramatically illustrated the vulnerability of Southeast Asian economies to global forces and their powerlessness in affecting critical decisions at the global level (Ba *forthcoming*). That sense of powerlessness and vulnerability inspired a search for alternative — or at least, supplementary — arrangements, as well as political leadership. "To this end," as the *Jakarta Post* put it, "ASEAN, while painfully recognizing its own institutional and geopolitical weakness, has acknowledged the fact that the East Asian region could be much stronger and influential in world affairs if the three major Asian powers up north are eventually brought into the picture" ("ASEAN Needs"; "Coming Together"). In this post-crisis context, East Asia became much more persuasive as an idea compared to the early 1990s when Mahathir first broached his East Asian Economic Group idea. One might also add that East Asia offers ASEAN an opportunity for new relevance.

Nor was ASEAN alone in finding "East Asia" more persuasive an idea than before, as evidenced by the heightened activity along East Asian lines from other actors since the financial crisis. Most notably, 1997 saw Japan —

perhaps the most ambivalent actor in the drama of East Asian regionalism —
propose the creation of an Asian Monetary Fund, "a regional facility that
would be prepared to disburse pre-committed emergency funds more promptly
than the resource-strapped IMF".[20] Created in response to "regional
dissatisfaction both with global multilateral solution and with the US reaction",
the AMF has been characterized as an attempt at "regional self help" (in
response to "no help") (Rapkin 2001, p. 375; Chang and Rajan 1999, p.
273). Specifically, the AMF aimed to both prevent and manage future crises.[21]

The AMF also received wide support from regional economies, receiving
as much as $100 billion in contributions (Chang and Rajan, 1999, p. 273).
In 1999, at meetings in Manila, Japan expressed its explicit support for the
APT process, again a contrast to its previous hesitancy. Even though Japan
remains extremely wary of any attempts to give the process a more formal and
prominent institutional form, there is acknowledgement that 1) global
governance arrangements are not enough; and 2) there has been a sea change
in regional attitudes about East Asian processes since the crisis. Specifically,
Japan saw that the crisis has created enough consensus on the desirability,
indeed the necessity, of East Asian co-operation on certain issues that Japan
has little choice but to participate if it wants to have any role in directing the
process or if it is to effectively respond to China's growing influence.

Since the advent of the crisis in 1997, ASEAN+3 meetings have
consequently met on a regular basis every year, but perhaps even more
significant have been the activities at lower ministerial and working group
levels. In addition to the annual APT meeting of East Asian leaders, there are
regular meetings between finance, foreign, and economic ministers, as well as
regular senior officials meetings. Greatest activity has been in areas of finance
and monetary co-operation towards strengthening policy dialogues, increasing
regional activities in areas of capital flows monitoring, self help and support
mechanisms and international financial reforms. The Chiang Mai Initiative
(CMI), an expanded ASEAN swap arrangement that requires co-operation
among East Asia's central banks, especially stands out. Paul Bowles has
described the CMI as "a *de facto* AMF, providing a mechanism to meet the
aims of an AMF but avoiding the more politically difficult task of establishing
a formal institution which might encounter U.S. opposition" (Bowles 2002).

There is also growing talk about lessening the region's dependence on the
U.S. dollar as the main trade and settlement currency. Especially as intra-
regional trade increases, there is growing talk about adopting a regional
currency like the Japanese Yen. Though most also see a monetary union and
exchange rate co-operation as a long term, not short term, goal, they argue
that the adoption of a common regional currency will be important to

preventing competitive devaluations, stabilizing currency values, and lowering the cost of doing intra-regional trade (Sussangkarn 2003).

Most notably, these activities go beyond the market-led integration that characterized regionalization processes during the 1980s and 1990s. While it would be incorrect to say that states in the 1980s and 1990s played no role in facilitating trade and economic linkages (as in the case of ASEAN and China, where China's state owned enterprises have been ASEAN's primary trade and investment partners) or in the creation of regional production networks (as in the case of Japan with Southeast Asia), governments have generally been less enthusiastic (even resistant) about supporting explicitly East Asian integration proposals. Since 1997, however, East Asian governments have taken a much more active, leadership role in leading and facilitating regional co-operation and integration along East Asian lines. To quote Shujiro Urata, there has been a "shift from market-led to institutional-led regional economic integration in East Asia" (Urata 2002). Yu Yongding similarly observes that, "Up until the onset of the Asian financial crisis, there was virtually no serious discussion on monetary co-operation, especially on institutionalized monetary co-operation, in the East Asian region" (Yu 2001). Thus, even though U.S. objections successfully blocked the AMF's creation, there remains notable consensus about the need for an additional regional line of defence and support in times in trouble and crisis.

Perhaps most interesting have been China's views on East Asia. Already mentioned are China's changing views of ASEAN and ASEAN-led processes. Though scholars may disagree about China's intentions and long-term goals, it is difficult to deny that China's attitudes towards regional multilateral processes have undergone some significant changes. China's heightened involvement in regional processes, recent initiatives like ACFTA as well as the Shanghai Co-operation Organization (also China-initiated), all suggest China's higher comfort level in participating in such processes, if not appreciation for multilateral/institutional processes (or at least, particular kinds of multilateral processes) (Zhang 2002, pp. 217–18). Some Chinese participants of Track II processes have been most explicit about regional processes performing important reassurance functions towards mitigating Asian security dilemmas not only in terms of China-ASEAN relations, but also Japan and the wider East Asia (Tang 2002; Zhang and Tang 2003; Zhang 2002; Zhang 2003).

At the same time, while China has been increasingly more comfortable with ASEAN and ASEAN-led regionalism, its objections to Japan's original AMF proposal also illustrated that it was not necessarily comfortable with *all* regional multilateralisms. According to Yu, China was both suspicious of Japan's intentions in proposing the AMF and uncertain about the need for such a proposal. China's suspicions stemmed from the fact that there had been no communication between Tokyo and Beijing about the proposal, which consequently "caught [Beijing] by surprise." Also, China had been affected differently than the other economies. According to Yu:

> during the Asian financial crisis, the impact of the crisis on the Chinese economy was mainly via the reduction of demand for China's exports, which in turn was mainly a result of the slowdown of the global economy. Consequently, China's attention was focused on global solutions. (Yu 2001)

Moreover, "due to its relatively secure position *vis-à-vis* possible international speculative attacks, China was not clear what benefits China can get from participating in such institutionalized arrangements at the expense of the sovereign control of a significant portion of its foreign exchange reserves" (Yu 2001). By this argument, China felt that it had the capacity to protect itself; it also was not at all sure that others would uphold their commitments in such an arrangement.

In the few years since the crisis, however, China's views on East Asia also appear to have evolved some potentially significant ways. Some believe that China's changed attitudes on East Asian financial co-operation, like Japan's, are the product of the realization that "if it does not play a positive role in the process, it will be kept out by other countries".[22] Paul Bowles has argued that China's changed position reflects Chinese unhappiness with the U.S. failure to acknowledge China as a responsible and meaningful member of the international community (Bowles 2002). Meanwhile, in China, some Chinese scholars have framed arguments for East Asian integration in terms similar to those being put forth by many ASEAN elites — that is, East Asian integration is necessary if East Asian economies are to be prepared for competing in a tough global economy and the next crisis. While trade and technological co-operation is considered more important, Yu has argued that the region must think more about co-operation on exchange rates. As Yu puts it, such co-operation is necessary if they are to discourage states from engaging in competitive devaluations, which he describes as "dangerous" (Yu 2001, p. 7).

Other observers have argued that an East Asian economic group has been China's goal all along. While ACFTA did aim to reassure a nervous ASEAN, for example, China may also have seen ACFTA as a stepping stone to building an East Asian free trade area. Zhang Yunlong offers this assessment, "China will not just stop at this [ACFTA] arrangement. Its larger interest lies in EAFTA" (Zhang 2003). One Malaysian economist argues that the China-

ASEAN FTA was pursued first simply because ASEAN is easier to "bully" and that once ASEAN is on board the others (Japan and Korea) will soon follow. In other words, ASEAN makes similar agreements by others with China more politically palatable.

As for why China would want an East Asian free trade area, Zhang explains, "China believes that East Asian regional co-operation and integration could help to create a stable and co-operative environment, which is crucial for realizing its ambitious modernization dream" (Zhang 2002, p. 223). Zhang also sees East Asian processes as important for long-term confidence building, a conclusion that echoes ASEAN's characterizations of regional processes and thus seems reflective of ASEAN's influence over China's changing views of regionalism. As he puts it, "East Asia needs political and security co-operation" in the interest of building trust but political circumstances mean that it must be done "cautiously and gradually" (Zhang 2002*b*). Until East Asian states feel more comfortable with one another, they may have to settle for a more "pragmatic approach" — pragmatic meaning different kinds of arrangements, bilateral and multilateral, intra-regional and inter-regional, and in areas where progress is possible (Zhang 2002, p. 220).

While there does appear to be growing consensus in China about the necessity of East Asian integration in some form, it is less clear how China sees ASEAN's long-term role and place in this East Asian political economy. At very least, Chinese scholars have envisioned different kinds of arrangements. Some, for example, prioritize Northeast Asian co-operation; some have even suggested the possibility of joint leadership between China and Japan (Sheng 2003). For advocates of a Northeast Asia first approach, Japan and Korea also can offer China more in the way of capital and technology transfers. Others, however, are more worried about China's disadvantaged position *vis-à-vis* Japan, especially, and prefer to focus more on ASEAN first. Even here, however, there are some differences in terms of ASEAN's role and place in such an East Asian framework. Zhang Yunlong and Tang Shiping, both of the Chinese Academy of Social Sciences in Beijing and both participants in regional Track II processes, for example, agree on the necessity of East Asian integration, but they differ somewhat in how they conceive ASEAN's role in that process. Zhang seems to advocate moving away from "ASEAN plus" framework to a more explicit "East Asian" process. He writes:

> As an important step, we must consider moving from the TPT [Ten plus Three] structure to a regional organization, e.g, an Organization of East Asian Co-operation (OEAC) within three to five years. The OEAC will

have a secretariat and functional committees. The Organization will not only continue the current activities, but also develop new functions as well. The annual leaders meeting will be a core activity. (Zhang 2002, p. 221)

In contrast, Tang seems to find the "ASEAN Plus" more favorable because he sees it as the only option given political constraints, and the only way to encourage integration. Similarly, Zhang notes, as long as China continues to have concerns about other Northeast Asian actors and "the direction of the process", "China is probably confident in negotiating a comprehensive deal with ASEAN, but not yet so with Japan or South Korea, nor for any East Asian regional agreement" (Zhang 2002, p. 218). At least in the near future, "East Asia" will be built upon multiple processes — specifically, a "four wheel" process involving more circumscribed activities (APT, Ten Plus One, Northeast Asia, and intra-ASEAN) that are not yet ready to come together under one East Asian rubric but can nevertheless be seen as mutually supporting processes in the interest of regional stability, long-term co-operation, and securing a more influential voice and greater protection in the global political economy (Zhang 2002c).

CONCLUSION

East Asia has been adapting to post-Cold War changes in the regional economy that include new concerns about global multilateral trading arrangements, as well as shifting relations with both the United States and China. While both China and ASEAN today are far from being each others' most important trading or economic partners, there is evidence to suggest that China will become more important, not less, and that the regional economy that has been driven by the U.S. market is already reorienting itself around China. For ASEAN, especially, China offers important opportunities and an additional motor for Southeast Asian growth, even at the same time that it represents an immense economic challenge. Again, there appears to be a growing sense that economic co-operation with China may be the only way for ASEAN to remain economically competitive and attractive to potential investors and businesses.

While there is a general consensus in East Asia that economic trends will likely make "East Asia" more compelling over time, politics and distrust continue to pose significant obstacles in the way of regionalization processes. Indeed, the discussion above highlights how *all* the principals involved have important reservations about "East Asia", but also how developments since the 1997–99 financial crisis have also created new consensus about the need to co-operate in certain areas, especially in the area of monetary co-operation. Consequently, there has been far more activity along East Asian lines since 1997 and moreover East Asian governments have taken a much more involved role in guiding and facilitating East Asian co-operation and activities.

With respect to the China-ASEAN relationship in particular, relations have seen much improvement but they have not been enough to completely eliminate concerns, especially ASEAN's concerns about China. For ASEAN, these concerns provide arguments both for and against East Asia. On the one hand, "East Asia" offers a way to mitigate Chinese influence and concerns about an asymmetric bilateral relationship; on the other, ASEAN worries that its voice and identity would be completely lost in larger grouping with larger powers. As for China, it has clearly been very attentive to ASEAN and over the last decade has come to see regional processes as performing important reassurance functions. Regional stability is critical to China's development and security objectives. At the same time, while China has an interest in improved relations with Japan and Korea, as well as ASEAN, it has been easier to work with ASEAN first. In this sense, ACFTA may very well turn out to be a stepping stone to a broader East Asian trade area and just one chapter in an ongoing drama that is "East Asia".

Notes

1. Namely, China, Japan, Korea (North and South), Indonesia, Malaysia, Philippines, Singapore, Thailand, Brunei, Vietnam, Laos, Myanmar, and Cambodia.
2. Savetsila was referring to a "warning" conveyed by Secretary of State Schultz in 1987.
3. Womack points out that to do otherwise almost certainly would have been interpreted by ASEAN states as aggressive and would have reacted competitively. See Womack (2003–04).
4. According to Felker, Indonesia skews the numbers because Indonesia accounts for about 60 per cent of the decline in FDI to SEA from 1996–2001 (Felker 2003, p. 280; See also Vatikiotis 2003).
5. For example, Dell, NEC Corp., Minolta. The *Nihon Keizai Shimbun* report pointed to a growing trend by which "Japanese manufacturers with operations in South-east Asia are increasingly shutting down their factories and moving production to China." See, for example, Perlez 2002; "Japanese Firms Saying Hello China…" 2002; "China Defends 'Win-Win' Surge…" 2002.
6. According to JETRO, 99 per cent of Japanese TNCs already invested in ASEAN did say that they did not intend to relocate their operations, though this did not preclude their expanding operations in China (UNCTAD 2002, pp. 44–57).

7. Regarding development, Indonesia, then-Malaya, Thailand all benefited from the war-time demand for rubber and tin, as did Singapore as Southeast Asia's main entrepot for those commodities. Of the Southeast Asian economies, Singapore and Malaya benefited most from the Korean War (due in part to certain British policies), while Thailand benefited especially from the Vietnam War, during which U.S. aid was instrumental to the early development of Thailand's national infrastructure and administrative structure and capabilities (Stubbs 1989).

8. For a good discussion of the flying geese model and its problems, see Bernard and Ravenhill (1995); Hatch (1996).

9. Another growing concern is the numbers of Taiwanese moving to the Mainland. By one estimate, there are now about one million Taiwanese (of Taiwan's population of twenty million) living in China. See Callick (2003).

10. Voon and Ren (2003).

11. ASEAN exports to China increased 55.5 per cent (to US$20.47 billion), while Chinese exports to ASEAN increased 32.4 per cent to US$13.77 billion during the first half of 2003. "China-ASEAN Trade…"

12. For details, see ASEAN website: <http://www.aseansec.org/13999.htm>. A list of proposed and actual regional trading arrangements involving East Asian countries can be found in Pangestu and Gooptu (2003), p. 83.

13. Singapore's *Business Times*, for example, wrote: "The overriding impression given by Japan's decision to pursue bilateral accords selectively is that it is trying to steal a march on China in its diplomacy towards South-east Asia." "Japan's Regional Grand Design" 2002.

14. Confidential Interview with author, Ministry of Industry and Trade, Kuala Lumpur, August 2002.

15. "ASEAN Considers Strengthening 'ASEAN plus 3' Co-operation" (27 July 2002). See also comments of Philippine Foreign Minister Siazon Abdullah (29 July 2002).

16. Ravenhill argues that in the case of Japan and Korea, their agreements are motivated more by a desire to protect certain domestic industries and sectors by offering a regional "alternative to the political pain caused by multinational trading negotiations" (Ravenhill 2003).

17. See comments of K. Kesavapany, Director of ISEAS and Singapore's former High Commissioner to Malaysia (Kesavapany 2003). See also, Daniel (2002).

18. Zhang 2002*b*. See also comments of Masaki Ishikawa, Executive Director of Industrial Resarch, JETRO Singapore, in Daniel (2002).

19. See, for example, arguments made by Mohd Haflah Piei, Deputy Director of the Malaysian Institute of Economic Research (Piei 2003).

20. Rapkin, 2001, p. 375. For a discussion of Japan's motivations behind the AMF proposal, see Altbach (1997).

21. The AMF's primary functions were identified as being: the promotion of policy

dialogue, the creation of emergency financial support, and the prevention of future crisis.

22. Pangestu and Gooptu paraphrasing arguments of He Fan (Pangestu and Gooptu, World Bank 2003).

References

ASEAN-China Expert Group on Economic Co-operation. *Forging Closer ASEAN-China Relations In the Twenty First Century*, 2001. The full report is available at <www.aseansec.org>.

"ASEAN Needs East Asian Regionalism". *Jakarta Post*, 30 August 2000.

" 'ASEAN Plus 3' Should be Called E. Asia Economic Group". *Japan Economic Newswire*, 4 August 2003.

Ba, Alice D. "China and ASEAN: Renavigating Relations for a 21st Century Asia". *Asian Survey* 43, no. 4 (2003): 622–47.

Ba, Alice D. "Contested Spaces: The Politics of Regional and Global Governance". In *Contending Perspectives on Global Governance*, edited by Alice D. Ba and Matthew J. Hoffmann. London: Routledge. Forthcoming.

Bernard, Mitchell and John Ravenhill. "Beyond Product Cycles and Flying Geese: Regionalization, Hierarchy, and the Industrialization of East Asia". *World Politics* 47, no. 2 (1995): 171–210.

Bowles, Paul. "Asia's Post-Crisis Regionalism: Bringing the State Back In, Keeping the (United) States Out". *Review of International Political Economy* 9, no. 2 (2002): 244–77.

Callick, Rowan. "Exiting the Dragon's Shadow". *Australian Financial Review*. 17 October 2003.

"China-ASEAN Trade Volume Grows in 1st Half of Year". *People's Daily Online*, 17 August 2003.

"China Defends 'Win-Win' Surge in Japanese Investment". *Deutsche Press-Agentur*, 14 August 2002.

"China's Hu Jintao Urges Talks With ASEAN on Fee-Trade Zone". *South China Morning Post*, 27 April 2002, p. 7.

Choi, Won-Mog. "Regional Economic Integration in East Asia: Prospect and Jurisprudence." *Journal of International Economic Law* 6, no. 1 (2003): 49–77.

Choong, William. "China Can Fuel Demand for Asian Exports". *The Straits Times*, 18 December 2001.

"Coming Together". *Asiaweek*, 4 August 2000, p. 73.

Daniel, Patrick. "ASEAN's Historic Opportunity". *Business Times* (Singapore), 2 May 2002.

Felker, Greg. "Southeast Asian Industrialization and the Changing Global Production System". *Third World Quarterly* 24, no. 2 (2003): 255–82.

Gordon, Bernard K. "A High Risk Trade Policy". *Foreign Affairs* 82, no. 4 (2003).

Hatch, Walter. *Asia in Japan's Embrace: Building a Regional Production Alliance.* New York: Cambridge University Press, 1996.

Hill, Cameron J. and William T. Tow. "The ASEAN Regional Forum: Material and Ideational Dynamics". In *Reconfiguring East Asia*, edited by Mark Beeson. London: RougledgeCurzon, 2002.

Ho, Khai Leong. "Rituals, Risks, and Rivalries: China and ASEAN in the Coming Decades". *Journal of Contemporary China* 10, no. 29 (2001): 683–94.

Leung, Eddie. "Southeast Asia-China: Threats, Opportunities". *Asia Times*, 2 August 2003.

Loh, Hui Yin. "AFTA Will Ensure Better Fit With China". *Business Times* (Singapore), 16 April 2002.

Kaur, Hardev. "Japan, Playing Catch Up With China". *New Straits Times*, 6 November 2002.

"Japan's Regional Grand Design". *Business Times,* 22 October 2002.

"Japan Will Not Slash Aid Budget for East Asia". *The Straits Times* (Singapore), 13 August 2002.

"Japanese Firms Saying Hello China, Sayonara Southeast Asia". *Deutsche Press-Agentur*, 14 August 2002.

Kesavapany, K. "Reconciling National and Regional Security Interests". *IDSS-Perspectives* (January 2003). Available at <http://www.ntu.edu.sg/idss/Perspective/research_050301.htm>.

Kim, Wan-Soon. "China: Opportunity or Threat?" *Korea Herald*, 29 January 2004.

Krumm, Kathie and Homi Kharas. *East Asia Integrates: A Trade Policy for Shared Growth*. Washington, D.C.: World Bank, 2003.

Leow, Jason. "Taiwan to Push ASEAN for More Trade Deals". *The Straits Times*, 18 October 2003.

Lien, Jennifer. "PM Goh Offers to Share FTA Experience with ASEAN States". *Business Times* (Singapore), 10 May 2003.

Nebeshima, Keizo. "Diplomatic Prowess for Less". *Japan Times,* 26 August 2002.

Ong, Eng Chuan. "Anchor East Asian Free Trade in ASEAN". *Washington Quarterly* 26, no. 2 (2003): 57–72.

Pangestu, Mari and Sudarshan Gooptu. "New Regionalism: Options for China and East Asia" (Chapter 3). In *East Asia Integrates: A Trade Policy for Shared Growth*, edited by Kathie Krumm and Homi Kharas. Washington, D.C.: World Bank, 2003.

Piei, Mohd Haflah. "Beware of Proliferation Trade Initiatives". *New Straits Times,* 17 May 2003.

Perlez, Jane. "China Races to Replace U.S. as Economic Power in Asia". *New York Times*, 28 June 2002.

Ravenhill, John. "The New Bilateralism in Asia and the Pacific". *Third World Quarterly* 24, no. 2 (2003): 299–317.

Richardson, Michael. "China Seen by ASEAN as Market". *International Herald Tribune*, 26 April 2002.

Richardson, Michael. "How to Compete with China — And Like It". *International Herald Tribune*, 7 November 2003.

Rowley, Anthony. "Why ASEAN Still Appeals to Japan Despite China". *Business Times* (Singapore), 22 August 2002.

Savetsila, Siddhi. "Current Trends: Implications and Repercussions on Thailand's Foreign Policy". Address to Foreign Correspondents Club of Thailand". Bangkok, Thailand, 27 January 1988. In *Collection of Speeches 1988*.

Sheng, Lijun. "China-ASEAN Free Trade Area: Origins, Developments, and Strategic Motivations". ISEAS International Politics and Security Issues Working Paper no. 1, 2003.

Siazon, Domingo. "The Emergence of Geoeconomics and Its Impact on Regional Security". *Kasarinian* 10, no. 3 (First Quarter 1995).

Stubbs, Richard. "Geopolitics and the Political Economy of Southeast Asia". *International Journal* 44 (Summer 1989): 517–40.

Sussangkarn, Chalongphob. (President, Thailand Development Research Institute). "East Asian Financial Co-operation". Presentation to First East Asian Congress, 2003.

Sutter, Robert. "China and Japan: Trouble Ahead?" *Washington Quarterly* (Autumn 2002).

Tang, Shiping. "Institution Building Under 10+3: Tackling the Practical Issues". *Global Economic Review* (Seoul) 31, no. 4 (2002): 3–16.

Tang, Shiping. "Last Chance for East Asian Integration". *The Straits Times*, 17 November 2002.

Terada, Takashi. "Constructing an 'East Asian' Concept and Growing Regional Identity: From EAEC to ASEAN+3". *Pacific Review* 16, no. 2 (2003): 251–77.

UNCTAD. *Trade and Development Report, 2002*. New York: United Nations, 2002.

Shujiro Urata. "A Shift From Market-led to Institution-led Regional Economic Integration in East Asia". Paper presented at Conference on Asian Economic Integration. Research Institute of Economy, Trade, and Industry, United Nations University. Tokyo. 22–23 April 2002.

Vatikiotis, Michael. "Catching the Dragon's Tail". *Contemporary Southeast Asia* 25, no. 1 (2003): 65–79.

Vatikiotis, Michael. "Outward Bound". *Far Eastern Economic Review*, 5 February 2004, pp. 24–27.

Voon, Jan P. and Ren Yue. "China-ASEAN Export Rivlary in the US Market". *Journal of Asia Pacific Economy* 8, no. 2 (2003): 157–79.

Wanandi, Jusuf. "East Asian Regionalism: The Way Ahead". *The Straits Times*, 4 December 2000, p. 21.

Womack, Brantly. "China and Southeast Asia: Asymmetry, Leadership, and Normalcy. *Pacific Affairs* 76, no. 4 (2003/4).

Wong, John and Sarah Chan. "China-ASEAN Free Trade Agreement". *Asian Survey* 43, no. 3 (2003): 507–26.

Yu, Yongding. "On East Asian Monetary Co-operation". Working Paper Series no. 2. Research Centre for International Finance, Institute of World Economic and Politics/Chinese Academy of Social Sciences. Available on line: <http://www.iwep.org.cn/english/index.htm>, 2001.

Zhang, Yunling. "East Asian Regionalism and China". *Issues and Studies* (June 2002): 213–23.

Zhang, Yunling. "East Asian Co-operation and Integration: Where to Go?" Paper available at <http://www.iapscass.cn/English/Publications/showcontent.asp?id=67>, 2002*b*.

Zhang, Yunling. "Toward an East Asian Community: Still a Long Way to Go". Paper presented at Asian Economic Integration: Current Status and Future Prospects." Tokyo, Japan, 22–24 April 2002*c*.

8

ASEAN+1 OR CHINA+1?

Regionalism and Regime Interests in ASEAN-China Relations

Ho Khai Leong

INTRODUCTION

China's rise as an economic power in a rapidly changing international environment and stagnant global trade negotiations has had a great impact in ASEAN. The after-shock of the 1997–98 Asian financial crisis, Japan's decade-long economic slump and the consequences of U.S.-led war against terrorism in the Southeast Asian region were three accompanying events that changed ASEAN's perceptions of intra-regional and international relations. The financial crisis exposed the weak fundamentals inherent in the economic systems and flaws within the corporate structures of the ASEAN states; Japan's economic decline culminated in the questioning of its leading role in ASEAN and the loosening of trade and investment ties between Japan and ASEAN;[1] and the Islamic terrorist threat continues to haunt the region, with their latest terrorist acts in Indonesia.

ASEAN's economic landscape has been transformed due to China's diplomatic offensive in the last two years, especially its aggressive push in signing the Free Trade Area (FTA), thus making it the first Northeast Asian nation to join the ASEAN+3 along with Japan and Korea. To a great extent, China is attempting to consolidate its "insider" role in the region, against

United State's military and economic presence. The China-ASEAN FTA includes the promotion of trade and investment, the realization of free trade within a decade (by 2010) and the development of the Mekong sub-region (which involves Yunnan, Myanmar, Laos, Thailand, Cambodia and Vietnam).

These developments raise many important questions: How far would the China-ASEAN FTA go in bringing about regional integration? What would regional integration bring to ASEAN? What are the implications of China's participation in AFTA and the ASEAN economic community (AEC)[2]? How should ASEAN respond to regional integration? While it could be speculated that an integrated region may well strengthen regional stability and reduce the likelihood of conflict, it is as yet too soon to determine whether it will be worth the efforts of all parties involved. However, as an interdependent economic community, ASEAN needs to be more wary of the political as well as the economic consequences. Ironically, in spite of the consequences of being too regionally integrated, ASEAN does not seem to have many alternatives.

For the present, ASEAN's most important goal is to consider proposals with the potential to enhance its economic security and promote its growth in the short to medium term. Proposals for an integrated economic community in ASEAN (in the from of AFTA) and in Asia (in a vague framework of the so-called Asian Economic Community) are but means to achieve these goals. Simply put, regionalism is a means to sustained economic development, not an end in itself. A rapidly developing China is both a "promised land" and "turbulent sea" for it is both a competitor and a partner to the ASEAN economies.[3] In this stage of development, China competes head to head with ASEAN in foreign direct investment (FDI) and export markets, but at the same time, despite the rivalry, the ASEAN economies cannot ignore the potentials of the China's enormous market.

This is more so given the fact that China will be an important determining factor in the outcome of the ASEAN economies' painful process of restructuring and change.[4] This chapter will therefore assess the recent developments of trade relations between ASEAN and China (ASEAN+1), and examine the proposals of the China-ASEAN FTA and how it would impact regional integration. It will also highlight some of the potential challenges in China-ASEAN relations in the near future. The major argument posited by this chapter is the cautious pursuit of the necessary and urgent adjustments between China and ASEAN so as to enable them to keep pace with each other, thereby allowing them to reap the benefits of regional integration.

CHINA-ASEAN RELATIONS: BEYOND MULTIPOLARITY, TOWARDS REGIONALISM

International politics underwent a fundamental transformation at the end of the Cold War. The demise of the Soviet Union in the late 1980s and the dominance of United States, Japan and NATO prior to the September 11 terrorist attack shaped an international system best described as a multipolarity, where powers are distributed in different geographical entities. But the September 11 incident ushered in an international system where the United States exercised its military might indiscriminately in the name of national interest in its crackdown on terrorism. In the face of this ongoing conflict between the United States and the terrorist networks, the Asia-Pacific with its many Islamic countries (such as Indonesia, and to a lesser extent, Malaysia) has become entangled in the increasing tensions between its Muslim populations and United States' determined effort in its war on terror. Most ASEAN states, with the exception of Singapore and the Philippines, called for opposition to unipolarity and unilateralism, that is, dominance of United States in world affairs.

How does this new paradigm shift apply to China's role in the Southeast Asian region? As far as security arrangement is concerned, China-ASEAN relations have indeed made major strikes. Relations between ASEAN and China have reached a stage of development of "nascent security community." Recent policy developments certainly reinforced this trend. In 19 August 2003 in Wuyishan, Fujian province, Chinese senior officials and the ten ASEAN countries signed the 1976 Treaty of Amity and Co-operation (TAC).[5] ASEAN Secretary General Ong Keng Yong hailed this as a "trailblazing step" in confidence building between China and ASEAN.[6]

Rapid transformations are also simultaneously occurring on the political and economic fronts. During this period, Beijing sees China's promotion of its economic relations with the ASEAN states as a means to serving China's economic interests because Southeast Asia provides important export outlets and sources of foreign capital and raw materials. In providing China with the capital and market, Beijing deems Southeast Asia instrumental in China's drive towards economic modernization. China's initial opening in the 1980s and liberalization in the 1990s have resulted in its rapid export growth. The impact was less significant then as ASEAN was also experiencing rapid growth. By the end of 1990s, however, things were different. ASEAN economies were weakened by the financial crisis, and China turned increasingly to the regional and global markets as oversupply mounted and domestic prices nosedived. It was in this context that China expressed keen interest in joining AFTA.

Almost all parties involved agreed that the potentials for further development of China-ASEAN economic relations are great. A China-ASEAN free trade area would be the largest in the world, with a combined market of 1.7 billion people and a GDP of US$2 trillion and total trade estimated at US$1.23 trillion. China's entry into WTO almost certainly stimulated the growth of bilateral trade between the two regions, thus proving that the opportunities for trade and investment as well as other areas of co-operation are enormous.[7]

These developments, however, were met with some apprehension in the ASEAN states. Philippines Trade and Industry Secretary, Manuel A. Roxas II, for example, was one of the more sceptical ASEAN policymakers expressing reservations about China's presence in AFTA as it was difficult to weigh the pros and cons in light of the fact that China was only accepted into the WTO recently in 2001. It remains to be seen how China will comply with its commitments under a free trade regime.[8] So far, not all China's trading partners are satisfied with it. Another major concern is China's lack of legal and regulatory frameworks; for instance, it did not have an effective bankruptcy law. Although it is almost certain that the free trade area would force China to further reform its regulation and goods circulation system, the effectiveness of these reforms in policy formulation and implementation remains uncertain.

CHINA-ASEAN FTA: HASTE AND COMMITMENTS

On 4 November 2002, the "Framework Agreement on Comprehensive Economic Co-operation between the Association of Southeast Asian Nations and the People's Republic of China" was signed in Phnom Penh, a year after China introduced the idea. China, it seems, is more ready than ASEAN for regional integration.

There are many reasons for ASEAN's hasty move in acceding to China's proposal of regional integration in spite of its initial suspicions. It is a reflection of increasing economic interests on both sides; they would naturally want to view it as a positive-sum game. The strategic competition of the United States and Japan ranks among the most obvious factor propelling China's intense diplomatic offensive in the region. In addition, the spill over effects of these superpowers cannot be discounted. United States proposed the Enterprise for ASEAN Initiative (EAI) to enable the ASEAN states to establish FTA along the lines of the USA-Singapore FTA. Japan, too, unwilling to stand at the sidelines, announced the "Joint Declaration of the Leaders of ASEAN and Japan on the Comprehensive Economic Partnership" on 5 November 2002, in Phnom Penh.

These developments should be viewed in a positive light as they have had the effect of drawing the attention of these economic superpowers on ASEAN, thereby providing them with the impetus to put their acts together so as to effectively respond to such rapid developments.

Although the proposal was hurriedly agreed to, both parties were cautious in its implementation. The China-ASEAN FTA framework's main target was to have zero tariffs with ASEAN-6 and the rest of ASEAN for "normal track" products by 2010, and 2015 respectively. Thus, while both sides have adopted a gradual approach to achieve their objectives, it is as yet unclear how this negotiation will proceed. It is expected that some ASEAN states would put some sectors on the "sensitive track" to gain additional advantages in negotiations with China.

China responded by implementing the "Early Harvest Programme" (EHP) in 2002. The three-year programme is largely a Chinese concession dispensing early benefits to the ASEAN states through tariff reductions on a host of agricultural and manufactured goods before the actual implementation of the FTA on 1 January 2005. Agricultural communities are generally uneconomical in scale, technologically backward. In essence, they are small estates in need of government assistance. Products covered are live animals, meat and edible meat offal, fish, dairy produce, other animal products, live trees, edible vegetables and edible fruits and nuts. The ASEAN states reciprocated by giving China tariff concessions under a so-called tariff harmonized system for agricultural products like meat, fish, fruit, vegetables and milk. Countries such as Malaysia, Thailand and the Philippines whose economies have some comparative advantage in agriculture were pleased to be part of this scheme. For example, under the auspices of this programme, Malaysia has gained substantial benefits for it managed to reach an agreement with China exempting a package of 590 products, including unprocessed agricultural products as well as vegetable oils, cocoa products, detergents and glass envelopes from tariff elimination.

The predominantly agricultural Philippines, however, is more troubled by the agreement than the other ASEAN states. It fears that lowering the agricultural tariffs would damage the Philippine agricultural sector because it would open the way for a flood of cheap Chinese food products. There are reports indicating that the so-called "gray market" food imports from China into northern Luzon are already having negative consequences, which the Philippine Government did not want to see in the first place.[9]

While many agree that this programme is an economic confidence measure of some sort, the political and diplomacy dimensions are not missed. China's proposal puts it across as an economic leader and as such, it is able to stand out from the other economic powers and replace Japan's role as the leader in regional co-operation. This hypothesis is supported by analysts' observations that Japan is unlikely to offer something similar, as it is extremely protective of its own domestic agricultural market.

Many are optimistic about the outcome of the ASEAN-China FTA. By 2010, the average duty within the ASEAN-China FTA, if realized, will vary between zero and five per cent, and internal trade and investment barriers will be eliminated. The free trade area will then control 40 per cent of the world's foreign exchange reserves and more than US$2 trillion in gross domestic product, 10 per cent of the world's total.

ASEAN+1 OR CHINA+1? TENSIONS/CHALLENGES BETWEEN CHINA AND ASEAN

China's entry into WTO has major significance for its domestic economy and regional economy. Many analysts have noted that China's entrance into the WTO will encourage its incipient movement toward economic freedom. It is believed that the China-WTO agreement would reduce the command-and-control elements of government authority in China and add momentum in its move towards increased economic liberalization. This will in turn ensure China's further commitment in reducing the role of government in the economy and moving forward with market-based reforms.[10]

For ASEAN, China's entry into the WTO is timely as the 1997 currency crisis left the Southeast Asian states in need of the expansive Chinese market's demands for their goods and services when their economies pick up momentum. If ASEAN were to use export as their strategy to resolve some of their economic problems, they required access to the Chinese market. However, while the Chinese market is undoubtedly Asia's second largest, it is also the most protected. Therefore it is in ASEAN's interest to promote reforms and the liberalization of China's economic, trade, and investment sectors so as to bind China to the WTO's rules of international commerce as soon as possible.

Hence, in light of these numerous future challenges, it would behove the parties involved if they were reminded of the rocky road ahead. There are at least two areas requiring consideration: foreign investment and labour market.

Foreign Investment

One major complaint among ASEAN countries is that a growing China is hollowing out investments which should be theirs. Indeed, despite the trade surplus and political advantages ASEAN members enjoy, they have not been as successful as China in attracting foreign investment. This, therefore, has been a bone of contention with almost every ASEAN state.

It is probably more evocative to conceive the competition between China and ASEAN from the perspective of foreign investors. Although there are discrepancies in terms of decision-making between the central and the provincial governments, China is still effectively one country, and as such, the unitary sovereign state allows the foreign investors to conceive it as one totality. ASEAN's small, fragmented markets, on the other hand, are not as attractive to investors as the large Chinese market and more integrated regions elsewhere in the world.[11] Indications point to MNCs' investment strategies as being China+1 rather than ASEAN+1, thus giving priority to China rather than ASEAN. ASEAN+1, unfortunately, is a purely ASEAN conjecture and perspective. ASEAN needs to break away from its inherent belief in its self-importance and realize that the competition between the region and China is indeed intense.

So, one major issue to overcome in the China-ASEAN agreement would be the fair allocation of these investments. In order to ease ASEAN's fear in the short-term, China may need to conceptualize a formula that would allow ASEAN a fair share of FDI. However, giving/granting concessions to ASEAN is problematic because poorer ASEAN countries such as Cambodia and Laos are pressing China for greater concessions. Can China then extend such concessions to other better-off ASEAN countries as well? Would these countries demand similar concessions? Should China extend these concessions to all the ASEAN member states? Is China willing to forgo these investment inflows especially for its inland and western regions? Economic competition will no doubt feature permanently in the relations between China and ASEAN in the foreseeable future. Indeed, free trade versus fair trade is not merely an issue between industrialized countries and developing states, it is also an issue between developing economies in the Asia-Pacific region. Poorer ASEAN countries such as Vietnam, Laos and Cambodia, may not complain because they are able to lure foreign investment and take advantage of the free investment environment due to their significantly lower labour costs.

One way out of this quandary would be the Chinese Government's encouragement of its more successful businesses to go southward, just as Taiwan did in its "Southward Policy". While Chinese investors are increasingly moving offshore as China's economy strengthens, the present Chinese investment in ASEAN is still extremely modest.[12]

ASEAN's chief challenge is to regain the confidence of foreign investments that are traditionally centred in the region. Japanese investments, which have been an important partner in the region's development, should be courted. Japan's commitment to the region should not be underestimated by ASEAN. Its assistance to Thailand and Indonesia in the 1997–98 financial crisis reflects its willingness to continue to exert its presence in the region. This is especially important given China's minimal FDI in ASEAN. ASEAN's traditional partners, that is, Japan, the United States, EU, and the Asian NICs, continue to constitute a major portion of foreign investment in the region. While this may change in the near future, Chinese FDI does not look set to displace ASEAN's traditional trade partners.

Labour Market

As foreign investments are pouring into China, ASEAN workers are being displaced at an alarming rate. ASEAN and China have similar export industries, and in the past, its member states have been concentrating on labour-intensive export industries. A further reduction in export and the relocation of manufacturing and foreign direct investment would put additional pressure on these economies. In the face of competition from the Chinese market, many ASEAN countries are now facing the difficulties of structural adjustments in industries affected either directly or indirectly by China's entry into WTO. Vietnam and Indonesia's textiles and garment producers and Malaysia and Thailand's electronic equipment producers are already feeling the impact.

Many analysts have argued that the impact of such labour dislocation is short- to medium-term. Once the right structural adjustments have been made and are fully instituted, the ASEAN economies will be in a better position to compete with China. It, however, remains to be seen whether the ASEAN economies are able to adapt as quickly as the growth of the Chinese economy.

ASEAN FTA: Disputes and Common Ground

ASEAN nations are diverse and different, in terms of population size, economic development and political systems. The competing interests and individual considerations have sometimes put the ASEAN-FTA in disarray. Disagreements range from disputes over discrepancies in bilateral trade figures (for example, Singapore does not publish trade figures featuring Indonesia)[13] to the ultimate goal of AFTA. ASEAN needs to find a common ground and move away from its shaky one, in doing so, its relations with other members states in AFTA would render the region more attractive to foreign investment. While there is no lack of exchanges, policymakers have had great difficulties in coming to terms with the kind of integration that ASEAN is striving towards. It is unclear if the end product or vision is a common market of an economic union or a single market. The uncertainties engendered by these issues would continue to plague ASEAN while China's economy is taking off.

Another reason is that AFTA is deemed by many ASEAN states to be of secondary importance to their own economies. While AFTA contributes to the increasing confidence and stability of the region, studies have found that its effects on these countries' development are not as important as the dynamic interdependence between ASEAN and the other East Asian economies, such as Korea, Japan and China.[14] This would also explain why individual countries are pursing bilateral agreements with these big economic powers.

China's growing influence has placed ASEAN in the limelight by bringing the region to the attention of major powers, such as India, Japan and Russia in their competitive interest in Asia. India, with its "Look East Policy", is considering building a railway route linking existing ASEAN rail plans and connecting New Delhi to Hanoi (and not incidentally, with the pan-Asian rail system being pushed by China). It also planned to produce a framework agreement for an India-ASEAN free trade area. Russia has also signed its first agreement with ASEAN in June 2003 and is presently considering whether it should adhere to the 1976 ASEAN Treaty of Amity and Co-operation. Japan and ASEAN have also agreed to launch free trade agreement talks.

These developments suggest that there are challenges as well as opportunities for ASEAN FTA. Members of the FTA are each other's major trading partners, and the elimination of trade barriers removes discrimination between partner countries and domestic firms. While intra-ASEAN trade has expanded, ASEAN trade with non-partner countries in East Asia has expanded at a higher rate. This trend looks set to continue and integration with the China, Japan and Korea will offer additional opportunities for the region's economic development.

REGIME INTERESTS AND REGIONAL INTEGRATION

How shall both sides view regional integration from the perspective of national interests? Economic integration typically refers to the extent to which goods and services, and financial capital are free to move between countries. The ASEAN and China economic integration may well be the answer to the region's future economic growth. It is also a viable strategy of dealing with emerging regionalism around the world. The region's geographic proximity, complimentary resources and industrial structures and historic and cultural ties, all suggest that China and ASEAN can work together towards the objective of an integrated economic region. For China and ASEAN, economic regionalism begins on their own turfs; one need only look at China's many "regions" to understand how the integration of these regions is a priory for Chinese policymakers. China-ASEAN economic integration, especially for the fragmented ASEAN nations, offers hope for expanding market opportunities.

Theoretically, an integrated economic zone makes sense in the face of competition. However, in practice, it will only make good sense if ASEAN is in a healthy position to meet the challenges arising from it. At the moment, ASEAN is ill equipped to meet the challenges of embarking towards a free trade zone with China due to the many existing internal divisions within ASEAN. First of all, there are difficulties over policies of internal trade liberalization because of gaps in the economic levels of the AFTA members. In addition, these countries' dependence on foreign markets also contribute to the lack of consensus in policy actions.

Former ASEAN Secretary General, Rodolfo Severino, once complained that regional economic integration seems to have become stuck in framework agreements, work programmes and master plans. This is true given that the reluctance of some countries to make changes had stalled the integration of the entire group. Citing studies on integrating capital markets, adopting an ASEAN currency unit, liberalizing financial services and removing restrictions on capital account transactions, Severino hinted that consensus appeared out of reach. At present, this remains true and as such, there is no clear indication where plans for regional economic integration are headed.[15]

Another issue to contend with is the relevancy of AFTA *vis-à-vis* the prominence given to ASEAN FTA with China. Analysts have argued that if AFTA were to remain relevant for ASEAN in the achievement of its objective of sustained economic growth, it is important that it is strengthened rather than weakened so as to achieve a larger degree of integration.[16]

Another indication that ASEAN has no concerted strategies is the fact that many individual countries are pursuing FTA with China. This trend is likely to accelerate, especially after Singapore initiated the process. On 31 October 2003, Singapore's Trade and Industry Minister George Yeo announced that Singapore has begun negotiations with China for a FTA.

This move came after the historic FTA with the United States in 2003. The proposal included removing tariffs and the liberalization of services. Four other areas were mentioned:

- Singapore is to work with Chinese firms intending to go global;
- Boost co-operation in high-tech areas;
- Strengthen co-operation in human resource training and development; and
- Work to develop China's western regions.

Such an effort to enlarge its web of free trade agreements is not surprising given the competition within ASEAN for resources for sustained development. Undoubtedly economic gains from China will be unevenly distributed among the ASEAN nations and the countries that will benefit most are those possessing economies with a competitive edge. Bilateral negotiations clearly arose from competitive considerations between countries in the region. Singapore has denied that this would bring about negative impact on ASEAN; Yeo argued that Singapore's FTAs "are intended to bring in the rest of ASEAN eventually."[17] But whether the rest of ASEAN views the bilateral deals with similar outcome remains to be seen.

It has been observed that the proliferation of FTAs largely reflects the difficulty in satisfying all WTO member countries. If individual countries are signing such FTAs, the challenge is to ensure consistency between the various agreements. If they can build upon each other and the multilateral system then a win-win situation may emerge. Otherwise, a series of framework agreements with different terms would add more cost to business transactions. It is time perhaps to consider the plausibility of a Common Framework Agreement for every ASEAN+1 FTA.

THE EVOLUTION OF INTEGRATION

What is the form of economic integration that ASEAN and China are envisioning? At present, we are able to bear witness to the evolution of the model by looking at the integration of Hong Kong and China. Free trade relations between China and Hong Kong under what is known as the Closer Economic Partnership Agreement entail primarily the liberalization of trade in both goods and services and the simplification of investment and trade. Hong Kong, for its part, expects that CEPA will have a boosting effect on economic growth. The removal of customs tariffs and the early expansion of the service sector into China promises significant merits not only for Hong Kong but also for Hong Kong-based foreign companies.

Whatever the model, economic integration in ASEAN and China-ASEAN is unlikely to fall into one neat pattern. There are several considerations for this phenomenon.

One, differentiation of products will continue and the gaps between ASEAN-4 and ASEAN-6 would probably get bigger. Analysts have stressed that special and differential (S&D) treatment and flexibility for the ASEAN-4 (Cambodia, Laos, Myanmar, and Vietnam) will be necessary to enable a more effective participation by the newer members in the proposed ASEAN-China FTA.[18] Specialization of products and labour and the building of each country's individual niche should be anticipated. There are proposals made for enhancing domestic entrepreneurship and inter-firm networking, and for monitoring and benchmarking supply capabilities and competitiveness at the enterprise level within ASEAN and China.[19]

Secondly, if integration is progressing from bilateral to sub-regional to regional, then we are witnessing a very haphazard and chaotic process. Bilateral, regional agreements are simultaneously ongoing. ASEAN is in the midst of establishing their own free trade area, and is planning to sign a FTA pact with India, the world's second most populous nation, as well as an agreement with Japan with provisions for a FTA. While AFTA is evolving, there are a number of regional proposals with the potential of leading the region to a larger integrated arrangement. At the present moment, the process seems too chaotic and muddled for comfort.

Third, the fact that there is no consensus among ASEAN states to act in concert with the interest of the member states in mind is very distressing and worrying. "The beauty of the ASEAN process is that there is a structure allowing for differences while we move forward", as Philippines' Trade and Industry secretary, Manuel Roxas most optimistically explains.[20] But the fact remains, that without a common strategy, ASEAN is unlikely to get the most out of their interests in the negotiation process.

CONCLUSION

In an increasingly inter-connected economic system, regions have few choices but to be regionally and ultimately internationally integrated. As an economic region, the Southeast Asian countries interact with the rest of the world at three levels: the global level, the regional level (Asia-Pacific) and the sub-regional level (ASEAN). For ASEAN, the global trade negotiations in WTO will doubtlessly be supplemented by regional and sub-regional negotiations. If ASEAN were to concentrate on trade, investment and finance, it would be rendered more competitive and would thus be on the path to achieving regional and sub-regional integration. The most important thing for ASEAN now, is to consolidate AFTA before moving on to the proposal of the Asian economic community. But because AFTA is too shallow, it is unable to sustain long-term economic growth of ASEAN. Since the Asian financial crisis, the ASEAN nations' recoveries have been barely perceptible. Their economic foundations are still weak and major problems such as bureaucratic corruption and improving corporate governance have not been fully addressed. Ironically, ASEAN's desire towards economic co-operation and integration has intensified in the face of its member countries' slow growth and abounding political and economic problems.

In this equation of regional integration, China is still an enigma. Its emergence as an economic powerhouse and its accession into the WTO is closely watched. China's entry into WTO has already yielded two important impacts: one, the acceleration of the process of trade liberalization, and two, it has enabled the Chinese economy to maintain a relatively high growth rate. ASEAN will continue to tap into this huge potential market in China, as the latter creates business opportunities for ASEAN enterprises. Much of this, however, will depend on the methods China uses to deal with its own economic, social and political problems. Furthermore, political, social and economic risks from China must be factored into the equation. Economic integration would mean that ASEAN would not be able to insulate itself from the socio-political and economic fallout from China, if it occurs. Given the non-interference policy and the relative weak bargaining power, ASEAN is unlikely to have any leverage or influence on China's reforms. This has made economic integration with China even more risky.

Hence it is useful to remind ASEAN that regional integration is but a means to an end of sustained economic growth. It should not be pursed at all costs. Economic integration is but part of the puzzle of development. Political capacity and security issues are also at the heart of the political process. The ASEAN states will have to find their own niche based on their natural comparative advantages as well as taking care of their political and security interests. Finding an equilibrium between national interests and regional integration and security would be the ultimate challenge for the political leaders in the individual ASEAN states. Then and only then, can they come together for the purpose of equitable free trade.

Acknowledgement

The author would like to acknowledge support from the Institute of Southeast Asian Studies, Konrad-Adenauer-Stiftung and National Sun Yat-sen University. Thanks go to K. Kesavapany, Stefan Friedrich, Sharon Loo and Samuel Ku for their comments. An earlier version of this chapter has been presented as a paper at the International WTO-conference "China and her Trading Partners within WTO — New Issues, New Developments," jointly organized by the Konrad-Adenauer-Stiftung and the Shanghai Institute of Foreign Trade (SIFT), Shanghai, China, 9 December 2003.

Notes

1. ASEAN countries have traditionally served as low-tech manufacturing units for Japan. Importing Japanese capital and intermediate goods and exporting final goods primarily to the United States and Europe have resulted routinely in trade deficits with Japan. Recently this imbalance has eased because Japan's domestic financial difficulties have caused it to invest less in the region and also the devaluation of the ASEAN currencies have discouraged imports while encouraging exports.

2. The ASEAN Economic Community (AEC), first proposed by Singapore's Prime Minister Goh Chok Tong in 2002, was agreed upon the SEAN leaders in Ninth ASEAN Summit Meeting in Bali, 2003. The AEC is to be realized by 2020. It is envisaged that the AEC will have a single market and production base with free flow of goods, services, investment, capital and skilled labour.

3. Among the many commentators who share this view is Senior Minister of Singapore, Lee Kuan Yew. He argued that China's entry into the WTO will initially make it more of a competitor to ASEAN, but as the country advances into high-tech industries, FDI will pour into the region and China will become a good business partner. Interestingly, he did not give a timeframe for his prediction. See "China will be competitor and partner for ASEAN", 1 August 2002, <www.sedb.com/edbcorp>.

4. Singapore, for example, is restructuring its economy at a very fast pace. Now the city-state is concentrating on biochemical products and away from electronics, the lifeblood of the economy, which now make up about 30 per cent of total manufacturing, down from 50 per cent five years ago, as cheaper Chinese exports take market share. Singapore aims to double its biomedical output to S$20 billion by 2010, or about 12 per cent of the island's economy, and raise its share of manufacturing to 15 to 20 per cent by 2005 from 7 per cent in 2003.

5. TAC is a general framework that commits the parties to respect the independence, sovereignty, and territorial integrity of the parties, not to interfere in their affairs, to settle dispute peacefully, and to renounce the threat or use of force. ASEAN

opened the treaty to outside accession in 1998. The other country that has joined is Papua New Guinea.

6. Lyall Breckon, "On the Inside Track", *Comparative Connections* (Third Quarter 2003). <http://www.csis.org/pacfor/cc/0303Qchina_asean.html>.

7. Thitapha Wattanapruttipaisan, "ASEAN-China Free Trade Area: Advantages, Challenges, and Implications for Newer ASEAN Member Countries", *ASEAN Economic Bulletin* 20, no. 1 (2003).

8. "Philippines: Study China Entry into AFTA", *Inquirer News Service*, 3 February 2002. <http://www.inq7.net/bus/2002/feb/04/bus_2-1.htm>.

9. Lyall Breckon, "On the Inside Track", *Comparative Connections* (Third Quarter 2003). <http://www.csis.org/pacfor/cc/0303Qchina_asean.html>.

10. "The Case For China's WTO Accession", revised text of delivered remarks by Gene B. Sperling, Director, National Economic Council at the White House and Assistant to the President for Economic Policy, delivered at the Economic Strategy Institute, Washington, D.C., 23 February 2000. See also, Stuart Harris, *The WTO and APEC: What Role for China?* (Canberra: Australia-Japan Research Centre, Research School of Pacific and Asian Studies, The Australian National University, 1997).

11. "China and ASEAN to Sign Trade Pact as AFTA Falters", *Reuters*, 4 November 2002.

12. Chinese investment is growing at a rapid pace. In 2000, the Chinese Government approved US$108 million in new investments to be channelled to the ASEAN region, a 50 per cent jump from 1999, and actual Chinese investment totals are certainly higher as many Chinese companies try to circumvent official foreign currency controls by investing through offshore entities.

13. Singapore does not publish trade data on Indonesia due to a mutual agreement of the two countries' leaders in 1974. But, in spite of this agreement, the city-state has handed its annual data to Jakarta over the past twenty-nine years.

14. Tran Van Tho, "AFTA in the Dynamic Perspective of Asian Trade: Towards a Closer Co-operation Between ASEAN and Korea, Japan and China", *The Journal of the Korean Economy* 3, no. 1 (Spring 2002).

15. "China and ASEAN to Sign Trade Pact as AFTA Falters", *Reuters*, 4 November 2002.

16. Helen Nesadurai, "Is AFTA Still Relevant?" <http://www.ntu.edu.sg/idss/Perspective/research_050304.htm>.

17. "Singapore Pursuing Trade Pact with China", *The Straits Times*, 31 October 2003.

18. Thitapha Wattanapruttipaisan, "ASEAN-China Free Trade Area: Advantages, Challenges, and Implications for Newer ASEAN Member Countries", *ASEAN Economic Bulletin*, 20, no. 1 (2003).

19. Ibid.

20. "ASEAN and China Launch First Stage of Free Trade Plan", *Agence France-Presses*, 6 October 2002.

References

Ba, Alice D. "China and ASEAN: Renavigating Relations for a 21ˢᵗ Century Asia". *Asian Survey* 43, no. 4 (2003): 622–64.

Cai, Kevin G. "The ASEAN-China Free Trade Agreement and East Asian Regional Grouping". *Contemporary Southeast Asia* 25, no. 3 (2003): 387–402.

Haacke, Jurgen. "Seeking Influence: China's Diplomacy Toward ASEAN after the Asian Crisis". *Asian Perspective* 26, no. 4 (2002): 13–52.

Ho, Khai Leong. "The Changing Political Economy of Taiwan-Southeast Asia Relations". *The Pacific Review* 6, no. 1 (1993): 31–40.

———. "New Directions in Taiwan-Southeast Asia Relations: Economics, Politics, and Security". *Pacific Focus* 10, no. 1 (1995): 81–100.

———. "Threat, Trade and Tribe: PRC's Challenges in Southeast Asia". In *China and the Asia-Pacific Region: Evolving Interactions and Emerging Trends*, edited by Chen Wen-Chun. Taiwan: National Sun Yat-Sen University, 2001, pp. 301–19.

———. "Rituals, Risks and Rivalries: China and ASEAN in the Coming Decades". *Journal of Contemporary China* 10, no. 29 (2001): 683–94.

Suryadinata, Leo. *China and the ASEAN States: The Ethnic Chinese Dimension*. Singapore: Singapore University Press, 1985.

Thitapha Wattanapruttipaisan. "ASEAN-China Free Trade Area: Advantages, Challenges, and Implications for Newer ASEAN Member Countries". *ASEAN Economic Bulletin* 20, no. 1 (2003).

Wang, Gungwu. *China and Southeast Asia: Myths, Threats, and Culture*. Singapore: Singapore University Press, 1999.

Wong, John and Sarah Chan. "China-ASEAN Free Trade Agreement: Shaping Future Economic Relations". *Asian Survey* 43, no. 3 (2003): 507–26.

Zha, Daojiong. "The Politics of China-ASEAN Economic Relations: Assessing the Move Toward a Free Trade Area". *Asian Perspective* 26, no. 4 (2002): 53–82.

9

ASEAN-CHINA RELATIONS
Legacies and Future Directions

Reuben Mondejar and Wai Lung Chu

GENERAL CONSIDERATIONS

There is no doubt in anyone's mind that China's attempts to become globally competitive continues to gather momentum at breakneck speed. This chapter posits the view that in this globalization process, the relationship between China and ASEAN constitutes an important element, ASEAN being right in the heart of China's own backyard. That being the case however, much still has to be done. There is a lingering impression, gaining its own momentum, that the rise of China means that it has taken over the former role of Japan, as the region's prime growth engine. It is in this light that ASEAN and China have to get their relations right in order for both entities to derive profit from this shifting axis in the region.

ASEAN for its part has much home work to do if it is to enter profitably into a positive relationship with China. For one, it needs to demonstrate that it is advancing in its cohesiveness, that all the ten member countries are at the same level of organizational confidence. In the least, such unity will be a boost to ASEAN's bargaining power in its dealings with China.

There are several considerations which serve as background for China-ASEAN integration. First, there is the significance of a combined 1.8 billion market, large enough by any standard, with all the economic implications that such size commands. Indeed, there is the accepted notion that China has now become the biggest factory in the world, a kind of a seedbed of another Industrial Revolution of sorts. It is a huge factory for the production of other people's goods and a global provider of numerous commodities. ASEAN on the other hand can claim to a market of about 560 million people with a US$330 billion consumer market, equal to China's coastal region. For ASEAN and China, this means first and foremost that their competing exports don't lead to mutual disaster and disadvantage, rather, that they become more complementary, or put more simply, whatever competition they have should end up enriching both entities. Complementation will mean that both ASEAN and China can ride on each other as both entities endeavour towards economic progress. It has to be noted that between the two entities, there has been a remarkable surge in intra-trade. China's trade with ASEAN countries have already hovered around US$100 billion in 2004, surging by over 35 per cent from the year before. Imports jumped 51.7 per cent to $47.33 billion, while exports correspondingly leapt 31.1 per cent, logging US$30.93 billion. China is definitely on course to comfortably surpass the target set by Premier Wen Jiabao of US$100 billion in annual trade with the 10 members of the ASEAN by 2005. Current combined gross domestic product of China and the ASEAN countries is estimated at about US$2 trillion.

Second, there is the perceptible changing Asian model of political governance, whereby authoritarianism is regarded as outmoded and the acceptance of the notion that economic growth and political legitimacy go together, even inseparable as lips to teeth.

Third, not only is China being swept by the winds of globalization, but the ASEAN member nations themselves are also grappling with the same forces. One consequence of these forces is the shift in FDI interests in the region. A McKinsey report in March 2004 found that investment in Southeast Asia shrunk 66 per cent since the 1997 Asian economic and financial crises, and its collective economic growth has dropped 50 per cent, underscoring the need for even further regional economic integration.

EARLY ASEAN-CHINA RELATIONSHIP

China's relationship with Southeast Asia, and in particular with present-day ASEAN states dates back several centuries. It is well known that the Chinese have historically thought of themselves as the centre of world order, in other words, that the world was Sino-centric. China was at the centre of civilization and everybody else outside its concentric hierarchy was seen as contending for the blessing of a suzerain relationship with the Celestial Empire. The scholar John Fairbank points out in fact, China's relations with other peoples and countries can be grouped into three main zones.

First, there is the so-called "Sinic Zone", consisting of the most nearby and culturally similar tributaries such as Korea and Vietnam, parts of which had anciently been ruled within the Chinese empire. Included in this category are the Ryukyu Islands (now part of Japan), and even Japan itself. Second, there is the "Inner Asian Zone", consisting of tributary tribes and states of the nomadic or semi-nomadic peoples of Inner Asia, who were not only ethnically and culturally non-Chinese but were also outside or on the fringe of the Chinese culture area, even though sometimes pressing upon the Great Wall frontier. Third, there is the "Outer Zone", at a further distance over land or sea. Here is included Southeast Asia . Also included are the countries of South Asia and even beyond such as the Middle East and Europe, that were supposed to send tribute when trading.

In theory, all the non-Chinese states and peoples were expected to be properly tributary to the Son of Heaven (the Chinese emperor), in the Central Country (that is, China). It was through this ancient tribute system that the Celestial Empire once sought to dominate Asia. As could be expected, that view would not always find coincidence in the minds of the non-Chinese world. The worldview that there is only one world (unipolar in today's jargon) and that China had the exclusive mandate of its governance did not square with how the others saw it. In the case of Southeast Asians, with the exception of the Vietnamese, who were in the first Sinic Zone, they did not on the whole consider themselves part of the Chinese world system as the Chinese believed them to be. Another scholar, Lucian Pye contends that "from the earliest times the Southeast Asians, living on natural maritime crossroads, conceived of the world as multipolar. Indeed, they were far more sensitive to other civilizations than the Sinic: politically they modelled their governments after the Hindu concept of the state; in religion they embraced Buddhism, Islam, and Christianity; and culturally they borrowed very little from the Chinese, a fact which has punctured Chinese pretensions of superiority towards Southeast Asians" (Pye 1981, p. 218).

That, however, did not mean that China had no influence. In fact, several of the principal kingdoms of Southeast Asia at one time or another periodically sent tribute missions to the Han court. Jumping back and forth in a scale, as it were, China had varying degrees of influence over the Southeast Asian kingdoms at different historical epochs.

On the whole, China, with its imperial history and a civilization that dates back earlier than 4,000 BC, and thus ranks among the world's oldest, was likely to have a presence of some sort in the surrounding territories of Asia, including Southeast Asia. Archaeological findings of Chinese artifacts in Malaysia, Singapore, Java, Sumatra, and Borneo are proof or a Chinese presence in present-day ASEAN states. Anthropologists have also established the imprints of Chinese influence in terms of technology (for example, the potter's wheel, use of paper money, gunpowder) and absorption of Chinese words into the languages of the now ASEAN states. Chinese historical sources reveal that diplomatic missions and trading expeditions were much in evidence, for example, the establishment of commercial relations between the Chinese emperor Sui Yang-ti (AD 607) and the kingdom of Siam, present-day Thailand (Purcell 1965, p. 11). Between AD 756 and 779, three envoys from Java (now Indonesia) arrived at the court of the Emperor of China as one more mark of the then prevailing trade relations between them. The king of Brunei is recorded to have sent envoys to the Chinese court in the year 977.

During the Ming dynasty (1368–1644), historians have noted a kind of acknowledgement by some of the Southeast Asian kingdoms of China's role as peacekeeper and protector. For example, Emperor Hung-Wu (1368–98) demanded that the king of Brunei would have to send tribute to China rather than to Java which had saved Brunei earlier from an invasion attempt by the neighbouring Sulu kingdom (now spread across Malaysia and the Philippines). Brunei acceded despite Java's protests and in 1408, Brunei asked for fullest protection from China and agreed to a form of provincial status. Brunei also asked that Emperor Yung-lo mediate so that Java be prevented from obliging Brunei to pay tribute, to which Yung-lo (1402–24) declared that Java should exempt Brunei from tribute (Wang 1968). Another kingdom, the Srivijaya (in present-day Indonesia) also sent regular missions to the Chinese court and sought Chinese recognition to protect it from Java's threats.

The fourteenth and early fifteenth centuries show a significant China-ASEAN interaction with China wielding some kind of recognized superpower status, applying today's terminology retroactively. Witness for example the period from 1402 to 1424 when Emperor Yung-lo sent his bureaucrats to the various kingdoms of Southeast Asia. This period was known as the "Eunuch Diplomacy;" the emperor's trusted bureaucrats who acted as his envoys were eunuchs. Yung-lo's objective was to streamline his administrative reach in these Southeast Asian kingdoms. The policy was to "cut down rigid formalities, administrative restrictions, and Confucian scruples and to simplify the tributary relationship by making it between one ruler and another, not involving the submission of one government to another" (Wang 1968, p. 55). Yung-lo sent a recorded forty-eight missions in twenty-two years. Another keen China-

ASEAN observer has noted, "It was in July 1405, almost a century before Columbus, that the biggest fleet the world had ever seen set sail from China; 62 large ships and 255 smaller vessels, carrying nearly 28,000 men, making their way out of the Yangtze. Some of the large ships were 122 metres long. They reached Java, Sumatra and Vietnam. Subsequent voyages reached Aden on the Red Sea and Mogadishu in Africa. The purpose was trade, either willingly or with a certain degree of persuasion. On board the ships were the world's original "marines" — 10,000 of them — ready to encourage access to domestic markets. One could argue that the "marketing director" of China, the three-jewel eunuch Admiral Cheng Ho, had is eye on Chinese dominance of the international market. Cheng Ho, a Muslim from Yunan province and a eunuch since age 13, stood 2.3 metres (seven feet) tall, with a 1.6-metre (five-foot) waistline. He had glaring eyes, high cheeks and a high forehead, a small nose, and a voice like a huge bell..." (Batey 2002, p. 51).

The missions included such ASEAN countries as the Philippines, Brunei, Thailand, Indonesia, Vietnam, and others stretching to the Indian Ocean. The missions typically conveyed Yung-lo's wishes and greetings and articulating Ming China's superior place in the world. As already noted, these missions were supported by significant naval forces. As a result of these missions, China-Malacca relations grew; the Malacca kingdom being newly established at that time. China was quick to see Malacca's importance for any attempt to keep the sea lanes under control and offered Malacca protection against any threat from nearly kingdoms of Java and Siam, an offer which Malacca readily accepted. Brunei's king also made a personal appearance at Yung-lo's court in what we may call today a state visit. Other state visitors were the king of Malacca in 1411 and Paduka Pahala, king of Sulu (in present-day Philippines) in 1417. The Filipino monarch journeyed to China to establish a sort of diplomatic relations with Ming Emperor Zhu. Earlier, the king of Pahang (now part of Malaysia) sent envoys in accordance with the tributary relationship it had with China. Yung-lo is also recorded as having sent delegates to Luzon (northern Philippines) to discuss problems concerning sovereignty.

The Yung-lo missions extended the tributary system to thirty new countries by their definition of what a country is at that time. It should be noted however, that within twenty-five years from the time Admiral Cheng Ho began his naval adventures, China would put a stop to the voyages. An inward-looking succeeding emperor put an end to what could have been China's mightiest foray into regional hegemony.

Scholars of ASEAN-China history usually point out that the tributary relationship did not necessarily mean subordination by China of the Southeast

Asian kingdoms. In fact, many of these kingdoms also harboured self-centred worldviews but did not push them too far as to conflict head-on with China. As such, different self-centred views of superiority existed side by side. They derived from a variety of different sources, from Hinduism and Buddhism in Java and Cambodia, from Hinayana Buddhism in Thailand, from Islam in Sumatra and Malacca (Wang 1968, p. 56).

Indeed, China was only one of several entities with which the Southeast Asian kingdoms had foreign relations. The Arabs, Persians, and Indians were even more aggressive than the Chinese. But the Chinese were contented that their superiority was being acknowledged, even if only nominally, and thus did not find any added benefit in annexing the kingdoms of the Southern Seas (as Southeast Asia was then called) to the Chinese empire. Again, it seemed that the order of the day was that superiority did not mean domination but merely the acknowledgement of Chinese superiority as the holder of the mandate from Celestial Heaven.

At the beginning of the sixteenth century, the Southeast Asian arena saw the arrival of the Europeans. The first two centuries of European colonialism, however, did not bring about, on the whole, drastic changes in the prevailing China-ASEAN regional set-up. In the next two centuries, the eighteenth and the nineteenth, the Europeans would gradually provide the Western cosmopolitan aspect to what was already an operational regional foreign relations network. As the positions of world supremacy changed from one European power to another from the sixteenth to the nineteenth centuries (at various epochs alternated by the Spaniards, Portuguese, British, French, Dutch), the Southeast Asians interpreted such shifts in power as one more confirmation that the world was indeed not unipolar as the Chinese would have them believe it to be, but multipolar.

ASEAN FEAR OF CHINA AS SCHEMING DRAGON

Meanwhile in the Western hemisphere, the disruptions caused by the First World War was only a prelude to the new set-up that would result from the Second World War. Just as the former colonial countries of Southeast Asia gained independence and started their trek towards nationhood, the long protracted internal competition between feuding interests in China led to the establishment of the People's Republic of China. The victory of the communists in China inspired fear among the Southeast Asians who, perhaps because of religion and centuries of association with the capitalist West, did not find communist ideology attractive. However, the resurgence of nationalism, which was an offshoot of the decolonization process, provided China an opportunity to export the so-called wars of liberation. The ASEAN countries found themselves confronted with some pockets of communist-inspired insurgency movements just when their newly-born nations were struggling for survival. China was seen as a dragon scheming to devour the non-communist Asian countries. China on the other hand, supported and encouraged at various times and degrees, local communist movement in the ASEAN states. It is because of this that there existed a certain mistrust of China which maintained that "support and encouragement" to those local movements need not be a function attributed to the Chinese Government as such, but of party-to-party relations.

When ASEAN was formed in 1967 China interpreted the forging of the association as an immediate threat to its position. ASEAN was in fact accused of being an instrument of U.S. imperialism. Only two years earlier, China was announcing its desire to control Southeast Asia and ASEAN's birth was seen as an obstacle to that scheme. In August 1965, Chairman Mao addressed the Communist Party politburo in Beijing saying: "We must without fail get hold of Southeast Asia, including South Vietnam, Thailand, Burma, Malaysia, Singapore. Southeast Asia is a very rich region, it abounds in minerals. In the future it will be very useful for the development of Chinese industry. After we get hold of Southeast Asia, the wind from the East will prevail over the wind from the West." (Gahrana 1984, p. 7)

The historical restlessness of the ASEAN states over getting too close to China can be viewed from different angles. First, these new nations were zealous to protect their hard-earned independence. They were wary of big-power interference with their sovereignty, either in domestic affairs (including communist insurgency movements within their country), or foreign policy decisions. Second, it was a fact that most of ASEAN's populations are believers in God, with the majority professing the Islam or Christian faiths. Thus communism as an atheistic ideology had little appeal. ASEAN members would not be willing to exchange for friendship a threat to the glue that holds their populations together. From the economic standpoint, ASEAN states felt confident about their track record of economic development especially beginning the late fifties and the early sixties, believing that China at that time was not seen as a suitable model. China then had many products common to ASEAN countries and it was viewed as a potential competitor for future markets.

Finally, there was also the fear that the overseas ethnic Chinese populations in each of the ASEAN states were potential fiefdoms that China was manipulating to its advantage. The advent of the Cultural Revolution in China, and the Vietnam War would add another dimension to ASEAN's historical anxiety in its relations with China.

CHANGES IN RECENT DECADES

The aftermath of the Cultural Revolution which impaired China's image in the ASEAN states, the Vietnam War and China's involvement in helping Vietnam only to part ways with Vietnam later on, the meteoric economic growth in the ASEAN countries as a whole — all of these, inaugurated a new attitude among the ASEAN governments with regard to their relations with China. This attitude, turning positive on the whole, was bolstered by Deng's reforms and the opening up of China to the world in the late seventies. The decade of the eighties was a time for ASEAN's re-acquaintance with China.

A new era in China-ASEAN relations was already in practice at the start of the nineties. In July 1991 China began to attend the ASEAN Post-Ministerial Conference as a consultative partner. Up to 1990, some ASEAN members did not even have formal diplomatic ties with China. At the Twenty-fourth ASEAN Ministerial Meeting in Kuala Lumpur, former Chinese Foreign Minister Qian Qichen expressed China's interest in strengthening co-operation with ASEAN. This was received warmly by ASEAN. Since then, some milestones in China-ASEAN relationship followed. First, was the establishment of the ASEAN-China Joint Committee on Economic and Trade Co-operation, and the ASEAN-China Joint Committee on Science and Technology in July 1994. That same year, China became a member of the ASEAN Regional Forum with all parties agreeing to have consultations on political and security issues of common concern. Two years later, in July 1996, China became a full dialogue partner of ASEAN. Since 1997, China has been participating in the ASEAN+3 Summit (the three refers to South Korea, Japan, and China) paving the way for the holding of the annual ASEAN-China Summits. It is this summit which provided the framework for the two entities to discuss economic as well as political and security issues of common concern. The 2003 ASEAN-China Summit taking place on the heels of the Eighth ASEAN Summit in Phnom Penh was particularly productive. The summit saw the signing of the Framework Agreement on ASEAN-China Economic Co-operation which aims at the creation of an ASEAN-China Free Trade Area within ten years. China is the first ASEAN dialogue partner to sign such a pact with ASEAN.

China was also regarded as a favourable factor for ASEAN during the 1997–98 financial and economic crises. There was a regional sentiment that

China by refusing to devalue its currency has provided an oasis of stability in what was then a sea of financial, economic, and political turbulence. For ASEAN's part, various member states have reciprocated, for example, by providing diplomatic help to China in the resolution of the Korean refugee crisis by offering as the country transit points before the refugees were taken by South Korea.

In sum, China-ASEAN relations have gone a long way, formalized or not, officially acknowledged or not, since their several centuries of pre-history. The ASEAN states are in the "Sinic Zone" according to China's historical view, irrespective of whether ASEAN agrees or not. Also, the presence of overseas ethnic Chinese in the ASEAN states is a constant reminder of the historical links between them. It is worth noting that these ethnic Chinese populations have over time already integrated in their new homelands. These factors, among others, serve as a positive foundation for the future of China-ASEAN relationship without denying that there could be potential flashpoints and irritants such as the Spratlys and the Paracels territorial disputes.

CHINA HAS MUCH WORK TO DO

In dealing with China, ASEAN should take note that China has some internal homework to do, and thus calibrate its bargaining with China, knowing that some domestic chores are still being addressed. For one, it is no secret that China, for its part, has to grapple with the pangs of post-WTO entry. China continues to face such challenges such as the lack of immediate trade servicing software, people-skills, and other similar deficiencies which are needed in order to deal with the post-WTO era. It could be a case of too much opening up to the world, too soon. China's internal weaknesses could be exposed for all the world to see. China will need to continue to be willing to learn and adapt, including learning from mistakes.

The fast changing regional geopolitical conditions in Asia is also a source of challenge for China. In particular, the supposed previous "Asian Model" of state governance whereby benevolent authoritarianism was acceptable, is being severely challenged. Authoritarianism, benevolent or otherwise, is becoming outmoded. In many countries of Asia, people are demanding, whether openly or surreptitiously, that economic growth and political legitimacy go hand-in-hand. The conditions provided by globalization and its consequences on the flow of what is happening outside China only exacerbates this itch. The more China takes its share in the world spotlight such as holding of grand international conferences, hosting the 2008 Olympics, and similar world class events, the more will China feel the pressure to respond to the twinning of economic growth with political legitimacy. This will gather momentum as China goes global. We only have to remind ourselves that China continues to undergo transition politically, economically, socially, demographically, technologically, etc. It could be a case of having too much to handle. After all, China has to also consider that it has some baggage of more than fifty years, consisting among others, of the Great Leap Forward, the Let the Hundred Flowers Bloom, the Cultural Revolution, the Tiananmen Event — all of which have to simmer down.

There is no denying that China's leaders, both the recent past and current ones, are intent and determined to sustain the reforms and opening up process initiated by Deng Xiaoping in 1978. As in any reform process, both pluses and minuses get exposed collaterally. Thus, advantages and problems emerge for all (insiders as well as outsiders) to see. For example, the WTO mandate of removal of artificial barriers, for example, exchange controls — shall reveal both hidden strengths and hidden weaknesses.

SOME POTENTIAL CHINA PROBLEMS

Considering where China has come from since 1949, and more recently, since 1978, one can only admire China's current reputation for reform and progress. Yet, one cannot also shy away from some potential difficulties that China's transformation has bred. It might be worth considering some of these.

One is the perceptible increasing disparity among regional economies. There are occasional reports of frustration from less economically endowed provinces when they compare their plight with the blue-chip provinces. This could result in some social disorder.

Second is the issue of the debt-ridden financial sector coupled with uneven or even poor regulatory provisions, notwithstanding the fact that there are visible and credible banking reforms that are proceeding all over China.

Third is the perception reported in various media sources, in print or electronically, of selective or uneven application of the rule of law and legal regulations. China has to constantly demonstrate that there is a secure protection under the law for those who honestly engage themselves in lawful ventures.

Fourth, there is the potential fallout from industrial over-capacity coupled with the consequences of the closure of a substantial number of state-owned firms. This could result in some economic and social turbulence. The overcapacity also is felt in real estate resulting in a potential bubble burst with a disastrous aftermath.

Fifth, the One-Child policy began in 1978 has bred a curious situation whereby a larger portion of the population is depending on the productivity of a smaller portion of the demographic pie. This situation is bound to accelerate, not decelerate, unless some young people are injected into the population. One effect is the downsizing or even closure of industries that cater to the young with its social and economic consequences. It is a fact that primary schools are disappearing as there are fewer and fewer children to go to school. In a few more years, it will be the turn of high schools, middle schools, and secondary schools in general to suffer from the same phenomenon.

Sixth, some social and economic safety net is needed for the estimated up to 300 million migrant population. They can be a potential trouble source even if they also serve as a buffer to the uneven economic differences between the various provinces/counties.

Seventh, there exists several sub/mini-cultures within China with its fifty-six ethnic nationalities across the land. These mini-cultures have their own demands and peculiarities that have to be responded to in the implementation of government policies, economically, politically, and socially. If not handled carefully, there could be unwarranted trouble of sorts.

Eighth, reading China official statistics and economic figures is at times a source of difficulty for those trying to get an accurate picture of the economy. There are expressed sentiments that getting accurate statistics and economic data is a challenge because of restrained information flows, for example, state monopoly on financial/economic reporting. Paranoia and obsession with reporting only what is regarded as "helpful", "correct", or "politically comfortable" numbers and figures could lead bureaucrats to resort to overly creative accounting leading to inaccurate or even misleading pictures. This situation could also apply to other areas: witness for example the experience of how information flows transpired during the SARS crisis of 2003, and the bird flu of 2004.

While these potential problems could affect ASEAN only indirectly, a keen consideration of these could guide ASEAN on when and how much to push its relations with China.

CHINA SEEN THROUGH A LOOKING GLASS

As if the palpable problems are not enough, ASEAN would be well advised to be aware of seeming tensions that confront China, that is, (1) tensions between the central and provincial governments in terms of tug-of-war over power, jurisdiction, and resources, (2) tensions between state and private enterprises especially since the former are being downsized, (3) tensions between generational leaders, and (4) tensions between current elites and the aspiring ones. ASEAN would benefit by anticipating how China behaves when its unwritten priorities are at stake. Over the past three or four decades, there have been a few sensitive nerves that basically give a hint of China's behaviour. These are known as the "Five Ts and One R". In all of these issues, China has displayed a characteristic attitude which would be good to keep in mind. The five Ts are Taiwan, Tibet, Tiananmen, Trade, and Telecommunications. The one "R" is Religion. The first three Ts concern "face" and jurisdiction issues. Trade is still a touch-and-go despite the entry of China into the WTO. Remember that with the vast expanse of China and the multifarious trade levels that such an economy command, what is agreed to at the highest levels of officialdom may not necessarily be adhered to so faithfully at the lower rungs. How to police overall conformity is not an easy task for the size of China's economy.

Telecommunications is another nemesis of China's embrace of globalization since by definition, globalization means a two-way street. The desire for control on what the state allows its people to receive, hear, and see is negated by the desire to welcome the outside world to one's doors. With the current state of telecommunications, state censorship of sensitive areas becomes a much more expensive and difficult exercise to implement.

The same can be said of religion which is practically a sphere of the individual's spiritual aspect. To police one's beliefs, spiritual adherence, non-material longings will be impossible. The state may put barriers but they are only artificial and short-lived, as those who seek these will always find ways to hear about what they are seeking: indeed, if there is a will, there is a way. In today's conditions, state control of the mind, and much less, state control of one's spiritual beliefs will be impossible to sustain over the long run. China's bouts with Falungong, and the underground Christian churches are just two examples of China's challenges in this regard.

Again, ASEAN is only partly affected by these tensions, but if ASEAN ignores consideration of these issues, it will be at the peril of the solidity and future of China-ASEAN relations.

ASEAN HAS CHANGES TO MAKE

ASEAN has its own woes to deal with. The member states have such a wide disparity economically, territorially, political structure, population size, cultural background, and so on, that the fact they belong to one organization is almost a miracle. Of course, the only easily accepted common denominator is that all happen to be located in the same part of the globe; it is the waters around them that actually unite them.

Co-ordination among the members remains much to be desired. Strategic alliances among the members in significant industries and sectors are few and far between. For instance, since ASEAN's birth in 1967, it was only in January 2004 that the organization could agree to work to integrate eleven industry sectors as part of efforts to create a European-style single market by the year 2020 for ASEAN's 530 million people. It took ASEAN thirty-seven years to be able "agree to work to integrate"! And we have yet even to see the fruition of this intention. The association wants to achieve initial integration before 2010, if possible, in the sectors of wood, rubber, vehicles, textiles, electronics, agriculture, information technology, fisheries, health care, air travel and tourism. Indeed, unless ASEAN is literally able to get its act together, it will be left behind compared to other regional blocs.

The politically correct attitude of non-interference in a member state's internal affairs has also proven to be a bane for ASEAN's cohesion. Yet, there is no sign that this is going to disappear soon. It is clear that the member states are very reluctant to surrender any bit of its sovereignty to the hands of the organization. Every now and then, the member states' political leaders become too touchy and sensitive even to suggestions and comments on anything that pertains to a member state's domestic behaviour. The members claim this is the "ASEAN way" of doing things. This in fact could be an "ostrich's way" of facing challenges whereby the repercussions of one member's domestic troubles overflowing outside its borders harming eventually the entire organization, is left to the winds. A case in point is Myanmar's internal political troubles which has complicated the organization's dealings with the West, in particular the United States and the European Union. ASEAN members do not seem to accept that, like the European Union's experience, there is a give-and-take in being part of a regional organization; and its strength, life, and future depends to a great extent on this see-saw between how much balance can be had among the individual members *vis-à-vis* the organization as such, sovereignty-wise and otherwise. The arrival of modern-day terrorism which knows no geographical borders has awakened ASEAN, but just a bit. Hopefully, this awakening will snowball into more integration, rather than less. There are a lot of areas which can provide a platform for more co-ordination and integration: forest fires, migrant labour, piracy in the sea lanes, weather forecasting, crime and smuggling control, marine research, and so on.

In the history of ASEAN, there were times of determined leadership, especially during those years when the Domino Theory as regards communism was hovering in the air. But the decade of the nineties demonstrated very weak or even absent regional leadership, what with several member states experiencing political haemorrhage domestically. In ASEAN's heyday in the eighties, with some friendly foreign help and prodding, the organization practically forced Vietnam to get out of Cambodia, even if Vietnam had, then, the explicit support of the Soviets. Its reputation was on the upswing that it even began to engage the big powers including the United States, Japan, China, Russia, and the European Union in what would eventually be known as the ASEAN Regional Forum (ARF) and the Asia-Europe Meeting, respectively. But it did not take long before ASEAN's impotence was displayed, to the dismay of everyone. We only have to recall the on-and-off-again forest fires in Indonesia which blanketed a good part of ASEAN territory. There was nothing the organization could do to stop the almost annual calamity. The East Timor crisis was another example of ASEAN organizational powerlessness. More recently, we have seen how the organization sat passively as one member state after another roiled into the cauldron of economic paralysis caused by the regional economic crisis that struck Thailand first in 1997. What began as a financial crisis soon became a comprehensive economic crisis, turning further into a political crisis of government. After a spurt of daring by rapidly expanding the membership to accommodate countries of varying political systems and wide disparities in stages of economic development, ASEAN did not seem able to handle the resulting difficulties. The saddest part is perhaps the impression given by ASEAN that its members could not even agree on what the problems really were, their magnitude, and much less how to overcome them.

FURTHER TASKS FOR ASEAN

For the organization to upgrade its relations with China, it needs to show that it is more tightly-knit, speaking with one voice, and each member state's general approach to China should be co-ordinated with the others. The recent trend to establish bilateral economic treaties between China and some ASEAN member states is something that has to be done without detriment to an overall ASEAN-China integration, in whatever form and degree. The temptation to do what could be considered practical and best for each individual country rather than as a group is quite strong. Indonesia for example could claim every reason why it needs to develop its abundant natural resources and undercut the other ASEAN countries by capitalizing on its still cheap manufacturing labour force and deal with China directly. Singapore could also claim that its edge in biotechnology could be sufficient reason to strike deals with China directly.

The need to have a unified co-ordinated approach also applies to the various chambers of commerce, and business federations of the member states. They have to mobilize inputs of labour, capital, technical knowledge, and to pool resources, if need be. ASEAN entrepreneurs have to continuously develop, for example, the sense of cost control, minimize inefficiency losses which usually arise from wasteful misplaced political lobbying and corruption in their home countries. These entrepreneurs, being motors of China-ASEAN integration, have to remain focused despite turbulences in individual ASEAN countries caused at times by political regime changes, economic challenges, on top of natural calamities. ASEAN has to upgrade and refine the quality of its products and services; it is easier to curtail corruption when one is confident about the quality of goods that can be offered.

ASEAN would have to be prepared to deal with the fact that China-made products could easily match ASEAN-made products, either in cost or quality. There is room for manufacturing co-operation between China and ASEAN enterprises. Intra-trade between the two entities could still be boosted further from the estimated less than 10 per cent of China exports going to ASEAN (China accounts for less than 5 per cent of ASEAN's exports).

There is no stopping the move towards China (and away from ASEAN) of foreign direct investment (FDI). The opportunities in China is just overwhelming for ASEAN to compete for FDI. ASEAN, however, can co-opt this phenomenon by offering itself as production sites for some of these FDI-invested ventures, making it a tripartite arrangement.

PROGRESS IN RELATIONSHIP AMIDST TRANSITION

Both China and ASEAN are undergoing transitions — politically (including state governance), socially, economically, among others. Precisely because of these transitions, windows of opportunities open up that could upgrade and intensify China-ASEAN relations. Witness for example how China, after many years of insisting to deal with the Spratlys and Paracels dispute on a state-to-state bilateral basis, all of a sudden agreed in 2002 to sign with ASEAN the Declaration on the Conduct of Parties in the South China Sea. This took place in addition to China's signing of the Framework Agreement on Comprehensive Economic Co-operation with ASEAN, and China's agreement to work towards China-ASEAN Free Trade Area. In October 2003, China signed with ASEAN in Bali a Treaty of Amity and Co-operation which covers a broad framework that includes renouncing the use of force in settling disputes as well as calls for greater economic and political co-operation.

There is no doubt that Asia's new regional gravitational centre — geopolitically, economically, and even militarily — is China. It is in China's interest to be seen as the major player in the area, and it is for this reason, among others, that China is interested in gathering the various countries in Asia within its regional geographical vicinity towards a mutually comfortable relationship. It is good for China to be seen as an indirect protector, promoter, and enhancer for all of the neighbouring countries in the region with due respect to the sovereignty of each individual country. For example, there could be instances in the international relations arena where China would rather prefer that another country forwards a particular motion or point of view rather than China doing it herself. And once the motion is on the table, China is among the first to support it. This could be a subtle game of diplomacy which could go a long way in developing a *modus operandi* of goodwill between China and its ASEAN neighbours. It is not in China's interest to be a cut-throat competitor with ASEAN, but to be in fact above competition. For example, while China offers itself as a venue for high-volume, low-margin goods in the Pearl River and Yangtze deltas, its unquenchable appetite for raw materials and semi-finished goods means that this precisely is one window of opportunity where it complements with the neighbouring countries who produce these half-finished goods. Also, with proper niche matching, while ASEAN firms might find it cheaper to move their factories to China, Chinese enterprises could be seeking technology and services that might not otherwise be available in the Mainland. It is this interdependence and complementariness that would forge supply chains criss-crossing China and ASEAN many times before the product is finished. This could be one of the centrifugal forces that would pull ASEAN and China together. After all, entities that exploit each other positively for mutual advantage, rather than fear each other, will propel themselves to greater heights.

THE WAY FORWARD

With China's historical links with ASEAN, it is just natural that China and ASEAN should have a continuing fruitful relationship and be integrated in some form. Yet, even with that as background, some traditional rules could serve both China and ASEAN: (1) where there is risk, there are returns as well, (2) both entities should find ways of complementariness in economics, politics, diplomacy, and security, (3) keeping an eye on opportunities is not enough, opportunities must be created, (4) both ASEAN and China must be ready to learn some things, and to unlearn others, (5) although there could be thorny issues ahead, and either party (or both) can make mistakes, but integrate they must over the long run, and try they must with persistence. Whatever problems there are should be solved through dialogue, containment, and prudent management.

Herein lies the challenge that is in the heart of China-ASEAN relationship. It should be a boon, rather than a bane.

References

Ba, Alice D. "China and ASEAN: Renavigating Relations for a 21st Century Asia". *Asian Survey* 43, no. 4 (2003): 622–47.

Batey, I. *Asian Branding*. Hong Kong: Prentice Hall, 2002.

Gahrana, G.K. *China, Asia and the World*. New Delhi: New Delhi Publications, 1984.

Ho, Khai Leong. "Rituals, Risks, and Rivalries: China and ASEAN in the Coming Decades". *Journal of Contemporary China*, 10, no. 29 (2001): 683–94.

Ku, Samuel C.Y. "The Political Economy of Taiwan's Relations with Southeast Asia". *Contemporary Southeast Asia* 17, no. 3 (December 1995): 282–97.

Purcell, V. *The Chinese in Southeast Asia*. London: Oxford University Press, 1980.

Pye, L.W. "The China Factor in Southeast Asia". In *The China Factor: Sino-American Relations and the Global Scene*, edited by R.S. Solomon. Englewood Cliffs, NJ: Prentice Hall, 1981, p. 218.

Wang, G.W. "Early Ming Relations with Southeast Asia: A Background Essay". In *The Chinese World Order*, edited by J.K. Fairbank. Cambridge, MA: Harvard University Press, 1968.

Part IV

CHINA, TAIWAN & SOUTHEAST ASIA
Diplomatic Balance
&
Strategic Engagement

10

TAIWAN'S DIPLOMACY IN SOUTHEAST ASIA:

Still Going-South?

Chen Jie

This chapter discusses Taiwan's relations with the ASEAN region in the politico-diplomatic sphere since the end of the Cold War, focusing on Taiwan's policies and increasingly difficult advancement in the region. Taking into account the broader cross-strait, regional and international circumstances, the chapter looks into the Lee Teng-hui administration and Chen Shui-bian's respectively, but contrasts and compares the two eras in order to highlight the current challenges that Taipei has faced in Southeast Asia.

A NEW TAIWAN IN SOUTHEAST ASIA: THE LEE TENG-HUI GOVERNMENT'S GO-SOUTH CAMPAIGN[1]

It is necessary at the outset to define Taipei's "pragmatic diplomacy" in general. Although this policy approach was first crafted and practised during the Lee period, the Chen administration of the pro-independence Democratic Progressive Party (DPP) has inherited the spirit and many practices despite having seemingly dropped the jargon itself. Despite the official differences between the Kuomintang and DPP on the issue of China unification, the two parties share a consensus that Taiwan or the Republic of China (ROC) should now be regarded by the international community as a sovereign entity separate from the PRC.

"Pragmatic diplomacy" seeks international recognition of Taiwan's national sovereignty. In most cases it has involved a strategy of creeping officiality, achieving partial recognition through broadened and upgraded diplomatic representation (bilaterally and multilaterally), increased international agreements, and proactive officials' visits. Although these are no substitute for full diplomatic recognition, incremental progress in the quality and quantity achieved in representation, agreements and visits can help reinforce Taiwan's profile as a legitimate sovereign state and raise Taiwan's international standing. Seeking acceptance of sovereignty is first and foremost aimed at international legitimization of the so-called "new Taiwan". Democratization and economic prosperity has meant Taiwanese society has diverged from China's in terms of political identity. Despite a common cultural heritage to China, Taiwan is nonetheless a separate nation with a distinct identity worthy of a separate statehood. International respect for national sovereignty is also perceived to be crucial to the security of vulnerable small entities situated in the shadow of suspicious and threatening big neighbours. Furthermore, legitimization of sovereignty is desired because as one of the major global investors and traders, Taiwan has found it increasingly necessary to involve government and diplomatic channels in dealing with a host of issues arising from its expanding trade and investment relations. More institutional and legal frameworks are needed for a plethora of demands ranging from provision of information and intelligence to the business sector, to protection of intellectual property and investment. In addition, as a result of its economic and social globalization, Taiwan has become closely linked to many nations in a range of non-traditional security issues including environmental and ecological problems, cross-border crimes, and health epidemics. Since those issues are transnational, solutions have to be sought through the Taiwanese Government strengthening its consultation with other governments and international organizations concerned — hence the importance of sovereignty recognition.

Thus seeking acceptance of sovereignty is not just a legitimacy quest of a new Taiwan, but also contributes to the country's more concrete national interests in security and economic areas and non-traditional security concerns. On the other hand, sovereignty cannot be projected without expanded relations with other countries in functional issue areas, particularly trade and investment. This is because such expansion strengthens Taiwan's significance to the countries concerned, and justifies the establishing and upgrading of representative offices, increased agreements, and more frequent and higher leadership visits.

And this was the crux of the Lee Teng-hui administration's policy towards Southeast Asia.

Before Lee's presidency, ROC's politico-diplomatic visibility in Southeast Asia was negligible. While Taipei maintained its official relations with the Philippines and Thailand after the Kuomintang fled to Taiwan in 1949, South Vietnam became the only new diplomatic ally for Taipei in the entire East Asia in the post-1949 period. Meanwhile, Taipei maintained a Consulate General in Kuala Lumpur. It was closed down when Malaysia recognized PRC in 1974, and similar recognition by Manila and Bangkok in 1975 also led the two governments to abandon Taipei too. In the same year, the Saigon regime was eliminated. The Lee administration pursued what was in general a robust and consistent policy towards Southeast Asia, officially dubbed Go-South policy, in trying to upgrade its politico-diplomatic relations with the ASEAN states by manipulating Taiwan's newly acquired economic and trade clout in the region as an enticement. From the late 1980s, Taiwan saw a series of internal economic structural readjustments including the relaxation of foreign exchange controls and restrictions on investment abroad, the appreciation of the New Taiwan Dollar, rising labour costs, sky-rocketing land prices, robust labour unions, and mounting concern about industrial pollution. These made domestic environment unfavourable to the business sector, particularly regarding labour-intensive projects, and positioned Taiwan as a burgeoning economic upstart ready to expand internationally. Consequently, waves of manufacturing enterprises left Taiwan.

Southeast Asia became the largest recipient of Taiwan's out-bound investment, until China took over that position from the mid-1990s. Taiwan's huge investment capital, technical and managerial expertise complemented well with the regional countries' endowment in natural resources, industrial land, abundant labour, expanding market and the preferential treatment they enjoyed in Western markets. As a result, Taiwan's investment in the ASEAN countries expanded at a most staggering pace from 1988. Taiwan became a major foreign investor in almost every Southeast Asian country except Singapore. Though the pace of growth of Taiwanese investment in the region started to slow down since the mid-1990s due to the lure of PRC, by June 1999 the accumulated total of Taiwan's regional investment reached US$39,705 million, making Taiwan the fourth largest international investor in Thailand, third largest in Malaysia, fifth in the Philippines, sixth in Indonesia and second in Vietnam.[2] Investment induced trade relations. Taiwanese enterprises based in Southeast Asia imported from Taiwan raw materials, parts and components and machines and equipment, and exported back to Taiwan some of the finished or semi-finished products. As a result, while it was insignificant as a trader in the region before, Taiwan became by the 1990s one of the top five or six trading partners for Southeast Asian countries except Singapore.[3]

Another major component in Taiwan's regional economic profile was the import of large number of migrant workers. Taiwan was in need of foreign labour because of the rising production cost caused by shortage of domestic labour in some traditional sectors in manufacturing, construction, fishing and domestic helping. The attractive wages, plus appreciation of its currency, made Taiwan a new destination of the labourers from its poorer neighbours. In particular, the steep rises in production costs created an urgent need for changes in industrial structure in order to remain competitive in the international markets. Taiwan must restructure its economy by moving into higher value-added, more skill-intensive, and capital-intensive manufacturing, and into business and services, as well as transferring some traditional manufacturing operations overseas. To alleviate labour scarcity, measures to increase labour supply such as importing workers from abroad were also considered essential.[4] Considering that importing mainland Chinese workers was out of the question, policies and regulations were made regarding the import of contract labourers from Southeast Asia. According to the statistics of ROC Council of Labour Affairs, by the end of 1995, the total of legally imported migrant labourers in Taiwan was 189,051. It jumped to 309,424 by June 2000. Of this, 140,487 workers came from Thailand, 109,279 from the Philippines, 55,779 from Indonesia, 3,743 from Vietnam, and 136 from Malaysia.[5]

Taiwan's regional economic profile laid a solid foundation for the government's quest for a higher politico-diplomatic status. On the other hand, facilitation and protection of Taiwan's national interest in business and migrant labour also called for upgraded politico-diplomatic status. In addition, many non-traditional security issues necessitated formal dealings with the regional governments. Taiwan had become a key target as well as a transit point for regional trafficking in weapons, narcotics, humans, and endangered species. So far as health epidemics was concerned, the increasingly dense flow of population involved several large high-risk groups such as migrant labourers in Taiwan, Taiwanese business people as permanent residents in the region (estimated to be more than 150,000 by 2000), and Southeast Asian brides in Taiwan (estimated to be more than 71,100 by 1999).[6]

As in dealing with most other countries, it was clear to Taipei that creeping officiality through semi-official relations with the ASEAN states would probably never reach full officiality (diplomatic recognition) short of miracles in China. Numerous agreements, an expanding network of representative offices, and more frequent leadership visits among other diplomatic initiatives, became tools to maximize the official substance of semi-official relations, rather than feasible stepping stones to full diplomatic relations. Here advancements were substantial during Lee Teng-hui's presidency, though still far away from what Taipei hoped.

The status of Taiwanese representative institutions in the region and their regional counterparts in Taipei were noticeably upgraded through the change of names and expanded functions and privileges. It is clear from Tables 10.1 and 10.2 that the names of those institutions changed from being obscure to being more official. It is true that the official state name "Republic of China" was removed from Taiwan's representation in Singapore with Singapore's recognition of Beijing, yet the new name "Taipei Representative Office" was one of the best scored by Taipei in its informal diplomatic representation in the world. Without words like "economic and trade", the new name implies a full representation of a government. Moreover, in June 1992, a "Taipei Economic and Cultural Office" was established in both Hanoi and Ho Chi Minh City. Vietnam reciprocated the following year by setting up a Vietnam Economic and Cultural Office in Taipei. Breakthrough with Vietnam demonstrated Taipei's remarkable pragmatism. Since its ally in Saigon was annihilated in 1975, Taipei's relationship with Vietnam degenerated to a zero level. With respect to the unified Vietnam, Taipei applied its standard policy during the Cold War of not having any relations with any member in the communist bloc — not even private trade and postal contact. Thus, even when Hanoi became the only Southeast Asian country whose relations with Beijing actually deteriorated since the mid-1970s and indeed, became China's chief enemy in the region, Taipei still maintained its self-defeating policy of blacklisting Hanoi. On the other hand, blacklisting seemed to be mutual. In fact, during the Cold War, no socialist state thought about developing relations with Taipei, no matter how traumatic their relationship with China became. To side with Moscow, not Taipei, was their standard diplomatic punishment against Beijing. In this sense, the warm-up between Taipei and Hanoi since the late 1980s was one of the key symbolic events indicating the end of the Cold War ideological barrier in this part of the world.

Trappings of officialdom increased also because Taiwanese representative institutions and their regional counterparts expanded their governmental operations and gained more diplomatic privileges. In international practice, normally twelve categories of privileges and immunities are given to foreign diplomatic officials. They include: hospitality for residence, free tax on tobacco and wine, free tax on salary, free tax on automobile, consultation for public

TABLE 10.1

Changing Names of ROC Representative Institutions in Southeast Asia: 1988 – Present

Host countries	Names in Jan. 1988	Set-up date	Names at present	Renaming date
Indonesia	Chinese Chamber of Commerce to Jakarta	Apr. 1971	Taipei Economic and Trade Representative Office	Oct.1989
Malaysia	Far East Travel and Trade Centre	Aug. 1974	Taipei Economic and Cultural Office	July 1992*
The Philippines	Pacific Economic and Cultural Centre	July 1975	Taipei Economic and Cultural Office	Dec.1989
Thailand	The Far East Trade Office	Feb. 1980	Taipei Economic and Trade Office	May 1992
Singapore	Trade Mission of the Republic of China	Mar. 1969	Taipei Representative Office	Sept.1990
Vietnam	No representation		Taipei Economic and Cultural Office	Nov. 1992 (set-up date)

*Renamed first as Taipei Economic and Cultural Centre in June 1988.

Sources: Republic of China Yearbook (Government Information Office, Taipei), relevant years.

TABLE 10.2

Changing Names of Southeast Asian Representative Institutions in Taipei: 1988 – Present

Represented countries	Names in Jan. 1988	Set-up date	Names at present	Renaming date
Indonesia	Indonesian Chamber of Commerce to Taipei	Jun. 1971	Indonesian Economic and Trade Office	Jan. 1995
Malaysia	Malaysian Airline Taipei Branch; and Malaysian Culture and Trade Exchange Centre	1977; 1983*	Malaysian Friendship and Trade Centre	Jun. 1988
The Philippines	Asian Exchange Centre, Inc.	Mar. 1976	Manila Economic and Cultural Office	Dec. 1989
Thailand	Thai Airways International Ltd. Office	Feb. 1976	Thailand Trade and Economic Office	Sept. 1992
Singapore	Office of the Singapore Trade Representative	Jun. 1979	Singapore Trade Office	Sept. 1990
Vietnam (set-up date)	No representation		Vietnam Economic and Cultural Office	July 1993

*Exact month unknown in both cases. In 1988, the two institutions were merged to become Malaysian Friendship and Trade Centre.

Source: *Republic of China Yearbook* (Government Information Office, Taipei), relevant years.

affairs, official identification, free inspection on luggage, airport courtesy, communication in secret code, free inspection for official postal bags, communications with own government, and issuing visas.[7] Before the late 1980s, Taiwan's offices in the region enjoyed limited diplomatic functions and privileges, and this treatment was also true the other way round as a result. While Singapore and the Philippines were relatively friendly to Taipei, the other countries only let Taiwanese diplomats enjoy three to five of those items mentioned above.[8] However, one research suggests that by the mid-1990s, except for the public use of state name and national emblem and outdoor hanging of the national flag, Taiwan's offices had enjoyed most of those twelve privileges and immunities in all countries.[9] The exact situation with each country is impossible to verify with foreign affairs establishment due to political sensitivity. One official information source from Taipei in early 2000 presented a broad picture of the state of functions and privileges of Taipei's diplomatic representations in the original five ASEAN countries plus Vietnam. It claimed that of the twelve categories, most host countries' governments issued ROC diplomats appropriate ID documents, while the other eleven categories were enjoyed by ROC offices in all countries.[10]

In terms of reciprocal officials' visits, Lee's era represented a totally different time from Chiang Ching-kuo's. Visits at the ministerial level proliferated, though there were differences depending on individual countries' relations with China. Due to historical and geopolitical factors, mainland Southeast Asian countries (Thailand and Vietnam) were more cautious with Taiwan than maritime countries. The ASEAN governments did a great service to Taipei in the visits to the region by its Foreign Minister which carried far more diplomatic symbolism than visits by ministers in charge of more functional business. On public record, if one excludes some dubious transit visits, a Taiwanese foreign minister (under Lee Teng-hui) only ventured to three non-diplomatic allies outside Southeast Asia, namely Jordan, United Arab Emirates and Belgium (the visit to Brussels by John Chang in 1996 was one to the European Parliament). However, counted together, foreign ministers under Lee Teng-hui travelled to Singapore, Thailand, Indonesia, Malaysia and the Philippines. A system of bilateral annual economic talks at the ministerial level was also established with Singapore (since 1990), Indonesia (since 1990), the Philippines (since 1991), Thailand (since 1991; suspended since 1992), Vietnam (since 1993; suspended since 1995), and Malaysia (since 1997). Taiwan's Central Bank joined the Association of Directors of Southeast Asian Central Banks (in the name of the Central Bank of China, Taipei) in 1992, and the association's 1994 annual meeting was held in Taipei.

In the more significant realm of visits above ministerial level, achievement was also remarkable. This was most clearly demonstrated by Taiwanese leaders' visits to the region. During the Chiang Ching-kuo period, there were only two cases of top level visit, namely Premier Sun Yun-suan's visit to Indonesia in 1981, and Premier Yu Kuo-hwa's visit to Singapore in 1987. During the Lee era, Taiwanese leaders travelled widely in the region. President Lee visited Singapore, the Philippines, Indonesia and Thailand. Lien Chan visited Malaysia and Singapore as premier, and visited the two countries again as vice-president. Premier Hau Pei-tsun visited Singapore in December 1990, and Premier Vincent Siew visited Malaysia, the Philippines and Indonesia in 1998. Thus each premier under Lee Teng-hui except Lee Huan (May 1989–May 1990) visited Southeast Asia, a record shared by no other region or country, not even by Taipei's diplomatic allies during Lee's presidency. Record of regional leaders visiting Taipei was less impressive. They included prime ministers (Singapore and Malaysia), vice-president (the Philippines), vice prime ministers (Thailand, Singapore and Malaysia), and Senior Minister Lee Kuan Yew from Singapore.

In Taipei's calculation to chase symbolism of sovereignty through bilateral agreements with foreign countries, two kinds of agreements were seen to carry the largest dose of such symbolism. One was investment protection agreement and another, double taxation avoidance agreement. They entail mutual recognition of the legitimacy of legal systems, financial systems, and currencies, among other political and sovereignty implications. Taiwan signed the former with Singapore (April 1990), Indonesia (December 1990), the Philippines (January 1992), Malaysia (February 1993), Vietnam (April 1993), and Thailand (April 1996). By 1999, the latter agreement had been signed with Thailand, Malaysia, Singapore, Indonesia, and Vietnam.[11]

Ultimately, Taipei's Go-South policy was legitimized, and also facilitated by, an observable "Southeast Asia consciousness" which was in the making in Taiwan throughout the 1990s. It emphasized a new and deepened sense of shared neighbourhood with the region. This had been propelled by increased interactions with the region — trade, investment, migrant labours and transnational marriages had brought about ever closer human and societal enmeshment. Another essential contributor to this new sense of neighbourhood was Taiwan ridding itself of the "One-China" pretension in Lee's era. On the other hand, the "Taiwanization" of ROC had also been facilitated by this developing "Southeast Asia consciousness". The Kuomintang's traditional self-righteous and condescending China-centred view of Southeast Asia had been challenged. This traditional view celebrates the regional entities' tributary relations with Chinese imperial courts and emphasizes — in fact vastly exaggerates — early Chinese settlers' "civilizing" influence over the indigenous peoples. The China-centred perspective stresses the region's role in various dynastic transformations in China as a major shelter for the rebels, and in the modern revolution led by the Kuomintang itself. It boasts ethnic Chinese communities' contribution to, and "domination" of, regional economies, as a sign of cultural and business superiority. It looks at the region as a major ground to promote the great Chinese culture so that the "overseas compatriots" would not be "tainted" by the local cultures, and stresses the local Chinese communities' linkages to their ancestral land.

Other than those considerations closely related to the Greater China project, the region matters little in ROC's traditional view of Southeast Asia. Under this grand China scheme, Taiwan's own inherent relations with the region is overshadowed, suppressed or just mentioned in passing as a tiny footnote to China's relations with the region. An emerging new view of the region, which is not lacking in cultural and racial superiority towards non-Chinese peoples in Southeast Asia, takes a broader and deeper look into the region itself and its ties with Taiwan. Stressing geographical proximity and climate, ecological and biological similarities, it highlights Taiwan as a member of the maritime world of Southeast Asia while also celebrating Taiwan's linkages to mainland China and Northeast Asia. It rediscovers Taiwan's shared history with Southeast Asia, including common experiences with Western colonialism. It emphasizes the similarities in the method and timing of mainland Chinese migrants coming from the same provinces to both Southeast Asia and Taiwan during the early centuries, as coolies or political exiles. It highlights the significance of commercial relations, historical and contemporary, between Taiwan and the region. It looks into the similar challenges faced by both in their economic, political and social development. In this Taiwan-centred scheme, there is also the celebration of Taiwan aborigines sharing the same ethnic and linguistic origin with a number of indigenous peoples in Southeast Asian archipelagoes. Both are racially of southern Mongoloid stock, speaking different varieties of Austronesian languages. This emerging regional identity provided further legitimacy to the government's diplomatic quest, while leading to the fine-tuning of some of the foreign policy tactics.

When it came to dealing with Taiwan, the ASEAN countries except Singapore were interested mostly in economic benefit, while Taipei played up the politico-diplomatic significance of such dealings and often tried to play one government against another when it was most sought after. Regional governments would expand quasi-official relations and frameworks with Taipei, when doing so was technically or legally necessary for facilitating business relations, but with extreme precaution due to China's pressure. Otherwise, they would be loath to deal with Taipei at a high governmental level. Sometimes, particularly at a time of economic difficulties, Southeast Asian governments would take initiatives to provide Taipei some politico-diplomatic trappings to please Taipei so that real business dealings could be made easier. More often than not, just as economic strength gave Taipei the instrument to push for upgraded governmental relations, Taipei's anxiety to promote diplomatic profile also gave Southeast Asian governments the opportunity to manipulate Taipei's vulnerability for economic interests. Ups and downs in politico-diplomatic relations closely coincided with the ups and downs in Taiwan's perceived economic value as well as the changing China factor in regional politics.

Though the Lee administration significantly raised Taipei's politico-diplomatic position in Southeast Asia, achievements were still short of Taipei's own expectations, not just bilaterally but particularly regarding Taipei's role in the ASEAN-centred multilateral forums. It was during the first half of the 1990s that Taipei's diplomatic achievements in the region were most impressive. After all, Taipei's investment protection agreements with the regional governments were all signed before 1995, except the one with Thailand. All ministerial forums with the regional governments started before 1995, except the one with Malaysia. Also, twenty-five out of the thirty-seven bilateral agreements Taipei signed with regional governments from January 1998 to December 1998 were signed before July 1995.[12] In addition, the status of Taipei's quasi-diplomatic offices was apparently all upgraded before the mid-1990s. The single most triumphant event in Taipei's regional diplomacy, namely Lee Teng-hui's trips to the region, materialized in 1989 and 1994. This issue of timing means that Taipei's diplomatic accomplishments and setbacks cannot be fully understood without analyzing the changing nature of international and regional relations, particularly with respect to China's interactions with Southeast Asia.

During the first several years since the late 1980s, coinciding with Lee Teng-hui's rise to power, two developments provided Taipei with a favourable external environment to achieve its diplomatic goals. First, Beijing lost its pivotal position in the so-called strategic triangular relationship of Moscow, Washington and Beijing, thus its diplomatic significance to the Western world was reduced. Politics in China's own region also mirrored this development. While the ASEAN states had relied on China's support for the regional proxy Cold War in Cambodia, the post-Cold War solution of the Indochinese conflict reduced Beijing's regional strategic leverage. Second, the

1989 Tiananmen massacre damaged Beijing's international image and isolated the Chinese Government for the first time since the early 1970s. As a result of these developments, Beijing's key foreign policy need became the regaining of international respectability and ending of Western sanctions. This made China more willing to compromise with other countries regarding their relations with Taiwan. China had to compromise with Western powers, because China needed to repair relations with them. And China had to compromise with some developing countries (particularly those in Southeast Asia) because their political relations with Beijing during 1989–92, largely unaffected by the Tiananmen killings, were the only façade which helped boost Beijing's international respectability.[13] Meanwhile, improved relationship between Beijing and Taipei themselves from the beginning of the 1990s made it easier for many countries to reassess their commitment to the "One-China" principle. A "private" Straits Exchange Foundation (SEF) was created in Taipei in 1990 to make unofficial contacts and negotiations on non-political matters with the PRC. SEF's mainland counterpart organization, the Association for Relations Across the Taiwan Straits (ARATS), was created in 1991. A historic meeting took place between SEF Chairman Koo Chen-fu and the ARATS Chairman Wang Daohan in Singapore in April 1993. These advantageous circumstances made both Taipei and the ASEAN states diplomatically adventurous.

However, since the mid-1990s the situation shifted against Taipei. The Chinese Government weathered the 1989 domestic political crisis successfully and proved that it was far from being just another collapsing communist regime. On the contrary, the Eighth Five-Year Plan period (1990–95) saw the fastest economic growth in China since 1949, particularly in the coastal regions. The world's memory of the awful events of Tiananmen receded. Meanwhile, from tension in Korean Peninsula, multilateral disputes in the South China Sea, proliferation of weapons of mass destruction to a range of other global issues, China's new strategic weight became incontestable. China had eventually emerged from the end of the Cold War with considerable new strategic and economic latitude, a status further boosted by the handover of Hong Kong. The perception of China as a giant, impoverished pariah shifted dramatically to one which saw China as an emerging political and economic superpower set on a colliding course with the United States, though both perceptions were simplistic. After China's strong reactions to the U.S. visit by Lee Teng-hui and the Sino-U.S. conflict over China's military exercises across the Taiwan Strait in 1995–96, "strategic engagement", aimed at further integrating China with the established rules of the international security and economic systems, became the norms for major Western powers and China's neighbours. China forged "strategic partnerships" with all the major powers, so as to conduct more institutionalized consultation on common security and economic issues and interests, as well as to project itself as a force to be reckoned with by Washington in the new world order. China's military exercises further convinced the ASEAN governments that China was not to be provoked on issues of nationalism. Those military actions were not only reactions to Lee's U.S. visit, but also warnings against Taiwan's new diplomacy in general. Since then, China started to engage in a global diplomatic offensive against Taiwan with a degree of intensity not seen since the mid-1970s, demonstrating unprecedented flexibility and sophistication. Money diplomacy, manipulation of veto power in the UN Security Council, professional lobbying, overseas Chinese connections, political party diplomacy and parliamentary diplomacy were all used *vis-à-vis* the countries concerned. On the other hand, the ASEAN countries' ever-increasing willingness to engage China (bilaterally and multilaterally) and the marked progress achieved in that regard reduced Taiwan's room for diplomatic manoeuvring. With the strategic stake increased in their relations with China, the ASEAN countries generally found their Taiwan connections to have become even more sensitive. It became more difficult for Taiwan and Southeast Asian governments in their relations.

The ASEAN countries care deeply about security across the Taiwan Strait. Broad strategic and commercial significance of the strait and Taiwan's economic partnership with the region make all Southeast Asian governments hope for peace and stability in that region. Officials in Singapore often claimed that both China and Taiwan were their friends, that damage to either side by a serious confrontation would hurt Singapore, and that the hurt would be double if both sides suffered damages. To varying degrees, this sentiment could also be true of other regional governments since all had significant national interests in both Taiwan and China. However, Southeast Asian governments cannot do anything substantive on the Beijing-Taipei conflict other than quiet and toothless diplomacy. Their leverage on China is extremely limited. If the regional governments are hesitant to interfere in each other's domestic affairs, there is even less courage to interfere in what they have already acknowledged to be China's "domestic conflict". On the contrary, during moments of cross-strait tension, the ASEAN governments would find it necessary to show Beijing where they stand, trying their best to avoid being seen to be openly siding with Taipei.

The Asian financial crisis in 1997–98 raised Taipei's diplomatic hope, since of all East Asian economies, Taiwan's was one of the few which survived the crisis relatively unscathed and became the envy of all governments in the region. However, despite some ASEAN countries waving back at the olive branches waved by Taipei, substantive diplomatic achievements were limited compared to the first half of the 1990s. The crisis not only projected Taiwan's economic strength, but also highlighted China's contribution to regional economies. Beijing's firm commitment not to depreciate the value of the renminbi (PRC currency) was profoundly appreciated by the regional governments, since to do otherwise could cause disastrous consequences to the already troubled regional economies. The Chinese Government's contribution of US$5.5 billion (Hong Kong contributed another US$1 billion) to the IMF-led rescue packages for Indonesia and Thailand also won gratitude from the region.[14] Apart from taking part in the IMF package, Beijing also provided an unspecified sum of export credit to Bangkok and Jakarta, and an extra US$300 million low-interest loans to Jakarta.[15]

By the end of Lee Teng-hui's presidency, one could reach a definitive impression regarding Taipei's regional diplomacy. Namely, with China's heightened diplomatic pressure and changing regional politics, and with regional financial crisis failing to create real diplomatic miracle for Taipei, it seemed that Taiwan's politico-diplomatic relations with Southeast Asia were starting to enter a stage of holding on to — and struggling to repeat — what was already achieved. However, this struggle was to become very difficult in the Chen Shui-bian era.

THE DPP GOVERNMENT'S FOREIGN POLICY: HOW IMPORTANT IS SOUTHEAST ASIA?

Before analyzing Taipei's relations with ASEAN since Chen Shui-bian in the next section, it is important to clarify the Chen administration's general foreign policy. The aim in this section is not to discuss foreign policy or specific policy approaches, but to project developments and issues which particularly highlight the considerably reduced priority given to the ASEAN region. The Chen administration has mostly focused on: improving relations with the United States, sustaining relations with formal diplomatic allies, and mobilizing civil society's linkages with transnational networks as a vital complement to the government's foreign policy pursuits. These indeed were also among Lee's top priorities. However, as explained in the following, domestic, cross-strait and international circumstances surrounding the Chen administration have led Chen to spend far more diplomatic energies to pursue these priorities, consequently reducing the importance of the ASEAN region in the overall foreign policy. Comparatively, Lee's foreign policy was more of an all-out global campaign to promote Taiwan's separate statehood. After all, lots of new initiatives in Lee's pragmatic diplomacy started in

Southeast Asia before they were practised in other countries. Lee's visit to Singapore in March 1989, the first visit to a non-diplomatic ally by a ROC head of state, provided the first litmus test for the government's rhetoric on diplomatic pragmatism. This pragmatism was to send Lee to the Philippines, Indonesia and Thailand in 1994. Lee's informal 1995 visit to the United States was modelled on these Southeast Asian adventures. In terms of bilateral ministerial forums, the first shot of pragmatic diplomacy was also fired in Southeast Asia. In the pre-Lee days, Taipei operated such mechanisms only with diplomatic allies. Since the 1990s, this was extended to other countries, of which Singapore and Indonesia were the first and second to open such systems with Taipei (both in 1990). The experiment led to the opening of a regular vice ministerial forum with the United States starting in 1995. Also, Taipei's investment protection agreement signed with Singapore in April 1990 was the first such agreement Taiwan signed with a non-diplomatic ally. Furthermore, Vietnam represented the opening of Taipei's governmental dealing with the then socialist world, and it created a model for similar dealings with others.

The victory of Chen Shui-bian in the March 2000 presidential elections signified the transfer of national political authority from the Kuomintang to the opposition in half a century. Though Washington has always been the centerpiece of Taipei's foreign policy, it has become more so for the DPP government. As a first-timer in national leadership, the Chen team must focus more on what is most important to the country. It has to cultivate Washington's confidence to establish a solid base in international relations in general. More importantly, however, there have been major events, uncharted waters and consecutive periods of high anxiety in Taipei-Beijing-Washington triangular manoeuvring which have made the Chen administration preoccupied in ways and to an extent which did not characterize its predecessor's dealings with Washington. Taipei must be eager to learn both the limits and opportunities in those triangular relations which have become far more eventful and delicate for Taipei than they were during the 1990s. Nine months after Chen's electoral victory, the White House also changed hands. Another nine months later all parties in the delicate Taipei-Beijing-Washington triangle were caught off guard by the terrorist attacks on New York and Washington. Amid the global anti-terror fanfare, the Chinese leadership transition, from the third generation Communist Party officials with Jiang Zemin at its core to a third generation group centred upon Hu Jintao, was partly completed at the party's Sixteenth National Congress in November 2002 and National People's Congress in March 2003. Frustrating stalemate characterized the Chen administration's relations with the departing Clinton administration, whose anxiety became evident in the lead-up to the March 2000 elections, considering the DPP's long-standing commitment to Taiwan independence. Chen was aware that the United States remained to be convinced regarding both himself and his party. He then saw the beacon of light in George W. Bush's White House, with the latter's reassessment of China as a potential threat to regional security and challenger to U.S. primacy in the Asia-Pacific as well as a key economic partner. However, the September 11 attacks made Taipei fear a U.S.-China co-operation on anti-terrorism at its own expense. In the lead-up to war in Iraq, Taipei was concerned with Beijing's lukewarm approach in the UN Security Council where it privately pledged not to block U.S. military action but publicly sided with France and Russia in calling for protracted UN inspections. Taipei suspected a Chinese attempt to wait and cut a deal with Washington against Taipei. After the war was officially declared over, Taipei's worry became whether Washington would be ready to compromise its support for Taiwan to get China's help in persuading Pyongyang to give up its nuclear weapons programme. However, the time-consuming nature of Taipei-Washington relations since mid-2002 also resulted from Chen's own more reckless efforts to project Taiwan's separate statehood, particularly in the lead-up to the 2004 presidential elections. His proclamation that there was "one country on either side" of the Taiwan Strait, his push for referendums and his promise of a new constitution in 2006, made Taipei-Washington-Beijing relations more delicate and tense, thus further reducing the relative importance of other items in the diplomatic agenda.

Taipei's diplomatic allies, mostly small and impoverished states, are the key supporters of its bidding for membership in Inter-Governmental Organizations (IGOs) and provide the only façade of full international recognition of ROC's state sovereignty. But there have been also other and newer reasons accounting for the Chen government making far greater efforts than its predecessor to consolidate relations with diplomatic allies. There was the anxiety not to give Beijing a chance, at a time of volatile political transition in Taipei, to sabotage Taipei's long-standing relations with allies in Central America, the Caribbeans, West Africa and South Pacific by using its veto power over the UN peacekeeping missions and financial assistance packages. Taipei's anxiety was best symbolized by Chen's trip to some of the ROC's diplomatic allies in South America and Africa (the Dominican Republic, Nicaragua, Costa Rica, The Gambia, Burkina Faso and Chad) in August 2000, less than three months after he took office and despite all the domestic emergencies associated with the leadership transition. This was the first time a ROC president visited these countries.

Subsequent leadership visits to the allies further proved this point. These visits were unprecedented in terms of their frequency and the fresh nature of some tours. Thus in September 2000, Vice President Annette Lu visited Salvador, Honduras, Belize and Guatemala. Chen travelled in May–June 2001 to Salvador, Guatemala, Panama, Paraguay and Honduras. In September the same year Premier Chang Chun-hsiung visited Saint Christopher and Nevis, the Commonwealth of Dominica, Saint Vincent and the Grenadines, and Grenada (Chang was the first ROC premier to visit these Caribbean allies). In December that year Lu visited the Gambia, and toured Nicaragua and Paraguay in January 2002. In July that year Chen visited Swaziland and became the first ROC president to visit Senegal, Sao Tome and Principe, and Malawi. In the following month, Premier Yu Shyi-kun travelled to Haiti, Panama, Costa Rica and Belize. Thus two years into office Chen visited fifteen of the twenty-seven diplomatic allies, whereas during his twelve years as president (1988–2000), Lee visited only eight (Nicaragua, Costa Rica, South Africa, Swaziland, Panama, Honduras, El Salvador, Paraguay). In addition, while Chen, Lu, Chang and Yu all chose diplomatic allies to make their first overseas visits, their predecessors favoured non-diplomatic allies, particularly the ASEAN states.

Another indicator of the Chen administration's anxiety to sustain the existing ties with allies is that while the Lee government was keen to sabotage Beijing's diplomatic relations with small and poor states, the Chen government has generally not taken any such action. It was estimated that between ten and twenty of Beijing's allies were "winnable" by Taipei if it tried hard, [16] but so far Taipei appears to have only taken action with Kiribati, which defected to Taipei in November 2003. Indeed, it may well be because of Taipei's strengthened efforts — at the expense of other priorities such as Southeast Asia — that the defection of diplomatic allies has not been as spectacular as worried about. It is true that Macedonia severed ties with Taipei in June 2001, followed by Nauru in July 2002 and the Commonwealth of Dominica in March 2004. However, this is insignificant considering that in 1997–98, a total of five allies (St. Lucia, Bahamas, Republic of Central Africa, Guinea-Bissau, and Tonga) "fell" to Beijing.

To systematically mobilize Non-Governmental Organizations (NGOs) in the pursuit of the state's diplomatic goals was one of the trademarks of Taipei's foreign policy during the 1990s. Influenced by its own ideological tradition of mobilizational authoritarianism, the Kuomintang government's utilitarian approach towards civil society also reflected diplomatic reality. First, as a result of democratization, the number and strength of NGOs had expanded dramatically in Taiwan, and their participation in the transnational civil society had become increasingly robust. Second, it suited the interests of both the government and NGOs to co-operate in promoting the politico-diplomatic status of the state, since the marginalization of the ROC state similarly posed obstacles to NGOs' own participation in international forums, particularly those forums hosted by the UN. Third, Ministry of Foreign Affairs (MOFA) and NGOs were complementary in that the former could assist the latter in financial resources, diplomatic training and information gathering, while the latter were expected to use their connections with major International Non-Governmental Organizations (INGOs), particularly those with consultative status in the UN, to promote the state's profile and interests through back doors. According to Taipei's statistics, there were about 45,674 INGOs by 2001, more than 1,000 of them enjoying UN consultative status. On the other hand, Taiwan had about 4,000 registered NGOs, and more than 1,000 INGOs had Taiwanese organizations as members.[17]

Though the Chen administration inherited the mantle of its predecessor on the front of NGO diplomacy,[18] as a former solidarity partner of Taiwan's grassroots social movements, the DPP has more faith in civil society groups, professing more emphasis on mutual benefit.[19] The DPP government is not only pragmatic enough to continue to subsidize and make good use of those organizations which were traditionally pro-Kuomintang and established as that party's corporatist organizations, but has also enlisted the support from the more authentic activist organizations which were not favoured in the Lee government's NGO diplomacy due to their unreserved criticism of the government in international forums. In addition, the DPP government's approach appears to be more institutionalized, focused and proactive. MOFA established a NGO Affairs Committee in October 2000, with ten of its fifteen board members selected from NGOs.[20] The NGO Affairs Committee has actively facilitated Taiwanese NGOs' relations with the relevant INGOs, encouraging Taiwanese activists to become elected for the leadership positions in the key INGOs and/or persuade those INGOs to stage their grand events in Taipei, which would enable MOFA officials to make poignant propaganda to a broad international audience.

However, compared to Lee's approach, Chen's NGO diplomacy is further geared towards priorities in relations with the United States, diplomatic allies and international organizations, particularly World Health Organization (WHO), a key diplomatic target after Taipei joined World Trade Organization in January 2002. The Chen government pays special attention to humanitarian aid and human rights NGOs, since their international activism helps project the image of a humanitarian and democratic Taiwan, which would boost its position in the above priorities. Human rights NGOs are encouraged and subsidized to deepen their relations with the Western-dominated INGOs such as Human Rights Watch, Amnesty International, International League for Human Rights, International Federation for Human Rights. These efforts are expected to project in the United States and the Western world in general an image of Taiwan as a pro-human rights new democracy, thus scoring diplomatic points. So far as the aid NGOs are concerned, MOFA has been mobilizing, co-ordinating and subsidizing the main players such as Buddhist Tzu Chi Charity Foundation, World Vision Taiwan, Taiwan Root Medical Corps, and Eden Social Welfare Foundation to fulfil their international humanitarian missions. This to serve relations with diplomatic allies since natural disasters and civil strife are trade marks of Taipei's allies except the Vatican. Taipei has made elaborate plans to incorporate humanitarian and medical NGOs in the government's aid programmes to supplement the latter's limited resources and expertise. A top-down model, characterized by understanding and friendship forged at societal levels, is believed to be able to place the governmental relations on a more solid ground. Aid NGO diplomacy is also intended to endear the United States. After all, Afghanistan and Iraq are the two "priority zones" of Taipei's humanitarian relief mission. In addition, the medical dimension of international aid has been particularly stressed since it helps win the international — particularly Washington's — support for Taipei's bid for an observer status with the WHO.

THE DPP GOVERNMENT AND SOUTHEAST ASIA

Under the circumstances discussed above, the DPP government's approach towards the ASEAN region has not shown the kind of consistency, comprehensiveness and potency as demonstrated during the Lee era. There have been occasional outbursts of important rhetoric, without follow-up measures. The various issues of the *ROC Foreign Policy Yearbook* published by MOFA clearly show that in the original ASEAN-5 plus Vietnam, Taipei's politico-diplomatic profile has stagnated, if not deteriorated. The Lee era's advances in bilateral representations have apparently remained, and the overwhelming majority of the agreements in operation since 2000 were signed during the Lee era. On the other hand, except for Vice President Lu's August 2002 to Indonesia and Senior Minister Lee Kuan Yew's visits to Taipei (2000, 20002), no above-ministerial level visits have been recorded either way. In fact even the ministerial level exchanges have also decreased demonstrably. Most of the visitors are deputy ministers, parliamentarians and local government officials. Lu's visit to Indonesia was disrupted due to

China's pressure (she was barred from entry into Jakarta, went to Bali instead, and then managed to slip into Jakarta) and the Philippine Government categorically refused to accept any possible visit by Chen regardless of his visiting capacity.[21] In September 2002, Chen, speaking at a meeting of the Council of Taiwanese Chambers of Commerce in Asia, itself established by the Lee government as an organ in the Go-South campaign, tried to rekindle the Go-South rhetoric. He called for efforts to expand Taiwan's economic relations with Southeast Asia to reduce the country's dramatically increasing economic dependence on China, a dependence seen to jeopardize Taiwan's national security and weaken its position in negotiations with China.[22] The mainland-bound investment had snowballed, and by the end of 2001, China also replaced the United States as Taiwan's largest export market, with 23 per cent of Taiwan's total export going to China (21 per cent to the United States).[23] However, if Chen believed that his Go-South declaration was to generate some diplomatic benefit, he was to be totally disappointed. In December 2002, Beijing's pressure forced the cancellation of a secretly arranged trip by Chen to Indonesia just within hours of his departure.[24] Similar pressure was not always successful during the 1990s.

Taipei's problem is not just that it has been constantly preoccupied with other priorities. The above frustrations and lack of politico-diplomatic advancement in the region also reflect new developments in China-ASEAN relations, China-Taiwan relations and the DPP government's own structural weakness in the Southeast Asian context, as discussed below.

The state of the region's relations with China has become considerably different from that during the 1990s, making the diplomatic playing field far less favourable to Taipei, reinforcing the similar trend which started during the late years of the Lee era. While Taiwan's domestic partisan bickering has been hindering its diplomatic momentum since 2000, China has become more assertive and self-confident in conducting its foreign policy, regionally and internationally, particularly under the Hu leadership. China's relations with the ASEAN states and the ASEAN organization have become the strongest since the 1970s. Proliferating mechanisms of dialogues and co-operation in multiple issue areas have been built upon the existing structures such as China's membership in ASEAN Regional Forum (since 1994), ASEAN-China Senior Officials' Meetings (since 1995), China's dialogue status with ASEAN (since 1996) and the Ten+3 summit series (since 1997). In November 2002 China signed with the ASEAN states a Declaration on the Conduct of Parties in the South China Sea, and a Joint Declaration of ASEAN and China on Co-operation in the Field of Non-Traditional Security Issues. These issues were defined to include trafficking in illegal drugs, people smuggling, sea piracy, terrorism, arms smuggling, money laundering, international economic crime and cyber crime. Also, in October 2003, China acceded to the 1976 Treaty of Amity and Co-operation in Southeast Asia, and signed a Joint Declaration of the Heads of State/Government of the Association of Southeast Asian Nations and the People's Republic of China on Strategic Partnership for Peace and Prosperity.[25] To mention these events is neither to overstate ASEAN's importance or unity, nor to play down the lingering traditional suspicions between China and the region. However, since China-ASEAN relations set an overarching parameter for Taiwan's diplomacy, the recent warm-up in these relations has significantly reduced the leeway for Taipei's regional policy.

As well proven during the Lee period, evolution of Beijing-Taipei relations influences regional governments' approach to Taipei. Improved atmosphere across the Taiwan Strait would make things easier for Southeast Asian governments in dealing with Taipei. On the other hand, in a crisis between Beijing and Taipei, no ASEAN country would want to be seen to be siding with Taipei though private sympathy may be expressed for Taipei, as testified during the March 1996 crisis. If forced to express their stand, the ASEAN governments would invariably chant the "One-China" slogan. In this sense, the Chen Shui-bian era is probably the worst time for the ASEAN governments in terms of dealing with Taipei. In the lead-up to Taiwan's presidential elections in March 2004, ASEAN foreign ministers were obliged to declare a consensus on the issue, warning that Taiwan's coming referendum would worsen the situation across the strait, urging Taipei to avoid such an act.[26] This was the first time for the ASEAN countries to collectively warn Taipei on its domestic politics.

China's trade with the ASEAN countries has increased more rapidly than Taiwan's. This has further raised China's leverage in the region, though China (not including Hong Kong) cannot match Taiwan's regional significance as an investor and labour importer. Trade between China and the ASEAN states amounted to US$8,865 million in 1993, rose to US$16,692 in 1996 and US$31,150 million in 2000, then jumped to US$45,512 million in 2001. On the other hand, Taiwan's trade with the ASEAN countries was valued as US$14,304 million in 1993, US$24,114 million in 1996, US$23,514 million in 2000, and US$15,605 million in 2001.[27] On the basis of the previous China-ASEAN mechanisms such as Joint Committee on Economic and Trade Co-operation, Joint Science and Technology Committee (both formed in 1994), and ASEAN-China Joint Co-operation Committee (1997), institutionalized co-operation has expanded. In November 2002 an agreement was sealed setting the timetable for the establishment of the world's largest free-trade zone by 2010–15.

Apart from political and economic interests in Southeast Asia, China's recent moves to beef up relations with the region are also intended to serve broader strategic concerns. Taipei may have been suffering from some collateral damages. Post-September 11, China has become more concerned with the perceived expansion of American unilateralism and a unipolar world. In particular, the United States had achieved stronger diplomatic and military presence in China's peripheral regions after the Afghan campaign. It acquired military bases in Tajikistan, Kyrgyzstan and Uzbekistan, thus effectively driving wedges between members of the Shanghai Co-operation Organization, which was just officially inaugurated in June 2001 under Beijing's initiatives to precisely counterbalance the U.S. global supremacy. The United States had also established a pro-American regime in Afghanistan, beefed up relations with China's chief Muslim ally Pakistan, increased arms sales to India, held joint military exercises with India, strengthened its defence profile with the Philippines and reinforced the U.S.-Japan military alliance. All these developments increased Beijing's sense of uncertainty about its surrounding security scenario at a time of leadership transition. Beijing has seen the ASEAN Regional Forum (ARF) and ASEAN's consultation systems with its dialogue partners as a useful diplomatic counterbalance against the U.S.-led, newly re-enhanced, bilateral security networks in Asia. At least China could use those Southeast Asian mechanisms to make the U.S. networks look increasingly anachronistic. Beijing has made it clear that while the regional dialogue (led by the friendly ASEAN and based on the principle of consensus) is a good example of new international co-operation in the post-Cold War era, the U.S.-dominated security alliances in Asia are examples of Cold War power politics.

The DPP government's policy instruments in Southeast Asia are considerably less and weaker than the Kuomintang's. During the 1990s, Taipei was still providing financial aid to Southeast Asia. Such aid, mainly in the form of low-interest loans, was provided by MOFA-controlled International Co-operation and Development Fund (ICDF) to Vietnam, the Philippines and Indonesia. These lending programmes were intended to help Vietnam's road building, industrial park development projects, small and medium sized enterprises (SMEs) development and agricultural projects, Indonesia's industrial parks in Batam and Medan and agribusiness enterprises, and the Philippines' Subic Bay Industrial Park, SMEs development, upgrading of food processing and agricultural machinery. A total of US$174.38 million had been lent to the three governments (US$71.58 million for Manila, US$66.90 million for Hanoi, US$35.90 million for Jakarta).[28] These projects facilitated the overall Go-South diplomacy. For example, the Taipei-funded Subic Bay Industrial Park (the Philippines) and Tan Thuan Export Processing Zone (Vietnam) significantly boosted Taiwan's investment in the two countries. However, generosity has been stopped since the DPP. Taiwan's national economy plunged into recession since 2000, with very low growth rate, high unemployment rate and expanding government budget deficit. This has imposed limits on overseas financial assistance. Furthermore, Taipei has to pull the available resources together to consolidate relations with diplomatic allies. Normal trade and investment with those poor and distant allies are too weak to be diplomatically useful, so Taipei's economic diplomacy in these cases can literally boil down to just loans and cash/material donations. Yet "money diplomacy" has already become Beijing's distinct advantage over Taipei, globally as well as in Southeast Asia. For example, in 2002 China provided a low-interest loan of US$120 million to Vietnam, and US$400million to Indonesia.[29]

It is true that Taiwan remains one of the major traders and investors in the region. For example, in 2001 Taiwan invested US$336 million in the region, making it the fourth largest extra-regional source of investment in the year, after the EU-15, the United States, and Japan. In the same year, Taiwan was ASEAN's seventh largest export market and eighth largest import origin.[30] Taiwan still employs 303,684 Southeast Asian workers.[31] However, Lee's more successful Go-South diplomacy was never just about manipulating impressive statistics at ministerial forums. It was also a personal and private diplomacy. More often than not, individual tycoons and their conglomerates from both Taiwan and Southeast Asia played a more decisive role in some diplomatic adventures, in the shadowy milieu of government-business collaboration on both sides. Yet this strategy was more of Kuomintang's advantage than the DPP's in dealing with the region.

Pursuit for personal connections is vital to Taipei's foreign policy. Since informal diplomacy is played out in gray areas, and since its governmental relations with foreign countries is least institutionalized of all, private personal connections have become important as diplomatic instruments. Although this is a key in Taiwan's dealings with all countries, yet it has been more so with Southeast Asia than with the Western governments. In Lee's era, personal diplomacy, sweetened with business benefit, was a crucial lubricant in diplomacy with Southeast Asian countries, authoritarian, democratizing or socialist. While dealings with the Western governments could be obstructed by suffocating legalistic rigidity, political transparency and legislative predictability, wheeling and dealing with Southeast Asian politicians and their business protégés provided the Lee government with real potentials for progress. While Taiwanese officials were keen to lobby the legislative bodies in the West, they spent hard efforts working on opportunities provided by crony capitalism and cultural emphasis on personal ties in Southeast Asia. Prominent Taiwanese tycoons who had invested heavily in Southeast Asia and cultivated intimate personal relations with the local political elite and politically connected business figures often spoke proudly of their "people diplomacy", namely using their own relations to contribute to the Kuomintang government's diplomatic goals. These capitalists were often pro-Kuomintang, since many of Taiwan's large private enterprises emerged and grew under the tutelage of the Kuomintang regime. Also indicative of a legacy of Taiwan's own political history, Kuomintang-operated enterprises and state-owned enterprises (SOEs) (both were effectively banned from investing in China) collaborated with the Lee government for diplomatically motivated investment projects in Southeast Asia. This was important since the government could not control the private sector in terms of the latter's decisions concerning overseas investment. This was particularly the case with the countless SMEs — the majority of Taiwanese investors in Southeast Asia. However, if SOEs had already become more autonomous throughout the 1990s due to democratization, the DPP government's reform in government-business relations have made SOEs even less of an instrument for diplomatically motivated mega-projects overseas. President Chen certainly saw the diplomatic value of the business elite. For example, despite the DPP's past accusation of Kuomintang's cronyism, not long after his 2000 inauguration Chen sought the support from Jeffrey L.S. Koo, a leading Taiwanese tycoon and Chairman of Taiwan's biggest privately owned bank (Chinatrust Commercial Bank). He was one of the most important business collaborators with the Kuomintang government's foreign policy. Koo was asked to remain in his position as an ambassador-without-portfolio in order to help the DPP government facilitate back-door diplomacy. It is nonetheless fair to argue that in general, and particularly in the Southeast Asian context, the DPP government's usable diplomatic resources in capitalists and conglomerates are considerably less than the Kuomintang's. The DPP and its elite have never been part of the long-standing shadowy interactions between Taiwanese government-business world and its Southeast Asian counterpart.

Partly because of its manipulating the business-government relations in both Taiwan itself and Southeast Asia, and partly because of its long tenure in office, the Kuomintang and its leaders enjoyed close relations with some Southeast Asian leaders and/or their families. Again this was an advantage the DPP does not possess with today's Southeast Asian leaders. Such relations facilitated Taipei's Go-South diplomacy, though these regional leaders found the balancing act (between Taipei and Beijing) increasingly difficult to perform during the 1990s. Leaders known to be friendly to the Kuomintang government included Suharto, B.J. Habibie, King Bhumibol Adulyadej, Corazon Aquino, Fidel Ramos, Joseph Estrada (and the current Philippine President Gloria Arroyo's fond memory of Taiwan derived from experiences with the Kuomintang's old ROC, not new Taiwan). On the other hand, relations between Taipei and Chiang Ching-kuo's old soulmate Lee Kuan Yew has become a thing of the past, because Lee regularly criticized Taipei's campaign for separate nation-statehood. In short, the DPP government and its people are largely new in the political establishment in Southeast Asia. As a party, the DPP's major political connection with the region seems to be a solidarity built with some small opposition parties and groups within the framework of Council of Asian Liberals and Democrats (CALD; Chen Shui-bian was sworn in as CALD's new chairman in March 2004).[32]

This weakness is compounded by the DPP's lack of relations with ethnic Chinese communities in Southeast Asia. The Kuomintang's ties with such communities were strong historically. After all, Southeast Asia or *Nanyang* was used by Sun Yat-sen and his followers as the most important base for revolutionary mobilization of *Huaqiao* (overseas Chinese emigrants). During the two Chiangs' time, *Qiaowu* (overseas Chinese affairs) was a chief instrument used by the ROC government in its recreation of a political and cultural Great China on Taiwan. The policy was a self-legitimizing tool used by the Kuomintang to impose a "One-China" myth upon the Taiwanese people and propagate its own historic contribution in China's modern history. Relations with the global ethnic Chinese communities functioned as a symbol of the self-claimed central government interacting with the whole of China. Democratization and political nativization during Lee Teng-hui's era progressively eroded *Qiaowu's* revolutionary and nationalistic functions, shifting its priorities towards Taiwan's own core national interests. As a result, diplomatic objectives became supreme in *Qiaowu* practices, and Taiwanese emigrant communities assumed a much higher profile. During the Lee era, Southeast Asian *Qiaowu* became an instrument in the pragmatic diplomacy of the Go-South Policy, aimed at seeking politico-diplomatic influence in the region through an institutionalized ethnic framework. On the other hand, the DPP campaigned against the Kuomintang's *Qiaowu* from its own perspective of Taiwan independence. Since coming to power, the DPP officials seem to have watered down such radical rhetoric and started to see some of the diplomatic value of the global Chinese communities, but particularly the recent Taiwanese migrant groups. During the authoritarian era, many of today's DPP activists thrived in the overseas Taiwanese groups which were nonetheless overwhelmingly based in the United States and Japan, not in Southeast Asia. Overall it is true that the DPP's connections with the overseas Chinese communities in Southeast Asia is very recent, focused on the disparate Taiwanese investors themselves and their associations, and aimed at mobilizing potential supporters to vote in the elections in Taiwan itself.

CONCLUSION

The Lee government's informal diplomacy in Southeast Asia benefited from China's domestic and international troubles as much as from Taiwan's own newly gained popularity, significance and self-confidence. With China's all-out diplomatic campaign, coupled with Beijing's changed international and regional relations, Taiwan started to become defensive since the mid-1990s. Its foreign policy initiatives started to increasingly become counter-actions against Beijing's actions, in an effort to hold the ground it had already gained.

While Taipei's diplomatic environment in Southeast Asia has continued to deteriorate over the recent years, the country's position in the region has also suffered from the DPP government's own relative side-lining of the region and its lack of diplomatic instruments. As a result, Taiwan's politico-diplomatic relations with the individual ASEAN states at the beginning of the new millennium have stagnated if not worsened. Meanwhile, Taiwan remains isolated from all ASEAN-centred dialogue forums. Broadly, it is also not part of ASEM (Asia-Europe Meeting), and plays a less-than-equal role in APEC. Taiwan's position in the Track II diplomacy of the Council on Security Co-operation in the Asia Pacific has also remained emasculated. Yet like any other regional country, Taiwan has substantial interests in strategic, military, territorial, political, economic and transnational issue areas, and the facilitation and protection of such interests must be built upon a higher politico-diplomatic status. For example, to combat SARS and avian flu, Taipei needs to join regional inter-governmental efforts. To secure the country's future economic well-being, Taipei needs to sign Free Trade Agreement with Southeast Asian countries. Most importantly, there is the continual "Southeast Asia consciousness" in Taiwan reflecting the maturing of a new identity. As Chen Shui-bian himself declared in his 20 May 2004 inauguration speech, Southeast Asian brides (about 280,000 today) and workers "who labour under Taiwan's blazing sun" were just like other communities in Taiwan in that they had all "made a unique contribution to this land and each has become an indispensable member of our 'New Taiwan' family".[33]

Notes

1. Discussion in this section is partly based on Chapters 1–2 of my book, *Foreign Policy of the New Taiwan: Pragmatic Diplomacy in Southeast Asia* (London: Edward Elgar Publishing Limited, 2002).
2. Southeast Asian governments' statistics complied by Investment Commission, Ministry of Economic Affairs, Taipei.
3. *Direction of Trade Statistics Yearbook* (International Monetary Fund, Washington), various years.
4. Ching-lung Tsay, "Taiwan", *ASEAN Economic Bulletin* 12, no. 2 (November 1995): 177–79.
5. Website of Council of Labour Affairs, Taipei.
6. For human and societal enmeshment between Taiwan and Southeast Asia, see "Exploring the Human Dimensions of Taiwan-Southeast Asia Economic Interdependence: Migrant Labourers, Ethnic Chinese and Alien Wives", in Samuel C.Y. Ku, ed., *Southeast Asia in the New Century: An Asian Perspective* (Kaohsiung, Taiwan: National Sun Yat-Sen University Press, 2002), pp. 83–124.
7. Kuo-hsiung Lee, "The Republic of China and Southeast Asia: More Than Economy", in Yu San Wang, ed., *Foreign Policy of the Republic of China on Taiwan* (New York, Westport and London: Praeger Publishers, 1990), p. 99.
8. C.Y. Ku, *Taiwan's Political and Economic Relations with Southeast Asia: Favorable and Unfavorable Environment in the Development of Complex Interdependence* (Taipei: Fengyun Forum Publisher, 1998) (in Chinese), p. 122.
9. Ibid., pp. 122–23.
10. Information provided by Department of East Asian and Pacific Affairs, Ministry of Foreign Affairs, Taipei, January 2000.
11. *ROC Foreign Policy Yearbook* (Ministry of Foreign Affairs, Taipei), various years.
12. *ROC Foreign Policy Yearbook*, various years.
13. Chen Jie, "Human Rights: ASEAN's New Importance to China", *The Pacific Review* 6, no. 3 (1993): 227–37.
14. *Renmin ribao* (*People's Daily*), Beijing, 17 November 1998.
15. Ibid., 30 July 1998.
16. Interview of Parris Chang, Chairman, Committee on Foreign Relations, Legislative Yuan, Taipei, 22 December 2001.
17. Liao Wei-ping, "Annual Review and Prospect of MOFA's NGO Affairs

Committee", in Asia-Pacific Public Affairs Forum, ed., *Taiwan NGOs: Marching Towards the 21ˢᵗ Century* (Kaohsiung, Taiwan: Asia-Pacific Public Affairs Forum, September 2001) (in Chinese), p. 16.

18. For a comprehensive discussion of NGO diplomacy during the beginning period of the DPP government, see *Taipei Journal*, 27 October 2000.

19. Interview of Lo Chih-Cheng, Chairman, Research and Planning Board, Ministry of Foreign Affairs, Taipei, 17 December 2001.

20. Liao Wei-ping, op. cit., pp. 17–21.

21. *Taipei Times*, 21 August 2002.

22. Ibid., 11 September 2002.

23. *Zhongguo Shibao* [*China Times*], Taipei, 15 April 2002.

24. *Taipei Times*, 23 December 2002.

25. For the progress in China-ASEAN relations up during the recent years, see the websites of ASEAN and China's Ministry of Foreign Affairs.

26. *Zhongguo Shibao*, 6 March 2004.

27. *ASEAN Statistical Yearbook, 2003*, in ASEAN website.

28. *International Co-operation and Development Fund Annual Report*, various issues, in ICDF's website.

29. *Taipei Times*, 9 July 2002. Apart from the open shop of ICDF, Taipei also provides loans and grants more secretly from MOFA's confidential budget, but the recipients have long been diplomatic allies.

30. *ASEAN Statistical Yearbook, 2003*, in ASEAN website.

31. Website of The Council of Labour Affairs, Taipei.

32. For the DPP's transnational solidarity, see Chen Jie, "The Influences of Democracy on Taiwan's Foreign Policy", *Issues & Studies* 36, no. 4 (July/August 2000): 1–32.

33. Website of Taiwan's Presidential Palace. The figure of Southeast Asian spouses is from the Ministry of Home Affairs, reported in *Zhongguo Shibao*, 7 May 2004.

11

THE CHANGING POLITICAL ECONOMY OF TAIWAN'S AND CHINA'S RELATIONS WITH SOUTHEAST ASIA

A Comparative Perspective

Samuel C.Y. Ku

INTRODUCTION

China has been divided since October 1949 when the People's Republic of China (PRC) was established in Beijing, and the Republic of China (ROC), established on 10 October 1911, was forced to move its government to Taiwan. Since then both Chinese governments have been in conflict with one another over the representation of China around the world,[1] a key element for the survival of both governments. To develop and establish a close network of international relations then has become crucial for both the ROC and the PRC. The United States has been a major power since the end of World War I in 1918 and a global superpower since the end of World War II in 1945, and thus the United States has always played a crucial role in the ups and downs of Taiwan's and China's foreign relations in the world.

Things have changed a little, however, since the end of the Cold War in the late 1980s. While the United States continues to play a crucial role in the development of foreign relations for both Taiwan and China, Southeast

Asia has become another major arena for both Taiwan and China in competing with one another. That is to say that the governments on both sides of the Taiwan Strait have placed more and more emphasis on their relations with neighbouring countries in the region, thanks to the rising regionalism since the late 1980s. It is evident that a big China and a small Taiwan are not comparable in many aspects, including population, market, economic resources, and more importantly, international status. Interestingly, while China, having so many advantages, is advocating a strict policy in blocking Taiwan's international development, the island continues to play a relatively important role in the international community, particularly in the economic arena.

Accordingly, several questions are raised. Why is Taiwan able to survive under the shadow of China's political blockade and military threat? Without having formal diplomatic relations with any Southeast Asian nation, how does Taiwan develop its political economy with countries in the region? Is economics really meaningful in the development of Taiwan's and China's relations with Southeast Asia? While China's economy is rising due to expanding regionalism since the mid-1990s, can Taiwan continue to develop its substantial political economy with Southeast Asia in the years ahead? And, how have Taiwan and China changed their political economy with Southeast Asia in the last two decades?

This chapter uses the theory of interdependence to examine the changing trends in the development of Taiwan's and China's relations with Southeast Asia since the late 1980s. The foreign policies of both governments are to be examined, which are the foundations of the changing political economy between Southeast Asia and the governments on both sides of the Taiwan Strait. This chapter argues that Taiwan has changed its foreign policy from the so-called one-China policy to a flexible diplomacy, using multiple channels in developing the network of the island's international relations. While China still insists on the "One-China" policy, the PRC has also been emphasizing an economic role in its foreign relations, particularly since the mid-1990s.[2] That is to say that Taiwan, in order to reduce both the sensitivity and vulnerability of the island's diplomatic survival, emphasizes non-political ties with Southeast Asian nations, but China continues to stress political primacy, trying to block the possibility of Taiwan's foreign moves. While China's economic integration with Southeast Asia is getting stronger, a positive trend for China's rising economy, Taiwan will face the challenge of fostering its own economic growth and competition from China as well. While Taiwan continues to move towards democratization and democratic consolidation, a positive trend toward meeting the universal standards on human values, China will face the challenge of its own political democratization.

I. THE APPLICATION OF INTERDEPENDENCE THEORY

In their famous book — *Power and Interdependence*, Robert Keohane and Joseph Nye have proposed a theoretical framework on the development of foreign relations,[3] which is particularly relevant for small and minor countries like the ROC on Taiwan. The relationship of interdependence between two countries is not only one of multiple interactions and exchanges between the two; rather, these flows of interaction between the two countries could create the effects of constraints and costs. Interdependence among nations, however, does not necessarily mean a symmetrical one; it also can be an asymmetrical interdependent relationship. For Keohane and Nye, most interdependent relationships fall in between. Countries that are less dependent are more able to use one issue to influence other issues than those countries that are more dependent. Thus, the ability to use the relationship of interdependence is actually a source of power.[4]

Keohane and Nye have indicated that the use of power in a situation of interdependence is shaped by sensitivity and vulnerability. Sensitivity reflects the degree of survival capability prior to the change of a specific policy framework, whereas vulnerability has to do with the survival capability after the change of this policy framework.[5] Accordingly, sensitivity to interdependence involves the changes of various aspects of international affairs, including economics, politics, and social events, while the degree of vulnerability depends upon the flexibility of policy adjustments. The more capable a country is in facing the external challenges from policy changes, the lower its vulnerability. On the contrary, if a nation is not able to adjust its policy when external environment changes, this country's vulnerability will be high.

In the case of the development of foreign relations for both the PRC and the ROC, the two rival states have experienced both sensitivity and vulnerability since the early 1950s. For the ROC on Taiwan, for example, sensitivity and vulnerability have always been two key concerns and elements in the island's foreign relations. Due to the island's limited political and economic resources, Taiwan is always sensitive towards external political and economic changes, particularly towards the changes from China and the United States. Taiwan's vulnerability to the changing international environment was high prior to the mid-1970s, but Taiwan's vulnerability has been lowered as its economy has kept growing since the early 1980s. China's sensitivity towards any change in Taiwan's status has also been high, particularly towards America's alliance with Taiwan, although the United States established full diplomatic relations with the PRC in 1980. Like Taiwan, China's vulnerability to the international political economy began to change from a higher level to a lower one, but this change has come about since the early 1990s, however, because of its growing economic strength and resulting greater political influence.

Evidently, one thing that has changed is that both governments now have a lower degree of vulnerability, but one thing unchanged is that both Taiwan and China maintain a high sensitivity towards changes of each other. This means that both Taiwan and China are now more capable in managing international affairs. In addition to greater economic strength, the regimes on both sides of the Taiwan Strait are still antagonistic toward one another, politically and militarily. Leaving politics and military affairs aside, both governments are now promoting their economic relations with countries in Southeast Asia, trying to empower economic resources in exchange for political gains.

In addition to their interpretation of interdependence, Keohane and Nye have also brought about the idea of complex interdependence, showing a different perspective from the realist perspective on international relations. While realism stresses that the nation-state is the subject of international society, complex interdependence emphasizes the importance of multiple channels among nations, in which the nation-state, international organizations, multinational corporations and even civilian elites could play a role in international affairs. Keohane and Nye also point out that all issues are equally important when dealing with international affairs, that is, an absence of hierarchy among issues, as compared to the view of realists who promote security as a concern superior to all other issues. Finally, complex interdependence downgrades the role of military force in the management of international affairs, in contrast with the important role assigned to armed force by realism.[6]

Simply said, complex interdependence promotes the notion that all actors and sectors are able to play a role in international affairs. This pretty much reflects the regional environment in Southeast Asia after the end of the Cold War, which also relatively replicates the current situation of Taiwan's relations with Southeast Asia. While the PRC maintains formal diplomatic relations with all Southeast Asian countries, Taiwan does not have such a diplomatic relationship with any country in the region. This means that the ROC Government is not a recognized actor in the community of Southeast Asia, simply because Southeast Asian nations do not treat the ROC on Taiwan as a sovereign nation-state. However, Taiwan continues to maintain relatively substantive relations with these neighbouring countries, thanks to multiple channels between the two parties, an absence of hierarchy among issues in the region, and the minor role of military force in this part of the world.

II. THE CHANGING POLITICAL ECONOMY OF TAIWAN'S RELATIONS WITH SOUTHEAST ASIA

1. Taiwan's Weak Political Economy with Southeast Asia, Prior to 1987

Before 1975, the ROC Government had actually maintained formal diplomatic relations with several Southeast Asian countries, namely Thailand, South Vietnam, and the Philippines.[7] Since the admission of the PRC to the United Nations in October 1971, the diplomacy of the ROC Government began to suffer in global society. When South Vietnam was taken over by the North in April 1975 (the unification of Vietnam), the ROC Government's diplomacy in Southeast Asia suffered a major setback from having been forced to cut off its diplomatic exchanges with all countries in the region. Since then up till the mid-1980s, the ROC on Taiwan experienced a dark period of ten years in developing its diplomatic relations around the world in general and with Southeast Asian nations in particular. For example, the former Embassy of the ROC in the Philippines was renamed the Pacific Economic and Culture Centre in Manila in July 1975. The Embassy of the ROC in Thailand was also changed to the Office of the Representative of China Airlines in Thailand in September 1975 and to the Office of Far East Trade in Thailand in February 1980. In addition to diplomatic setbacks, Taiwan's economic relations with Southeast Asia were also very weak before the mid-1970s.

However, the name of the ROC has gradually been replaced by the name of Taiwan since the mid-1970s, partly because of the downgrade of the ROC's international status and partly because of the island's shining economic achievement since then. The volume of bilateral trade between Taiwan and Southeast Asia, for instance, expanded from US$1,172 million in 1976, to US$3,302 million in 1985 and to US$5,013 million in 1987, mostly in Taiwan's favour.[8] As for Taiwan's investment in Southeast Asia, the figure was very low in 1976 (roughly US$3 million), but this figure was expanded to US$35 million in 1987.[9] Clearly, Taiwan's economic performance has continued to attract attention from most Southeast Asian countries, despite the ROC's political status of a sovereign nation-state being not recognized in the region. This economic performance has presented a channel for Taiwan to survive in Southeast Asia in particular, and in the world in general.

2. The Rise of Taiwan's Political Economy with Southeast Asia, 1988–97

Taiwan's political economy with Southeast Asian countries began to be transformed in the late 1980s, thanks to Taiwan's continual expansion of economic ties with countries in the region. While Southeast Asian nations are becoming more dependent on Taiwan's economic resources, Taiwan is empowered to strengthen its relations with countries in the region. When the ROC's Executive Yuan (Cabinet) passed the "Operation Outline for Strengthening Economic and Trade Relations with Southeast Asia" in March 1994, the Southward Policy originated,[10] further strengthening Taiwan's substantive relations with Southeast Asia. According to the Operation Outline, Taiwan intended to achieve the following four objectives: (1) expanding two-way economic, trade and investment relations with Southeast Asian countries, (2) assisting Taiwan's enterprises in finding beneficial production and distribution bases in Southeast Asia and reducing the degree of trade dependence on mainland China, (3) helping Southeast Asian countries create job opportunities, raise people's annual incomes and encourage economic prosperity, and (4) participating in the activities of international economic organizations in Southeast Asia.

The Southward Policy entered its second stage from January 1997 to December 1999 as the Executive Yuan passed the "Practical Programme for Strengthening Economic and Trading Relations with Southeast Asia" in March 1997, with an attempt to achieve four objectives.[11] This time the Southward Policy was expanded to include other neighbouring countries in the region, including Laos, Myanmar, Australia, and New Zealand. Although the second wave of the Southward Policy, under the shadow of the Asian financial crisis, was not very successful, the ROC Government has shown its political will in influencing trends of Taiwan's multidimensional relations with Southeast Asia, going against the principles of free market.

Accordingly, Taiwan's economic relations with Southeast Asia significantly expanded during the ten years between 1988 and 1997. The volume in bilateral trade increased from US$7,073 million in 1988 to US$29,673 million in 1997, which was all in Taiwan's favour in each year during this decade.[12] Taiwan's investment in Southeast Asia was even more significant during these ten years. According to Taiwan's official statistics, Taiwan's investment in Southeast Asia in 1988 was roughly US$60 million, but this figure jumped to US$621.8 million in 1997.[13] However, these figures, based on those of local governments, were much larger; Taiwan's investment in Southeast Asia in 1997, for example, was US$4,849 million.[14] It is estimated that Taiwan's investments in Southeast Asia have created at least 50,000 job opportunities in the region.

In addition to the contribution of private enterprises, the ROC Government on Taiwan has extended a series of loans and grants to Southeast Asian governments, particularly Vietnam, Indonesia, and the Philippines. In May 1993, for example, the ROC Government issued a loan of US$30 million to Vietnam for the construction of the No. 5 Road, whereas the Philippines obtained two loans (nearly US$42 million in all) for the development of the Subic Bay Industrial Park in 1993 and 1995.[15] Taiwan has also dispatched agricultural and technical teams to Indonesia and Thailand, helping local farmers on agricultural reforms, and thus, local farmers have greatly increased production in the crops they plant. This project has given Taiwan a good reputation among the two governments and local citizens in these two countries.

Southeast Asian countries also benefit from sending immigrant labour to Taiwan. Since 1994, the ROC Government on Taiwan began to allow foreign labour on the island, and almost all of these foreign workers are from Southeast Asian countries, including Indonesia, the Philippines, Thailand, and Vietnam (since 1999).[16] When this policy was first introduced in 1994, for example, 151,989 workers from Southeast Asia were allowed to work in Taiwan, but this figure almost doubled in the year 1999. The number of foreign workers in Taiwan reached its peak at 326,515 in 2000, and since then it has gradually declined to 303,684 in 2002. Up to the end of 2002, Thai workers (111,538) were ranked the highest in the number of Taiwan's foreign workers, followed by Indonesian workers (93,212) and Philippine workers (69,426).[17] These foreign workers take their earnings home at the end of their employment, which has contributed to the economies of their motherlands.

Apparently, in the asymmetrical relationship of interdependence between Taiwan and Southeast Asia, the latter is more dependent on the former, thus empowering Taiwan to improve its substantive relations with Southeast Asia, particularly in the political realm. Taiwan is one of the few countries around the world that is successful in using its economic resources in exchange for political gains.[18] For instance, the names of all of Taiwan's Offices in Southeast Asia have changed from ambiguous ones to new names under the title of

Taipei, the capital city of the ROC. In the Philippines, Taiwan's Pacific Economic and Culture Centre was renamed the Taipei Economic and Cultural Office in the Philippines in December 1989, while Taiwan's Office in Indonesia was changed from the Chinese Chamber of Commerce to the Office of Taipei Economic and Trade Representative in October 1989. The new names of Taiwan's Offices in Southeast Asia are politically significant mainly because they imply that Taiwan's political status in the region has been upgraded and the treatment of Taiwan's officials in Southeast Asia has been promoted to a higher level similar to those of officials from international governmental organizations like Asia-Pacific Economic Co-operation (APEC).[19]

The upgrading of the status of Taiwan's Offices in Southeast Asia is just one example. Taiwan's high-level government officials were also frequently invited to visit Southeast Asia during the ten years from 1988 to 1997. In February 1994, for example, former President Lee Teng-hui visited the Philippines, Indonesia, and Thailand, and held meetings with leaders of these three Southeast Asian countries. Although this visit was under the name of vacation diplomacy, this was the first time that the ROC president paid a visit to countries without the exchanges of diplomatic recognition. In addition, former Vice President Lien Chan, former Premier Vincent Hsiew and other ministers in the cabinet also had visited countries in Southeast Asia in the 1990s, and some of them had even visited Southeast Asia several times.[20] Similarly, high-level officials from Southeast Asia were also frequently invited to visit Taiwan during the 1990s. Taking former Indonesian President B.J. Habibie as an example, we find that when Habibie was State Minister for Research and Technology, he was invited to visit Taiwan three times between 1991 and 1996.

One more indicator of Taiwan's improving relations with Southeast Asia is the international agreements signed between Taiwan and its counterparts in the region. Theoretically speaking, the signing of agreements among nation-states implies the practice of the sovereignty they represent. Taiwan does not conduct formal diplomatic exchanges with Southeast Asia, meaning Taiwan would not have the opportunity to sign official agreements with countries in the region. Practically speaking, however, Taiwan has gone beyond the boundary of formal diplomatic relationships. For example, Taiwan signed at least eight agreements with the Philippines during the 1990s, including those agreements and memorandums on Promotion and Protection of Investment, Aviation, Fishing and Agricultural Co-operation, Customs Co-operation, Science and Technology Co-operation, Avoiding Double Taxation, and so on. Taiwan also signed similar agreements and memorandums with other Southeast Asian countries during the same period of time.

In short, Taiwan's economic resources have significantly helped the island's substantive relations with Southeast Asia since the late 1980s. Evidently, economic ties were meaningful and, to some extent, successful in upgrading Taiwan's political status in the region, making the island more capable of surviving in the region as well as around the world.

3. Taiwan's Declining Political Economy with Southeast Asia since 1997

Taiwan's political economy with Southeast Asia has, since 1997, gradually declined, however, in spite of the extension of the Southward Policy from October 2000 to December 2003.[21] This development was shaped by two factors. The first one is external, that is, change in the regional political economy, whereas the other one is domestic, that is, the changing political economy in Taiwan.

Changes in the political economy in the region took place with the outbreak of the Asian financial crisis that struck in mid-1997, which seriously hit most countries in Southeast Asia, including Malaysia, Thailand, Indonesia, Vietnam, the Philippines, and even Singapore. Southeast Asia was regarded as an investment paradise during the years from the mid-1980s to the mid-1990s. Due to the rising economic openness in the region, many Southeast Asian countries relaxed financial controls, designated related policies and legislation to encourage foreign investment, and thus their markets were opened up to the world. Taiwan investors, following in the footsteps of Japanese businessmen, entered Southeast Asia and became one of the leading group of investors in the region. During the ten golden years of foreign investment, Southeast Asian countries did progress in the area of public infrastructure and private wealth.

When development opportunities arise, corruption follows in Southeast Asia where transparency and legal institutions are not well established.[22] As key foreign investors desired not to play money politics with government officials in Southeast Asia, they stopped extending loans and pouring money into Southeast Asia, and then the financial crisis took place. Suddenly, currencies greatly depreciated in most Southeast Asian countries, foreign investors were forced to move out, factories were closed, and inflation and unemployment rates were rising. Southeast Asian nations were then seeking help. At this crucial moment, while Western countries and the West-oriented financial organizations like the World Bank and International Monetary Fund hesitated to issue loans and assistance, China stood firmly to support Southeast Asian countries in two ways. One was to keep the

Chinese currency, the renminbi, stable, and the other was to extend loans to Southeast Asian countries.[23]

While Southeast Asia was hit hard by the Asian financial crisis, China was on the rise, particularly because of its stable currency, huge market, comparatively better quality of human resources, and resulting development opportunities. Accordingly, foreign investors moved from Southeast Asia to China, giving more potential to the rise of China's economic hegemony. But, this was not the case with Taiwan. Taiwan's economy performed quite well during the crisis, which stirred up feelings of admiration and a little bit of jealousy in Southeast Asian countries. Taiwan actually intended to issue loans to specific Southeast Asian countries through governmental mechanisms,[24] in exchange for political gains from Southeast Asia. Yet, Taiwan after all is not comparable to China. The Asian financial crisis set the stage for the rise of China in its strengthening relations with Southeast Asian countries, while Taiwan was not able to play a comparable role in the region.

The changing political economy in Taiwan was also played an important role in Taiwan's relations with Southeast Asia since 1997. Economically speaking, Taiwan's economy then, unlike that in the 1980s and 1990s, gradually declined during the turn of the century, mainly because of the impact of global economic recession and a domestic decision to terminate the construction of the Fourth Nuclear Power Plant in late 2000.[25] The island's economic growth rates, for example, went down, and they were even negative in the years of 2001 and 2002, the first time ever since the ROC Government moved its seat to Taiwan in late 1949. The unemployment rate kept rising, which was above five per cent in the years of 2001, 2002 and 2003, as compared with less than two per cent in the thirty golden years of Taiwan's rapid economic growth between 1970 to the mid-1990s.

Accordingly, Taiwan's trade with Southeast Asian countries did not perform well; the volumes of bilateral trade in the years of 1998(US$24,521 million)and 1999(US$28,770 million) were even lower than that in 1997(US$29,673 million).[26] This figure grew a little, however, in the next three years, that is, US$38,706 million in 2000, US$30,953 million in 2001 and US$32,476 million in 2002, but the degree of the growth of bilateral trade was not significant compared to that in the 1980s and 1990s. Significantly, however, Southeast Asia began to enjoy trade surpluses since 1998 in contrast to its trade deficits with Taiwan before 1997. For example, Southeast Asian countries enjoyed a favourable trade volume of US$780.6 million in 1998, and this figure expanded to US$1,043 million in 2000 and reduced a little to US$719.3 million in 2002.[27]

Taiwan's investment in Southeast Asia has declined even more greatly as compared to Taiwan's trade with countries in the region. Although Taiwan has maintained its position as one of the leading foreign investors in Southeast Asia, Taiwan's actual investment in Southeast Asia has greatly declined since 1998, from US$4,849 million in 1997 to US$1,420 million in 1998, to US$1,329 million in 2000, and to only US$692 million in 2002.[28] Apparently, Taiwan's economic strength has been eroding gradually in Southeast Asia, which certainly has had an impact on the bilateral relations between the parties.

Politically speaking, Taiwan experienced the first ever power turnover in May 2000 when Chen Shui-bian, the former opposition leader, was sworn in as the tenth President of the ROC on 20 May 2000. The Kuomintang (Nationalist Party) had ruled the ROC Government since its creation in October 1911, but now the Democratic Progressive Party (DDP), advocating Taiwan's eventual independence, replaced it as Taiwan's ruling party. While in power, the DPP is certainly using every means to achieve its political goal, in spite of the political sensitivity of the issue of Taiwan's independence. The new political agenda of the DPP has certainly had an impact domestically on Taiwan's citizens, who had been under the rule of the Kuomintang for more than five decades, as well as internationally on countries like the United States and those in Southeast Asia.

For Southeast Asian nations, stability and prosperity have become a common value since the end of the Cold War. While Taiwan's economic performance in the 1980s and 1990s was confirmed worldwide, Southeast Asian countries also would like to observe stable and peaceful development on the Taiwan Strait. Given the reality of having to maintain diplomatic ties with the PRC, Southeast Asian countries certainly support the so-called One-China policy, although policymakers in the region fully understand that Taiwan is not under the control of the mainland. Ruling leaders in Southeast Asia do not want Taiwan to provoke China by offending the sensitivities of the mainland on the issue of the One-China policy. In the second missile crisis on the Taiwan Strait in March 1996, for example, the then Malaysian Prime Minister Datuk Seri Mahathir Mohamad said in public that Taiwan should play the role of an economic entity, instead of a nation-state; if not, the island would cause some problems.[29] Therefore, Southeast Asian countries are quite alert towards Taiwan's diplomatic moves led by the DPP government since its coming to power in May 2000.

In addition to a different political ideology, the DDP also has a different approach to developing Taiwan's foreign relations. Due to the lack of ruling experience at the central government level, the DDP does not fully trust the civil servants in the Ministry of Foreign Affairs that have close ties with the Kuomintang; as a result, the DPP leaders in power desire to do things their own way. This then has become a significant weakness of the ruling DPP in its foreign policy, because the gap between officials of the Foreign Ministry and DPP leaders is widened. Very often this gap becomes a barrier to Taiwan's foreign relations with Southeast Asian countries. Vice President Annette Lu's visit to Indonesia in early September 2002 is one example. Due to the communication gap among officials of the Presidential Hall, Ministry of Foreign Affairs, and Indonesian officials, Lu's visit was not a successful one; she was not even allowed to visit Jakarta.[30] Worse than that, Indonesia's foreign minister, under the pressure of the PRC Embassy in Jakarta, even said in public that Indonesia does not recognize the government of Taiwan and does not welcome the visit of high-level government officials from Taiwan.[31] Lu's visit to Indonesia did not strengthen Taiwan's relations with the Muslim state, but rather damaged the existing linkages between the two countries.

The final change in the political economy in Taiwan was that the DPP did not win a majority of seats in the Legislative Yuan in the 2001 nationwide legislative elections, which has resulted in a series of disputes between the ruling DPP and the two major opposition parties, namely the Kuomintang and the People's First Party (PFP).[32] Political struggles have then kept breaking out between the ruling party and the opposition parties during the four years of the DPP's reign from 2000 to 2004. There was even a motion, for example, to impeach President Chen in late 2000 because of the termination of the construction of the Fourth Nuclear Power Plant.[33] As a result, the DPP government was not able to pay too much attention to foreign affairs. Taiwan's high-level officials rarely visited Southeast Asia between 2000 and 2004 and *vice versa*,[34] and fewer agreements were signed between the two sides. Since the incident involving Vice President Lu, Taiwan's relations with Southeast Asia seem to have fallen to a new low.[35]

III. THE CHANGING POLITICAL ECONOMY OF CHINA'S RELATIONS WITH SOUTHEAST ASIA

1. China's Weak Political Economy with Southeast Asia Prior to 1990

Due to its internal chaos in the 1960s and 1970s, China did not maintain a thriving political economy with most Southeast Asian countries prior to

1980. Instead, most countries in Southeast Asia kept a certain distance away from the PRC, even though some countries like Malaysia established full diplomatic relations with the PRC in 1975.[36] Even Indonesia, a country that had exchanged diplomatic recognition with the PRC in January 1950, became hostile toward the Chinese Communist regime since October 1967.[37] Vietnam, a previous diplomatic partner of the PRC before 1975, also had been antagonistic towards the mainland since 1976 when Vietnam began to lean towards former Soviet Union. Accordingly, Myanmar, Laos and Cambodia were the only Southeast Asian countries that maintained relatively good relations with the PRC before 1980.

Although China initiated the so-called Open Door policy in 1979, its political economy with Southeast Asia had not changed at all in the 1980s. China's internal political economy began to transform a little, however, since the early 1980s, mainly because of the incoming foreign investments. Politically, there was a little political reform in China at the township level by conducting direct elections for township delegates, whereas there were some infrastructure improvements and more business activities in economic terms. Even though China's international trade was expanding in the 1980s, it was not significant at all in the world picture. As the world was watching China's changing political economy, the Tiananmen Massacre on 4 June 1989 shocked the world, and, as a result, China's growing economy was damaged.

2. The Rise of China's Political Economy with Southeast Asia, 1990–96

Things have gradually changed since the beginning of the 1990s as China began to be politically stabilized and foreign investors began to return to the largest market in the world. China also started restoring its foreign relations with major countries as well as its neighbouring countries in Southeast Asia. While Taiwan began to strengthen its relations with Southeast Asia in the 1990s, China's efforts were not in vain. When the Fourteenth People's Congress was convened in Beijing in October 1992, strengthening China's economic relations with Southeast Asia was for the first time on the agenda of China's national economic policies, proposed by former Secretary General of the Chinese Communist Party Jiang Zemin. Since then, China has gradually expanded its economic linkages with countries in Southeast Asia, partly because of its growing economic strength in the region and partly because of China's continuing political stability.

China's trade with Southeast Asian nations was particularly significant. According to China's official statistics, the volume of the mainland's trade with Southeast Asia in 1990 was US$7,202 million, but this figure gradually expanded to US$9,020 million in 1992, to US$14,242 million in 1994, and to US$19,204 million in 1996.[38] Certainly, the volume of China's trade with each Southeast Asian country kept expanding simultaneously during the same period of time, but the significance is that the share of China's trade with Southeast Asia in China's entire trade picture also slightly increased in the first half of the 1990s. Taking China's trade with Indonesia as an example, one finds China's trade volume with Indonesia in 1990 (US$1,205 million) was 1.07 per cent of China's entire trade volume, but this proportion slightly increased to 1.279 per cent in 1996.[39] A similar trend is reflected in China's trade relations with Thailand, Vietnam, Malaysia, the Philippines and Singapore, demonstrating China's closer economic linkages with Southeast Asia.

One more thing to be noted is that the balance of bilateral trade between China and Southeast Asia in the early part of the 1990s was tilted in China's favour. According to the statistics of the ASEAN Secretariat, Southeast Asia's trade deficits with China were US$455.1 million in 1994, US$928.8 million in 1995, US$1,743.4 million in 1996, and US$4,314.9 million in 1997.[40] Compared with Taiwan's favourable trade relations with Southeast Asia in the first half of the 1990s, China's trade picture with Southeast Asia was similar, but China's expanding trade relations with the neighbouring countries in this region has proved its increasingly significant economic role in Southeast Asia. In other words, while Taiwan was strengthening its economic relations with Southeast Asia in the 1990s, China was gradually catching up, narrowing the economic gap between the two.

China's investment in Southeast Asia was not significant in the early 1990s. While Taiwan had became a leading foreign investor in Indonesia since the late 1980s, for example, China's investment in Indonesia did not even appear in Indonesia's official statistics. It was only in 1994 that the figure for China's actual investment in Indonesia began to be recorded in the report of the Investment Co-ordinating Board (BKPM), Indonesia's official agency in charge of foreign investment. China's actual investment in Indonesia in 1994 was only US$2.1 million, and this figure increased to US$68.4 million by December 1996.[41]

Nevertheless, China's economic relations with Southeast Asia were on the rise in the first half of the 1990s. Ruling leaders of Southeast Asian countries, like most other leaders around the world, certainly have noticed and, to some extent, confirmed China's changing political economy. China's political ties with Southeast Asia then have strengthened since the early 1990s; exchanges of visits among high-level government officials between the two sides have frequently taken place at the same time. For instance, Malaysia's former Prime Minister Mahathir Mohamad led a large delegation of 290 officials and businessmen on a state visit to China in June 1993, while Singapore's Senior Minister Lee Kuan Yew also led a large delegation of officials and businessmen to visit China in late August 1995. Similarly, high-level officials from China, including former President Jiang Zemin and former Premiers Li Peng and Zhu Rongji, were also invited to pay a state visit to most Southeast Asian nations during the first half of the 1990s.

3. China's Hegemonic Political Economy with Southeast Asia Since 1997

China's political economy with Southeast Asia has dramatically changed since the outbreak of the Asian financial crisis in mid-1997. Prior to the crisis, China was merely regarded as a huge market with great economic potential, but China has achieved economic hegemony in Asia after the crisis, not to mention China's traditional political dominance in the region. Compared to Taiwan's declining political economy with Southeast Asia since 1997, China's political economy with the region is even more significant.

Looking at bilateral trade relations, for example, the volume of Southeast Asia's trade with China has kept growing since the crisis, from US$22.6 billion in 1997 to US$45.8 billion in 1999 and to US$55.3 billion in 2001.[42] One thing significant is that the volume of Southeast Asia's trade with China has exceeded that of Southeast Asia's trade with Taiwan since 1999, and the gap between the two has kept on widening. In 1999, for instance, the gap between the two (that is, Southeast Asia-China trade vs. Southeast Asia-Taiwan trade) was US$17.1 million (US$45.8 billion and US$28.7 billion, respectively), and it was expanded to US$22.8 billion (US$61.5 billion and US$38.7 billion, respectively)in 2000 and to US$24.4 billion(US$55.3 billion and US$30.9 billion, respectively)in 2001.[43] Another significant development is that the year 1999 has also brought the beginning of Southeast Asia's favourable trade balance with China. In 1999, Southeast Asia enjoyed a surplus of US$7,064 million from its trade with China, and it was US$8,553 million in 2000 and US$7,719 million in 2001. Interestingly, Southeast Asia also began to enjoy a favourable trade balance with Taiwan since 1998, demonstrating Southeast Asia's greater dependence on markets in both Taiwan and China for its exports.

China's investment in Southeast Asia has greatly expanded since the mid-1990s, although it is not significant compared to that of Taiwan's investment in the region. According to the ASEAN Secretariat, China's investment in Southeast Asia was US$114.3 million in 1995, but this figure jumped to US$302.4 million in 1998 and US$135.8 million in 1999.[44] China's cumulative investment in ASEAN during the period from 1995 to 2001 was already US$821.36 million, similar to Sweden's investment in ASEAN during the same period of time.[45] Although this figure is not significant compared to that of Taiwan's, South Korea's and Hong Kong's investments in ASEAN, China's investment capability has shown great potential in ASEAN. It is anticipated that Southeast Asian nations will continue to attract more investments from China in the coming years.

China's tourism to Southeast Asia is another important indicator showing the mainland's economic hegemony in the region. Prior to 1994, the ASEAN Secretariat did not even record the number of visitors arriving from China in ASEAN nations, but things have dramatically changed since 1995 because of the increasing number of tourists from China going to Southeast Asia. Before 1998, the number of Chinese visitors to Southeast Asia was not significant compared to those of other major sources of tourists to the region. But since 1999, China has gone beyond Taiwan and become the second largest source of foreign visitors to Southeast Asia, next only to Japan. Significantly, the gap between China's visitors to ASEAN nations and Taiwan's tourists to ASEAN countries has been widening since 1999, that is, 179 million (1,919 million and 1,740 million, respectively) in 1999, 375 million (2,312 million and 1,937 million, respectively) in 2000, and 498 million (2,433 million and 1,935 million, respectively) in 2001.[46]

In addition, China has played a more hegemonic role in the regional economic development since 1997, leaving Japan behind. In February 1997, China and ASEAN, under the PRC's initiative and leadership, established a joint co-operation committee (Ten+1), which brought about closer economic ties between the two parties. They have held annual conferences since then. In November 2002 after the Ten+1 Summit, China and ASEAN signed a framework agreement on Free Trade Area (FTA) between the two, which outlined plans to set up an FTA between China and ASEAN in ten years. If this FTA is achieved in ten years, China and ASEAN will become the second largest FTA around the world, next only to the European Union. It is anticipated that ASEAN countries will continue to strengthen their economic integration with China as time goes on, and China's economic role in the economic development of ASEAN countries will also become more significant in the years ahead.

In order to quicken its economic recovery after the Asian financial crisis, ASEAN countries also held another summit with the three East Asian countries (that is, China, Japan and South Korea) in late 1997. This so-called Ten+3 conference has been held annually since then. In November 1999, during the third non-official ASEAN summit, Southeast Asian countries decided to establish a Free Trade Area in 2002 and to include China, Japan and South Korea inside its FTA. Apparently, the expansion of ASEAN's FTA helps to expand markets for the products of Southeast Asian countries, which is crucial to promoting economic development in the region. This is also a major reason for the changing structure of Southeast Asia's trade with China from previous deficits to current surpluses since 1999, as stated earlier in the chapter.

With these mounting economic resources, China is certainly empowered to strengthen its political ties with countries in Southeast Asia. While Taiwan and Southeast Asian nations have reduced the number of the exchanges of visits among high-level officials since the Asian financial crisis, China and Southeast Asian countries have continued to exchange the visits of high-level officials between both sides in recent years. Similarly, while Taiwan has slowed down in its signing of agreements with Southeast Asian countries, the mainland has kept expanding its ties with countries in the region since the turn of the century. While Southeast Asian countries were more dependent upon Taiwan's economic resources before the Asian financial crisis, Southeast Asia's asymmetrical dependence has transformed into one of leaning towards the mainland after the Asian financial crisis.

CONCLUSION

In the game of confrontation between the two governments on the Taiwan Strait, Southeast Asia has presented a new arena for the development of foreign relations for both the ROC and the PRC. During the era of the Cold War, political and military confrontation was the dominant philosophy for both Taiwan and the mainland in the development of their foreign relations, but now economics is the main theme for policymakers on both sides of the Taiwan Strait. Politics is vital, because it represents sovereignty and boundaries. Economics is probably even more important, because it goes beyond sovereignty and boundaries, thus providing multiple channels of interactions among nations.

Without having diplomatic relations with all the Southeast Asian nations, Taiwan's successful economy has demonstrated its capability in developing substantive relations with countries in the region through various channels, thanks to the minor role of military force and the absence of hierarchy among issues in the region since the end of the Cold War. Because of Taiwan's success in wielding the power of interdependence with Southeast Asian countries, Taiwan has transformed its high vulnerability in the 1950s, 1960s and 1970s to a low vulnerability since the mid-1980s. Also, Taiwan's democratic consolidation helps the island become more confident in winning support from major countries like the United States as well as countries in Southeast Asia. This means Taiwan is now more capable of managing foreign affairs in the region in particular and in the world in general, despite Taiwan's slightly declining political economy with Southeast Asia since 1997. However, the challenge now for the island is still economics. Regardless of mounting economic competition from China, Taiwan would continue to maintain its substantive ties with Southeast Asia should the island's economy keeps growing. On the contrary, Taiwan would be economically isolated should regional economic integration develop well in the near future.

As for the PRC, the mainland did not have a positive political economy with Southeast Asian nations in the 1950s, 1960s, and 1980s, in spite of China's traditional political hegemony in the region. China's vulnerability was also high in the first three decades after WWII, because of its confrontation with first the United States and later the former Soviet Union. However, the mainland's high vulnerability kept decreasing since the early 1990s as China's economy began to rise. The PRC has even become a political and economic hegemony since the outbreak of the Asian financial crisis as China's political economy with Southeast Asia has continued to expand since 1997. Although China's sensitivity towards the changes in Taiwan remains high, the Chinese Government seems to worry unnecessarily about the economic competition from Taiwan in the years ahead.

However, while Taiwan has become a consolidated democracy after a series of political reforms since the mid-1980s, China will face the challenge of political reforms from the pressure of its own citizens. China's economy seems to have great potential to grow, but China does not seem ready to face resulting political changes. Given some grave internal problems, for example, corruption, huge numbers of laid-off workers, the economic gap between the coastal provinces and inland provinces, etc., China would be in crisis should the world's largest market not be managed well. Economics will continue to remain a high priority in the agenda of China's future relations with Southeast Asia. China would continue to maintain its political and economic hegemony in Southeast Asia should regional economic integration develop well in the foreseeable future.

Notes

1. Since Lee Teng-hui's proposal of a special state-to-state relationship between Taiwan and China in September 1996, Taiwan has gradually placed more emphasis on its survival, dignity and sovereignty over the people of Taiwan only, no longer including the Chinese people on the mainland.

2. The main thrust of the One-China policy is that there is only but one China, and Taiwan is part of China. However, the PRC recently has revised the one-China policy a little, saying that there is one China and both Taiwan and the mainland are part of China.

3. Robert Keohane and Joseph Nye, *Power and Interdependence* (New York: Harper Collins Publishers, Second edition, 1989).

4. Ibid., p. 10.

5. Ibid., pp. 11–12.

6. Ibid., pp. 23–28.

7. The ROC Government also had a General Consul office in Kuala Lumpur before 1975, a semi-official relationship with the Malaysian Government.

8. In 1980, for instance, Taiwan enjoyed a surplus of US$222 million from its trade with Southeast Asia, and this figure was US$996 million in 1983, US$787 million in 1985, and US$1,734 million in 1987. (Bureau of Statistics, *Monthly Statistics on Exports and Imports in the Taiwan Area,* Taipei: Bureau of Statistics, Ministry of Finance, December 1988, pp. 13–22.)

9. These figures were approved by the ROC Government, but the actual investment figure was usually at least five times larger. (Investment Commission, *Statistics on Overseas Chinese & Foreign Investment,* Taipei: Investment Commission, Ministry of Economic Affairs, December 1992, pp. 51–52.)

10. The Southward Policy was originally aimed at six Southeast Asian countries, namely Singapore, Thailand, Indonesia, Malaysia, the Philippines, and Vietnam, but later it was expanded to all countries in Southeast Asia.

11. These four objectives are: (1) to encourage the China Import and Export Bank to increase loans for overseas investment, (2) to hold trade shows for Southeast Asian products in Taipei in order to increase bilateral trade, (3) to request that the central banks of the Southeast Asian countries give payment warranties so that large Taiwanese enterprises and state-sponsored enterprises can import more easily large amounts of raw materials from Southeast Asian, and (4) to ask the China Import and Export Bank to provide an insurance premium of NT$10 billion (roughly US$300 million) for Taiwanese licensed exporters' claims for losses while exporting to the Southeast Asian countries.

12. For instance, Taiwan enjoyed a favourable trade balance of US$3,044 million with Southeast Asia in 1990, and this figure was US$2,871 million in 1994 and US$2,875 million in 1997. (Bureau of Statistics, *Monthly Statistics on Exports and Imports in the Taiwan Area,* Taipei: Bureau of Statistics, Ministry of Finance, December 1988, pp. 13–22.)

13. These figures are for Southeast Asia, only including the six major countries in the region: Singapore, Malaysia, Indonesia, Thailand, the Philippines, and Vietnam. Investment Commission, *Statistics on Overseas Chinese & Foreign Investment* (Taipei: Investment Commission, Ministry of Economic Affairs, December 1998), pp. 41–42.

14. Local investment agencies are BOI in Thailand, MIDA in Malaysia, BOI in the Philippines, BKPM in Indonesia, EDB in Singapore, MPI in Vietnam and CIB in Cambodia.

15. Ministry of Foreign Affairs, the Republic of China.

16. There is a series of reports and analyses on Taiwan's immigration policy and the lives of foreign workers, including Westerners, in Taiwan. For details, see *Taiwan Review* 53, no. 10 (October 2003): 4–25.

17. The figures in this paragraph are from the Employment and Vocational Training Administration, Commission of Labour Affairs, the Republic of China. <http://163.29.140.81/htm1/htm/311040.htm>, 8 March 2004.

18. Samuel C.Y. Ku, "The Political Economy of Taiwan's Relations with Southeast Asia", *Contemporary Southeast Asia* 17, no. 3 (December 1995): 282–97.

19. The treatment of diplomats in foreign countries can be simply divided into three categories. The first category belongs to diplomats among friendly countries with the exchange of diplomatic recognition, who usually enjoy full diplomatic privileges (more than fifteen cases). Representatives and officials of international governmental organizations fall into the second category, who enjoy a little fewer diplomatic privileges than those in the first one. The third category belongs to officials in countries without diplomatic relations, who enjoy only a few diplomatic privileges. During the dark decade of Taiwan's diplomacy, the island's officials dispatched to most countries without diplomatic ties with the ROC only enjoyed a few diplomatic privileges (the third category). But now, with the improvement of foreign relations with these countries, Taiwan's officials can enjoy more diplomatic privileges, almost similar to those diplomats of countries with diplomatic exchanges (the second category).

20. Vincent Hsiew and Frederick Chien (former Minister of Foreign Affairs), for example, had visited Indonesia three times during the 1990s.

21. The ROC's Executive Yuan passed a resolution in October 2000 to continue carrying out of the Southward Policy.

22. According to Transparency International and the Hong Kong-based Political and Economic Risk Consultancy Ltd., Indonesia, Thailand, Vietnam and the Philippines have been on the list of either the most corrupt countries or those with poor governance in recent years.

23. China co-operated with the International Monetary Fund and the Asian Development Bank.

24. For example, Taiwan was about to issue a loan to Malaysia in early 1998 when former Deputy Prime Minister Anwar Ibahim paid a private visit to Taipei. But

later, due to Malaysia's political concerns, Taiwan's plan of assistance came to an end.

25. The Legislative Yuan has already approved the budget for the construction of the Fourth Nuclear Power Plant, but the ruling DPP terminated the project by an executive order in October 2000. The cost was tremendous, because Taiwan not only terminated numerous job opportunities but also lost its political and economic credibility in the world, particularly with multinational corporations.

26. Bureau of Statistics, *Monthly Statistics of Exports and Imports in the Taiwan Area* (Taipei: Bureau of Statistics, Ministry of Finance, the Republic of China, various years.)

27. Ibid.

28. These figures are from local governments, that is, Thailand's BOI, Malaysia's MIDA, Philippine's BOI, Indonesia's BKPM, Singapore's EDB, Vietnam's MPI, and Cambodia's CIB.

29. Dr. Mahathir's talks were delivered during the Asia-European Summit in early March 1996.

30. While intentionally skipping over the communication with Taiwan's Representatives in Jakarta, Vice President Annette Lu's visit was arranged by H.Z. Kong, a local Chinese Indonesian, who had close ties with high-level officials in the DPP government.

31. For details, see the *China Post*, Chinese edition, 2–5 September 2002.

32. The People's First Party was established by James Soong right after the 2000 presidential elections.

33. The opposition parties almost organized an impeachment movement against President Chen, but later the opposition leaders, for the sake of political stability in Taiwan, blocked the motion.

34. The most significant one was former Foreign Minister Tien Hong-mao's visit to Thailand in 2001.

35. In mid-January 2004, the DPP government dispatched a team to several Southeast Asian countries to promote Taiwan's plan for the first referendum on 20 March 2004, but the Thai Government declined the entry of this official team from Taiwan.

36. The Malaysian Government, for example, did not allow its citizens born in China or those having relatives in China to visit their motherland before 1980; this policy has now been discarded.

37. The Indonesian Communist Party initiated an abortive coup on the eve of 30 September 1965, and Indonesian Government officials believed the PRC was involved in the coup. (Justus van der Kroef, "The Sino-Indonesian Rupture", *the China Quarterly*, no. 33 (January–March 1968): 23.

38. China Statistical Publishing House, *China Foreign Economic Statistical Yearbook*, various years.

39. Ibid.

40. ASEAN Secretariat.
41. Investment Co-ordinating Board (BKPM), *Monthly Investment Report* (Jakarta: Investment Co-ordinating Board, various issues).
42. ASEAN Secretariat.
43. ASEAN Secretariat and Bureau of Statistics, *Monthly Statistics of Exports and Imports in the Taiwan Area* (Taipei: Bureau of Statistics, Ministry of Finance, the Republic of China, various years.)
44. ASEAN Secretariat: ASEAN FDI Database.
45. ASEAN Secretariat: ASEAN FDI Database.
46. ASEAN National Tourism Organizations <http://www.aseansec.org/7607.htm, 16 February 2004.

12

BALANCING, BANDWAGONING, OR HEDGING?:

Strategic and Security Patterns in Malaysia's Relations with China, 1981–2003

Joseph Chinyong Liow

INTRODUCTION

Over the past decade, there has been extensive interest in the field of security studies in Southeast Asia for the political and strategic ramifications of the emergence of China as a great power. The extant literature however, has focused primarily on the so-called "Strategic Triangle" of U.S.-China-Japan relations and how its dynamics might have an impact on the region.[1] Significantly fewer attempts have been made at looking at the policies of individual Southeast Asian states towards China. This chapter is an attempt to address this lacuna by studying Malaysia's foreign policy towards China over the past two decades of the Mahathir administration. This time period has been chosen for three reasons. First, there is a dearth of scholarship on Malaysia-China relations that covers the post-Cold War era. Second, it has been over the last twenty years that the academic and policy community in East Asia began to view China as a major power with the potential to affect the regional, if not global, distribution of power. This impression has certainly gained greater urgency in the post-Cold War years with certain circles in the International Relations community viewing China as the successor to the Soviet Union as the United State's main political and strategic adversary. Finally, the past twenty years has itself proven to be somewhat of a watershed in the study of Malaysian foreign policy, for it was during the Mahathir administration that the Malaysian Government took on a more active profile and role in international affairs, a development that is poignant to Malaysia-China relations.

Given that it has been suggested on several occasions that Southeast Asian states appear to be bandwagoning with China, this chapter begins by exploring some conceptual paradigms relevant to the understanding of Malaysia's posture towards China.[2] Following this, the study investigates Malaysia-China relations in terms of the continuity and change in its China policy over the last two decades, but focusing primarily on the post-Cold War era. In the main, the chapter contends that a discernible shift has taken place in Malaysia's China policy over the last decade, which in turn demonstrates how Kuala Lumpur is seeking to secure its own interests by navigating closer to Beijing.

THEORIZING HEDGE DIPLOMACY: A VIABLE POLICY FOR SMALL STATES?

International politics, the prominent International Relations theorist Kenneth Waltz once declared, is based on great powers.[3] Yet despite the claims of Waltzian "grand theorists", a literature on the role of small states in international politics has grown considerably.[4] Summarizing the vast scholarship on this topic would be beyond the scope of this chapter. What is being suggested however, is that the concept of bandwagoning, ironically enough extrapolated from the neorealist school of International Relations theory which Waltz himself was pioneer and progenitor, provides conceptual insights as to how smaller states can adopt policies to preserve and advance their interests vis-à-vis great powers. There are however, variations in bandwagoning behaviour that need to be illuminated.

A common belief among neorealists is that under conditions of power disparity, weaker states tend to coalesce with other like-states against the powerful to preserve security and try to affect either the distribution of power or in response to threat perceptions.[5] As the oft-quoted Kenneth Waltz articulated: "secondary states, if they are free to choose, flock to the weaker side; for it is the stronger side that threatens them".[6] This proposition was later refined by Stephen Walt, who argued that "states balance against threats rather than against power alone".[7] While Walt conceded that power was an important factor in assessing trends in military alignment, he introduces geographic proximity, offensive capabilities and perceived intentions in order to augment his argument that states do not balance against power *per se*, but threat.[8]

The logic of bandwagoning, on the other hand, suggests that states in such situations in fact align themselves with the stronger. Many neo-realist scholars further suggest that acts of bandwagoning, which they maintain are less frequent than balancing, are motivated by the assumptions that 1) the stronger state is the greater threat, and 2) weak states are too far behind the strong to be able to influence the distribution of power even if they chose to balance. Underlying these assumptions is the contention that weak states are helpless in the greater scheme of things (that is, great power rivalries in an anarchical international political environment), and hence are forced to look to strategies of bandwagoning with stronger, more threatening powers, as a security strategy. In other words, small states are coerced by systemic forces into bandwagoning.

Such a definition of bandwagoning however, may not capture the essence of the concept in terms of the policy options available to small states seeking to survive and thrive amidst great power rivalries in an anarchical society, nor does it recognize high degrees of variation in bandwagoning behaviour. Most notably, packaged and presented in the above manner, bandwagoning seems to spell the necessary compromising of the interests of smaller states that, while unwilling to do so, are nevertheless helpless to resist "systemic pressures" and hence bandwagon in the hope for the best. Yet there is another dimension to bandwagoning which sees small states adopt such behaviour proactively, not because of a sense of helplessness in the face of an acute threat, but rather as a carefully calculated and calibrated response in order to capitalize on great powers' need for friends and allies and advance their own political, economic, and strategic interests. This form of bandwagoning is motivated not by fear or threats, but by incentives and benefits. The work of Randall Schweller has expanded the conceptual scope of bandwagoning in such a manner.

Using Walt's position that bandwagoning is the diametrical opposite of balancing and pursued out of a sense of threat and limited options, Schweller's postulation of bandwagoning assigns greater scope for intent and initiative to "weak" states. Taking an analogy from domestic politics, Schweller suggests that "positive sanctions are the most effective means to induce bandwagoning behaviour, (and) states, like delegates at party conventions, are lured to the winning side by the promise of future rewards".[9] In further contrast to Walt,

Schweller also contends "the presence of a significant external threat ... is unnecessary for states to bandwagon".[10] Instead, the most important determinant of alignment decisions is "the compatibility of potential goals, not imbalances of power or threat".[11] Elsewhere, Schweller introduces another aspect of bandwagoning worth noting — he suggests that bandwagoning is often directed at challenging a prevailing international order. Here, he writes that "unlike defenders of the status quo, revolutionary states will not hesitate to offer other dissatisfied nations substantial gains in territory and prestige as a reward for helping them to create a new order".[12] In other words, revisionist powers that hope to challenge a preponderant international order or world power will look to potential bandwagoning allies to share in their crusade, providing incentives for such co-operation along the way. While the "profit" dimension of this aspect of bandwagoning may not be tangible (given the ideological character that such challenges usually assume), it still remains an appealing option for smaller states dissatisfied in one way or another with the current order to bandwagon with a rising major power that shares similar beliefs and reservations towards the inequality of the prevailing international order (whether it succeeds in revamping or transforming the prevailing order is, of course, another matter altogether).

The bandwagoning thesis that shifts attention to rewards (as opposed to constraints) as a motivating factor has been further refined by Kevin Sweeney and Paul Fritz.[13] In their study on great power alliances, Sweeney and Fritz observe that despite claims that bandwagoning behaviour is rare, "there are many examples from the past two centuries where a, or many, Great Power(s) opted to join the stronger side".[14] Moreover, they argue that what determines this mode of alliance formation is not the distribution of power, but rather the calculated interests of the weaker party(s).[15] Along with Schweller, what Sweeney and Fritz have done is to manoeuvre bandwagoning away from the structural confines of neorealism; to them, bandwagoning is no longer a systemic outcome of power preponderance but rather a policy choice of smaller states.

What is of further consequence in Sweeney and Fritz's appreciation of the factors that give rise to bandwagoning behaviour is their expansion of these factors beyond the military dimension. With theoretical roots in the literature on military alliances, it is not surprising that many theorists of bandwagoning focus on alliances and military capabilities. Hence, while scholars have differed over motivations, in the main the primary focus of the literature has been the act of bandwagoning as a military/strategic activity.[16] The taxonomy of bandwagoning however, need not be limited to purely military factors. Bandwagoning, and indeed balancing, can also be seen as non-military behaviour.[17] As Sweeney and Fritz observed as they introduced their argument that states bandwagon according to interests, "in considering state interests, we must include both security and non-security issues".[18] While their adoption of the concept of interest leaves them open to criticism given the ambiguity and vagary of that term itself, it does allow them to expand factors of consideration beyond the purely military dimension. This accords with post-Cold War trends, where new kinds of power configurations are being premised less on outright conquest of territory and more on economic and political preponderance. This has especial resonance in the Asia-Pacific, where analysts have noticed that China and the United States have been engaged in a carefully calibrated political, diplomatic, and ideological, as opposed to military, contest for favour and influence in the region.[19]

The previous point that the United States and China are currently engaged in political, diplomatic and ideological rivalry in East Asia draws attention to another feature of bandwagoning, where small states may actively bandwagon with both the preponderant as well as the rising power as they navigate an uncertain but stable strategic environment. Contrary to conventional neo-realist wisdom, pursuing closer relations with both preponderant and emerging powers are not mutually incompatible policies, and are particularly evident during strategic epochs of stability, when great power military conflict has not materialized. There are several premises to this contention. First, it accommodates the findings of theories of bandwagoning that allow small states to proactively engage great powers not out of fear or distress, but in pursuit of profit and in order to fulfil their own political, economic, and strategic interests in a low-risk environment. Second, particularly in a security environment such as the post-Cold War where new structures of relations are anticipated but have yet to result in strategic conflict, an important hedge against such uncertainty for a small state is the ability to court major powers without being committed to either party, in so doing safeguarding their interest should the security situation change for the worst. Hence, if Stephen David conceptualizes multiple-balancing or "omni-balancing" strategies as a viable policy option for small states in times of distress (that is, placating one source of threat to balance against another), than what is being proposed here is that during times of relative strategic calm, small states can practice hedge diplomacy premised on a strategy of "multiple bandwagoning".[20] As a variation of bandwagoning then, hedge diplomacy can be viewed as a move not only to avoid becoming a strategic pawn of great powers, but also to capitalize on economic, political, and diplomatic rivalry between great powers in a manner that furthers a small state's own interests and does not foreclose policy options.

Extrapolating from the extant theoretical literature thence, there are two key elements to the application of the concept of bandwagoning for present purposes. First, motivations for bandwagoning behaviour can arise from both a sense of insecurity, which is derived from a perception of an immediate threat, or from a state's calculated pursuit of interests. The latter is of particular interest in the context of more recent scholarship on the question of bandwagoning, which as the above discussion has shown, has identified that such behaviour has been more prevalent in international politics than initially thought. Moreover, by suggesting that a state can pursue bandwagoning policies under such conditions we can ascribe some measure of initiative to small or "weak" states, rather than accept wholesale the adage that international relations is about the politics between great powers and small states have to, as Thucydides once claimed, "suffer what they must". Second, indicators of bandwagoning behaviour need not necessarily be confined to military activities, but can pertain to policies in the economic, political, and diplomatic realms as well.

In sum, Walt's position that bandwagoning strategies are defensive and "worst-case" scenarios represent the extreme end of a bandwagoning spectrum, where small states have little choice, and their policy options and behaviour are dictated by the forces of an international system dictated by great powers. Schweller, along with Sweeney and Fritz, takes a more nuanced view that bandwagoning strategies can be consciously and deliberately chosen by small states for purposes of advancing their own goals and interests. To them, bandwagoning is not so much a function of systemic politics as it is a policy choice available to small states attempting to manipulate, rather than to be victimized by, great power politics. Finally, the notion of hedge diplomacy introduced here is located at the other end of the spectrum where bandwagoning-like policies towards a range of major powers are a conscious calculated choice of small states made not out of security concerns, but rather as a means to advance their own interests. In essence, while Walt's neo-realist reading of bandwagoning straightjackets small states and reduces their options to an act which is in truth that of capitulation, further down the spectrum one sees that there are other variations of bandwagoning behaviour that permit room for independent action and do not entail the acquiescing of small states to the will of great powers. It is the case here that hedge diplomacy best captures Malaysia's emerging strategy *vis-à-vis* China.

MALAYSIA'S CHINA POLICY: 1981–2003

By the time Mahathir Mohamad assumed the prime ministership of Malaysia in June 1981, Malaysia had already enjoyed seven years of normalized ties with the Peoples' Republic of China. Even so, there was little doubt that Kuala Lumpur still harboured much distrust towards Beijing, and this had been reflected succinctly in the extant scholarship on Malaysia's relations with China.[21] Some scholars have maintained that residual distrust continues to define Malaysian perceptions of China in the post-Cold War era.[22]

For most of the Cold War, the primary concern for Malaysian leaders was China's reluctance to categorically renounce all forms of support for the CPM (Communist Party of Malaya). These concerns were not mitigated by the normalization of ties in May 1974.[23] Consequently, at the outset of the Mahathir administration, the influential Malaysian Foreign Minister Ghazali Shafie articulated his government's position on China in the following manner:

> I would like to state very categorically ... that the Chinese global position is circumscribed and should not be construed to include a role by China as the sole restraining hand for the security of Southeast Asia. I say this with the firm conviction that China has dangerous ambitions of her own in the region which she has refused to renounce.[24]

While Malaysia's concern for China's support of a local communist insurgency and stewardship of the overseas ethnic Chinese community have dissipated by the end of the Cold War,[25] to some the China threat had merely morphed into an external threat:

> The Malaysian perception of China as a threat has however, over the last ten years, increasingly externalized to the point where the Chinese navy is currently considered as a serious, direct military threat in the South China Sea.[26]

While the commentator might have been overly pessimistic in his swift indictment of China, his observation is nevertheless noteworthy for its interpretation of Malaysian perceptions of China in the post-Cold War era.

Paradoxically, Malaysian policy circles have also been aware of the fact that an engagement policy towards China would be prudent in the wake of the end of the Cold War. In explaining this logic of engagement to the United States, former Malaysian Foreign Minister Abdullah Badawi commented:

> Close relations and co-operation between Malaysia and China would alleviate any attempt by China to resort to military action because that would also be detrimental to China ... If there is no co-operation, there is a possibility China may resort to military action (against Malaysia) or cause a conflict here because it will not lose anything. We want to create a choice (for China).[27]

At first glance, the vacillation in Malaysia's policy towards China would be enigmatically obvious. On closer inspection however, one can identify subtle shifts in Malaysia's policy towards China that, while perhaps merely symbolic at the time, nevertheless demonstrate a gradual shift in Malaysia's posture towards China.

BILATERAL TRADE

As with most states in the region that were cautiously looking for opportunities to engage China in order to ascertain or mitigate Beijing's political and strategic ambitions in the region, the logic of economics and trade underscored Malaysia's initial approaches to Beijing.

Bilateral trade between Malaysia and China over the past two decades however, did not begin auspiciously as far as the former was concerned. In fact, for much of the 1980s, much of the trade was one-way, as Malaysian products experienced difficulties penetrating the Chinese market. Since the early 1990s, Malaysia-China trade has increased significantly, and the economic benefits of Kuala Lumpur's engagement policy have begun to have a substantial positive impact for the Malaysian economy.[28] More importantly, the trade balance with China that was so unfavourable towards Malaysia in the 1980s has begun to turn to Malaysia's advantage.

In June 1993, Mahathir led a 290-strong delegation to Beijing, and secured the signing of thirty-six MOUs worth RM$8 billion.[29] A subsequent visit by then Deputy Prime Minister Anwar Ibrahim in September 1994 bagged more joint-venture projects.[30] Trade statistics further verified this upturn in bilateral economic relations. Bilateral trade jumped from US$910 million in 1988 to US$2.2 billion in 1994, and China had become Malaysia's tenth largest trading partner. The economic benefits of the relationship were taken several steps further with Mahathir's visit to China in August 1999. An outcome of the visit was China's signing of a Memorandum of Understanding in which it committed investments into a pulp and paper plant in Sabah, the cost of which was US$1 billion. At that time, this proved to be China's largest investment outside of the mainland. Earlier, in May 1999, Malaysian Foreign Minister Syed Hamid Albar's visit to China resulted in the signing of a Joint Statement on Future Bilateral Co-operation with his Chinese counterpart, Tang Jiaxuan. This document blueprinted the future of bilateral relations based on a wide scope of co-operation, from economics to education to defence, and was at the time arguably the most comprehensive agreement signed between China and a Southeast Asian country.[31]

Trade and investment between Malaysia and China has continued to increase in more recent times. In 1999, bilateral trade stood at US$4.264

billion, which was already a twenty-fold increase since bilateral ties were established in 1974. By 2003, this figure had jumped to US$18.04 billion.[32] Of equal significance was the fact that in 2003 Malaysia had overtaken Singapore (long believed to enjoy a foothold on the Chinese economy given its substantial ethnic Chinese population and economic wealth) as China's largest trading partner within ASEAN.

POLITICAL COLLABORATION

International political developments since the end of the Cold War have witnessed a remarkable convergence of the worldviews of both Malaysian and Chinese leaders. The Mahathir administration was a regular critic of prevailing Western-dominated international political and economic orders. The fact that China shares some of these grouses has meant that a close relationship with China based on this shared opposition to the current international order enhances Kuala Lumpur's interests and international status. Indeed, the words and deeds of Malaysian leaders demonstrate the utility of courting China. While in 1985, Prime Minister Mahathir spoke of how "much more needs to be done before common ground is reached (on issues of common concern)"; in 1990 he stated candidly that "mutual confidence and trust", terms never before used to describe Malaysia's relations with China, had enabled both countries to take a "common stand" on a host of international and bilateral issues.[33] Where once Chinese and Malaysian leaders diverged considerably in their worldviews, the end of the Cold War and the heralding of a new international order injected evident coherence. Both countries openly identified with and supported each other on issues of democracy, human rights and the increasingly important role of the Third World in international politics in opposition to Western and American dominance. Since the early 1990s, a whole range of bilateral initiatives such as the Malaysia-China Friendship Society, the Bilateral Meeting between Foreign Officials of Malaysia and China and the Beijing Dialogue on Malaysia and China Partnership has fostered this congruence in perspectives.

Together with this wide range of bilateral institutions, the leaders of both countries have also substantially increased the number of high-level contacts in the post-Cold War period. According to Mahathir himself:

> In the absence of satisfactory solutions to these issues, close scrutiny appears to be given to our relations only during high-level visits such as this. Instead of becoming a continuous process, the development of our relations has hinged upon the visits we make.[34]

To that extent, the increase in visits in the 1990s should not go unnoticed, as they have in fact become part of this "continuous process". Mahathir's first visit to Beijing, in 1985, was also his only visit in the 1980s. Subsequently, after 1989, he made four other visits (three of them over a four-year period) in June 1993, May 1994, August 1996 and August 1999. Chinese leaders too, have reciprocated with more visits in the 1990s. This trend alone is revealing of the improved complexion of bilateral relations.[35]

Through these bilateral linkages, both parties further refined their support for each other's international political initiatives such as Malaysia's proposal to establish an EAEC,[36] China's entry into the WTO,[37] the creation of a new international financial order,[38] and collective proposals for the restructuring of the UN Security Council.[39] This agenda against the prevailing order heightened in the wake of the regional financial crisis of 1997–98, which had brought Malaysia's economy to a standstill and constituted a fundamental threat to the economic security of the nation. To that effect, Mahathir openly displayed appreciation of China's unilateral decision not to devalue their currency, whilst being highly critical of American and European reluctance to assist the stricken Asian economies, and their continued nonchalance toward the activities of their hedge fund traders. In a move with symbolic undertones, Chinese President Jiang Zemin met with Mahathir on the sidelines of the 1998 APEC Summit in Kuala Lumpur, after the latter was snubbed by the leaders of the United States, Canada and Australia.[40]

Events following September 11 have fostered further coherence between the international postures of China and Malaysia, strengthening their political relations. Malaysia's opposition to American hegemony and unilateralism has resonated with Chinese strategic and political concerns, and Beijing has reciprocated by supporting Malaysia's vocal leadership of international opposition to Washington's conduct of the war on terror. In the main, China's support of Malaysia's opposition to American and Western cultural, political, and economic dominance has undoubtedly augmented Kuala Lumpur's role and status as a Third World leader. Corralling with China on such terms clearly allows Malaysia to "increase, not just preserve, their core values and to improve their position in the system".[41]

POLITICS ON THE DOMESTIC FRONT

Close co-operation with China has not only brought about broader international political benefits, but has also paid dividends on the domestic front for the Mahathir administration. With a substantial ethnic Chinese population that remains protective of its cultural identity, close relations with

China has had the effect of codifying the support of this community for the ruling *Barisan Nasional* coalition. It certainly was no coincidence that Mahathir's last visit to China as prime minister took place in August 1999, three months before a major general election that eventually saw the ruling coalition retain its position on the back of Chinese electoral support.[42]

A month before taking over at the helm of the Malaysian Government in October 2003, then Deputy Prime Minister Abdullah Badawi visited Beijing and reaffirmed that China was not viewed as a threat in Malaysia.[43] That visit proved timely once again, for the ruling Malaysian Government was widely expected to hold general elections in the first half of 2004.

The discussion thus far has demonstrated the substantial changes that have occurred in the political and economic realms of Malaysia-China relations. While the seeds for the convergence of political and economic interests was sewn in the 1980s, it was really after the Cold War that they began to discernibly bear fruit. That said, these developments, though significant, on their own still remain insufficient indicators of a perceptible shift in Malaysian security perceptions of China. To ascertain this, one must inevitably discuss the China factor in the context of Malaysia's emerging post-Cold War strategic concerns.

THE SOUTH CHINA SEA STRATEGIC IMPERATIVE

It should come as no surprise that Malaysian policymakers factor China into their security policy equation. The extent to which China is considered a threat, and a greater one compared to Malaysia's other neighbours, however, is something that as yet cannot be convincingly determined. Certainly, if China continues to be perceived as a "serious, direct military threat in the South China Sea" as one observer suggested in 1991,[44] then Malaysia's strategies of dealing with this "threat" would be of both academic and policy interest.

According to some analysts, security planners in Kuala Lumpur are circumspect regarding China's role and interpretation of the geopolitics and regional order of the Asia-Pacific, fearing that China's territorial claims in the South China Sea are aimed at transforming it into an "internal lake".[45] Indeed, the South China Sea case seems to provide the clearest evidence of Malaysian, and Southeast Asian, apprehension toward China's intentions. To that end, others have noted that "the prevailing sentiment seems to be that China is 'the threat' to the *status quo*, peace and stability of the South China Sea region". This view was justified with a quote from Zakaria Ahmad, a Malaysian strategic analyst: "Don't forget, they (the Chinese) have a track record of using force in that part of the world".[46] Later, after the 1995

Mischief Reef incident, it was noted that for Malaysia, "it is China which is perceived as the likely belligerent at some point in the future".[47]

While China has no doubt developed a track record of aggression in the South China Sea, several issues need to be taken into consideration. Chinese aggression has primarily been targetted at Vietnam, with which it has a long history of animosity.[48] As for Malaysia, it must be recognized that China's response to Kuala Lumpur's counter claims have been much more benign:

> When the Vietnamese Army chief-of-staff and the vice-president of the Council of State made inspection tours of the Vietnamese-held Spratlys in May 1989, Beijing sternly condemned this "flagrant provocation" of China's territorial integrity. However, it remained silent over the visit to the Malaysian-occupied atoll of Terumbu Layang-Layang by Malaysia's Sultan Azlan Shah and Queen Bainun in May 1992. China had launched a strong protest against Vietnam's "illegal" construction of a "Science, technology and economic zone" on some Spratly islands and reefs in mid-1989, but when Malaysia started to develop Terumbu Layang-Layang into a tourist resort in 1991 … China's reaction was conspicuously moderate.[49]

Furthermore, in a leaked confidential speech to the PLA general staff, President Yang Shangkun stated that China was prepared to use military means to settle its South China Sea disputes with Vietnam. No mention of other claimants was made in the text.[50]

On their part, Malaysian leaders, at least in declaratory terms, have categorically denied that China is a threat. Moreover, they have often come to Beijing's defence repeatedly by arguing that China had never made incursions into foreign soil. Reflecting this, Mahathir articulated in 1994 that "… historically China has not exhibited any consistent policy of territorial acquisitiveness … full invasion and colonization has not been a feature of Chinese history".[51] Paradoxically, Mahathir himself had earlier declared in 1984 that Malaysian policymakers warned that a strong China could well "revert" to hegemonic policies, a move which, "from a historical perspective", was a concern for Southeast Asia.[52] The change in language and tone here may perhaps be telling of a more substantive shift in perception. Such a perspective was further reinforced by Syed Hamid Albar, who in his capacity as defence minister in 1996 observed, in response to a question on China's intentions in the Spratly Islands, that:

> China's claims in the South China Sea have been looked upon by extra-regional powers as the greatest destabilizing factor in Southeast Asia and have provided the seemingly irrefutable evidence for their China threat

theory. But we in Southeast Asia generally feel that China has so far been a sober and responsible regional player. Its advocacy of joint exploitation of South China Sea resources with other regional states and its recent indication of readiness to abide by the international law in resolving the Spratlys issue have made us feel that it wants to co-exist in peace with its neighbours.[53]

Of course, it is possible for one to attribute such comments from Malaysian leaders to diplomatic rhetoric. Yet even so, one should be kept in mind that traditionally, Malaysian leaders such as Tunku Abdul Rahman, Ghazali Shafie and Mahathir Mohamad have had no qualms publicly proscribing their Chinese counterparts and drawing public attention to the China "threat" if it indeed accorded with their perceptions.[54] Again, it should be noted that early in his tenure, Prime Minister Mahathir was himself a firm believer in the China threat theory, and often made this known publicly. To the extent that this is true, such statements are telling indicators of changing Malaysian attitudes toward China. Of equal significance is the fact that opinions of forthcoming Malaysian analysts themselves seem to have also demonstrated a discernible shifted since the mid-1990s. For instance, J.N. Mak noted in 1991 that "no matter what twists and turns Sino-Malaysian relations may take, it can be argued that Malaysia has, and will in the forseeable future, regard China as its greatest threat in one form or another".[55] By 1996, Mak, along with B.A. Hamzah, had somewhat conceded to a Malaysian strategic *volte face vis-à-vis* China when they acknowledged that "China is no longer regarded as a direct and immediate threat".[56]

Another notable, if subtle, shift in Malaysia's posture towards China over the South China Sea pertained to their position on multilateral approaches to settling the disputes over the islands. In 1995, when China was discovered to be building structures on Mischief Reef, Malaysia's immediate response was to partake in the consolidated concern expressed by ASEAN. Reflecting Malaysian views at that time, Noordin Sopiee, Director General of the government-linked Institute of Strategic and International Studies (ISIS) in Kuala Lumpur, acknowledged that the February 1995 discovery of Chinese structures on Mischief Reef "had a very substantial impact on how we (ASEAN) look at China".[57] Subsequently, ASEAN's response calling for restraint was seen by Jawhar Hassan (Deputy Director General of ISIS) as "a collective response which in no uncertain terms will register with China that there are certain rules of the game".[58] On hindsight however, it has become evident that this may well have been more a knee-jerk reaction to the suddenness of the Mischief Reef incident rather than the crystallization of a united ASEAN stand in response to China.[59]

Since the Mischief Reef incident and ASEAN's alarmist response, it has become clear that its members harbour different opinions as to how to confront China over the South China Sea issue. Some, like the Philippines, called for ASEAN to take a more proactive position against China, whereas other non-claimant countries preferred to take a lower profiled and more cautious approach. As for Malaysia, contrary to conventional wisdom, they have since the Mischief Reef episode demonstrated a decided preference to primarily engage China on bilateral terms.

Malaysia has clearly preferred and pursued bilateral engagement of China in general, and on the South China Sea in particular, even as they continue paying lip-service to the cause of multilateralism.[60] At Track II (non-governmental) level discussions on the South China Sea, it has been observed that Malaysian representatives have regularly stonewalled the multilateral initiatives of ASEAN counterparts.[61] At Track I (official) level, Malaysia even rejected proposals for multilateral discussions of the South China Sea issue at the 1999 ASEAN Ministerial Meeting in Singapore. Then Malaysian Foreign Minister Syed Hamid Albar, in a move that surprised many, categorically rejected Filipino requests to discuss recent South China Sea incursions at the ASEAN Regional Forum (a regional security dialogue set up precisely to deal with security issues such as South China Sea contingencies), opining instead that it was "a bilateral issue to be discussed bilaterally".[62] In doing so, Syed Hamid had echoed a Chinese statement made prior to the meeting:

> The South China Sea issue should be settled through bilateral negotiations … It would only make a bilateral issue of dispute more complicated if the issue is internationalized. Therefore, China holds that the ARF is not an appropriate occasion to discuss the South China Sea issue.[63]

Much in the same vein, Kuala Lumpur's subsequent rejection of a proposed code of conduct for the South China Sea mirrored Chinese attitudes toward the issue.[64] Malaysia's nonchalant attitude toward ASEAN and the ARF on this matter was not lost to fellow ASEAN members, especially the Philippines, whose Foreign Secretary Domingo Siazon disclosed: "among the ASEAN members, it is really just Malaysia now that has some second thoughts".[65]

This difference of opinion between two of ASEAN's founder-members carried important implications. First, Syed Hamid's response was nothing less than an endorsement of China's long-held preference for bilateral approaches to the South China Sea problem. Second, Malaysia's response was also a conspicuous contradiction of ASEAN's common stand on the importance of multilateral dialogue with China. Third, in making this statement, Syed Hamid had in fact publicly slighted a fellow ASEAN member, an act that was uncharacteristic of ASEAN-style diplomacy. Indeed, this entire episode has led many observers, including those from within ASEAN, to speculate that Malaysia and China were "cutting a deal".[66] In a move that further hinted of a collusion of sorts, it was Malaysia that proposed at the July 2002 ASEAN Ministerial Meeting an ASEAN-China political declaration in place of a Code of Conduct.[67] This was significant as Beijing had until then staunchly resisted any attempt to draw China into signing a Code of Conduct on the South China Sea. Indeed, it was this initiative that set the stage for China's subsequent signature on the Declaration on the Conduct of Parties in the South China Sea and accession to the ASEAN Treaty of Amity and Co-operation at the Phnom Penh Summit in November 2002. In sum, it can be seen that recent developments over the South China Sea clearly calls into question previous opinions that Malaysian policymakers were opting for the multilateral approach in dealing with China.[68]

The case of the South China Sea demonstrates the "profit-seeking" dimension of Malaysia's recent policies towards China. With China insisting on its unquestioned sovereignty over the Spratly islands, Malaysian policymakers will be keenly aware of the fact that only three options exist for them as far as their interests in the South China Sea are concerned — they can either abandon their claims, prepare to confront the Chinese (either unilaterally or multilaterally) politically, diplomatically, and militarily should the latter chose to press their claims, or align themselves with Beijing in the hope that the latter will be less adamant about its claims in future *vis-à-vis* Malaysia.

For reasons of sovereignty and national pride, the first option, Kuala Lumpur's abandonment of their claims, is not likely to materialize. As far as the second option is concerned, the chances of accruing political and/or military success from a confrontation with China are also slim. Given that some ASEAN members are themselves involved as counter-claimants, the chances of a united ASEAN bringing any significant political weight to bear against China on the issue is highly unlikely. Certainly, it can be said that China's recent accommodation of ASEAN-style multilateralism had less to do with successful ASEAN lobbying as it did a change in China's regional strategy. Much in the same vein, without the "balancing potential" of another major power, the potential of a successful collective ASEAN military response in the event of Chinese aggression is also remote at best. Even then, such conjuncture pre-supposes that ASEAN would be able to come together as a military alliance in the first place. Simply put then, given China's unwavering claims of ownership to the islands, should China decide to pursue their claims aggressively in future, the option of military or political confrontation would likely entail substantial costs for Kuala Lumpur, probably more than it can or is willing to bear.

In view of such circumstances, the prudent option for Malaysia's interests may well be to draw closer to China now, when the opportunity avails and the major power bandwagon is still responsive. Indeed, Malaysia's most recent reactions to the developments in the South China Sea seem to indicate that this is precisely the strategy Kuala Lumpur is pursuing *vis-à-vis* China in the hope of securing its long-term interests.

MILITARY MODERNIZATION IN CHINA: RE-READING MALAYSIA'S RECENT RESPONSES

Perhaps the most controversial dimension of Malaysia's relations with China is its position on Beijing's increased military capacities. Keeping in mind a suggestion made in a detailed study of the politics of the South China Sea counter-claims that "maritime disputes are primary determinants in defence priorities" of the counter-claimants, another clear indicator of Malaysian perspectives on China would be their response to China's emerging strategic maritime capabilities.[69] Extrapolating from this, Malaysian threat perceptions, insofar as they exist (and if neorealist forecasts are anything to go by), should conceivably be expressed in an increase in maritime capabilities and a naval buildup.

China's military modernization programmes have long been recognized as a potential source of instability given the ambiguity of Beijing's strategic ambitions. Certainly, scholars such as Mak and Acharya have been cognizant of this, and have in their writings suggested that this military buildup has intensified Malaysian concerns.

No doubt, China is larger, and its military power far greater in quantitative terms than Malaysia, or the rest of Southeast Asia, for that matter. Consequently, if China's southward expansion was deemed a matter of considerable concern, Malaysian "internal balancing" in the form of a naval build-up would be an obvious response (as predicted by neo-realist theory), and likewise a clear demonstration of Malaysia's acute threat perceptions towards China (indeed, this is the logic that underpins arguments such as Mak [1991] and Acharya [1999]). To the extent that the Malaysian Armed

Forces had indeed focused on enhancing their maritime capabilities in the early 1990s, this logic seemed to hold true. However, more recent arms procurement plans have not really affirmed this wisdom.

It is striking that while a Malaysian naval build-up was evident in the late 1980s and early 1990s,[70] it had been scaled down in the late 1990s even as tensions in the South China Sea persisted.[71] Analysts of Malaysian defence spending have in fact noted that:

> Under the 6MP (Sixth Malaysia Plan), it was clear that the RMAF and RMN benefited from increased defence spending to a far greater extent than the army. The distribution is likely to be reversed or at least become more balanced in the late 1990s.[72]

The introduction of the Seventh Malaysia Plan in 1996 saw defence expenditure concentrate on artillery, air defence systems and armoured fighting platforms and logistics equipment. In other words, defence spending prioritized the needs of the army and air force at the expense of the navy.[73] Although defence expenditure has increased across-the-board under the Eighth Malaysia Plan of 2001, which includes the purchase of submarines and the upgrading of frigates, what remains fascinating was Malaysia's reluctance to take immediate measures to buffer its naval capabilities in the late-1990s, which coincided with increasing tension in the South China Sea.[74] In essence then, Malaysia's military build-up does not seem commensurate to an acute perception of a Chinese threat. In fact, it has been suggested in certain quarters that Malaysian military procurement appears to be a response to military build-ups taking place in its immediate neighbourhood, and belie a perception of a land-based, not maritime, threat.[75]

In the main, what is being suggested here is that while Chinese policy of force projection into the Spratlys remains to some extent unclear, it is important to look at the politics of the South China Sea and the force modernization strategies of China and Malaysia, and the rest of the counter-claimants, in perspective. Analysts studying maritime force modernization trends in the region have drawn attention to the difficulty of equating military build-ups to concerns over China, given that through the 1990s China has gradually displayed "responsible" international behaviour.[76] As some have noted, "China, until today, has not developed any real power projection capability. Moreover, countries like Malaysia are convinced that China is becoming an increasingly responsible international player".[77] This certainly appears to be the case with Beijing's recent accession to the ASEAN TAC and signing of the Code of Conduct.

THE UNITED STATES AS MALAYSIA'S
COUNTERVAILING STRATEGY?

Proponents of balance of power strategies would certainly argue that however strong Malaysia's defence posture, it is not likely to be an effective deterrent against China if undertaken unilaterally. Indeed, most would suggest that Malaysian security would be better preserved through bilateral and multilateral alliances or security arrangements. The close defence relationship that Malaysia enjoys with the United States and Australia would seem to demonstrate some measure of "balancing" behaviour. Yet there are several important reasons why Malaysia is not likely to be balancing China.

There should be little doubt that despite recurring political differences, Malaysia enjoys historically strong bilateral defence relations with both Washington and Canberra. That said, there are also notable problems in Malaysia's relations with the United States and Australia that hamper the realization of the full potential for collaboration. Political and diplomatic friction is a matter that has been well documented elsewhere.[78] In a revealing study of Malaysia's defence relations with the United States, J.N. Mak observed that the two key motivating factors behind Malaysia's continued pursuit of close ties with Washington despite political differences have been the benefits Malaysia can accrue in terms of transfers of technology, and a belief in Kuala Lumpur circles that an American presence will continue to be a key factor to regional stability.[79] However, Mak also alludes to the economic-political security threat that the United States poses to Malaysia. Given the emphasis of the Mahathir administration on a comprehensive understanding of security, he suggests that the Malaysian Government harbours strong reservations towards Western, and in particular American, neo-liberal economic and political values, which pose a threat to Malaysian internal/domestic security. Consequently, Mak argues that one reason why Malaysia-U.S. functional co-operation has been kept out of the public eye is the fact that Mahathir viewed "the West, and especially America, as a source of threats to the Malay community with its emphasis on the rights of minorities and its perversion of values. Even more dangerous was its neoliberal economic agenda and its attempts to control the world market and undermine the competitiveness of Eastern countries".[80] It can be said that this inherent tension in Malaysia-U.S. relations has come into greater relief in recent years. The economic crisis of 1997 aggravated Mahathir's perceptions of a need for East Asia to stand up against Western-dominated international financial institutions (something he had already championed in his staunch opposition to APEC). Further to that, Malaysia has stood at the forefront of international condemnation of

Washington's unilateralist foreign policy in the wake of the campaigns in Afghanistan and Iraq.[81] While much of Mahathir's hostility towards Washington was polemical, there have been recent signs that the line between rhetoric and practice may have been transgressed. Firing a broadside at the Mahathir administration's continued castigation of American foreign policy, Marie Huhtala, U.S. Ambasssador to Malaysia, articulated in no uncertain terms to an audience in Kuala Lumpur that "these are not helpful statements by any standard, and I'm here to tell you that Washington does take note of them. They are bound to have a harmful effect on the relationship".[82] The tone of the response would be of particular interest for its severity; it being arguably the first time American government officials in Malaysia publicly voiced Washington's disapproval of Kuala Lumpur's antagonistic posture towards them by insinuating that these responses "are bound to have a harmful effect".

China's emergence as a key strategic player in the region thence, and Malaysia's response to this, needs to be understood in context. In this regard, several issues need to be considered. First, unlike the 1980s, China does not appear to pose a clear, direct threat. Instead, it can be said that China is beginning to endear itself to Southeast Asia, and Malaysia seems to be leveraging on this to further its own interests. Second, given Malaysia's inclination to prioritize economic security, its most obvious "balancer" from a strategic perspective, the United States, looks equally "threatening" from an economic and political perspective. If anything, it appears that despite the historically-close relations between the United States and Malaysia, the recurrence of political and economic tension indicates that Kuala Lumpur may well be "free-riding" on the more stable relations between the United States and Thailand, the Philippines, and Singapore, all of which arguably serve as stronger assurances of American interest in, and commitment to, the region. Third, Malaysia also has a range of disputes with several of its neighbours that appear much more intractable. Unlike China however, where the potential for conflict might only be aggravated by factors relating to geographical proximity, Malaysia's sometimes turbulent relations with several of its Southeast Asian neighbours carry a great deal of historical baggage, and hence the animosity is likely to be more deep-seated, and differences harder to resolve.

CONCLUSION

The security environment that Malaysia operates in today is markedly different from that of the Cold War. While concerns in the immediate post-Cold War era were that China would pose a strategic threat to Southeast Asia, on hindsight there has been little to substantiate such claims. In fact, it can be argued that Beijing has ingratiated itself to Southeast Asia by taking on board the practices of ASEAN-style multilateralism it had eschewed in the early 1990s. The highlight of this transition was China's signing of the Code of Conduct for the South China Sea and accession to the ASEAN Treaty of Amity and Co-operation.

China's rise to the status of great power is inevitable. Consequently, the concerns for states in the region like Malaysia will be less how to stop this development than how to deal with it. It has been argued here that Malaysia's policies towards China, particularly in recent times, have to be viewed in the context of the current strategic milieu, where it has been precisely the relatively stable strategic environment that offers small states such as Malaysia much more manoeuvring room in its relations with great powers. Not only is the lack of a clearly-defined external threat a definitive feature of the prevailing strategic milieu for Malaysia, under present conditions one finds great powers endearing themselves to smaller states in the search for friends and bandwagons as they engage each other in contests for political, economic, and diplomatic primacy. In other words, while the role of the great powers is undoubtedly vital to regional order and stability, this study has shown how states like Malaysia can proactively capitalize on periods of tranquility, fortify their bargaining positions, and secure their interests by pursuing bandwagoning-like behaviour with the major players.[83]

It is important to emphasize however, that while bandwagoning-like behaviour can certainly be identified in the case of Malaysia's China policy, and probably a host of other Southeast Asian states, the empirical evidence indicates that Malaysia's orientation towards China is part of a policy of hedge diplomacy towards the two major powers, Washington and Beijing, and which is premised with engagement strategies towards both the preponderant and the rising power. Furthermore in relation to China, this behaviour is motivated not so much by threat perception as by Kuala Lumpur's intention to capitalize on the potential political, economic, and strategic benefits associated with the rise of China, which affiliation with Beijing might entail.

Notes

1. Some examples include Paul Dibb, *Towards a New Balance of Power in Asia*, London: Oxford University Press, 1995; Michael Leifer, *The ASEAN Regional Forum* (London: Oxford University Press, 1996); Thomas Christensen, "China

and the U.S.-Japan Alliance", *International Security* 23, no. 4 (Spring 1999); Ted Osius, *The U.S.-Japan Security Alliance* (Washington D.C.: Praeger and CSIS, 2002).

2. Phar Kim Beng and Wei Kiat Yip observe these tendencies in regional economics, while David Kang attempts to argue this in regional security and politics. See Wei Kiat Yip, "Prospects for Closer Economic Integration in East Asia", *Stanford Journal of East Asian Affairs* 1 (Spring 2001); Phar Kim Beng, "Southeast Asia Losing FDI Fight to China", *Asia Times*, 12 November 2002; David Kang, "Getting Asia Wrong: The Need for New Analytic Frameworks", *International Security* 27, no. 3 (Spring 2003).

3. Coincidentally, Malaysia was cited explicitly as an example of a state around whose policies and perceptions of international affairs it would be "ridiculous to construct a theory of international politics". See Kenneth Waltz, *Theory of International Politics* (Reading, Massachusetts: Addison-Wesley, 1979), p. 73.

4. Some more sophisticated studies include Annette Baker Fox, *The Power of Small States: Diplomacy in World War II* (Chicago: University of Chicago Press, 1959); Robert Rothstein, *Alliances and Small Powers*, New York: Columbia University Press, 1968; Charles Glaser, "Realists as Optimists: Co-operation as Self-Help", *International Security* 19, no. 3 (Winter 1994–95). More recent studies would include Charles Kupchan, *End of the American Era: US Foreign Policy and the Geopolitics of the Twenty-first Century* (New York: Alfred A. Knopf Inc, 2002).

5. Waltz, *Theory of International Politics*, pp. 116–28; Stephen Walt, Origins of Alliances (Ithaca: Cornell University Press, 1987), p. 33.

6. Waltz, *Theory of International Politics*, p. 126.

7. Walt, *Origins of Alliances*, p. 5.

8. Ibid, pp. 1–22.

9. Randall Schweller, "Bandwagoning for Profit: Bringing the Revisionist State Back In", *International Security* 19, no. 1 (Summer 1994): 88–89.

10. Ibid, p. 74. In fact, Schweller criticizes Walt's assumption that bandwagoning behaviour is inspired by threat perception by arguing that Walt had departed from the common usage of the term and only focuses on the coercive and compulsory aspect of bandwagoning, and that Walt's purported explanation seemed to equate bandwagoning to "capitulation". Ibid., p. 81.

11. Ibid, p. 88.

12. Randall Schweller, "Managing the Rise of Great Powers: History and Theory" in *Engaging China: The Management of an Emerging Power*, edited by Alistair Iain Johnston and Robert Ross (London: Routledge, 1999), p. 11.

13. Kevin Sweeney and Paul Fritz, "Jumping on the Bandwagon: An Interest Based Explanation for Great Power Alliances", *Journal of Politics* 66, no. 2 (May 2004).

14. Sweeney and Fritz, "Jumping on the Bandwagon", p. 1.

15. Sweeney and Frtiz suggest that one of the key "interests" that bandwagoning states aim to protect is the status quo of a prevailing international system.

16. Aside from Waltz, Walt and Schweller, see also Robert Jervis and Jack Snyder, eds., *Dominoes and Bandwagons: Strategic Beliefs and Great Power Competition in the Eurasian Rimland* (New York: Oxford University Press, 1991).

17. See for example, Mark Kramer, "Neorealism, Nuclear Proliferation, and East-Central European Strategies" in *Unipolar Politics: Realism and State Strategies After the Cold War*, edited by Ethan Kapstein and Michael Mastanduno (New York: Columbia University Press, 1999). Ralf Emmers provides an insightful and innovative interpretation of the political (as opposed to military and strategic) functions of the balance of power factor. See Ralf Emmers, *Co-operative Security and the Balance of Power in ASEAN and the ARF* (London: Routledge, 2003).

18. Sweeney and Fritz, "Jumping on the Bandwagon", p. 7.

19. See for example, Evelyn Goh, "A Chinese Lesson for the U.S.: How to Charm South-east Asia", *The Straits Times*, 31 October 2003; Amitav Acharya, "China's Charm Offensive in Southeast Asia", *International Herald Tribune*, 8–9 November 2003; Evan S. Medeiros and M. Taylor Fravel, "China's New Diplomacy", *Foreign Affairs* (November/December 2003).

20. See Stephen David, "Explaining Third World Alliances", *World Politics* 43, no. 2 (January 1991).

21. See Stephen Leong, "Malaysia and the People's Republic of China in the 1980s: Political Vigilance and Economic Pragmatism", *Asian Survey* 27, no. 10 (October 1987); Zainuddin Bahari, "Malaysia-China Bilateral Relations" in *ASEAN and China: An Evolving Relationship*, edited by Joyce Kallgren, Noordin Sopiee and Soedjati Djiwandono (Berkeley: University of California-Berkeley, Institute of East Asian Studies, 1988).

22. Mak Joon Nam, "The Chinese Navy and the South China Sea: A Malaysian Assessment", *Pacific Review* 4, no. 2 (1991); Amitav Acharya, "Containment, Engagement, or Counter-Dominance: Malaysia's Response to the Rise of China" in *Engaging China*, edited by Johnston and Ross.

23. SWB FE/5969/A3/2, 15 November 1978, "Malaysia's Foreign Policy and Teng Hsiao-ping's Visit".

24. Ghazali Shafie, keynote address at the Conference on "ASEAN — Today and Tomorrow" at Fletcher School of Law and Diplomacy, Boston, USA, 11 November 1981.

25. The end of the Cold War also marked the end of the communist insurgency in Malaysia. On 2 December 1989, CPM leader Chin Peng signed an agreement with Thai and Malaysian officials which marked the laying down of arms of the Malaysian communists. Also, in 1989, China passed the Law on Citizenship, which effectively severed China's ties with overseas Chinese.

26. Mak, "The Chinese Navy and the South China Sea", p. 150.

27. FBIS-EAS-93-159, 19 August 1993, BK1708110293.

28. See Joseph Chin Yong Liow, "Malaysia-China Relations in the 1990s: The Maturing of a Partnership", *Asian Survey* 40, no. 4 (July/August 2000).

29. FBIS-EAS-93-21, BK 2406110193, 25 June 1993.
30. "Malaysia Assumes Larger, More Vital Role in Regional Affairs", *Straits Times*, 15 September 1994.
31. See "China and Malaysia Sign Joint Statement for Future Co-operation", *BBC Worldwide Monitoring*, 31 May 1999.
32. *Business Times*, 14 January 2004. Available at <http: www.btimes.com.my/ Current_News/Btimes/Wednesday/Nation/20040114000843/Article>.
33. For his 1985 comment, see Mahathir Mohamad, speech entitled "The Return Banquest in Honour of H.E Premier Zhou Ziyang", Beijing, 22 Movember 1985. For his 1990 comment, see Mahathir Mohamad, speech entitled "*Majlis Makan Malam Meraikan Tuan Yang Terutama Li Peng, Perdana Menteri Republik Rakyat China*", Kuala Lumpur, 10 December 1990.
34. Mahathir Mohamad, untitled speech given in Beijing, 20 November 1985. See *Foreign Affairs Malaysia* 18, no. 3 (December 1985): 392.
35. An exhaustive list of high level visits both ways can be found on the website of the Ministry of Foreign Affairs of the People's Republic of China. Available at <http: www.fmprc.gov.cn>.
36. "Chinese President Yang says EAEC will Benefit Region", *Japan Economic Newswire*, 11 January 1992.
37. "KL Supports Beijing Entry into WTO", *Business Times Malaysia*, 20 August 1999.
38. "Joint Effort with China to Establish New Financial Order", *New Straits Times*, 2 June 1999.
39. FBIS-EAS-94-219, 14 November 1994, BK1111135494.
40. "Jiang to Meet Snubbed Dr. Mahathir", *South China Morning Post*, 17 November 1998. The snub was a symbolic registration of protest against the incarceration of former Deputy Prime Minister Anwar Ibrahim.
41. Schweller, "Bandwagoning for Profit", p. 87.
42. "In Campaign Mode", *Asiaweek*, 16 July 1999.
43. "China Not a Threat to Asia: Malaysian DPM", *People's Daily*, 16 September 2003.
44. See also "China Still Seen as a Threat to Our Security", *New Straits Times*, 7 December 1991.
45. See B.A. Hamzah, "Jurisdictional Issues and the Conflicting Claims in the Spratlys: What Can be Done in Enhancing Confidence-building Measures", paper presented at *the Workshop on Managing Potential Conflicts in the South China Sea* in Bali, 22–24 January 1990.
46. See Ang Cheng Guan, *The South China Sea Dispute Re-visited*, IDSS Working Paper No. 4, Singapore: Institute of Defence and Strategic Studies, 1999, p. 2. Ang quotes Zakaria Ahmad from "China's Warning on Spratlys Raises Spectre of Armed Clashes", *The Straits Times*, 11 March 1992.
47. Derek Da Cunha, "Southeast Asian Perceptions of China's Future Security Role

in its 'Backyard' ", in *China's Shadow: Regional Perspectives on Chinese Foreign Policy and Military Development*, edited by Jonathan Pollack and Richard Yang (Washington D.C.: Rand Corporation, 1998), p. 116.

48. Though there have been rumours of Chinese warships firing on Philippine naval vessels as well, the author has not been able to verify nor document this information.

49. See Chen Jie, "China's Spratly Policy — With Special Reference to the Philippines and Malaysia", *Asian Survey* 34, no. 10 (October 1994): 901.

50. See "Reports Show China To Develop Strong Navy", *Periscope Daily Defence News Capsules United Communications Group*, 16 December 1992.

51. See, for example, Mahathir Mohamad's speech entitled "The 1994 China Summit Meeting", Beijing, 11 May 1994.

52. "Malaysia, Seeing a Threat, Urges US to Stop Building Up Power of China", *New York Times*, 10 July 1984.

53. "The ADJ Interview: Dato Syed Hamid Albar, Malaysia's Defence Minister", *Asian Defence Journal*, April 1996.

54. For example, throughout much of the 1980s, Mahathir Mohamad was adamant that China's intervention into the Cambodian crisis by invading Vietnam was a clear signal that China was a threat to the region. See "Malaysians Depict China as a Threat", *New York Times*, 23 August 1981. See also "Threat? What Threat? Mahathir Causes Diplomatic Stir by Implying that Vietnam is not the Biggest Danger to ASEAN", *Far Eastern Economic Review*, 21 August 1981, p. 13.

55. Mak, "The Chinese Navy and the South China Sea", p. 150.

56. J.N. Mak and B.A. Hamzah, "The External Maritime Dimensions of ASEAN Security" in *The Transformation of Security in the Asia-Pacific Region*, edited by Desmond Ball (London: Frank Cass, 1996), p. 128. Mak and Hamzah were quick to add that China remains a factor in regional security, a fact that this author does not dispute.

57. "ASEAN Taking a More Active Role in Spratlys Dispute", *Straits Times*, 8 April 1995.

58. "Neighbours Challenge Beijing's Claim — ASEAN Presents a United Front to China in Ocean Boundaries Dispute", *Asian Wall Street Journal*, 17 April 1995.

59. To substantiate this, one needs only to look at the number of intra-ASEAN disturbances that have occurred over the Spratlys since 1995.

60. See for example, Rajmah Hussain, "A Southeast Asian Perspective: View from Malaysia" in Michael Everett and Mary Sommerville, *Multilateral Activities in Southeast Asia* (Washington D.C.: National Defence University Press, 1995), pp. 53–62.

61. One such example has been Malaysian participation in the South China Sea workshop series organized by Indonesia. See Dino Djalal, "Indonesia and Preventive Diplomacy: A Study of the Workshops on Managing Potential Conflicts in the South China Sea", Ph.D. dissertation submitted to London School of Economics, 2000, pp. 190–96.

62. "Hamid: Spratlys Issue not for ARF discussion", *New Straits Times*, 23 July 1999.
63. FBIS-CHI-1999-0715, 15 July 1999, OW1507143899.
64. See "Regional code of conduct now referred to working group", *New Straits Times*, 21 July 1999.
65. FBIS-EAS-1999-0723, 23 July 1999, BK2307075799.
66. SWB/FE/3594/B/5, 22 July 1999. See also "ASEAN Security Forum Support Talks on Spratlys Row", *Businessworld*, 23 July 1999.
67. The significance of this lay in the fact that in conventional diplomatic practice, a political declaration would be less binding than a Code of Conduct, which is a legal document that requires national ratification.
68. Acharya, "Containment, Engagement, or Counter-dominance".
69. Liselotte Odgaard, *Maritime Security between China and Southeast Asia*, Aldershot: Ashgate, 2002, p. 138.
70. See Richard Stubbs, "Malaysian Defence Policy: Strategy vs Structure", *Contemporary Southeast Asia* 13, no. 1 (June 1991).
71. Defence spending in general was reduced from the Sixth Malaysia Plan, even as economic growth had increased. See International Institute of Strategic Studies, *The Military Balance 1997/1998* (London: Oxford University Press, 1997), p. 168.
72. See "Malaysia's Armed Forces in the Late 1990s: Aiming for Credible Conventional Capability", *Asian Defence Journal*, April 1996.
73. That having been said, it must be noted that both the navy and air force have also managed to procure new platforms such as two Italian missile corvettes and MIG-29 and F-18 interceptors, and the navy had planned an extensive modernization program that has since been shelved for lack of funds. However, a lot of these purchases may have been paid for as part of the earlier Sixth Malaysia Plan.
74. See Abdul Razak Baginda, "Malaysia: Security and Military Profile". Available at <http: www.global-defence.com/1997/Malaysia.html>.
75. See Andrew Tan, "What's Behind Malaysia's Defence Build-up?", *IDSS Commentaries*, June 2003.
76. Sam Bateman, "ASEAN's Tiger Navies: Catching Up or Building Up?", *Jane's Navy International*, April 1997.
77. Mak Joon Nam, "Maritime Priorities in the Asia-Pacific" in *Asian Defence Yearbook, 1999–2000* (Kuala Lumpur: Asian Defence Journal, 2000), pp. 30–31.
78. For the most recent studies on these relationships, see Rita Camilleri, *Attitudes and Perceptions in Australia-Malaysia Relations: A Contemporary Profile* (Sydney: INT Press Publishing, 2001); Pamela Sodhy, "U.S.-Malaysian Relations during the Bush Administration: The Political, Economic, and Security Aspects", *Contemporary Southeast Asia* 25, no. 3 (December 2003).
79. See J.N. Mak, "Malaysian Defense and Security Co-operation: Coming Out of

the Closet" in *Asia-Pacific Security Co-operation: National Interests and Regional Order*, edited by See Seng Tan and Amitav Acharya (Armonk, N.Y.: M.E. Sharpe, 2004).

80. Ibid., pp. 142–43.
81. See Joseph Liow, "Malaysia's Opposition to the Iraq War: A Matter of Principle or Exigency?", *IDSS Commentaries*, April 2003.
82. Marie T. Huhtala, address entitled "Let's Move Forward the U.S.-Malaysia Bilateral Relationship" delivered at the ASLI Strategic Issues Forum, 23 May 2003.
83. Of course, given that one of the key conditions for hedge diplomacy as defined in this chapter is a period of strategic calm, the obvious question is whether such a posture towards the major powers can still be sustained when tranquillity gives way to serious strategic competition between these powers.

13

SINGAPORE'S REACTION TO A RISING CHINA

Deep Engagement and Strategic Adjustment

Evelyn Goh

INTRODUCTION

Singapore is a minute island-state that has managed to punch above its weight in the regional and international arena because of its remarkable economic achievements and its active diplomacy. In terms of strategic security in the Asia-Pacific, Singapore's perspective and thus its attitude towards China, is shaped by four factors:

1. The Economic Imperative

In the rapidly developing Southeast Asian region, Singapore's influence derives from its capacity to attract foreign trade, investment and finance, and to invest in turn in its neighbours. Continued economic development and wealth is also a vital prerequisite and foundation for stability within Singapore.

Thus, national interest is more often than not defined by the economic imperative. Regarding China, as Khong notes, the critical issue for Singapore is "how to 'manage' China's growing power such that peace and stability, the prerequisites of rapid economic growth, can be maintained in the Asia

Pacific".[1] Viewed through this lens, a rising China is regarded by Singapore leaders as both an opportunity (particularly in terms of the China market and China's potential as the new, massive engine for regional economic growth) as well as a challenge (consider Chinese competition for foreign direct investment, and in the manufacturing, financial and even technologies sector; and potential Chinese revisionism towards the strategic *status quo*).

2. Strategic Relevance

Singapore's foreign policy elite operates out of an acute awareness of its limited size and international significance. As a direct consequence, they have forged an activist foreign policy, particularly in response to perceived potential changes in the international system. In the wake of the Cold War, the fear of American withdrawal from Southeast Asia and concerns about potential Chinese hegemony have combined with a certain frustration with the perceived introspection of its ASEAN partners to produce a sustained bout of diplomatic activism from Singapore. By initiating and sponsoring the ASEAN Regional Forum [ARF] and strongly supporting APEC, Singapore has tried, through the aegis of ASEAN, to retain influence over the nature of the emerging regional security architecture. In this battle to reaffirm Southeast Asia's strategic relevance, the engagement of the major powers is a vital element. Singapore has used regional institutions to capture and justify great power interest and involvement in the region; to promote security dialogue between them; and to highlight the important facilitating role smaller regional states have to play in developing regional confidence and diplomacy. In this sense, Singapore is a prime practitioner of middle power activism.[2]

3. Preference for U.S. Preponderance

The Singapore Government has a positive assessment of the U.S. role in region, and a marked preference for a regional security structure guaranteed by American preponderance of power. Prime Minister Goh Chok Tong has, in various speeches, declared the United States a "reassuring and stabilizing force" in Southeast Asia and the American presence a "determining reason for the peace and stability Asia enjoys today".[3] In a 2001 speech in Washington, he said:

> The US' involvement has had a profound impact on this history of East Asia's development. America maintained an 'open-door' to China, twice transformed Japan, and spilt blood to hold the line against aggression

and communism. The US constructed and maintained the post-World War II international order that allowed East Asia to flourish. America's victory in the Cold War and its technology driving the new economy are continued influences. In the strategic sense, therefore, the US is very much a part of East Asia. It has been, and still is, a positive force for stability and prosperity.[4]

At a concrete level, Singapore has acted upon this rhetoric by offering to host the American naval logistics command centre (WESTPAC LOGCOM) and increasing access to American vessels and aircraft, after the closure of U.S. bases in the Philippines in 1992. Additionally, Singapore has built a new naval base at Changi that can accommodate U.S. aircraft carriers (the Kitty Hawk was the first foreign warship to dock there in March 2001), and Singapore also co-operates with U.S. forces in military exercises.

Senior Minister Lee Kuan Yew, in a 1996 speech in Washington D.C., referred to a "fallback position should China not play in accordance with the rules as a good global citizen", and suggested that the U.S. position would be to father a new alliance of Japan, Korea, ASEAN, Australia, New Zealand and Russia.[5] Some analysts have suggested that this reflects the likely choice for Singapore if the crunch comes it would choose the U.S. side.[6]

4. Realism and Soft Institutionalism

Singapore's foreign policy elite concentrates on great power *realpolitik* and the calculation of national interest based on power. However, in spite of this apparently realist outlook, there is also a real belief in the value of dialogue in and of itself, as an integral part of "confidence building measures"; and an attendant preference for informal relations over formal institutions. Singapore is a key proponent of the "Asian way" of engagement, which is fundamentally based on the hope of socialization through "soft" institutionalism.[7]

Thus, unlike other states such as the United States, the Singapore Government has hardly paused to grapple with the debate about whether China is a rising revisionist power that ought to be contained, or a potentially constructive member of international society that should be engaged with.[8] Singapore recognizes that its relationship with China contains elements of opportunity for mutual co-operation and gain, as well as economic competition and conflicting strategic aims. There is grave uncertainty about Chinese intentions in the medium to long term, but also the fundamental conviction that China shares the economic imperative and wants to concentrate on domestic development. Thus, Singapore leaders think that there is time to develop a constructive relationship with Beijing while guarding against the possibility of a revisionist regime in the longer-run. Hence, Singapore's China policy consists of a combination of "shaping" and "hedging" strategies.[9] On the one hand, Singapore emphasizes economic and political engagement with Beijing; while on the other, it is modernizing and augmenting its military strength and cultivating closer security relations with the United States.[10] In pursuing and developing this two-pronged policy, Singapore has used its central role in ASEAN to try to cultivate cautious deep engagement as the broad Southeast Asian approach to China as a whole.[11]

CHINA'S APPROACH TO SOUTHEAST ASIA

China's approach to Southeast Asia is under-girded by its desire to maintain stability in its surrounding regions, which would allow Beijing to concentrate on economic development.[12] China's strategy towards Southeast Asia may be described as one of "counter-hedging" and "counter-engaging".[13]

At the most basic level, Beijing wants to ensure that there are no conflicts with Southeast Asia which would compromise Chinese sovereignty, territorial integrity and national security. In this regard, the South China Sea (SCS) disputes are an important element of tension. China wants to resolve the issue with as much advantage to itself as possible, and has made firm but cautious moves to stake claims in the SCS.[14] This opportunism has been combined with calculated openness to negotiations. Southeast Asian perspectives vary, with the Philippines and Vietnam most worried, but there is an almost determined effort to stress progress in ASEAN dialogue to resolve the issue, and the conviction that China will not go to war over these islands.[15] After much wrangling over the scope of a potential code of conduct, China and ASEAN signed a Declaration on the Conduct of Parties in the South China Sea on 4 November 2002 at the ASEAN summit in Phnom Penh. While this has signified progress, Beijing has not withdrawn its territorial claims in principle to the whole of the SCS, and other disputed islands such as the Paracels are not included in the declaration.[16]

Beyond that, Beijing also wants to ensure that Southeast Asia is not alienated to another power antagonistic to China (that is, the United States or Japan). Thus, as Chung suggests, Beijing has adopted a "counter-hedging" strategy towards Southeast Asia which emphasizes the weakening of regional support for the U.S.-Japan security alliance and other American bilateral alliances; and the opposing of any heightening of Japan's security role in the region and of the deployment of Theatre Missile Defence system in or around Japan. Recently, Beijing's concern has been expanded due to Australia's announcement in December 2003 that it would join the American missile defence shield programme.

In positive diplomatic terms though, Beijing hopes to cultivate benign perceptions of China in Southeast Asia. It is aware of existing suspicions about Chinese intentions and sensitive to suggestions about "the China threat". Thus, an important part of China's Southeast Asia strategy is to engage with the region through bilateral and multilateral dialogue; a very conscious cultivation of a benign image of China's role in the region; the articulation of a co-operative attitude to a range of regional issues such as transnational crime; an emphasis on mutual benefits in China's economic development and the idea of China acting as an engine of economic growth and putative financial backer for the region; and the occasional play of common anti-Western sentiments.

SINGAPORE'S APPROACH TO CHINA

Acting from the realist assumption that small states might well be dispensable in the international system, Singapore's policymakers constantly try to make the country "useful" to the major powers in their quest for security. Thus, the middle levels of the Singaporean foreign policy establishment are wont to emphasize the importance of Singapore as an "interlocutor" for China, particularly *vis-à-vis* the United States. The idea is that the Chinese apparently recognize that Singapore — while possessing close military ties with the United States — is a fairly "independent", "objective" voice in international relations. Thus, it provides a useful bridge between the "Asian way" and the "Western style" of diplomacy and politics, and acts as an "honest broker" and even "interpreter" for the two sides. This view perhaps somewhat overstates Singapore's influence in both Beijing and Washington. However, it is true that Beijing has come to regard ASEAN in general as a trusted forum, and the "Asian way" as a comfortable and not too taxing method of international engagement.[17]

At a more mundane political level, China seems to be interested in learning from Singapore's experience in aspects of effective governance, such as fighting corruption, running grassroots organizations, and even state regulation of prostitution. Chinese delegations routinely visit Singapore on fact-finding missions. In economic terms, the Singapore leadership thinks that Beijing has a lot to learn from Singapore in terms of development strategy, managerial systems, and investment. Deng Xiao-ping was reputed to have glimpsed China's economic future during a visit to Singapore in 1979; Singapore was an ideal model because it showed that rapid economic growth was not inconsistent with tight central government control. Singapore has been playing advisory and investment roles in China's economic modernization since the 1980s. Goh Keng Swee, who devised Singapore's economic strategy, was appointed special adviser to two special economic zones in China, and the Singapore Government built an industrial township in Suzhou in 1993, though with limited success because of competition from a nearby development. It has since been invited to undertake a similar project for a technology park in Xian, in Beijing's drive to develop the inland western provinces.[18]

Economically, China is motivated by larger concerns of wanting to engage with Southeast Asia for two reasons: first, to maintain a stable periphery and so safeguard its economic development; and second, to pursue Southeast Asia as a critical economic constituency which would expedite China's economic reforms and development. Singapore leaders believe that these motivations are secured by a new generation of Chinese leaders who are essentially technocrats (like themselves), more open, and who want to learn from Singapore. As Goh Chok Tong put it, this younger generation "does not have a communist mindset. They have taken to heart Deng Xiaoping's dictum: 'To get rich is glorious'".[19]

Essentially, Sino-Singaporean engagement has been successful because of the coincidence of interests on both sides. Singapore has a real economic interest in China, and the Singapore Government believes that by giving China a stake in the economic and institutional processes in the region, Beijing might be socialized into accepting the prevailing norms and acting as a responsible major player in the region. Thus, Singapore has been particularly active in arguing the need for engaging China in regional fora and mitigating perceptions of the China threat.

Singapore's hope is first for a developing, prosperous and internally-stable China that may act as a regional economic growth engine, enjoying co-operative and mutually-beneficial economic ties with its neighbours. In this sense, recent developments, including the agreement to establish a China-ASEAN FTA within ten years, and Hu Jintao's message in his April 2002 visit to Malaysia and Singapore, have struck exactly the right cords. Hu assured his audiences that China's economic expansion is "a positive force for making for an economically stronger and more stable Asia". He promised that with WTO membership, China would provide its trading partners with opportunities worth at least US$1.5 trillion over the next five years, and open its services to more foreign investment.[20] Singapore and Thailand have pushed for those members of ASEAN who are ready to go ahead and sign trade pacts with China, and in June 2003, Thailand signed an FTA for fruits and vegetables with China.

Second, it wants to see China enmeshed in regional norms, acting responsibly and upholding the regional *status quo*. As Prime Minister Goh put it, "If China grows, and plays by international rules on such issues as weapons proliferation, international trade, freedom of navigation and environmental protection, it can become a constructive player." [21]

Finally, it places great importance on China becoming a second benign great power in the region, balanced tacitly by, and enjoying a *modus vivendi* with, the benign superpower. Singapore is realistic about the potential effects of China's growing power. Goh conceded that since "a corollary of strong economic growth is strengthened strategic weight", with China's growth, "some reconfiguration of the regional order, therefore, seems inevitable."[22] But it is not too sure about future Chinese intentions, and so it retains a firm belief in balance of power to constrain China. Goh affirmed, "I believe it is in everyone's interest if East Asia remains in balance even as China grows. The U.S. can help to provide this balance. Balance does not mean confrontation. It means that as China grows and becomes stronger, other countries in Asia too should grow and become stronger, buttressed by a strong U.S. presence. It does not mean conscribing China's growth or containing its power. It means mutually beneficial growth."[23]

SINGAPORE'S ASSESSMENT OF CHINA'S IMPACT ON SOUTHEAST ASIA

The following aspects of Chinese policies are viewed as potentially destabilizing for the region:

1. China's Military Modernization and Development Programme

As part of their hedging strategy, Southeast Asian states have also engaged in arms procurement and modernization. However, the 1997 financial crisis has slowed down these programmes, in most countries, except for Singapore.

2. The South China Sea Disputes

China and Vietnam had clashed over some Spratlys reefs in the late 1980s, but Beijing really worried its Southeast Asia neighbours when it laid claim to the whole of the SCS in 1992. Thereafter, the Chinese occupied and built structures on reefs claimed by Vietnam and the Philippines (Mischief) in 1992, 1995 and 1999, the latter of which led to diplomatic confrontations and military tensions. Singapore, not being directly involved, holds an optimistic view of Chinese intentions, and attempts to use the ASEAN forum to encourage dialogue and mediation. Initially, Beijing preferred bilateral talks — a medium widely seen to increase its bargaining power — but in the last few years, it has submitted to having the issue discussed in ASEAN-China dialogue meetings. In spite of the Declaration of Conduct, there remain internal divisions within ASEAN on the issue, and Vietnam and the Philippines continue to be wary of Chinese encroachment. Still, many analysts of Southeast Asia appear to agree that all sides perceive a shared interest in maintaining stability in order to concentrate on economic development.[24]

3. U.S.-China Relations

As Goh told Hu Jintao in April 2002: "...the US-China relationship is crucial. If this relationship is stable, it will have a calming effect on the entire region. If it is upset, it will unsettle the region".[25] Basically, Sino-American tensions will upset Southeast Asia because this will disrupt the working premise of the 1990s that all major powers in the region shared an interest in maintaining regional stability. It will diminish ASEAN's role and room for manoeuvre in the region, and worse, might force Southeast Asia to take sides. Of course, many Southeast Asia states have moved towards closer security relations with the United States since the early 1990s, but Southeast Asia leaders are loathe to have to be too explicit about their choices.

4. Taiwan

Southeast Asia watches the Taiwan Strait carefully, as the main "hotspot" of Sino-American tensions. Singapore, in the form of Senior Minister Lee, has tried to play the role of interlocutor between China and Taiwan, and Singapore hosted the first official cross-strait talks in 1993. However, Singapore cooled notably towards Taipei since Lee Teng Hui's presidency, as his attempts to raise Taiwan's international profile were regarded as unnecessarily provocative.[26] In 2004, the new Prime Minister Lee Hsien Loong publicly warned Taipei that Singapore would not support a Taiwanese declaration of independence.

5. Japan

China's adamant opposition to a greater role for Japan in regional security is seen as another potential problem in U.S.-China relations that will affect regional stability. Southeast Asia worries about potential conflict between a strengthened Japan and China, although thinking on this issue appears to be muddy at the moment. On the one hand, Southeast Asia does not want to have to be forced to choose between China and Japan. On the other hand, a resurgent Japan would serve the purpose of balancing China, and hedging against future reductions in U.S. interest in the region. Indeed, ASEAN has welcomed the recent limited expansion of the Japanese role, particularly in its involvement in peacekeeping operations and co-operation against piracy. Aware of the need to maintain close U.S.-Japan alliance relations, Southeast Asian countries have also been relatively reticent in expressing concerns about the Japanese Government's decision to deploy troops to Iraq in 2004. Fundamentally, there is significantly less concern in Southeast Asian minds about possible Japanese remilitarization, for historical reasons, and also because of an implicit faith in the restraining power of the U.S.-Japan alliance.

Chinese policies, on the other hand, are seen to promote regional stability in two key ways:

1. *Regional Institutions.* China appears to have taken an increasingly positive approach towards regional institutions since the early 1990s. China became ASEAN's "consultative partner" in 1991, and was promoted to "full dialogue partner" in 1996. Sino-ASEAN co-operation was institutionalized with the creation of five dialogue mechanisms in the areas of political, scientific, technological, economic and trade consultations. In the second half of the 1990s, China began co-operating with ASEAN in its Mekong Basin Development Co-operation, on a range of issues including the control of illegal migration, drug trafficking, the spread of AIDS, and developing transport links in the basin which brings together China and mainland Southeast Asia. In 1994, China joined in setting up the ASEAN Regional Forum, in which it has participated in security dialogue (co-hosting the 1997 Inter-sessional Study Group on Confidence Building Measures in Beijing, publishing its first Defence White Paper in 1995). In 1997, China, together with Japan and South Korea, inaugurated a new framework for regional co-operation in the ASEAN+3 summit track. In general, concrete positive steps include China's signing of the protocol to make Southeast Asia a nuclear-free zone (ZOPFAN) in 2001, its willingness to negotiate the Spratlys dispute through ASEAN, and its formal subscription to the ASEAN Treaty of Amity and Co-operation in 2003.

2. *Economic Policies.* For Southeast Asia, the 1997 financial crisis remains the key regional turning-point of the post-Cold War period, and China's

reactions at the time contributed greatly to improving perceptions of Beijing's positive regional role. Its US$1 billion aid package to Thailand, assurances not to devaluate the renminbi, extension of trade credits and offers of humanitarian aid were all welcomed as signs of Beijing's earnest desire to play a constructive leadership role in the region. ASEAN hopes that China will continue to open its market to help enhance the slackening demand for ASEAN exports. With Beijing's successful bid for the 2008 Olympic Games, its healthy economic growth, and its entry into the WTO, ASEAN states have considerable expectations of China contributing to their economic well-being. In this regard, Beijing appears to be fulfilling these expectations, in its agreement to pursue a China-ASEAN FTA, and in Hu Jintao's reassurances about China acting as a ballast for Southeast Asia's economic growth.

Multilateralism

Singapore's assessment of regional multilateralism is overwhelmingly positive because it has been the prime mover for Chinese participation in these institutions. It is critical to bear in mind that in trying to assess China's role in regional institutions, Singapore leaders are simultaneously writing the report cards for the success of a key tenet of their regional strategy. Ostensibly, it is an attempt at "hegemonic entrapment", or, less antagonistically, a strategy to "socialize" China into adopting regional norms and by giving it a stake in regional goals and stability. This strategy accords well with ASEAN's "comprehensive security" concept, which emphasizes a multi-level and multi-issue approach to security concerns at the intra-states, intra-ASEAN and ASEAN-and-the-rest-of-the-region levels.[27]

From Singapore's particular perspective, however, these multilateral engagement policies derive from two basic needs. First, in order to downplay the element of ethnic affinity in Singapore-China relations, Singapore prefers to engage China through a wider Southeast Asian or Asian forum. It remains acutely aware of its neighbours' sensitivities on this point, and wants to avoid any identification with China and Chinese interests on the basis of ethnicity. Second, Singapore leaders possess an unusually broad worldview, in the strategic sense. In it vigorous promotion of regional institutions, Singapore looks firmly beyond its Southeast Asian neighbours to the ambitious aim of wanting to engage the interest and involvement of the major powers whose attitudes and policies have critical bearing on the region. The United States, China, Japan and now India, are obviously the key players, but Singapore has also looked to engage Europe for its economic influence. In judging the efficacy of fora such as the ARF in engaging

China, Singapore officials tend to be positive, partly because, as discussed before, China has become more comfortable and forthcoming in the forum; but also because the primary expectation was that the ARF would act as a confidence-boosting "talk-shop" for China and ASEAN, and, more importantly, for China and the United States.

Indeed, the second key aim of the ARF, from Singapore's point of view, was to provide a constructive basis for continued U.S. involvement in the region. Prime Minister Goh spoke candidly about this to an American audience in 2001:

> America's status as a key ASEAN dialogue partner entrenches US presence in the region... ASEAN has changed the political context of US engagement in Southeast Asia. The Post-Ministerial Conference, in which the US Secretary of State regularly participates, and the ARF are forums created and sustained by ASEAN. The Southeast Asian countries have exercised their sovereign prerogative to invite the US to join them in discussing the affairs of Southeast Asia. As long as this is so, no matter what other shifts may occur in the region, no one can argue that the US presence in Southeast Asia is illegitimate or an intrusion into the region.[28]

Currently, the ARF is experiencing some sense of drift, for it appears that the forum has not been able to move beyond the first stage of confidence building towards the further step of preventive diplomacy.[29] However, the most notable development in the area of Chinese participation in regional frameworks is the ASEAN+3 forum. It is essentially the grouping that was proposed by Mahathir as an anti-Western East Asian Economic Caucus in the early 1990s, but rejected at the time in favour of APEC by Southeast Asian states like Singapore. The ASEAN+3 forum, consisting of annual summit meetings, was spawned during the 1997 financial crisis, and is regarded as a reaction to the perceived lack of support from the United States and Western institutions. The most immediate outputs were the Chiang Mai agreement on regional monetary co-operation, a human resources action plan, and the Greater Mekong development project. The forum is still relatively new, and the members are concentrating on studying various channels of economic co-operation and co-ordination, particularly a regional monetary fund and exchange regime, regional institution building on economic and financial co-operation, and ways to strengthen regional identity. Its key substantial co-operative efforts in the form of the Chiang Mai Initiative currently consist of a series of bilateral currency swaps, and the prospects for closer monetary integration in East Asia is still contested.[30]

At a political level, ASEAN+3 is interesting because it is the first broad attempt by Southeast Asia to engage with the key players in Northeast Asia, to the exclusion of Western powers. In one sense, it is an attempt to gain bargaining power and influence for Southeast Asian states, to deal with the West from a position of strength on economic issues such as protectionism, in contrast to their haplessness during the financial crisis. From the Singaporean view, this East Asian engagement may also be interpreted as a warning to Washington that the United States risks being left out in the region's developing strategic structure. As Goh warned in 2000, in the wake of the financial crisis, the United States risked losing goodwill in the region, which would affect its political and economic interests.[31] There appears to be some recognition in Washington that the United States risks being left out of East Asia by recent developments. Jim Kelly, the Assistant Secretary for East Asian and Pacific Affairs, remarked on 4 April 2002:

> Americans have always been strong supporters of ASEAN, but now the time is ripe to do more.... Americans must realise that ASEAN countries have options — one big one being China — and to maintain our influence in the development of commerce and industry in ASEAN, we must participate to the fullest extent at every opportunity.[32]

The Chinese, on their part, were probably motivated to join ASEAN+3 as part of their goal of undermining the U.S. attempt to "contain" or "encircle" China through close bilateral security relations with Southeast Asian states. This ties in with what appears to be a quiet strategy of making the major powers recognize the strategic importance of Southeast Asia and urging some degree of competition between them for influence in the region.

China now appears to be particularly keen on promoting ASEAN+3 as the premier Asian regional institution. On the other hand, Japan and South Korea, being U.S. allies, are naturally concerned with Washington's opinion about ASEAN+3, while Southeast Asian states equally do not wish to see the process undermining U.S. commitments in the region. Thus, in spite of the occasional, pre-existing play on Asian solidarity (for example, Bandung Declaration on human rights), even proponents like Malaysia and Singapore have tried to play down the significance of ASEAN+3 and to emphasize instead the "ASEAN plus" principle of general "open regionalism" which is "not an attempt to shut out Washington". In fact, this pooling together of Northeast and Southeast Asia reflects a growing East Asian identity which would enhance peace and stability in the region.[33]

Singapore's subtle message to Washington was made clear in Goh's key policy speech in 2001. He first emphasized ASEAN's unique role as an acceptable interlocutor in East Asia, reminding America that "... the very sensitivity of their current relationships means that China, Japan and Korea could only come together in the context of ASEAN". However, "ASEAN alone has insufficient strategic weight to indefinitely maintain this equilibrium. Particularly as it tries to renew itself, it needs the help of friends and partners", especially the United States. Goh told his policy audience that basic U.S. interests were at stake, because "if U.S. attention on Northeast Asia causes Washington to neglect Southeast Asia, sooner or later, the centre of gravity of the ASEAN+3 process will shift northwards", that is, towards Chinese dominance. The message was clear: without decisive U.S. engagement in the multilateral process, Chinese influence in the region will grow, at Washington's expense. However, the positive part of the message was that Southeast Asia and the United Stats shared a common interest against this outcome. Thus, the "strategic importance" of the United States remained in the region, and lay in its role as the only power with "the strategic weight to maintain equilibrium between the two component parts of East Asia".[34]

The Economic Imperative

Economic development is the major consideration in the region: in this respect, China's rise presents opportunities as well as challenges. The shared economic imperative is regarded by Singapore and Southeast Asia as a key binding force for peace and a critical common interest that buys time for the process of engaging and socializing China. Indeed, economic engagement between China and Southeast Asia has gained a momentum of its own and in recent years, Singapore has used the instrument of negotiating bilateral and regional FTAs as a means by which to stimulate a great power contest for influence in Southeast Asia.

Nevertheless, on the negative side of the ledger, Southeast Asia worries primarily about China siphoning off foreign investments in the region: in the last few years, China has been attracting 50–70 per cent of the FDI in Asia (excluding Japan), as opposed to the 20 per cent which ASEAN gets. In addition, ASEAN faces Chinese competition in sectors like textiles, electronics, and telecommunications. Businesses generally see China as a huge seamless market, while ASEAN is still regarded as a fragmented market of ten separate countries. However, there are variations in the impact of China's economic growth on the different Southeast Asian states.

China and ASEAN (excluding Singapore), at their present stages of economic development, tend to be more competitive than complementary, in FDI and manufactured exports in the developed-country markets. The rapid expansion of China's non-traditional exports such as machinery, electronics and other high-tech products is having the most disruptive impact on Indonesia, Thailand, Malaysia and the Philippines. Compared to ASEAN,

China possesses a much larger pool of both skilled as well as non-skilled labour. Furthermore, it has a large domestic market to take advantage of the economies-of-scale effect. With lower marginal and average costs, China is thus able to enjoy a tremendous cost advantage over ASEAN. The average labour cost per hour in Malaysia and Thailand is about US$2, compared to only US 50 cents in China. These ASEAN countries need to address the real issue of restructuring and cost-cutting.[35] China's WTO membership will further expand its competitive advantage.

Singapore (like Japan, South Korea, Taiwan and Hong Kong) has been losing to China its comparative advantage in labour-intensive manufactured exports. But it can also capture the benefits of the growing Chinese economy by exporting high-tech products and by investing more in China to maintain their market shares. Singapore has certainly done so, and looks likely to eventually become more closely integrated with China's economy.

On the positive side though, China is the world's seventh largest exporting nation and the top producer of grain, coal, iron, steel and cement. In purchasing power parity GNP terms, it has the second largest economy after the United States (although in per capita terms, its GNP is US$900, compared to Singapore's US$30,000).[36] China's trade with Southeast Asia grew from US$8 billion in 1981 to US$41.6 billion in 2001. As the Chinese economy continues to grow, it will increase the demand for exports from ASEAN, particularly in terms of primary commodities and natural resources. Thus, some ASEAN countries, particularly Malaysia and Thailand, are taking the positive view that the rise of China in the long run could potentially operate as a new engine of economic growth for the region. With WTO ascension and the implementation of tariff cuts, Beijing estimates that it will provide extra trading opportunities for Southeast Asia worth US$1.5 trillion over the next five years.[37] If China's economy keeps growing at seven per cent a year and the Japanese economy does not pull out of recession, analysts are predicting that China will become a more important market for Asian exports within five years.[38]

At the end of 2001, China and ASEAN moved to begin exploring and expanding these trading opportunities in the form of a regional FTA within ten years.[39] If successful, the China-ASEAN FTA will be the world's largest free trade zone, comprising 1.7 billion people, a total GDP of US$2 trillion, and total trade exceeding US$1.2 trillion. It is estimated to have the potential of raising Southeast Asian exports to China by US$13 billion (48 per cent), and Chinese exports to ASEAN by US$11 billion (more than 55 per cent).[40]

The FTA was a Chinese initiative, and Beijing has tried to overcome ASEAN leaders' concerns about China's competitiveness by promising to agree to grant preferential tariff treatment for some goods from Cambodia, Laos and Myanmar. More importantly, China pledged to open up certain key sectors first to give ASEAN countries a head start. This will enable them to beef up their own competitiveness before opening their markets to Chinese competition. For Singapore, a bigger free trade zone means more trading and investment opportunities for manufacturing. But liberalization in the services sector is another story. China is likely to take a longer time to open this up, as it does not feel ready to take on foreign competition in, say, financial services.[41] In spite of the official endorsement, however, progress on negotiating the FTA is expected to be slow, as there is divergence in ASEAN on the scope and speed of the process, with various sectoral and domestic economic concerns about market displacement and FDI.[42]

Singapore has been trying to negotiate FTAs with key APEC countries since 1999. Goh has declared support for an APEC-wide FTA eventually, but thinks that: "Those who can run faster should be allowed to run faster. Why should you pull him back just because some critics are not prepared to run?" Singapore was resorting to these agreements because they were the building blocks for freer global trade and investment, and FTAs will accelerate the free trade process.[43] It would seem that this trend towards bilateral FTAs will prevail in the coming decade in Asia, with more than twenty FTAs being discussed with East Asia at the moment.[44]

Singapore seems to have been relatively successful in generating competitive pressures for FTAs. In 2000, the United States and Singapore announced talks for an FTA. Shortly after that, China announced a working group to explore a FTA with ASEAN (formally endorsed in June 2001). The China-ASEAN FTA has been presented by both Singapore and China as diversification away from the U.S. market. According to Goh, "For us to depend on the U.S. alone as a market for growth for East Asia will be much more difficult in future, because the U.S. economy is going to slow down. So we recognise the need to generate internal dynamism and that we should do it through further co-operation amongst ourselves." [45] Having said that, the Singapore-U.S. FTA was successfully negotiated much faster and signed at the end of 2003.

Singapore has elicited a response from Japan as well. In 1999, Goh advised Japan to "entrench" its relations with ASEAN so that if ASEAN trades more with China, the economic ties between ASEAN and Japan will remain strong. Singapore's success at the time in getting Japan to agree to do a study on a possible bilateral FTA was seen as part of the strategy to entrench

Japan in the ASEAN region.[46] The FTA — Japan's first — was signed when Prime Minister Koizumi visited Singapore in January 2002. The arrangement has been variously criticized as limited at best, and — by China — as "unfair and biased" at worst because Singapore does not have an agriculture sector and signing the agreement would not affect Japan's agriculture sector. (While Singapore would abolish all tariffs on Japanese goods, Japan would remove tariffs on only 94 per cent of Singapore's exports, with about 2,000 products still taxable.)[47] Goh's key rationale though, is that Singapore needs to boost Japan's declining share in regional trade and investment. The FTA was crucial because "strategically, it will anchor Japan in Southeast Asia". More importantly, "Japan plays an important role in anchoring the U.S. in East Asia... The U.S.-Japan Security Alliance contributes to regional peace and stability. It provides balance to the important Japan-U.S.-China triangular relationship."[48] Thus, FTAs are an integral part of the Singaporean strategic tool-kit, serving as a means to facilitate and consolidate regional strategic relationships and stakeholdership. Using the same rationale, the island-state is also in the process of negotiating such agreements with other major powers in the region, namely India and South Korea.

CHINA AND SINGAPORE'S PERSPECTIVE ON SOUTHEAST ASIAN SECURITY AFTER 9/11

The terrorist attacks of 11 September 2001 in the United States, and Washington's subsequent foreign policy postures and actions have led to significant changes in security structures and perceptions around the world. Within Southeast Asia, the threat of terrorism has surfaced to become one of the region's key security preoccupations. Singapore is one of the Southeast Asian states to have taken this issue most seriously, and policymakers there expect that terrorism will be a long-term threat to the region.[49] At the same time, in some ways, the terrorist attacks of September 11 helped to dampen the hostility of the Bush administration towards China. China's support for the "war on terror" and its toleration of the heightened U.S. military presence in Central Asia led Bush to identify China as a "partner" on some issues, and to seek a "constructive relationship" with it.[50] As part of co-operative counter-terrorism efforts, the FBI has opened a liaison office in Beijing, and Washington has also ceased to criticize Beijing's moves to suppress separatist movements in its far western provinces, instead designating the East Turkestan Islamic Movement a terrorist organization. On the other hand, many points of contention between China and America remain, particularly over Taiwan. To realists who focus on how the war on terror has reinforced U.S. power and U.S. relations with China's neighbours, these trends will only serve to deepen existing conflicts between the two countries beyond the short term.[51]

Singapore's room for manoeuvre has increased recently because of the terrorism agenda and the thawing of U.S.-China relations after 9/11. At the same time, Singaporean perceptions of regional security prospects have also been affected by Beijing's increasingly evident dynamic diplomacy in Southeast Asia. In this regard, President Hu Jintao and Prime Minister Wen Jiabao's "charm offensive" during the ASEAN and APEC summits in the region in October 2003 was widely noted by Southeast Asian nations.[52] Singaporean policymakers appear to appreciate these moves, which vindicate their early conviction that China did not and will not seek to disrupt the stability or security of the region because of its current developmental imperative. Nevertheless, there is some worry that China's deeper engagement with Southeast Asia will further polarize a region that suffers from inherent differences and divisions. That is, these policymakers are concerned that some Southeast Asian countries are leaning or will shift too far into China's orbit altogether, thereby destabilizing the regional balance of influence.

For this reason — and also because of their perceived coincidence of interest in the war against terrorism — Singapore is forging closer relations with the United States. The Singapore Government has publicly declared its support for the American war on terrorism; and it has provided police training and logistical military support for the Bush administration's war in Iraq. During President Bush's visit to Singapore on 21 October 2003, the two countries announced their intention to expand co-operation in defence and security, and to negotiate a Framework Agreement for a Strategic Co-operation Partnership in Defence and Security. This strategic framework agreement will expand upon the scope of current bilateral co-operation in areas of defence and security such as counter-terrorism, counter-proliferation of weapons of mass destruction, joint military exercises and training, policy dialogues, and defense technology. Singapore is also trying to persuade Washington to engage more constructively with the region as a whole, so as to help to maintain American influence as a counter-force.[53] The ever-present worry that Washington has little time and attention for Southeast Asia because its focus is traditionally set upon Northeast Asia, is nowadays compounded by the concern that the Americans find it difficult to look beyond the terrorism agenda.

CONCLUSION

Singapore, like most of Southeast Asia, has been pragmatic in dealing with China in its acceptance that China is intrinsically a part of Southeast Asia, and the challenge is to find ways to live peacefully with it and to develop areas of mutual benefit. Singapore has sought to engage China both politically and economically, and these efforts may be argued to be proving successful, if Chinese actions and attitudes towards the region, in the last few years especially, is anything to go by. However, China is beginning to assert greater diplomatic, political and economic influence in Southeast Asia, and it is thus starting to offer significant competition to the American hold on the region. This is occurring at a time when the United States is suffering some degree of unpopularity in Southeast Asia because of its unilateral actions, especially in the war against Iraq. Thus, Singapore is maintaining its basic engagement strategy to manage China's growth, but subtly adjusting its hedging policy by further emphasizing the need for the United States to develop more broad-based and deeper relations with the region to maintain a balance of influence. While Singapore policymakers are now more optimistic about the prospects for a peaceful China that is a responsible regional player, they are maintaining the fall-back position of developing their military capabilities and sustaining close ties with the United States.

Notes

1. Khong Yuen Foong, "Singapore: A Time for Economic and Political Engagement", in *Engaging China: The Management of a Rising Power*, edited by Alastair Iain Johnston and Robert S. Ross (New York: Routledge, 1999), p. 109.
2. On the potential for middle powers to affect the regional security community in East Asia, see Paul Dibb, *Towards a New Balance of Power in Asia* (London: IISS, 1995); K. Moller, "How Much Insecurity in East Asia", *Pacific Review* 9, no. 1: pp. 114–24.
3. Goh Chok Tong, "ASEAN-US Relations: Challenges", speech to the Asia Society, New York, 7 September 2000, <http://www.asiasociety.org/speeches/tong.html>.
4. Goh Chok Tong, keynote address to US-ASEAN Business Council annual dinner, Washington D.C., reprinted in *The Straits Times*, 15 June 2001.
5. Lee Kuan Yew, "How the United States Should Engage Asia in the Post-Cold War Period", acceptance speech on receiving the Architect of the New Century Award, Nixon Centre for Peace and Freedom, Washington D.C., 11 November 1996, reprinted in *The Straits Times*, 13 November 1996.
6. Khong, "Singapore", p. 121.
7. A positive assessment of ASEAN's institutional style this is found in Amitav

Acharya, *Constructing a Security Community in Southeast Asia: ASEAN and The Problem of Regional Order* (London: Routledge, 2001).

8. See Richard Bernstein and Ross Munro, "The Coming Conflict with America"; Robert S. Ross, "Beijing as a Conservative Power", in *Foreign Affairs* 76, no. 2 (March/April 1997): 19–44. Re-considerations of the engagement-containment debate can be found in Gerald Segal, "East Asia and the 'Constrainment' of China", *International Security* 20, no. 4 (Spring 1996): 107–35; and more recently in David Shambaugh, "Sino-American Strategic Relations: From Partners to Competitors", *Survival* 42, no. 1 (Spring 2000): 97–115.

9. The terms belong to Richard Weitz, "Meeting the China Challenge: Some Insights from Scenario-Based Planning", *Journal of Strategic Studies* 24, no. 3 (September 2001): 19–48.

10. See Khong, "Singapore", *passim*; Andrew Tan, "Force Modernization Trends in Southeast Asia", IDSS working paper no. 59, January 2004.

11. See Yong Deng, "Managing China's Hegemonic Ascension: Engagement from Southeast Asia", *Journal of Strategic Studies* 21, no. 1 (March 1998): 21–43; Ian James Storey, "Living with the Colossus: How Southeast Asian Countries Cope with China", *Parameters* (Winter 1999–2000): 111–25.

12. Michael Leifer, "China in Southeast Asia: Interdependence and Accommodation", in *China Rising: Nationalism and Interdependence*, edited by David Goodman and Gerald Segal (London: Routledge, 1997).

13. C.P. Chung terms China's strategy one of "counter-hedging" — see Chung, "Southeast Asia-China Relations: Dialectics of 'Hedging' and 'Counter-Hedging'", *Southeast Asian Affairs*, 2004, pp. 35–53.

14. On Chinese opportunism, see Ang Cheng Guan, "The South China Sea Dispute Revisited", *Australian Journal of International Affairs* 54, no. 2 (2000): 201–15.

15. See, for instance, Shee Poon Kim, "The South China Sea in China's Strategic Thinking", *Contemporary Southeast Asia* 19, no. 4 (March 1998): 369–87.

16. For contending assessments of the significance of the Declaration, see Mely Anthony, "Major Milestone in ASEAN-China Relations"; Ralf Emmers, "ASEAN, China, and the South China Sea: An Opportunity Missed", IDSS Commentaries, 2001.

17. Rosemary Foot, "China in the ASEAN Regional Forum: Organizational Processes and Domestic Modes of Thought", *Asian Survey* 38, no. (May 1998): 425–40.

18. Chua Lee Hoong, "S'pore Invited to Build Tech Park", *The Straits Times*, 13 April 2000; "Govt will Help Private Investment in Inland China", *The Straits Times*, 27 April 2000.

19. Goh, address to US-ASEAN Business Council.

20. "China Boom Will Boost Region's Prosperity", *The Straits Times*, 25 April 2002.

21. Goh, address to US-ASEAN Business Council.

22. Ibid.

23. Ibid.

24. Optimistic analyses may be found in Joseph Y.S. Cheng, "Sino-ASEAN Relations in the Early Twenty-first Century", *Contemporary Southeast Asia* 23, no. 3 (December 2001): 424–25, 439–43; Yong Deng, "Managing China's Hegemonic Ascension: Engagement from Southeast Asia", *Journal of Strategic Studies* 21, no. 1 (March 1998): 31–33; Qingxin Ken Wang, "In Search of Stability and Multipolarity: China's Changing Foreign Policy towards Southeast Asia after the Cold War", *Asian Journal of Political Science* 6, no. 2 (December 1998): 73–74.

25. "Stable US-China Ties Crucial for Region", *The Straits Times*, 27 April 2002.

26. Leifer, *Singapore's Foreign Policy*, p. 117.

27. James Shinn, ed., *Weaving the Net: The Conditional Engagement of China* (New York: Council on Foreign Relations, 1996); Alastair Iain Johnston, "Socialization in International Institutions: The ASEAN Way and International Relations Theory", in *International Relations Theory and the Asia-Pacific*, edited by G. John Ikenberry and Michael Mastaduno (New York: Columbia University Press, 2003); Pauline Kerr, Andrew Mack and Paul Evans, "The Evolving Security Discourse in the Asia-Pacific", in *Pacific Co-operation: Building Economic and Security Regimes in the Asia-Pacific Region*, edited by Andrew Mack and John Ravenhill (Boulder, CO: Westview, 1995), pp. 250–54.

28. Goh, address to US-ASEAN Business Council.

29. Simon, Sheldon, (2002) "The ASEAN Regional Forum Views the Councils for Security Co-operation in the Asia Pacific: How Track II Assists Track I", *NBR Analysis* 13, no. 4; Evelyn Goh, "The ASEAN Regional Forum in United States East Asian Strategy", *Pacific Review* 17, no. 1 (2004): 47–69.

30. Melina Nathan, "The Chiang Mai Initiative", paper presented at "The Emerging Economic and Security Architecture of Asia", IDSS-Asia Pacific Policy Programme, JFK School of Government Forum, Singapore, 9 May 2002; Natasha Hamilton-Hart, "The Origins and Launching of the Chiang Mai Initiative and the Prospects for Closer Monetary Integration in East Asia", paper presented at INSEAD-ASEF conference on Regional Integration in Europe and Asia, Singapore, 7–8 July 2003.

31. Goh, "ASEAN-US Relations".

32. James Kelly, "Some Issues in US-East Asia Policies", address to The Asia Society, 4 April 2002, <http://www.asiasociety.org/speeches/kelly2.html>.

33. "Two big ideas to boost East Asia", *The Straits Times*, 24 November 2000.

34. Goh, address to US-ASEAN Business Council.

35. John Wong, "Turning a Rising China into Positive Force for Asia", *The Straits Times*, 26 September 2001.

36. Ibid.

37. "China Boom will Boost Region's Prosperity", *The Straits Times*, 25 April 2002.

38. "China's Rise: Export Boon for SE Asia", *The Straits Times*, 29 April 2002.

39. "Now for the Big One", *The Straits Times* 9 November 2001.

40. "China's Rise: Export Boon for SE Asia", *The Straits Times*, 29 April 2002.

41. "Asean, China Plan FTA", *The Straits Times*, 7 November 2001; "Now for the Big One", *The Straits Times*, 9 November 2001.

42. Helen Nesadurai, "East Asian Trading Arrangements", paper presented at "The Emerging Economic and Security Architecture of Asia", IDSS-Asia Pacific Policy Programme, JFK School of Government Forum, Singapore, 9 May 2002.

43. "PM in favour of APEC-wide free trade pact", *The Straits Times*, 15 November 2000.

44. Nesadurai, "East Asian Trading Arrangements"; "Everybody's Doing It", *The Economist*, 26 February 2004.

45. "ASEAN Lauds Freer China Trade", 24 November 2000; "ASEAN Keen on Bolder Trade Link-ups", 11 June 2001; "A Rising China is Not a Threat", 10 September 2001, all in *The Straits Times*.

46. "Japan urged 'to entrench' ties with ASEAN", *The Straits Times*, 10 December 1999.

47. "Japan, S'pore Sign Landmark Trade Deal", *The Straits Times*, 14 January 2002; "China Daily Slams Japan-S'pore Pact", *The Straits Times*, 17 January 2002. On the other hand, proponents point out that the Singapore-Japan FTA not only slashed tariffs on a whole slew of goods, including electrical, electronic and pharmaceutical products, but also opened new doors to services such as telecommunications, finance and tourism. For example, that agreement will enable investment advisers in Singapore to gain access to Japan's public pension fund goldmine, estimated to be worth 150 trillion yen (S$2.1 trillion). "Singapore Eyes FTA with Hongkong", *The Straits Times*, 20 February 2002.

48. "Japan, S'pore Sign Landmark Trade Deal".

49. Andrew Tan, "Terrorism in Singapore: Threats and Implications", *Contemporary Security Policy* 23, no. 3 (December 2002): 1–18.

50. Yu Bin, "United States-China Relations and Regional Security after September 11", *Issues & Insights* no. 2-02 (2002), Pacific Forum CSIS.

51. See Aaron Friedberg, "11 September and the Future of Sino-American Relations", *Survival* 44, no. 1 (2002): 33–50.

52. Evelyn Goh, "A Chinese Lesson for the US: How to Charm Southeast Asia", *The Straits Times*, 31 October 2003; Amitav Acharya, "China's Charm Offensive in Southeast Asia", *International Herald Tribune*, 8–9 November 2003.

53. Note that "balance of influence" is distinct from "balance of power". The former refers to political-economic influence, at which China is rapidly developing its capability; while the latter refers to military capability, in which the United States is expected to retain its primacy for the medium term at least.